The Cambridge Introduction to
Victorian Poetry

LINDA K. HUGHES

Texas Christian University, Fort Worth, Texas

CAMBRIDGE
UNIVERSITY PRESS

CAMBRIDGE
UNIVERSITY PRESS

University Printing House, Cambridge CB2 8BS, United Kingdom

One Liberty Plaza, 20th Floor, New York, NY 10006, USA

477 Williamstown Road, Port Melbourne, VIC 3207, Australia

4843/24, 2nd Floor, Ansari Road, Daryaganj, Delhi - 110002, India

79 Anson Road, #06-04/06, Singapore 079906

Cambridge University Press is part of the University of Cambridge.

It furthers the University's mission by disseminating knowledge in the pursuit of
education, learning and research at the highest international levels of excellence.

www.cambridge.org
Information on this title: www.cambridge.org/9780521672245

© Linda K. Hughes 2010

First published 2010

A catalogue record for this publication is available from the British Library

Library of Congress Cataloging in Publication data
Hughes, Linda K.
The Cambridge introduction to Victorian poetry / Linda K. Hughes.
 p.   cm. – (Cambridge introductions to –)
ISBN 978-0-521-85624-9 (hardback)
1. English poetry – 19th century – History and criticism.   I. Title.   II. Series.
PR591.H84   2010
821'.809–dc22

                                                                2010000698

ISBN 978-0-521-67224-5 Paperback

For
Carroll, Colin, and Haley

Contents

Figures

Preface

While presenting an overview of the key developments, features, and preoccupations of Victorian poetry, *The Cambridge Introduction to Victorian Poetry* has two additional aims: to argue that Victorian poetry was inseparable from the mass print culture within which it found an audience, and to reinterpret the "rhetoric" of Victorian poetry in this context. Rather than surveying major authors, the *Introduction* maps formal practices and a series of social debates within which poems, both canonical and lesser-known, jostled against, answered, and challenged each other for aesthetic and cultural pre-eminence. It is a less tidy, occasionally even more discordant, account of poetry than is found in some literary histories, but is meant to highlight the liveliness and vibrancy of poetry in its day and to suggest sources of its continuing appeal.

I customarily pair works to indicate the dialogues in which poems engaged and those they initiated for Victorian audiences. I also indicate when poems were first published in periodicals, a medium that George Saintsbury, the prominent late-Victorian critic and literary scholar, termed the defining genre of the age in *A History of Nineteenth Century Literature* (1896). The frequency with which this notation occurs in following pages underscores Victorian poetry's wide circulation among readers (which has sometimes been underestimated) and poetry's intersection with other print forms in the first mass-media era.

Insofar as poetry is itself a medium, of course, it cannot be understood apart from its intrinsic aesthetic features. However briefly I take up a poem, I direct attention to the role of form in conveying its meaning, significance, and effects. Two appended close readings of narrative and lyric poems from mid-century and century's end extend this focus.

Acknowledgments

The writing of this book was supported by a National Endowment for the Humanities Fellowship (2006); any views, findings, conclusions, or recommendations expressed in this publication do not necessarily reflect those of the National Endowment for the Humanities. I thank Linda Peterson and Kathy Alexis Psomiades for their support of this project at an early stage; Florence S. Boos for advice about revisions; and Deborah Downs-Miers; Elizabeth Woodworth; Susan D. Bernstein; and graduate students at Texas Christian University, the University of Wisconsin, and West Virginia University for responses to preliminary chapter drafts. I am grateful to Loren Baxter for assistance with digital images; to Mark Samuels Lasner for permission to reproduce the cover design of *The Sphinx* and frontispiece of *Goblin Market* from materials in the Mark Samuels Lasner Collection on loan to the University of Delaware Library; and to the Harry Ransom Humanities Research Center, The University of Texas at Austin, for permission to reproduce the printing of Christina Rossetti's "Up-hill" in *Macmillan's Magazine*. Finally, I thank Linda Bree for her oversight, patience, and support, and Carroll Hughes for his continued sustaining presence.

Permission to quote these poems has been granted as follows: M. E. Braddon, "Delhi," by Jennifer Carnell; Emily Brontë, "No Coward Soul is Mine," by Oxford University Press; John Clare, "Sonnet" ("I am"), by Curtis Brown Group Ltd., London, on behalf of Eric Robinson (© Eric Robinson 1966); Gerard Manley Hopkins, "Spring and Fall," by Oxford University Press on behalf of The British Province of the Society of Jesus; and Christina Rossetti, "Up-hill," "A Better Resurrection," "Angels at the Foot," "Who Has Seen the Wind?" and "When I am dead, my dearest" by LSU Press.

Editions cited

Poems in this study are cited from the following editions (unless otherwise indicated in notes). Line numbers are given in the text.

Arnold, Matthew. *The Poems of Matthew Arnold*, ed. Kenneth Allott and Miriam Allott, 2nd edn., London: Longman, 1979

Blake, William. *The Poems of William Blake*, ed. W. H. Stevenson and David V. Erdman, London: Longman, 1971

Brontë, Emily. *The Poems of Emily Brontë*, ed. Derek Roper with Edward Chitham, Oxford: Oxford University Press, 1995

Browning, Elizabeth Barrett. *The Complete Works of Mrs. E. B. Browning*, ed. Charlotte Porter and Helen A. Clarke, 6 vols., New York: G. D. Sproul, 1901

Browning, Robert. *The Complete Works of Robert Browning, with Variant Readings and Annotations*, ed. Allan C. Dooley, Jack W. Herring, Park Honan, and Roma King, Jr., 17 vols., Athens: Ohio University Press, 1969–

Carroll, Lewis. *The Annotated Alice*, ed. Martin Gardner, New York: Clarkson N. Potter, 1960

Clare, John. *Selected Poems and Prose of John Clare*, ed. Eric Robinson and Geoffrey Summerfield, London: Oxford University Press, 1967

Clough, Arthur Hugh. *The Bothie*, ed. Patrick Scott, St. Lucia: University of Queensland Press, 1976

Clough: Selected Poems, ed. J. P. Phelan, London: Longman, 1995

Coleridge, Mary E. *Poems*, London: Elkin Mathews, 1908

Coleridge, Samuel Taylor. *The Collected Works of Samuel Taylor Coleridge*, 16 vols., *Vol. 16, Part I: Poetical Works I*, ed. J. C. C. Mays, Princeton: Princeton University Press, 2001

Cook, Eliza. *The Poetical Works of Eliza Cook*, London: Frederick Warne and Co., 1870

Davidson, John. *Ballads and Songs*, London: John Lane, 1894

Dickinson, Emily. *Final Harvest: Emily Dickinson's Poems*, ed. Thomas H. Johnson, Boston: Little, Brown, and Co., 1961

Dobson, Austin. *The Complete Poetical Works of Austin Dobson*, London: H. Milford, Oxford University Press, 1923

Dowden, Edward. *Poems*, London: Henry S. King and Co., 1876

Dowson, Ernest. *Verses*, London: Leonard Smithers, 1896
Field, Michael. *Long Ago*, Portland, ME: Thomas B. Mosher, 1897
  Sight and Sound, London: Elkin Mathews and John Lane, 1892
  Underneath the Bough: A Book of Verses, London: George Bell and Sons,
    1893
FitzGerald, Edward. *The Rubáiyát of Omar Khayyám: A Critical Edition*, ed.
    Christopher Decker, Charlottesville: University Press of Virginia, 1997
Gosse, Edmund. *The Collected Poems of Edmund Gosse*, London: Heinemann,
    1911
Gray, John. *Silverpoints*, London: Elkin Mathews and John Lane, 1893
Hardy, Thomas. *Wessex Poems and Other Verses; Poems of the Past and Present*,
    London: Macmillan, 1908
Hemans, Felicia Dorothea. *The Poetical Works of Felicia Dorothea Hemans*,
    Oxford: Humphrey Milford, Oxford University Press, 1914
Henley, William Ernest. *Poems*, 5th edn., London: David Nutt, 1907
Hood, Thomas. *The Complete Poetical Works of Thomas Hood*, ed. Walter Jerrold,
    London, New York: H. Frowde, Oxford University Press, 1911
Hopkins, Gerard Manley. *Gerard Manley Hopkins: The Major Works*, ed.
    Catherine Phillips, Oxford: Oxford University Press, 2002
Keats, John. *The Poems of John Keats*, ed. Miriam Allott, Harlow: Longman, 1970
Keble, John. *The Christian Year*, London: J. M. Dent and Sons Ltd., 1914
Kendall, May. *Dreams to Sell*, London: Longmans, Green, 1887
  Songs from Dreamland, London: Longmans, Green, and Co., 1894
Kipling, Rudyard. *Rudyard Kipling's Verse*, Inclusive Edition, 1885–1918, Garden
    City, NY: Doubleday Page, 1919
Landon, Letitia Elizabeth. *Poetical Works of Letitia Elizabeth Landon, "L. E. L.":*
    A Facsimile Reproduction of the 1873 Edition, ed. F. J. Sypher, Delmar,
    NY: Scholars' Facsimiles and Reprints, 1990
Lang, Andrew. *The Poetical Works of Andrew Lang*, 4 vols., ed. Leonora
    Blanche Lang, London: Longmans, Green, and Co., 1923
Lear, Edward. *Nonsense Books*, Boston: Little, Brown, and Co., 1904
Lee-Hamilton, Eugene. *The New Medusa and Other Poems*, London: Elliot Stock,
    1882
Levy, Amy. *A London Plane-Tree and Other Verse*, London: T. Fisher Unwin, 1889
  Xantippe and Other Verse, Cambridge: E. Johnson, 1881
Lyall, Sir Alfred. *Verses Written in India*, London: Kegan Paul, Trench, and Co.,
    1889
Massey, Gerald. *My Lyrical Life: Poems Old and New*, First Series, London: Kegan
    Paul, Trench, and Co., 1889
Meredith, George. *The Poems of George Meredith*, ed. Phyllis B. Bartlett, 2 vols.,
    New Haven: Yale University Press, 1978
Meynell, Alice. *The Poems of Alice Meynell*, London: Geoffrey Cumberlege, Oxford
    University Press, 1940
Milton, John. *The Complete Poetical Works of John Milton*, ed. Douglas Bush,
    Boston: Houghton Mifflin, 1965

Morris, William. *The Collected Works of William Morris*, 24 vols., London: Longmans, Green, and Co., 1910–15

Newman, John Henry. *The Dream of Gerontius and Other Poems*, Oxford: Humphrey Milford, Oxford University Press, 1914

Patmore, Coventry. *Poems*, London: G. Bell and Sons, 1915

Procter, Adelaide A. *The Complete Works of Adelaide A. Procter*, London: George Bell and Sons, 1905

Robinson, A. Mary F. *The Collected Poems Lyrical and Narrative of A. Mary F. Robinson (Madame Duclaux)*, London: T. Fisher Unwin, 1902

Rossetti, Christina. *The Complete Poems of Christina Rossetti*, ed. R. W. Crump, 3 vols., Baton Rouge: Louisiana State University Press, 1979–90

Rossetti, Dante Gabriel. *Dante Gabriel Rossetti: Collected Poetry and Prose*, ed. Jerome McGann, New Haven: Yale University Press, 2003

Scott, William Bell. *Poems*, London: Longmans, Green, and Co., 1875

Shelley, Percy Bysshe. *The Poems of Shelley*, ed. G. M. Matthews and Kelvin Everest, 2 vols., London: Longman, 1989

Stevenson, Robert Louis. *A Child's Garden of Verses*, London: Longmans, Green, and Co., 1885

Swinburne, Algernon Charles. *The Complete Works of Algernon Charles Swinburne*, ed. Edmund Gosse and Thomas J. Wise, 20 vols., London: W. Heinemann Ltd., 1925–7

Symonds, John Addington. *New and Old: A Volume of Verse*, London: Smith, Elder, 1880

Symons, Arthur. *Poems*, 2 vols., London: William Heinemann, 1902

Tennyson, Alfred Lord. *The Poems of Tennyson*, ed. Christopher Ricks, 2nd edn., 3 vols., Harlow: Longman, 1987

Turner, Charles Tennyson. *Collected Sonnets Old and New*, London: C. Kegan Paul and Co., 1880

Watson, Rosamund Marriott. *The Poems of Rosamund Marriott Watson*, London: John Lane, The Bodley Head, 1912

Webster, Augusta. *Portraits and Other Poems*, ed. Christine Sutphin, Peterborough, ON: Broadview Press, 2000

Wilde, Oscar. *The Complete Works of Oscar Wilde*, 4 vols. to date, Vol. I: *Poems and Poems in Prose*, ed. Bobby Fong and Karl Beckson, Oxford: Oxford University Press, 2000

Wordsworth, William. *Wordsworth: Poetical Works*, ed. Thomas Hutchinson and Ernest de Selincourt, Oxford: Oxford University Press, 1988

Introducing Victorian poetry

> Of the difficulties that waylay a Victorian anthologist two are obvious.
> Where is he to begin? – Where to end? … Wordsworth happened to be
> the first Laureate of Queen Victoria's reign … [A]fter many months spent
> in close study of Victorian verse … I rise from the task in reverence and
> wonder not only at the mass (not easily sized) of poetry written with
> ardour in these less-than-a-hundred years, but at the amount of it which
> is excellent.   Arthur Quiller-Couch, *The Oxford Book of Victorian Verse*[1]

One distinction of Victorian poetry is the degree to which serious work and
popular culture converged, as evidenced by snippets of poems now proverbial:
"'Tis better to have loved and lost / Than never to have loved at all"; "God's in
his heaven – / All's right with the world!"; "How do I love thee? Let me count
the ways." These lines, from Alfred Tennyson's *In Memoriam* (1850), Robert
Browning's *Pippa Passes* (1841), and Elizabeth Barrett Browning's *Sonnets from
the Portuguese* (1850) become reassuring clichés when shorn of their contexts.
The poems themselves offer less conventional assurance: *In Memoriam* involves
a male poet's impassioned grief for another man; Pippa's hope is sung against the
backdrop of adultery and murder; and Barrett Browning's larger sequence opens
by alluding to Theocritus and fleeing from love.

The best Victorian poetry is complex, challenging, and experimental, *and* it
was read widely, thanks to its circulation during the first era of mass media. For
Victorians, that mass medium was print. If Sir Walter Scott's *Marmion* (1808)
and *The Lady of the Lake* (1810) sold 50,000 copies by 1836, Tennyson's *In
Memoriam* sold 60,000 copies in three to four years and *Enoch Arden* 40,000
copies in mere weeks. Nearly 400,000 copies of John Keble's *The Christian Year*
(1827) had been purchased when its copyright expired in 1873. To instance
another print form, the *Edinburgh Review* and *Quarterly Review*, founded early
in the century, peaked at circulations of 13,000 in 1813–14. *Cornhill Magazine*,
in which poems by Tennyson, Barrett Browning, Matthew Arnold, and the
Brontës appeared, attained a circulation approaching 100,000 with its first
issue. And cheap papers aimed at working and lower middle classes, like the
Family Herald or *London Journal*, also published original poetry and sold

1

between 300,000 and 450,000 copies per issue in the 1850s. Wilkie Collins estimated the audience for serial stories in these papers in the millions.[2]

The boundaries of Victorian poetry, like the term itself, are unstable and somewhat arbitrary.[3] As Quiller-Couch observes, William Wordsworth was the first Poet Laureate appointed by Queen Victoria. Indeed, Wordsworth's greatest poem, *The Prelude*, appeared in the same year as *In Memoriam*, in 1850. If Wordsworth became a Victorian poet by virtue of longevity, neither did Romanticism end with the deaths of Byron and Shelley. The early Tennyson cannot be understood apart from John Keats, Robert Browning from Percy Bysshe Shelley, Barrett Browning from Lord Byron, or the Rossetti family from William Blake. The poems of Felicia Hemans and Letitia Landon (which also influenced Tennyson and Barrett Browning) are regularly included in anthologies of both Romantic and Victorian poetry.

The question of scope also complicates attempts to identify Victorian poetry. More than 275 poets are represented in the first *Oxford Book of Victorian Verse*, including seventeen North American poets (for example, Henry Wadsworth Longfellow, Emily Dickinson, Walt Whitman) as well as James Joyce, Ezra Pound, and William Butler Yeats. Far from deeming themselves Victorian poets, Joyce caricatured "Lawn Tennyson, gentleman poet," in the Proteus section of *Ulysses*; Pound termed the Victorian "a rather blurry, messy sort of a period" in 1913; and Yeats announced in a BBC radio broadcast of 1936, "My generation, because it disliked Victorian rhetorical moral fervour, came to dislike all rhetoric. In France, where there was a similar movement, a poet had written, 'Take rhetoric and wring its neck.'"[4]

In contrast to Quiller-Couch's inclusive sweep, Walter E. Houghton and G. Robert Stange included only sixteen poets (and no women) in *Victorian Poetry and Poetics* (1959), an anthology deeply influenced by modernism. Should Victorian poetry be conceived in terms of its historical diversity and amplitude, as Quiller-Couch would argue, or by the portion most relevant to a given decade's tastes, as the example of Houghton and Stange implies? A forced choice between these alternatives is spurious. This study examines the diversity of Victorian poetry as well as canonical texts, and insists upon specific historical conditions as well as the interests of twenty-first-century readers. Approaching Victorian poetry in the context of print culture furthers these aims and, without effacing its links to larger poetic tradition (including Romanticism and modernism), helps pinpoint what is specific to Victorian poetry.

Poetic forms and themes did not definitively change in 1832, when Great Britain first extended the franchise and embarked on a course of (uneven) reform, or in 1837, when Victoria ascended the throne. The Romantic refashioning of blank verse, ballads, sonnets, narratives, and more into vehicles for probing human psychology, political injustice, ontology, the built world, and nature was itself a form of modernity and led directly to Victorian innovations. Romantic poetry was also diverse and experimental, embracing the "Miltonic sublime" of Wordsworth's "Tintern Abbey," the deflating irony of Byron's *Don Juan*, and the mundane particularity of Mary Robinson's "Winkfield Plain." As Stuart Curran notes, the very title of *Lyrical Ballads* is an oxymoron and points to an experimental generic hybrid, a mix of narrative and lyric, of communitarian impulse with the expression of an isolated individual.[5]

Yet fundamental changes in the material, socio-political, and intellectual conditions of British life after 1830 affected the content, form, and function of poetry in the reign of Queen Victoria.[6] If, as Virginia Woolf alleged of post-impressionist painting early in the twentieth century, "on [*sic*] or about December, 1910, human character changed,"[7] in 1830 nature changed. On September 15 the first intercity railway journey originated in Liverpool, and the death that day of William Huskisson, MP for Liverpool, who miscalculated the speed of the approaching locomotive (the *Rocket*) and was run over, aptly symbolizes the death of older configurations of nature. Propulsion through space and time on land had hitherto depended on the muscles, feeding, and watering of animals or human pedestrians, who generally followed roads shaped by natural contours. In contrast, as Wolfgang Schivelbusch observes, the "mechanical motion generated by steam power is characterized by regularity, uniformity, unlimited duration and acceleration."[8]

Railway lines, moreover, cut across open land according to abstract engineering principles rather than local custom or the natural paths cut by flowing water. As the protagonist of *Aurora Leigh* (1856), by Barrett Browning, recounts,

> we passed
> The liberal open country and the close,
> And shot through tunnels, like a lightning-wedge
> By great Thor-hammers driven through the rock,
> Which, quivering through the intestine blackness, splits,
> And lets it in at once.   (7:429–34)

Such inventions not only gave Victorians new relations to time, space, and nature but also new sounds and new rhythms. Not coincidentally, the railroad had a profound impact on the circulation of print, radically speeding up distribution and ratcheting up demand, since travelers increasingly turned to reading to pass the time and retain a sense of privacy.[9] Fittingly, two of the passengers on board the *Rocket* on September 15, 1830 were the future Poet Laureate of England, who celebrated this new technology in "Locksley Hall" (1842), and the man whose early death would inspire *In Memoriam*, the poem that won Tennyson the Laureateship: Arthur Henry Hallam.[10]

Older constructs of nature took another blow in 1830 from geologists' hammers, when the first volume of Charles Lyell's *Principles of Geology* was published. Though James Hutton had already discovered "deep time" in the rock formations of Siccar Point, Scotland, in the late eighteenth century, Lyell systematized evidence that earth's timescale vastly exceeded biblical chronology and that earlier species had become extinct. Charles Darwin extended this impetus, remapping nature as the site of impersonal forces and a "struggle for existence" in *On the Origin of Species* (1859).[11] Darwin had no sooner published his magnum opus than its principal tenets were circulated to homes throughout England. In addition to widespread reviews, George Henry Lewes discussed Darwin's new book in successive chapters of *Studies in Animal Life*, serialized in *Cornhill Magazine* in 1860, while *Punch* ridiculed Darwin and the emergent discipline of social science in "Unnatural Selection and Improvement of Species. (A Paper Intended to be Read at our Social Science Congress by One who has been Spending Half-an-Hour or so with Darwin)."[12] Wordsworth's "impulse from a vernal wood" that might "teach" "more of ... moral evil and of good, / Than all the sages can" ("The Tables Turned," 21–4) became increasingly difficult to imagine when compelling new evidence pointed to a nature "red in tooth and claw / With ravine" (*In Memoriam*, 56:13–16).

The impact on traditional Christianity of such work also helps to define the Victorian era. If, predictably, these new paradigms drove some Victorian poets to unbelief or (to use the term coined by scientist Thomas Henry Huxley in 1869) agnosticism, a general sense that traditional religion was being renegotiated brought theology to the fore. Even love poems were likely to touch on religion: was earthly love a scintillation of divine, undying love or an animal instinct as transient as life? Coventry Patmore's scripting of domesticity in *The Angel in the House* (1854–63) enunciates a firm theology:

> This little germ of nuptial love,
>   Which springs so simply from the sod,
> The root is, as my song shall prove,
>   Of all our love to man and God.   (1:537–40)

George Meredith's antiphonal lesson in *Modern Love* (1862) that marriages, like love itself, can die is grounded in an opposing cosmology: "'I play for Seasons; not Eternities!' / Says Nature, laughing on her way. 'So must / All those whose stake is nothing more than dust!'" (13:1–3). Philip Davis rightly claims that "the serious relation between belief and unbelief in the period makes unbelief itself a religious phenomenon."[13]

Another factor that pressured poets to take positions on vital contemporary issues was the explosion of print culture into a mass medium from the 1840s onward. If the philosophical and political ferment of the French Revolution and succeeding Napoleonic wars did so much to define literary production from 1790 to 1825, changes in Victorian publishing were themselves "revolutionary."[14] Steam-driven technology that made railroads possible began to be widely applied to printing presses in the 1830s and 1840s, and *Chambers's Edinburgh Journal*, the first of the cheap "respectable" periodicals that combined news; fiction; poetry; and informative articles on science, technology, education, political economy, and more, appeared in 1832.

The possibilities of reaching a mass audience through print were further realized in the 1840s by illustrated papers such as the *Family Herald* and *The Illustrated London News*. Books were still expensive and usually purchased only by the few, but the extraordinary success of Charles Dickens's *Pickwick Papers*, published in twenty monthly shilling installments in 1836–7, created a new publishing trend; and much of the age's best literature reached audiences in serial form (whether in individual parts or in magazines and weekly papers).[15] This extended to poetry in some instances, and Robert Browning's decision to issue his *Bells and Pomegranates* in eight double-columned, sixteen-page numbers from 1841 to 1846 must be seen in relation to Dickens's publishing success.

The 1850s marked a further watershed in publishing. In 1855 taxes on newspapers (imposed earlier in the nineteenth century to limit the spread of radical thought among working classes) were abolished, and the drop in price along with technological improvements created a boom in periodicals directed to all sectors of the British reading public. In the 1850s far more Britons could also borrow reading material. Circulating libraries had long been a feature of Great Britain, but the fees charged by most excluded the masses; and even middle-class patrons had access only to limited selections if they lived outside London. In 1850 parliament passed a bill founding free libraries, and artisans in the northern industrial cities of Liverpool and Manchester soon benefited. For middle-class patrons throughout Britain, a key event was the opening in 1852 of Mudie's Select Library in New Oxford Street, an institution that made borrowing affordable. Fiction was its mainstay, but this and other libraries carried wide arrays of newspapers and magazines in which poetry first appeared or was reprinted, and best-selling poems were also on hand. Charles Mudie purchased 2,500 copies of Tennyson's *Enoch Arden* to lend out, for example.[16] The same year that Mudie opened his New Oxford Street quarters, W. H. Smith and Son opened railway bookstalls throughout the country, stocking one-volume novels that sold for one or two shillings, and a range of weekly papers selling for a penny or two.

In the 1860s print production became cheaper yet with high-speed rotary presses and paper made from esparto grass or wood pulp. For the rest of the century, according to Richard Altick, "periodical printing became one of the most highly mechanized of all English mass-production industries"; cheap reprints of books produced by the same methods, including volumes of recent or older poetry, put books in the hands of all who were interested.[17]

The effect on poetry of a surrounding mass medium of print is visible in two major poems published six years apart but composed in different eras, Wordsworth's *The Prelude* and Barrett Browning's *Aurora Leigh*. Both are first-person narratives of the poet's development. Aurora's "relations in the Unseen" nourish her poetic gift and enable her to draw "The elemental nutriment and heat / From nature" (1:473–5), a Romantic premise also evident in the poem's tacit argument that imaginative vision can transform the world. Wordsworth's alpine vision of "Characters of the great Apocalypse, / The types and symbols of Eternity," and his epiphany upon Mount Snowdon of "a mind / That feeds upon infinity, that broods / Over the dark abyss" (6:638–9, 14:70–2), are answered by Aurora's culminating, apocalyptic vision of "The first foundations of that new, near Day / Which should be builded out of heaven to God" (9:956–7).

But just as Wordsworth's world is innocent of the train that Aurora and Marion take from Paris to Marseilles, only Barrett Browning provides a publishing history as part of Aurora's poetic development,[18] giving due attention to the impact of critical reception and even the poet's resort to "magazines, / And weekly papers" (3:310–11) for money to support her vocation. The novel is also a palpable presence in Barrett Browning's poem as it is not in *The Prelude* – a symptom of poetry that still commanded public readerships and prestige but was emerging when the novel flourished. In *Aurora Leigh* Marion Erle's drugging and rape hark back to Samuel Richardson's *Clarissa*, while the blinding of Aurora's cousin Romney is indebted to Charlotte Brontë's *Jane Eyre*. Another divergence between *The Prelude* and *Aurora Leigh* is that the former is structured by the poet's formation, conversion to the cause of revolution, disillusionment, and recovery of poetic vision, whereas *Aurora Leigh* is ultimately structured by a debate – personal, philosophical, political – about how best to reform society.

Debate itself is fundamentally Victorian, revealing an assumption that more than one perspective marks any issue and that truth is subject to contestation.

Victorian poetry is characteristically dialogic, presupposing and even harboring the existence of multiple voices. Print materialized the many-voicedness of Victorian poetry, since one poem or volume was sure to be challenged by another and all participated in the roiling, unceasing, sometimes chaotic flow of print through millions of hands in the form of books, newspapers, magazines, or paperbound serial parts. Isobel Armstrong demonstrates that the multivocality of Victorian poetry was not just an effect of material culture, however. She terms the defining form of Victorian poetry the "double poem": one that expresses an emotion or point of view yet, through formal means, simultaneously calls into question the poem's grounds for representing its subject and who or what should figure in poetry. This philosophical skepticism is manifested as poetic technique, so that the double poem is intrinsically aesthetic yet opens a space for cultural politics. In so doing the double poem challenges Immanuel Kant's assertion that art exists unto itself, apart from politics. Rather, the debate that surrounds poetry in print culture (and informs its content) inhabits its aesthetic foundations.[19]

The dramatic monologue illuminates the point. A key Victorian contribution to modern poetic tradition, and most typically a "double poem" in Armstrong's sense, the dramatic monologue subjects the lyric utterance of an individual to a social context, positioning that speaker in relation to a specific time, place, situation, and tacit or explicit auditor. By doing so, the dramatic monologue calls attention to the artifice of lyric utterance, which can appear to be direct and unmediated yet emerges from a specific cultural perspective or location and constructs an implied response for its readers. The dramatic monologue also negates the presumption of a universal poetic "I" that speaks for all humanity since a specific individual speaks, and utterance readily becomes a site of investigation because its social context is legible to readers.[20]

To take one of the best-known examples, in Robert Browning's "My Last Duchess" an imperious duke with blood on his hands brazenly negotiates marriage terms for his next wife. His power and arrogance are clear, but whether he deliberately hints that he ordered the murder of his first wife, who was insufficiently impressed by his "nine-hundred-year-old name" (33), or inadvertently reveals his guilt is left for readers to resolve. If readers assume the former, they must also determine why he would implicate himself in murder. In thus calling attention to speech acts (the Duke even quotes himself in line 6), the monologue calls attention to, and questions, all monological, one-sided utterance. In Browning's poem not only the socially inferior envoy is excluded from speech, but also the last duchess whose two-dimensional portrait is jealously controlled by the Duke (9–10), and the next duchess who is intimately affected by but not a party to the negotiations governing her fate. The dramatic monologue thus acts not only to challenge the universality of Romantic lyric and subjectivity, but also to open poetic utterance to analysis of its power relations and consideration of those excluded from speech. Monologue is used to express the Duke's sensibility but, as a form, also turns against itself.

Still, the role of print culture in poetry's dialogism should not be under-estimated. The mass medium of the periodical and newspaper effectively trans-formed even brief lyrics into approximations of dramatic monologues, since the lyric placed on its own page or huddled into a column jostled against fiction, gossip, political argument, travel writing, news, satires, science reports, art criticism, sociological analysis, musical entertainments, theatrical notices, or snippets of the latest "intelligence." The lyric, no matter how complex or finely crafted, could in this context offer only a contingent rather than transcendent perspective, forced as it was to compete with other voices and views for authority.

One of Christina Rossetti's best-known lyrics, "Up-hill," can serve as a useful example:

> Does the road wind up-hill all the way?
>   Yes, to the very end.
> Will the day's journey take the whole long day?
>   From morn to night, my friend.
>
> But is there for the night a resting-place?
>   A roof for when the slow dark hours begin.
> May not the darkness hide it from my face?
>   You cannot miss that inn.
>
> Shall I meet other wayfarers at night?
>   Those who have gone before.
> Then must I knock, or call when just in sight?
>   They will not keep you standing at that door.
>
> Shall I find comfort, travel-sore and weak?
>   Of labour you shall find the sum.
> Will there be beds for me and all who seek?
>   Yea, beds for all who come.

To eyes accustomed to free verse, the dominant mode of serious poetry in the twentieth and twenty-first centuries, the regularity of Rossetti's qua-trains and *abab* rhyme scheme, as well as her occasional resort to archaisms like "morn" and "Yea," may seem most striking. Readers familiar with William Blake's *Songs of Innocence and Experience* will recognize one source of Rossetti's reliance on simple diction and question and answer to address the end of life's journey, just as Blake's "The Lamb" addresses its origins: "Little lamb, who made thee?" (1). The poem's focus on religion and its restrained tone are also consistent with the decorous piety that Victorian readers expected from the "poetess" in an era when Bible reading and sermons were part of daily life.

In all these ways "Up-hill" seems highly traditional. But Rossetti's lyric slips free from overdetermined patterns of form and meaning and repays close attention with successive surprises. The engraving Blake devised for "The Lamb" makes it clear that a little boy addresses a lamb in the song; Rossetti's questioner and respondent are ungendered and untethered. The length of the journey and a night-time arrival establish the "I" as a pilgrim-through-life seeking answers about death, but who answers? The echo in "Up-hill" of Matthew 7:7 ("Ask, and it shall be given you; seek, and ye shall find; knock, and it shall be opened unto you") may suggest that Christ responds in Rossetti's even-numbered lines. Yet this respondent claims the casual relation of mere "friend" to the poem's questioner and proffers assurance only that the long, hard struggle of life culminates in a place to lie down and sleep. Indeed, the respondent pointedly refuses certain knowledge to the anxious question, "Shall I find comfort ..?"; "Of labour you shall find the sum" may imply that the speaker's deeds of a lifetime will determine the conditions meted out in the afterlife, or the line may allude bleakly to Ecclesiastes, in which the implied answer to the question "What profit hath a man of all his labour which he taketh under the sun?" (1:3) is "nothing."

The poem, like its elusive respondent, throws the basic question of who is speaking back upon its reader. The poet herself could be the respondent, acting as the proverbial reader's "friend," who here provides answers about death. If so, the "poetess" abandons feminine humility and takes on the mantle of the prophet – an assertive intervention in an age that still denied women public authority in the church. Or the respondent might be death itself, a possibility that displaces piety and religious assurance in favor of irony and alienation as the inquiring pilgrim confronts the supremely confident figure of death awaiting its inescapable harvest. In this interpretive scenario death's successively stressed words of line 6, which mimetically retard the pace of "slow dark hours" and suggest the tolling of the death knell, might be read as taunting the questioner with death's grim approach and the tedium of eternity. The undecidable identity of the respondent shores up the mystery that surrounds life's end no matter how the poem is read, but whether the mystery is sacred, terrifying, or bitterly ironic remains unclear.

Nor is the poem always rhythmically stable, though its rhymes are perfect and their scheme unvarying. The questioner consistently speaks in lines of five feet, predominantly in iambic pentameter; the respondent's rhythms vary

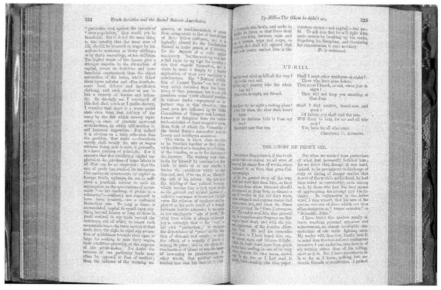

Figure 1   Christina Rossetti, "Up-hill," *Macmillan's Magazine*
(February, 1861), 324–5

unpredictably from the iambic trimeter that seems established in the first stanza. Line 6 has as many feet, while line 12, somewhat unnervingly, answers back in the same iambic pentameter used by the pilgrim to pose a question. Does the mirroring rhythm signify sympathetic harmony, empty echo, or parody? The respondent shrinks back to tetrameter in line 14 of the final stanza, then closes as in the beginning with a trimeter line, falsely seeming to assure the reader of stability where there is none.

Chiselled and chaste, the lyric "Up-hill" unleashes a surprising number of possible voices, tones, and perspectives. The lyric is structured as a dialogue to begin with, and the two speakers' possible identities bring divergent frames of reference to bear upon the exchange. For the poem's very first public readers, the lyric's opening onto a range of voices and competing beliefs would have been reinforced by its initial appearance in the February, 1861 issue of *Macmillan's Magazine* (see Figure 1).

Flanking articles on "Trade Societies and the Social Science Association" and "The Ghost He Didn't See" summon the very challenges and fallibilities that make life's journey an uphill battle indeed. "Trade Societies" closes by examining the rights of workers to organize based on the principle derived from political economy that "class-life is a battle"; "The Ghost He Didn't See" concerns a soldier back from the Crimean War whose kin seek no general accounts of battle because the "electric telegraph and express trains" and "Own Correspondent" of *The*

Times have made the details of war daily fare.[21] The relentless secularism surrounding the poem challenges the primacy it allots to mystery and eschatology, and introduces competing visions of what matters most in existence. This context so characteristic of Victorian poetry situates lyric, too, within a specific linguistic, rhetorical, and social milieu, registering – as in a dramatic monologue – other perspectives and an audience. To recover the materiality as well as the astonishingly varied and breathtaking language of Victorian poetry, then, is to realize how deeply it was intertwined with public and daily life, how significant a cultural medium it was for its readers.

This realization also underscores the reach of Victorian poetry in time and space. "Up-hill" circulated widely in America when *Living Age* reproduced the poem in its July 26, 1862 issue, in a notice pirated from *Eclectic Review*.[22] This transatlantic route to yet more readers may have fostered poetic cross-fertilization. Though Emily Dickinson never mentioned Rossetti, as she certainly did Emily Brontë and Elizabeth Barrett Browning, the uncanny pedestrian journey of Rossetti's questioner headed toward "A roof for when the slow dark hours begin" has a counterpart in Emily Dickinson's "Because I could not stop for Death," written around 1863, in which a carriage ride takes Dickinson's speaker to

> a House that seemed
> A Swelling of the Ground –
> The Roof was scarcely visible –
> The Cornice – in the Ground –   (17–20)

Though Dickinson's technique is the more obviously unconventional, the two poems share concision and a refusal to soften the strangeness or opacity of their authors' imaginative responses to death. Given such poetic kinship it is fitting that in the first *Oxford Book of Victorian Verse* Quiller-Couch places the two poets, both born in 1830, on the same page.[23] In such juxtapositions and poetic exchanges we glimpse not only the specificities of Victorian poetry but also its larger role in poetic tradition.

The remainder of this study examines the issues raised by "Up-hill" across a wide range of poems to illuminate the contours and achievement of this vibrant, diverse poetry in Victorian print culture. Part I, "The forms of Victorian poetry," looks at the role of experimental and inherited poetic forms – genres, metrical and stanzaic patterns, rhyme schemes – as well as the impact of classical tradition, modern tradition, and the mass medium of print on Victorian poetry. Part II, "The rhetoric of Victorian poetry," assumes poetry's coexistence and exchange with other print forms, just as the *Macmillan's Magazine* "Up-hill" enters a debate with surrounding articles over what battles of life have greatest significance. Chapters in Part II explore poetry's participation in Victorian considerations of science and technology, religion, affect, empire, and reform, as well as the aesthetic movement's growing skepticism about such public exchanges. A coda presents close readings of three poems to indicate ways that Victorian poetry might be read and to suggest why it remains vitally interesting.

Part I

The forms of Victorian poetry

Victorian experimentalism

> The shapes of things, their colours, lights and shades,
> Changes, surprises, –   Robert Browning, "Fra Lippo Lippi" (1855)

All literary writing is mediated by form, but poetry's very look on the page and sounds during recitation call attention to its artifice. Closely adhering to forms handed down over time might preserve and pay tribute to the past but can also stifle invention or dissent. Beginning with Wordsworth's preface to *Lyrical Ballads* (1802), nineteenth-century poets repeatedly argue for new ways of approaching poetic language and meter. In a century anxious about revolutions but also propelled by innovation in industry and the marketplace, the "new" became a desirable feature of poetry, especially as increased publishing opportunities required poets to distinguish themselves both from precursors and from numerous contemporaries. Modernity and a market-driven economy thus helped encourage what has always been a feature of memorable poetry: its ability to connect with readers yet repeatedly surprise them by unexpected turns in thought, image, language, or form. Experimentalism, then, is another defining feature of Victorian poetry. Because the dramatic monologue is so often cited as its distinctive development, I begin there.

Dramatic monologue

First-person utterances by fictive characters predate the Victorian era in Shakespearean and other dramatic soliloquy as well as in a long line of laments and declamations. The Victorian dramatic monologue departs from precedent insofar as it operates within a problematical epistemology and demands that readers negotiate a range of ambiguities. Does the poet agree with what the character is saying? Is the character sincere or self-interested? Does the auditor comprehend what the speaker is actually saying? Is the reader meant to take the utterance at face value, or is it ironized in keeping with the poet's desire to question how we know what we know and the social grounds on which utterance is predicated? Does even the speaker have command over the utterance and what it reveals?

The earliest dramatic monologues of Tennyson and Browning take up this last issue as part of an investigation of radical psychological states. As Ekbert Faas points out, the dramatic monologue and new scientific study of the mind and its processes emerged simultaneously, driven by intensified interest in introspection as both a philosophical and scientific method. A spate of treatises in the 1820s, including *Analysis of the Phenomena of the Human Mind* (1829) by James Mill (father to John Stuart Mill), as well as periodical reviews and essays, elicited further interest in psychological analysis and helped equip readers to comprehend mental process in poetry.[1] Thus when Tennyson's "Supposed Confessions of a Second-Rate Sensitive Mind not in Unity with Itself" appeared in *Poems, Chiefly Lyrical* (1830), W. J. Fox, editor of the *Monthly Repository*, could readily articulate its psychological interest in the *Westminster Review*, a periodical that James Mill co-founded:

> Mr Tennyson … seems to obtain entrance into a mind as he would make his way into a landscape … The author personates [in this poem] a timid sceptic, but who must evidently always remain such, and yet be miserable in his scepticism; whose early associations, and whose sympathies, make religion a necessity to his heart; yet who has not lost his pride in the prowess of his youthful infidelity; who is tossed hither and thither on the conflicting currents of feeling and doubt, without that vigorous intellectual decision which alone could "ride in the whirlwind and direct the storm" … we do honestly think this state of mind as good a subject for poetical description as even the shield of Achilles itself. Such topics are more in accordance with the spirit and intellect of the age than those about which poetry has been accustomed to be conversant.[2]

Fox accurately describes the fictional apparatus that distinguishes the speaker from Tennyson but adds that if the poet impersonates characters, "still it is himself in them, modified but not absorbed by their peculiar constitution."[3] From the first, then, the dramatic monologue was perceived as a site of multiple voices and perspectives. In the poem a governing trope of the sacrificial lamb introduced in the opening lines ironizes the speaker's utterance: "Men say that Thou / Didst die for me, for such as *me*" (2–3). But Christ as sacrificial lamb becomes linked to the spring lamb sacrificed only for human consumption rather than an afterlife (156–71) and the "lost lamb" his late mother would have wished safe in the fold of belief (105–6), suggesting both the egocentrism and near blasphemy underlying the speaker's timid fears.

The poet can also be detected in the dissonance of steady iambic tetrameter rhythm versus highly irregular rhymes, which suggest that the speaker's second-rate mind can only fitfully find harmony among clashing ideas. After the opening couplet, for example, the terminal "me" of line 3 finds no closure until line 8 ("misery"), and the poem is also notable for several half-rhymes (faith/scathe, tarn/forlorn, on/one, underneath/death), another experimental device used to psychological ends. Unsettled yet unrelinquished faith strands Tennyson's speaker in irresolution and makes the poem's end point as arbitrary as the diction is forced and artificial: "O damnèd vacillating state!" (190).

Browning, in contrast, depicts a mind unhinged by too much certainty and a doctrine that transmutes divine love into capricious love, hate, and injustice. "Johannes Agricola" first appeared in the January, 1836 *Monthly Repository*: the Unitarian, socially progressive journal edited by Fox, Browning's friend. The headnote Browning affixed to the poem – which identified Agricola as the founder of the Antinomians, who believed that "good works do not further, nor evil works hinder salvation; that the child of God cannot sin … that murder, drunkenness, &c. are sins in the wicked but not in him" – would have immediately established an ironic framework for readers.[4] More notable in the history of the dramatic monologue is the poem with which it was paired, "Porphyria" (later retitled "Porphyria's Lover"), which poses a test case of murder that Agricola and his followers are willing to overlook in a "child of God." Browning perhaps expected his title to recall Porphyry (*c*. 234–305), the Greek philosopher who authored *Against the Christians*, another repudiation of Christ's example. In 1842 Browning paired the monologues under the label "Madhouse Cells," providing another frame within which they were to be read. But the 1836 poem was more daring, thrusting readers into a murderer's mind before they could sense who the speaker was or where the poem was going.

After an odd account of nature's malevolence in the opening lines (1–4), the poem seems to settle into the tale of a privileged woman's tawdry affair with a cottager, and the poem momentarily swells from iambic tetrameter to a single line of pentameter in the moment Porphyria gives herself to the speaker (36). In unnervingly direct, ordinary terms the speaker then describes strangling his lover with her own blonde hair and the erotic fulfillment that follows:

> I warily oped her lids: again
> Laughed the blue eyes without a stain.
> And I untightened next the tress
> About her neck; her cheek once more
> Blushed bright beneath my burning kiss. (44–8)

Though told with the economy of a ballad, the poem generates a multitude of clues not easily synthesized, since gender and class relations complicate matters. Porphyria takes command of the love-making in the poem's first half, baring her skin and forcing the speaker to look up to her (17, 31); murder enables their positions to be reversed (50–3). Is the murder an act of monomaniacal possession or class revenge? Is Porphyria a fallen woman who brings her fate upon herself, a victim who proves the dangers of slumming? Did the murder even happen, since the lovers never exchange a word? Is the monologue a delusional fantasy? The only thing certain is the rhyme scheme, which takes a ballad pattern (*abab*) and adds a final rhyme (*ababb*) to create the compelling closure of a couplet: "And all night long we have not stirred, / And yet God has not said a word!" (59–60). The formal features again indicate the poet's presence in the poem, multiplying its perspectives and the uncomfortable questions it poses. Is Browning plumbing abnormal psychology disinterestedly, for its own sake, experimenting with how far he can push poetic content? Is he critiquing Antinomian dogma and the artifice of social distinctions, or possibly enjoying a lurid fantasy himself?

Browning went on to explore the criminal mind *in extenso* in Guido Franceschini, the murderous husband of *The Ring and the Book* (1868–9), the sole character along with the poet given two monologues. Browning could conceive of women criminals, too, as in "The Laboratory: *Ancien régime*," first published in *Hood's Magazine* in June, 1844. This jealous woman who purchases poison to destroy a successful rival is less complex than his other speakers, and it was left to William Morris to develop the possibilities of female criminal psychology in "Defence of Guenevere" (1858), though he takes his character from legend rather than history. The epistemology of "Defence of Guenevere" is again challenging. Guenevere may speak the truth in denying the charge of treason on grounds of adultery, argue casuistically that her beauty and passion are themselves higher truths than man-made laws, or simply stall for time until her lover comes to her rescue. Her daring and presence of mind reveal a woman of extraordinary intelligence as well as beauty, as she taunts Gawain with complicity in his mother's murder and critiques a social system in which she has been "bought / By Arthur's great name and his little love" (82–3). This taunting resistance, however, may simply mirror her other manipulations of men. The hybrid form of the monologue likewise complicates interpretation, for the poet repeatedly breaks in to set the scene or exalt her ("glorious lady fair!" [56]). Morris's rhyming tercets (*aba bcb*) establish a pattern of entanglement that suitably answers the poem's mixed evidence.

Swinburne took female capacity for lawlessness further, choosing another elevated, largely mythologized speaker, the Greek poet Sappho, who in

"Anactoria" (1866) expresses the desire to rend her lover Anactoria limb from limb, consume her body, and make poetry out of the cries of her lover's pain. This is a female murderer in sensibility if not in fact. The sheer distance of these speakers from feminine norms of purity, gentle nurturance, and abstention from self-interested rhetoric brings into question a range of ethical and biological assumptions as well as the very purpose of poetry and the grounds of beauty or pleasure.

An array of dramatic monologues by women poets explore unusual psychological states and social, theological, or philosophical problems with a crucial difference: it is not women who are perverse but the society that limits their choices and brands them as tainted goods if they resist. The dramatic monologue provided a space within which women poets could articulate alternative subjectivities, expand the multiple voices of Victorian print culture, and intensify the dramatic monologue's relativity of utterance by tacitly challenging monologues by male contemporaries. For example, both Felicia Hemans in "Properzia Rossi" (1828) and Amy Levy in "Xantippe" (*Dublin University Magazine* [May, 1880]) represent historical personages, just as do Tennyson in "St. Simeon Stylites" (1842) and Robert Browning in "Johannes Agricola," "Fra Lippo Lippi," "Andrea del Sarto" (1855), and *The Ring and the Book*.

In many respects Hemans's monologue enacts the role of the poetess, a performance of female loss and abandonment staged as the spontaneous outpouring of decorous female emotion.[5] But Hemans's subject matter – a female artist speaking in the act of creating art – simultaneously brings the poetess figure into question. Properzia is sculpting for her treacherous lover a statue of Ariadne, the mythic woman abandoned by Theseus after she helped him to slay the minotaur in the labyrinth on Crete: "I give my own life's history to thy brow, / Forsaken Ariadne!" (36–7). This expressive model of female creativity, which underlies reviews of women poets throughout the century, is belied by the fact that Hemans, the work's other artist, is patently not expressing herself but representing a sixteenth-century Bolognese woman. Along with the monologue's introductory lyric and rhyming pentameter couplets, Hemans's headnote referring to a rival depiction of Properzia by painter Jean-Louis Ducis likewise insists that female creativity is not spontaneous or artless but deliberate, grounded in form, and subject to competition with other creations.

Levy's choice of subject challenges the very making of history by men. Xantippe, the wife of Socrates, is so associated with shrill invective that her name is an English synonym for scold or shrew. But Xantippe emerges as a very different character in Levy's monologue, resembling Dorothea Brooke, the protagonist of George Eliot's *Middlemarch* (1871–2), in having married a scholar when unable to pursue knowledge in her own right. When she dares to question slighting comments about women's intellectual abilities that she overhears while serving wine to Socrates and his philosophical circle, she is dismissed because she lacks training in dialectic and in frustration hurls the wineskin to the ground, the spattered, blood-red wine symbolizing the death of her intellectual aspiration (210–22). Thereafter she steadily spins herself into the limited figure her society demands. Rather than ironizing the poetess, Levy's blank verse ironizes historical tradition, which demands reverence for Socrates and Plato, opprobrium for Xantippe. Her rival history asserts, as Simone de Beauvoir would in the mid twentieth century, that women are not born but made.

By positioning Eulalie, a prostitute, as the speaker of a 630-line blank-verse monologue entitled "A Castaway" (1870), Augusta Webster challenges the operative assumption that prostitution is an unspeakable subject in respectable literature, and brings before readers a psychologically interesting social deviant who is by turns angry, defiant, sarcastic, regretful, and terrified of what lies ahead. Like Xantippe, Eulalie is a by-product of society, and her utterance, though by no means transparent, is also positioned to elicit sympathetic response. Eulalie opens by reading from her girlhood diary, at once demonstrating the intimate link between a good middle-class girl and prostitute, the radical fissures to which identity is subject, and the problematic relation of texts (including Webster's) to stable truth. Webster's monologue, like Hemans's, also thwarts attempts to identify the female poet with her subject, since no self-acknowledged prostitute could have been published by a mainstream publishing house. If the dramatic monologue makes a prostitute's utterance possible, Webster's unconventional choice of speaker nonetheless risks, and possibly courts, identification with Eulalie, since she too makes money through sales in the literary marketplace.

Elizabeth Barrett Browning places a murderer at the center of "Runaway Slave at Pilgrim's Point," first published in the *Liberty Bell*, an American abolitionist annual, in 1848. Worse, the woman has murdered her own child. But categories of guilt, sanity, and justice are hopelessly complicated because she is also a slave woman raped by her white master, to whose child she has given birth. Having glimpsed in the baby's eyes "The *master's* look, that used to fall / On my soul like his lash … or worse!" (144–5), she now laughs at having smothered and buried the child:

> But *my* fruit … ha, ha! – there, had been
>   (I laugh to think on't at this hour!)
> Your fine white angels (who have seen
>   Nearest the secret of God's power)

> And plucked my fruit to make them wine,
> And sucked the soul of that child of mine
> As the humming-bird sucks the soul of the flower.   (155–61)

Her madness here seems confirmed. Yet she anticipates and refutes this charge, displacing like the poem itself the question of madness onto insane social institutions: "I am not mad: I am black" (218).[6] Her immediate situation also positions madness and hysteria as an effect, not cause, of her plight: the exhausted runaway has been relentlessly tracked to Plymouth Rock by slave hunters and speaks only when trapped. Even the insistent lyricism of her utterance is insanely inappropriate to her condition yet fitting, since her acts and psychological experience are predicated on the song she once made of her black lover's name. At every level, this dramatic monologue invokes radical psychological states, epistemological crises, and questions about form, while also unleashing powerful social protest. In general the dramatic monologue was one of the era's most important experimental forms, engaging key intellectual, philosophical, and social interests, and multiplying even when it rendered problematic the voices and perspectives brought to poetry by poets, fictional speakers, readers, and social conventions.

Hybrid forms

As narrative intrusions in "Defence of Guenevere" and the balladic refrains of "Runaway Slave" indicate, Victorian poets repeatedly experimented with hybrid forms, pushing discrete genres into new formations, often in response to new cultural experience ill-suited to inherited forms. Tennyson's long poem of 1847 announced its hybridity in the title: *The Princess: A Medley*. The rapidity with which Tennyson further complicated its form in a rapid succession of editions (1847–51) extended, by giving material expression to, its experimentalism. For Tennyson's contemporaries, the complete *Princess* comprised four successive volumes no more capable of easy combination than the medley itself. In all editions the prologue opens with a mechanics institute – an educational forum for workers provided by philanthropic reformers – on the estate of Sir Walter Vivian. The poem thus deliberately mingles classes as it also mixes a set of seven university men with women similarly privileged in class but denied men's educational opportunities. Following a spirited discussion of one of Sir Walter's forebears, a lady who donned armor and repelled an attack on her castle, the men propose to take turns narrating the tale of a princess and her radical innovations on behalf of "ladies' rights."

From the outset, then, the poem insists on multiple voices, a farrago of medieval fantasy and modern debates, and an unstable tone that varies from serious contemplation of reform to playful chaffing between the sexes. This deliberately fractured form suggests that no single perspective is adequate, and with authority decentered, Tennyson is free to imagine (as one option among others) a radically reconstituted society that integrates women into universities. The perplexity of an early reviewer indicates the risk Tennyson took in yoking highly finished style to a jumble of genres, tones, time frames, and subject matter: "Lecture rooms and chivalric lists, modern pedantry and ancient romance, are antagonisms which no art can reconcile." The poem attracted praise, too, both for its themes and formal innovations. But the consensus was that a medley posed a bar to artistic unity.[7]

Tennyson made substantive formal changes in 1850, when women were given singing parts in a series of lyrics that Tennyson now claimed to be "the best interpreters of the poem."[8] Imprinting modernity's rapid change, Tennyson also added to the conclusion an exchange between two college men who, rather than opting to mingle with the Institute crowd as in 1847, ascend to a higher vantage point, look to France, and debate whether the 1848 revolution there should be classed with the "wild Princess" of the tale as threats of anarchy, or whether "ourselves are full / Of social wrong; and maybe wildest dreams / Are but the needful preludes of the truth" (Conclusion, 62–74).

Retroactively these additions exposed the hidden exclusions of the 1847 edition. Tennyson preferred to contemplate radical changes in women's condition that were still safely far off, rather than entertain universal male suffrage or other points in the People's Charter being actively championed by workers as he composed *The Princess*. And of course, Ida's rejection of marriage to found a women's university that will help women lose "the habits of the slave" (II.77) is undone by women's maternal instincts and male conquest. Tennyson also retreated from formal experimentalism in 1850 when he deleted reference to "our compound story" and ascribed the written text to a sole poet-narrator: "The words are mostly mine" (Conclusion, 3). Now multiplicity was being effaced in order to promote a single vision after all.

Yet Tennyson undid the effect of greater decorum in 1851, when he experimentally inserted new psychological and gender instability into the prince, who had from the beginning sported girlish blond ringlets but now also suffered from the family disability of "weird seizures," a cross between the epilepsy suffered by Tennyson's father and radical epistemological crises that leave the prince unable to distinguish "The shadow from the substance" (I.5–18). The sheer weirdness of the device suggests magic realism and postmodern gender theory more than Tennyson's own era. Though perhaps unintentional, this new motif in the fourth edition also mirrors the disjunction between the poet's vision and its various material embodiments, each of which makes the other editions palpable yet inauthentic.

Tennyson would fashion another hybrid in his most controversial poem, *Maud* (1855), but in 1850 Arthur Hugh Clough was inventing an even more startling form in *Dipsychus and the Spirit*, published in 1865 after Clough's death. *Dipsychus* is a sustained dialogue between a divided mind (the "two psyches" of Dipsychus) and an opposing Spirit, embedded in a mix of closet drama, travelogue, Faustian psychomachia, and (in the prologue and epilogue) prose scenes that seem snatched from a novel. In the prose prologue a poet-nephew and his seventy-one-year-old uncle argue whether poetic form and meaning should be regular and stable or irregular and multivalent, a clue to the importance of form in the poem and the deliberateness with which Clough fashioned it. Whereas the uncle prefers "good plain verse" and complains that "Nothing is more disagreeable than to say a line over two, or, it may be, three or four times, and at last not be sure that there are not three or four ways of reading," the poet-nephew associates irregularity with vitality: "A rude taste for identical recurrences would exact sing-song from 'Paradise Lost', and grumble because 'Il Penseroso' doesn't run like a nursery rhyme.'" There follow Part I, seven external scenes set in Venice; Part II, seven inward dialogues; and the prose epilogue, in which nephew and uncle again argue about poetics, theory, and education until the nephew, echoing Ophelia (as T. S. Eliot would in the pub scene of *The Waste Land*), suddenly ends, "'Good night, dear uncle, good night'" (Epilogue, 94).

In the poem Dipsychus is divided between inability to believe in God and hope that God exists: "Hints haunt me ever of a More beyond" (2.4.39). In consequence he is also ambivalent about the temptations posed by casual sex and worldly convention, prompting the Spirit to retort,

> To see things simply as they are
> Here, at our elbows, transcends far
> Trying to spy out at midday
> Some "bright particular star" which may,
> Or not, be visible at night
> But clearly is not in daylight.
> No inspiration vague outweighs
> The plain good common sense that says
> Submit, submit.   (2.3.168–76)

The Spirit's tone and counsel that Dipsychus should "Enjoy the minute / And the substantial blessings in it" (1.1.53–4) allude to Byron's poetic travelogues and licentious episodes in Venice. Though Dipsychus addresses the Spirit as "Mephistopheles," to which the Spirit answers (2.2.43–4), the poet-nephew nonetheless remarks in the epilogue, "perhaps he wasn't a devil after all. That's the beauty of the poem; nobody can say ... the thing ... represent[ed] is the conflict between the tender Conscience and the World – now the over-tender conscience will of course exaggerate the wickedness of the world" (Epilogue, 12–16). The poet here repositions the divided mind, which in Tennyson's "Supposed Confessions" is associated with "Second-Rate" thinkers, as intellectual and interpretive virtue. The reader, too, is invited to become a "Dipsychus."

Interpretation is further complicated by the poem's experiments with genre, meter, and rhyme. Dipsychus' attempts to think precisely, without prejudice to either side of an argument, are mostly given in blank verse, the traditional medium of high seriousness. In contrast, the Spirit most often declaims in tetrameter rhymed couplets, a balladic jig into which he inserts multiple languages, oaths, colloquialisms ("Stuff!"), songs, nursery rhymes ("Little Bo Peep, she lost her sheep"), and nonsense-words ("Tooraloo, tooraloo tooraloo loo") (1.3.77; 2.7.48; 1.1.70). But Dipsychus, too, slips out of blank verse when he waxes sentimental in 1.5 ("In a Gondola") or uses words befitting the Spirit to recount a dream in which God has clearly exited the world:

> Ting ting, there is no God, ting ting
> Come dance and play, and merrily sing
> Ting ting a ding. Ting ting a ding.
> O pretty girl, who trippest along
> Come to my bed, it isn't wrong.   (1.6.16–20)

That Dipsychus adopts tetrameter couplets as Part II opens foreshadows his capitulation to the Spirit's sway.

Indeed, Clough's formal elements thwart clear-cut distinctions between Dipsychus and the Spirit elsewhere in Part II, just as the poet-nephew undoes moral binaries in the Epilogue. When Dipsychus reverts to blank verse to probe his conflicted beliefs (2.4.1–104), the Spirit *answers* him in blank verse (105–46) and later boasts, "I too have my *grandes manières* in my way. / Could speak high sentiment as well as you / And out-blank-verse you without much ado" (2.5.152–4). At every level, then, Clough's experimental language and mixed forms undermine the possibility of certitude. Even the poem's concluding echo of *Hamlet* ("'Good night, dear uncle, good night'") might connote madness, suicidal depression, action thwarted by introspection, or merely self-referential literary language and the text's arbitrary ending.

If Clough's *Dipsychus* represents an extreme case, experiments with hybridity are common in Victorian poetry. William Morris's *The Earthly Paradise*

(1868–70), for example, features a long narrative poem as prologue; in the poem proper each of twelve books opens with a continuing narrative frame and a month lyric, setting linear narrative against singing in place, before alternating a verse tale drawn from classical with one drawn from northern mythology. Hybrid form (including the novel in verse, discussed below) is especially feasible in long poems, but the dramatic monologue itself merges elements of drama, lyric, and narrative.[9] Similarly inventive combinations need to be assumed as a potential starting place for any Victorian poem.

Experiments in rhyme and rhythm

Though most Victorian poems feature patterned rhyme and rhythm, poets experimented with a range of variations. Tennyson, as noted above, adopted imperfect or half rhymes in "Supposed Confessions," a risky strategy since critics might assume technical incompetence rather than experimentation. This was especially the case for women poets, whose exclusion from higher education placed them at a disadvantage. Barrett Browning's half rhymes elicited attacks well into the twentieth century, yet she insisted that her imperfect rhymes were deliberate experiments founded upon Elizabethan precedent (as in John Donne's poetry).[10]

A favorite with Victorian readers, "Lady Geraldine's Courtship" (1844) abounds in half rhymes, though it is experimental in other respects as well. To represent love between a lower-class poet and upper-class woman, Barrett Browning borrows the trochaic octameter catalectic meter – which suppresses the last syllable in the eighth trochee – of Tennyson's immensely popular "Locksley Hall" (1842). She likewise depicts "palpitating engines" that "snort in steam across" landscapes (11), but she refashions Tennyson's catalectic rhymed couplets into quatrains that alternate feminine endings, in which the terminal syllables are unstressed, with masculine (i.e., catalectic) endings in an *abab* rhyme scheme. She thus adopts matter and a meter that are self-consciously modern, then modifies Tennysonian precedent by mixing feminine and masculine line endings. The poem's subtitle, "A Romance of the Age," also mixes masculine and feminine elements, pointing equally toward the aristocratic, masculine tradition of chivalric romance and romantic novels associated with women. Most of this epistolary dramatic monologue is "written" by Bertram, the poet, who overhears Lady Geraldine vow "Whom I marry shall be noble, / Ay, and wealthy" (263–4) and furiously declares his love for her while berating her for snobbery. At the end the monologue shifts to third-person narrative as Lady Geraldine comes to his room to declare her love for him. The poem's ambiguous title (which can signify an active or passive Lady) thus signals the equal role given to male and female wooing in the poem, a counterpart to its leveling of class distinctions.

Barrett Browning's half rhymes extend the poem's challenge to precedent. Though some half rhymes merely sustain the poem's general contestation of convention, others mark dissonant perception or action. For example, Barrett Browning rhymes "nature" and "satire" when obtuse aristocratic guests condescend to Bertram as a low-born man "gifted ... by nature" who poses no threat because "he writes no satire" (41, 43). Above all, half rhymes proliferate when Bertram misreads Lady Geraldine's obvious love for him, realizes that he has aggressively attacked while declaring love to her, and faints (261–350). The controlling poet of the Conclusion then overrides Bertram's limited vision, refashions Bertram's *abab* rhyme scheme into a new *abcb* pattern, and similarly rewrites romance plots to allow for new class and gender relations.

Other experiments in rhyme include "Goblin Market," in which Christina Rossetti innovates by piling rhyme up in such abundance and so unpredictably. Rhyme is lavishly indulged yet placed under suspicion, since its intensity of sonic pleasure parallels the sensuous temptations of luscious fruit offered by goblin men to Laura, who succumbs – as do most readers to the poem (see Figure 2).

Robert Browning interrogates rhyme through the contrary strategy of perfect rhymed couplets rendered almost inaudible by overriding speech rhythms in "My Last Duchess":

> That's my last Duchess painted on the wall,
> Looking as if she were alive. I call
> That piece a wonder, now: Frà Pandolf's hands
> Worked busily a day, and there she stands.
> Will't please you sit and look at her? I said
> "Frà Pandolf" by design, for never read
> Strangers like you that pictured countenance,
> The depth and passion of its earnest glance,
> But to myself they turned ...   (1–9)

The clash of eye and ear, the dissonance of seeing rhyme but hearing sentences, unlooses a distinctive poetic voice and tacitly theorizes the difference made by reading or hearing poetry in an era of mass print culture. The audience thus becomes a site of interrogation and contested claims as much as the text they consume.

Swinburne would later synthesize, as it were, the experiments of Browning and Rossetti by crafting verse so emphatic in sound and rhythm that poetry's sounding devices (alliteration, assonance, rhyme) repeatedly threaten to swamp cognition and thereby sense:

Figure 2   D. G. Rossetti, Frontispiece, in Christina Rossetti, *Goblin Market and Other Poems* (Cambridge: Macmillan, 1862)

> There is no change of cheer for many days,
> But change of chimes high up in the air, that sways
>   Rung by the running fingers of the wind;
> And singing sorrows heard on hidden ways.   ("Laus Veneris," 153–6)

In "Laus Veneris" (1866) and other poems, Swinburne, like Browning, emerges as a theorist of language who forces readers to consider language's potential opacity and obstruction of meaning as well as poetry's inherent artifice.

"Goblin Market" freely plays with line lengths and rhythms as well as rhyme. Even in the opening catalogue of luscious fruit the predominant dactylic dimeter unpredictably expands to four feet of trochees in line 30:

> Damsons and bilberries,
> Taste them and try:

> Currants and gooseberries,
> Bright-fire-like barberries,
> Figs to fill your mouth,
> Citrons from the South,
> Sweet to tongue and sound to eye;
> Come buy, come buy.   (24–31)

If goblin men sing here, the discourse of the good Lizzie is no more regular. In the act of plucking iris Lizzie even moves in the same dactylic pulse that marks the goblins' jingles: "Lizzie plucked purple and rich golden flags" (220). Rossetti not only establishes her fantasy world as a site of untrammeled play with language and rhythm but also uses meter (along with plot and symbol) to frustrate attempts to fix underlying order or meaning.

Several years earlier Tennyson experimented with varying line lengths as a psychological register. Tennyson described *Maud* (1855) – originally "Maud or the Madness" – as "'a little *Hamlet*,' the history of a morbid poetic soul, under the blighting influence of a recklessly speculative age."[11] Traumatized during childhood by the apparent suicide of his father after financial ruin, the unnamed speaker-hero understandably harbors jaundiced views of his society's obsessions with commerce and "progress." If he fears having inherited his father's mental instability, he also bears the family legacy of personal hatreds, since Maud's father, once the business partner of his own, "Dropt off gorged from a scheme that had left us flaccid and drain'd" (I.20). Yet when Maud returns to the family estate the speaker falls in love with her. The speaker ranges freely, at times wildly, from hysteria, paranoia, philosophical skepticism, and embittered fury to passionate exultation in new-found love. And, as Tennyson's contemporary, the physician Dr. Robert James Mann, declared of the poem, "The syllables and lines of the several stanzas actually trip and halt with abrupt fervour, tremble with passion, swell with emotion, and dance with joy, as each separate phase of mental experience comes on the scene. The power of language to symbolize in sound mental states and perceptions, has never before been so magically proved."[12]

Tennyson's experimentalism is especially clear in the first edition, which provides no part divisions or subtitle and immediately plunges readers into the rant of the opening lines:

> I HATE the dreadful hollow behind the little
>   wood,
> Its lips in the field above are dabbled with blood-
>   red heath,

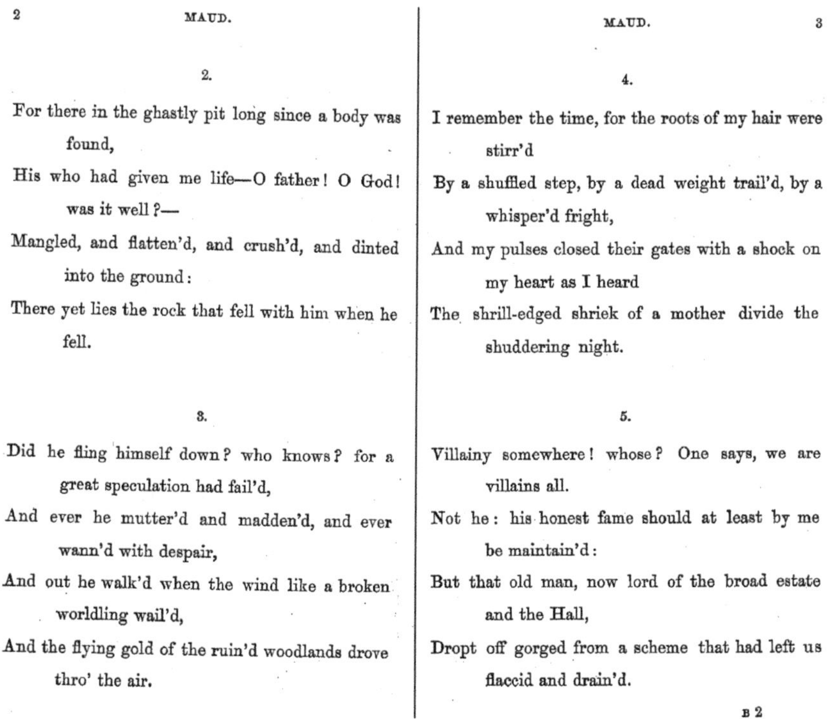

2.

For there in the ghastly pit long since a body was
  found,
His who had given me life—O father! O God!
  was it well?—
Mangled, and flatten'd, and crush'd, and dinted
  into the ground:
There yet lies the rock that fell with him when he
  fell.

3.

Did he fling himself down? who knows? for a
  great speculation had fail'd,
And ever he mutter'd and madden'd, and ever
  wann'd with despair,
And out he walk'd when the wind like a broken
  worldling wail'd,
And the flying gold of the ruin'd woodlands drove
  thro' the air.

4.

I remember the time, for the roots of my hair were
  stirr'd
By a shuffled step, by a dead weight trail'd, by a
  whisper'd fright,
And my pulses closed their gates with a shock on
  my heart as I heard
The shrill-edged shriek of a mother divide the
  shuddering night.

5.

Villainy somewhere! whose? One says, we are
  villains all.
Not he: his honest fame should at least by me
  be maintain'd:
But that old man, now lord of the broad estate
  and the Hall,
Dropt off gorged from a scheme that had left us
  flaccid and drain'd.

B 2

Figure 3   Alfred Tennyson, *Maud* (London: Edward Moxon, 1855), pp. 2–3

The red-ribb'd ledges drip with a silent horror of
    blood,
And Echo there, whatever is ask'd her, answers
    "Death."[13]

The odd meter – iambic hexameter rather than the dactylic hexameter of classical tradition – becomes more skittery with erupting anapests in shifting positions ("in the field," "-er is ask'd"). The very format of the lines (see Figure 3) bespeaks excess, a manic push of (textual) speech that spills into the space where another line ought to be.

After twenty-one pages of this, hexameters settle into tetrameters and the format resembles that of conventional lyric as the speaker hears Maud sing "A martial song like a trumpet's call" (p. 22). Later, in the ecstasy of his love, the speaker attains new lyric compression and order in "Go not, happy day" (pp. 54–5). The hero professes new-found identity born of patriotic dedication to war at the poem's end, but since the last page recalls the first in format, readers might question how far he has come. Variant line lengths, then, become a mobile register of the speaker's rising or quelled emotions.

The most radical Victorian experiments in meter and rhythm occur in the poetry of Gerard Manley Hopkins, which became an important influence on modernist poets after its posthumous publication in 1918. Hopkins, however, was known to late-Victorian readers through the eight poems included in *Poets and Poetry of the Century*, edited by Alfred Miles (1893). "The Starlight Night" was then reprinted in the first *Oxford Book of Victorian Verse*. The opening four lines of Hopkins's sonnet exemplify the principles of what Hopkins terms sprung rhythm, which is scanned according to stress rather than the more predictable patterns of conventional meters:

> Look at the stars! look, look up at the skies!
>   O look at all the fire-folk sitting in the air!
>   The bright boroughs, the quivering citadels there!
>   The dim woods quick with diamond wells; the elf-eyes![14]

Each line has five feet comprising one stressed syllable and anywhere from one to four unstressed syllables. As Hopkins asserts in his posthumously published Preface, sprung rhythm features "only one nominal rhythm" but carries the advantage of "twice the flexibility of foot."[15]

Sprung rhythm is indebted to the alliterative, four-stress line of Old English verse, with which Tennyson also experimented in a translation of "Battle of Brunanburh" in 1880. But Hopkins's sprung rhythm is a freer, more demanding form, since readers have no template to organize rhythm and must self-consciously negotiate conceptual "stresses" that inform accentual stresses and vice versa. How long, for example, are the pauses between "stars! look, look," which compose three of the five stressed syllables in line 1? Are the pauses mimetic, as imagined auditors crane their necks for a better "look" upward; hortatory, as the impassioned poet-priest implores his audience to gaze upon the wonders of God's creation; or epiphanic, as the revelation of the skies breaks on speaker and reader alike? Or are the pauses minimized in a rhythmic rush of theophanic joy?

Another innovation associated with the twentieth century but evident in Victorian poetry is free verse. Here the key figure is not British but the American Walt Whitman. According to William Michael Rossetti, cognoscenti in England were reading Whitman in imported American editions as soon as *Leaves of Grass* was published in 1855, despite hostile reviews that charged Whitman with formlessness and indecency. Rossetti published a selected British edition of Whitman in 1868 that opened with "Chants Democratic" and cut "Song of Myself."[16] If Rossetti effectively bowdlerized Whitman, he enabled his verse to be read in homes and libraries, and the *Athenaeum* pronounced "Out of the Cradle Endlessly Rocking" "noble poetry," while *Chambers's Journal*, with a circulation of between 60,000 and 70,000, printed liberal extracts and explained free verse to middle-brow readers: "he has invented a certain rolling changeful metre of his own, with, as his English editor truly remarks, 'a very powerful and majestic rhythmical sense throughout.'"[17]

If two results were Swinburne's rhymed poem "To Walt Whitman in America" (1871) and inclusion of Whitman in the first *Oxford Book of Victorian Verse*, a third was *In Hospital* by W. E. Henley. Henley lost one foot to tubercular infection and underwent treatment from 1873 to 1875 by Joseph Lister at the Royal Infirmary, Edinburgh, to save the other. Only the rhymed poems in his sequence were published in *Cornhill Magazine* in July, 1875, but in 1888 Henley published the whole in *A Book of Verses*. After depicting the pain, tedium, and people of hospital life in a range of tones and forms, the poem culminates in "Discharged." When the speaker is carried out he confronts the "stature and strength of the horses," the "flat roar and rattle of wheels," and the "smell of the mud in my nostrils" (5, 7, 10) until something more provocative arrests his attention:

> As of old,
> Ambulant, undulant drapery,
> Vaguely and strangely provocative,
> Flutters and beckons. O, yonder –
> Is it? – the gleam of a stocking!
> Sudden, a spire
> Wedged in the mist! O, the houses,
> The long lines of lofty, grey houses,
> Cross-hatched with shadow and light!
>   …
> Free …!
> Dizzy, hysterical, faint,
> I sit, and the carriage rolls on with me
> Into the wonderful world.   (12–20, 23–6)

Free verse admirably suits the exultant freedom of the discharged patient after the hospital's drab routines and allows for sharp cuts in focus as the speaker's eye riots in a chaotic sensory tableau. Dactyls convey the erotic charge of "undulant" clothing but are erased by the next sight and a new rhythm. The skeptical self-assessment in line 24 counterbalances the final line's "wonderful world" and reminds readers of the poet's underlying control as he represents the former hospital inmate plunged into a world of wonders.

Henley, who returned to free verse in *Rhymes and Rhythms* (1892), is its most important nineteenth-century British exponent. Otherwise free verse remained a rarity in Victorian England. Richard Le Gallienne uses it only to satirize decadence in "The Décadent to His Soul" (1893); Graham R. Tomson (later Rosamund Marriott Watson) uses it in "The Last Fairy" (1891), reprinted in *The Oxford Book of Victorian Verse*, to represent the modern forces that expel fairies from the world; and Edward Carpenter, a Whitman disciple, writes *Towards Democracy* (1883–1902) in free verse while affirming socialism and same-sex desire, thus paying homage to Whitman's Calamus poems and democratic vision. But only in the twentieth century did free verse become a readily accepted medium for serious British poetry.

Experiments in language, image, symbol

Robert Browning's bold expansion of the lexicon was a key contribution to modern poetic tradition. In the Preface to *Lyrical Ballads* (1802), Wordsworth advocates "the real language of men in a state of vivid sensation," and his lyrical ballads feature direct expression in service to philosophical elevation.[18] Even Wordsworth's evocations of humble life in "Simon Lee" or "We are Seven" seem a world away from Browning's "Soliloquy of a Spanish Cloister" (1842): "Gr-r-r – there go, my heart's abhorrence! / Water your damned flower-pots, do!" (1–2). The legacy of Browning's break with mellifluous tone and diction is immediately clear in the *Cantos* of modernist poet Ezra Pound: "Hang it all, Robert Browning, / there can be but the one 'Sordello'" (Canto 2, 1–2). Whitman was far more daring in his erotics than Browning but found sanction in the Victorian poet for his "barbaric yawp" and assumption that even the "pismire" and "tree-toad" were fit words for poetry ("Song of Myself," 31.2–3, 52.3).[19]

The same year that *Leaves of Grass* was published Browning pushed his own lexicon further in "Childe Roland to the Dark Tower Came," so fiercely imagining ugliness that it becomes a form of the sublime as the speaker stumbles directionless through a wasteland of leprous grass, "clay and rubble," "blotches rankling," and moss "like boils" (73–4, 150–1, 153). Hopkins's use of "May-mess" to describe the effect of orchard blooms in "Starlight Night" (10) is more comprehensible after Browning, as is the landscape in Thomas Hardy's "Neutral Tones" (1898), which seems "chidden of God" with its "few leaves" on "the starving sod" that "had fallen from an ash, and were gray" (2–4).

Browning, however, did not merely expand the lexicon of poetry by showing that discordant sound was as proper to poetry as euphony; he also experimented with compressed syntax, eliminating conventional bridges between thoughts, even parts of speech, as in these lines from "Fra Lippo Lippi," when the painter has been caught in the glare of watchmen's torchlight as he pads along alleys frequented by prostitutes and momentarily brazens out the situation:

> The Carmine's my cloister: hunt it up,
> Do, – harry out, if you must show your zeal,
> Whatever rat, there, haps on his wrong hole,
> And nip each softling of a wee white mouse,
> Weke, weke, that's crept to keep him company!   (7–11)

Ventriloquized squeaks interrupt a dependent clause describing the mouse, and agile reading is required to discern that the verb "nip" is attached not to "rat" but to the harrying "you," or that the momentary ambiguity allows Fra Lippo to imply their equivalence.

Such techniques explain repeated complaints that Browning was "obscure," but Hopkins and Emily Dickinson were instructed by Browning and pushed his syntactical compression even further. Note, for example, the second quatrain of Hopkins's "Starlight Night":

> The grey lawns cold where gold, where quickgold lies!
>   Wind-beat whitebeam! airy abeles set on a flare!
>   Flake-doves sent floating forth at a farmyard scare!–
> Ah well! it is all a purchase, all is a prize.   (5–8)

Successive similes for the starlit night function grammatically as appositives of "skies," but since Hopkins, as in "Fra Lippo," excises the grammatical links connecting lines 3 to 7 back to line 1, readers have to construct connections as they read. "Flake-doves" (7) represents an innovation that goes well beyond Browning's play with language. It compresses into a single noun phrase the agent and effect of an action, frightened doves flying and losing feathers that then float in the air, and the images of wonder (snow flakes) and decay (skin flaking off) these evoke by association.

Other Victorian experiments with language were less serious but no less complex, since the nonsense narrative verses of Edward Lear and Lewis Carroll demonstrate the inherent gap posited by twentieth-century semiotics between syntax and semantics, between the deep grammar of language and the meaning of individual words. "The Dong with the Luminous Nose" (1876), by Edward Lear, mimics pastoral laments of abandoned lovers but thwarts mimesis and the referentiality of language in the "Dong" and his "Jumbly Girl" (27–8). Lewis Carroll's "Jabberwocky," from *Through the Looking-Glass* (1872), is the more knowing, and famous, linguistic experiment. Here a few conjunctions and stative verbs provide the scaffolding for words that are not words; yet the oblique echoes of "brilliant" skies or "gambols" in "waves," as well as rhythm and sound, make reading the text a poetic experience:

> 'Twas brillig, and the slithy toves
>   Did gyre and gimble in the wabe:
> All mimsy were the borogoves,
>   And the mome raths outgrabe.   (1–4)

Experiments with image and symbol in the Victorian era are more closely tied than linguistic experimentation to distinct literary movements, especially Pre-Raphaelitism, aestheticism, and decadence. D. G. Rossetti was one of seven painters who banded together in 1848, that year of revolutions, to overturn stultifying conventions by drawing upon techniques that predated Renaissance perspective, color, and line. Since Raphael epitomized the achievements of Renaissance art, the young men dubbed themselves the Pre-Raphaelite Brotherhood and began signing "P. R. B." after their names on paintings. Rossetti also drew on medieval tradition in his poetry, especially from his namesake Dante. His first important poem, "The Blessed Damozel," appeared in the little magazine launched by the PRB in January, 1850 to advance its aesthetic agenda, *The Germ: Thoughts Towards Nature in Poetry, Literature and Art*. Rossetti's poem borrows its general situation from Dante, but rather than leading the poet heavenward to God, as Beatrice does in Dante's *Paradiso*, the damozel yearns toward earth and the lover left behind. "The Blessed Damozel" thus empties out the theology behind Dante's poem, replacing it with a religion of earthly love and desire.

Similarly, the poem appropriates religious images but empties them of traditional symbolic meaning. The damozel holds "three lilies in her hand"; "the stars in her hair were seven"; and "souls mounting up to God / Went by her like thin flames" (5–6, 41–2). But her desiring body negates spiritual transcendence:

> And still she bowed herself and stooped
>   Out of the circling charm;
> Until her bosom must have made
>   The bar she leaned on warm,
> And the lilies lay as if asleep
>   Along her bended arm.   (43–8)

Coleridge contends that the symbol participates in the meaning it conveys, just as Christ's incarnated body is both the vehicle and expression of divine love.[20] Rossetti's imagery, in contrast, becomes a heuristic tool, provoking questions about whether meaning can be transcendent or whether symbolic import is merely an effect of language or paint; such imagery returns the reader to the text rather than enabling spiritual or moral realization.

The point is even clearer in Rossetti's "The Woodspurge" (1870), which fixates on a flower comprising "three cups in one" (12) and announces Rossetti's poetics in its concluding stanza:

> From perfect grief there need not be
> Wisdom or even memory:
> One thing then learnt remains to me, –
> The woodspurge has a cup of three.   (13–16)

Grief opens no conduit to the Holy Trinity; the image is its own meaning – an assumption later crucial to aestheticism, which rejected the moral purpose on which so much prior verse depended for legitimacy.

Christina Rossetti appropriates Pre-Raphaelite symbol quite differently in "Goblin Market." The significance of the goblin-men seems stable; they are satanic figures who tempt the women to whom they purvey fruits. But Laura and Lizzie exceed traditional symbolic patterns. Laura, unlike Eve, recovers her innocence after her fall; Lizzie imitates Christ in undergoing torment to save Laura, but a female Christ is, within western religion, a contradiction in terms. Moreover, neither Lizzie nor Laura dies to the world; instead they set up homes within it.

Aesthetes were more likely to follow the model of D. G. than Christina Rossetti. A good example, quoted in full below, is "Cyclamens" (1893) by "Michael Field," the aunt and niece Katharine Bradley and Edith Cooper, who considered themselves *"closer married"* than the Brownings since they were lovers who wrote lyrics collaboratively:[21]

> They are terribly white:
> There is snow on the ground,
> And a moon on the snow at night;
> The sky is cut by the winter light;
> Yet I, who have all these things in ken,
> Am struck to the heart by the chiselled white
> Of this handful of cyclamen.

The imagery is a verbal counterpart to the impressionist painting *Symphony in White No. 1: The White Girl* (1862), by James McNeill Whistler, which experiments with white on white paint. The first and penultimate lines, however, are indebted to Rossetti, for though the images create a mood, they incite no revelation beyond the beauty of "cyclamens" as word and image.

In "Stella Maris," a poem in *The Yellow Book* (April, 1894), Arthur Symons pushes Rossettian image toward decadence. Symons identifies "intense self-consciousness, a restless curiosity in research ... a spiritual and moral perversity" as defining elements in "The Decadent Movement in Literature."[22] These elements also typify his *Yellow Book* lyric. "Stella Maris," or "sea-star," is an epithet of the Virgin Mary signifying her guidance, but the woman in Symons's poem is a prostitute whom the speaker recalls while watching the beacon of a lighthouse search a bay. More than simply suspending the traditional associations of "Stella Maris," Symons "perverts" them, and the image he ascribes to the haunting, wraithlike "Juliet of a night" anticipates the "sea-girls wreathed with seaweed" in T. S. Eliot's "The Love-Song of J. Alfred Prufrock" (*Poetry Magazine* [June, 1915]):

> I see your eyes
> Out of the empty night arise;
> Child, you arise and smile to me
> Out of the night, out of the sea,
> The Nereid of a moment there,
> And is it seaweed in your hair?
> O lost and wrecked, how long ago,
> Out of the drowning past, I know
> You come to call me, come to claim
> My share of your delicious shame.   (22–31)

Five years later Symons reworked "The Decadent Movement" into "The Symbolist Movement in Literature." French symbolists such as Stéphane Mallarmé and Gérard de Nerval, he argues, abandon a materialist rhetoric of exteriority for new symbolism that suggests and insinuates essences rather than relying on a fixed image. The self-conscious indirection crucial to the French symbolist movement is also evident in several Victorian poems, beginning with Morris's "The Blue Closet" (1858). Inspired by a watercolor of the same title that D. G. Rossetti was painting in 1856–7, Morris's poem is a form of ekphrasis, a verbal recreation of a visual artifact. Both poem and painting are evocative yet highly ambiguous. As in Rossetti's poems the components of his painting are self-referring: the title comes from the blue tiles of the inner chamber's walls and floor rather than referring to blue as the Virgin's color, though the women who sing and play instruments might (or might not) be engaged in devotions, another purpose of medieval closets.

Morris adds to Rossetti's scenario a narrative; however, this does not clarify but rather renders the poem more surreal. As in a court masque or drama, differing speakers are assigned passages: first two damozels, then in turn Lady Louise, Lady Alice, and all singing together. Italicized text signals a tolling death knell that might be sung by the women but seems outside their control, especially when, in response to their song of a lover feared dead in distant wars, the italics relate how a red lily "*With a patch of earth from the land of the dead*" shoots up through the floor and the women die at the end of their song (60–1, 77–9). Perhaps, as Lady Alice seems to declare, they are imprisoned women permitted to sing only once a year in the blue closet; perhaps they indeed die at the end. Or perhaps the entire poem is a performative singing of all this and no more. The blue closet thus takes on associations of imprisoned, frustrated female desire; macabre foreglimpses of death and the body's decay; love's mystery; the evanescent elusiveness of singing; and the decorative values of multiple type fonts. The poem, rich in implication, resists direct articulation.

Three decades later a sonnet by A. Mary F. Robinson first titled "In Affliction" (1888) and later "Neuraesthenia" (1902) approximates symbolism insofar as Symons claims that in symbolist literature "the visible world is no longer a reality, and the unseen world is no longer a dream."[23] Rather than narrating psychological malady, Robinson fashions a charged image that intimates entrapment, disorientation, and dysphoria. The speaker lacks energy to mix with "the happier people of the house" (1); rather,

> I watch them glide like skaters on a stream
> 　　Across the brilliant surface of the world.
> But I am underneath: they do not dream
> 　　How deep below the eddying flood is whirl'd.   (5–8)

John Gray, the beautiful young man who gave a last name to Oscar Wilde's Dorian, worked directly out of French *symboliste* poetry. "The Vines" (1893) cuts from hard-edged image to image, the relation among them left obscure. Only the horror inspired by the prospect of a clinging bride seems certain:

> "Have you seen the listening snake?"
> Bramble clutches for his bride,
> Lately she was by his side,
> Woodbine, with her gummy hands.   (1–4)

The obvious debt to Mallarmé and Jules LaForgue did not please some critics, nor had Symons yet published his symbolist manifesto. A year later Gray reconverted to Catholicism, eventually becoming a priest, and it was not until T. S. Eliot discovered Symons's 1899 essay in 1908 that the symbolist movement became an important force in Anglophone poetry.

Conclusion

I conclude with a poet who might seem least likely to embrace the "changes [and] surprises" (285) hailed by Browning's "Fra Lippo Lippi": John Henry

Newman. Best known as a brilliant leader of the Oxford Movement who left the Church of England, converted to Roman Catholicism, and ended life as a Cardinal, he was also an important theologian bent on grounding religious practice in authoritative doctrine. So much deference to precedent and origins seems an unpromising herald of experimentalism. Certainly *The Dream of Gerontius* is unexceptional in doctrine, and it was a Victorian favorite after its initial serialization in the Jesuit magazine *The Month* (April–May 1865), later inspiring the oratorio composed by Edward Elgar (1900). In Newman's work, Gerontius (Greek for "old man") dies and his soul is transported to heaven by his guardian angel. The soul encounters devils, heavenly choirs, and a searing moment in God's presence before the guardian angel leaves him in purgatory and reassuringly bids farewell: "Be brave and patient on thy bed of sorrow; / Swiftly shall pass thy night of trial here, / And I will come and wake thee on the morrow" (898–900).

If approached in terms of form rather than doctrine, however, the poem is decidedly experimental. Newman draws upon the traditions of medieval psychomachia and church oratorio, but the poem also shares many features of Victorian poetry discussed above. Most fundamentally, *The Dream of Gerontius* is filled with multiple voices: the earthly and then disembodied Gerontius, his earthly attendants, angels, demons, and souls in purgatory. The title, moreover, is deeply ambiguous, possibly signifying that Gerontius merely dreams of death and judgment or that the poet shares his own dream of an old man and his death.[24] The contingent status of the poem and principal character, especially if all takes place in the mind of Gerontius – who may suddenly wake – recalls the similar contingency of dramatic monologues and their speakers, as well as that form's emergence from interest in extreme psychological experience.

The poem is also a hybrid form, comprising interior monologue, dialogue, hymns, Latin ritual and prayers, and demonic chants. At one point the guardian angel notes divergent measures of time: "For spirits and men by different standards mete / The less and greater in the flow of time" (344–5). The poem is likewise marked by metrical variation so extreme that it introduces constant "change" and "surprise" into the text. The dying Gerontius begins by speaking in rhymed iambic pentameter (*abab*), followed by attendants whose lines vary from four to seven feet; when Gerontius resumes he speaks in alternating pentameter and trimeter couplets. As the moment of his death nears (108–29), the rhyme scheme and metrics of his utterance grow ever more irregular (half rhymes occur, for example, in lines 80 and 82). After his death, blank verse predominates in the dialogues between Gerontius and his guardian angel. But as they near God's judgment court the demons pent in the vestibule erupt into irregularly rhymed dimeter lines, formatted on the page to create visual disorder, in contrast to the steady preceding columns of blank verse. Reminiscent of Browning's "Soliloquy of a Spanish Cloister" or Clough's *Dipsychus*, the demons adopt direct, colloquial language to sneer at the truckling faithful to whom a despotic God transfers the crowns once reserved for fallen angels:

> Triumphant still,
> And still unjust,
>
> Each forfeit crown [given]
> To psalm-droners,
> And canting groaners,
> To every slave,
> And pious cheat
> And crawling knave,
> Who lick'd the dust
> Under his feet   (426–35)

After more blank verse dialogue, songs in English hymn measure, a hexameter prayer by the Angel of the Agony, and alternating rhymes and pentameter-dimeter lines as the soul nears God's presence, the moment of judgment comes. Immediately the poem cuts to souls in purgatory, whose utterance suggests litany or biblical prose. As poetry, however, it is tantamount to free verse, with a strong but irregular rhythmic pulse (871–84). The guardian angel then bids farewell, unexpectedly using imperfect rhyme ("given" "heaven," 893, 895). As the poem gathers to a close, Newman surprises again by adopting feminine endings for the second and fourth lines of his *abab* quatrains. Even the poem's final line relinquishes the masculine culmination considered most forceful and authoritative. Newman has no interest in Rossettian image or *symboliste* technique, and though it is unclear whether he represents authentic religious experience or only a dream, his religious imagery is traditional. Doctrinally sound, in form *The Dream of Gerontius* is a compendium of Victorian experimentalism.

Chapter 2

Victorian dialogues with poetic tradition

> Here Homer, with the broad suspense
> Of thunderous brows, and lips intense
> Of garrulous god-innocence.
> There Shakespeare, on whose forehead climb
> The crowns o' the world: O eyes sublime
> With tears and laughters for all time!
>
> Elizabeth Barrett Browning, "A Vision of Poets" (1844)

Poets' use of inherited subject matter and forms such as the ode, sonnet, or ballad entails a conversation with poetic precursors and consideration of how well readers will understand each adaptation or break with tradition. Drawing on tradition can impart authority or cultural prestige to new work, enable greater poetic force and economy through allusion, inspire poets to new inventiveness in meeting formal challenges, attract connoisseurs who appreciate the niceties of adaptation, foster a poet's expression of solidarity with a community or ideological orientation, or highlight local experimentalism within a larger bow to precedent. Poets thus offer competing visions of how tradition should be approached, entering into dialogue with the living as well as the dead. The first question to pose of a Victorian poem adapting inherited material and forms, then, is how the poet is appropriating poetic tradition and to what artistic and cultural end. Though references to classical and modern European precedent often overlap, as in Barrett Browning's citation of Homer and Shakespeare in "A Vision of Poets," they are treated separately below to give some shape to a broad, amorphous, yet vital issue in Victorian poetry.

Classical tradition

Adaptations of classical subject matter

Acquaintance with classical literature was an entrenched part of grammar school and university education for Victorian males, and household tutors sometimes extended instruction to sisters as well, as in the childhood home of Elizabeth Barrett Browning. But there were less exclusive means to knowledge of classical literature. As boys Thomas Arnold (father to Matthew) and John Ruskin, the Victorian art and social critic, immersed themselves in Alexander Pope's translation of Homer's *Iliad* (1716).[1] The stable manager's son John Keats famously went beyond Pope and lit upon the translation of Homer's *Odyssey* by George Chapman (1616–18), recording his wonder in "On First Looking into Chapman's Homer" (1816), and later adapted Greek myths for poems.

Beyond the classical legacy transmitted through Renaissance, Neoclassical, and Romantic poetry, additional forms of print culture acquainted readers with Greco-Roman literature and myth. Thomas Keightley, best known for his popular *Fairy Mythology* (1828), produced *Mythology of Ancient Greece and Italy* in 1831 (enlarged in 1838), while George Grote began his immensely influential twelve-volume *History of Greece* (1846–56) with two volumes on Greek myths and legends. Periodicals repeatedly included essays on classical matter to bring knowledge within the reach of frugal as well as privileged readers. "The Writings of Homer," for example, appeared in the *Penny Magazine* of 1838, and Thomas De Quincey's more esoteric "Homer and the Homeridae" in the October, 1841 *Blackwood's Edinburgh Magazine*. In the late 1860s Arnold's Oxford lectures on the needful "sweetness and light" of Greek culture were serialized in *Cornhill Magazine* before publication as *Culture and Anarchy* in 1869. As A. A. Markley comments, in the Victorian age "The cultures of Greece and Rome never strayed far from public consciousness."[2]

Victorian adaptation of Greek subject matter is usefully represented in three successive poems by Swinburne, Dora Greenwell, and Tennyson based on the myth of Demeter and Persephone. According to this myth Persephone (also known as Kore or Cora) is wrested away from her mother Demeter by Hades and taken to the underworld as his consort. The goddess Demeter then refuses to send life-giving crops to the earth until Zeus and the other gods intervene to allow Persephone to spend part of each year with her mother, part in the underworld. The myth thus offers a range of possible points of departure, from mother–daughter relationships to natural cycles to theology.

In 1865 Swinburne gained fame with *Atalanta in Calydon: A Tragedy*, a predominantly blank-verse drama based on the classical story of Meleager's doomed love for Atalanta. Swinburne returned to blank verse and high seriousness in "At Eleusis" in *Poems and Ballads* (1866). According to the ancient Homeric Hymn to Demeter, which George Grote describes in detail,[3] the goddess went to Eleusis in human guise while grieving for Persephone and nursed Demophoon, son of King Celeus and his wife Metaneira, until his mother discovered him in a purifying fire that would grant immortality and ended the transformation. A cult of Demeter developed in Eleusis, where secret Eleusinian Mysteries were enacted yearly. Swinburne's title thus has a double frame of reference. It places Demeter before the assembled citizens of Eleusis as she designates the grown babe (here conflated with Triptolemus, the traditional founder of agriculture) as her priest and promises to bless his followers. The title simultaneously suggests ritual enactment of an Eleusinian Mystery.

In her monologue Demeter narrates her anger at Zeus' collusion in the violent capture of Persephone, her thwarting of the gods' delight in human worship by destroying the cattle and crops that supplied sacrificial altars, and the limited human understanding that drove Metaneira to thwart her son's chance at immortality. It is thus a poem about human littleness contrasted with gods' divine powers, and since not even godhead protects Persephone from violent attack or Demeter from grief, fragile humanity seems more vulnerable still. The poem also emphasizes female power of a sort very different from that of the Christian intercessor Mary. In declaring that no crops will come until Zeus restores her daughter, Demeter adds, "For of all other gods is none save me / Clothed with like power to build and break the year" (51–2). Though she vows to "ease" the "harsh weight" of her curse for worshipers at Eleusis so long as they follow the rituals she has taught to Triptolemus, she also commands them to save "the choice of warm spear-headed grain" and sacrifice the "beasts that furrow the remeasured land / With their bowed necks of burden equable" (212–13, 218–23).

Humanity labors like the oxen they sacrifice for the goddess's pleasure but remains enslaved. Persephone is avenged by her mother, moreover, but not returned to her. In this poem religion offers no spiritual transcendence and, as Margot K. Louis observes, "The Eleusinian tale of disconnection and reconnection is turned into a tale of disconnection only." Herein lies its dialogue with tradition. Swinburne breaks with the Romantic precedent of seeking kindred elements in myth and Christianity and instead underscores the alterity of Greek culture. And while nothing in "At Eleusis" would prevent its being read aloud in a drawing room, it is placed in a volume of scandalous poems that, Louis asserts, suggest the orgiastic acts thought to characterize Eleusinian Mysteries.[4]

In "Demeter and Cora" (1876), Greenwell emphasizes the mother–daughter relationship: "Is't well with thee, my mother – tell?' / 'Is't well with thee, my daughter?'" (11–12).[5] Greenwell constructs a dialogue that expresses the abiding love of mother and daughter but also marks their severance: Demeter's thoughts reach Cora in Hades, but she cannot hear Cora, who resides apart in the realm of the dead. Domesticating Greek myth, the poem evokes the common Victorian experience of mothers' loss, including that of daughters leaving home to marry, and perhaps represents the wish that dead children continue to hear mothers' expressions of love. Greenwell also uses Greek myth to critique marriage and the daughterly submission recommended by Sarah Stickney Ellis in *Daughters of England* (1845). Cora has been forced into marriage and chafes in her confinement:

> too well
> He loves! he binds with unwrought chain.
> I was not born to be thy mate,
> Aïdes! nor the Queen of pain:
> I was thy daughter Cora, vowed
> To gladness in the world above.   (24–9)

Intriguingly, this daughter knows more, not less, than the mother, since Cora alone hears both sides of the dialogue and sets limits beyond which Demeter may not go: "'daughter, say, / Dost love Aïdes?' 'Now, too bold / Thy question, mother'" (36–8). Greenwell uses the Greek form of Hades ("Aïdes") but opts for "Cora" rather than Persephone, perhaps to echo "Corinne," the eponymous poet-protagonist of Madame de Staël's influential novel of 1807. For like a Romantic poet, Cora possesses special knowledge of an alien if richly beautiful realm, in which flowers are "fed with fire" and "kindle in a torch-like flame / Half ecstasy, half tender shame / Of bloom" (71–4). Greenwell, then, adapts Greek myth to express domestic affections yet also appropriates the strangeness of myth to question daughters' conventional roles.

Unlike Swinburne and Greenwell, who emphasize severance, Tennyson opens "Demeter and Persephone (In Enna)" (1889) at the moment Mercury escorts Persephone up from Hades to her waiting mother. Depicting both reunion and resurrection, the poem synthesizes theology and domesticity, the twin thrusts of Swinburne's and Greenwell's poems, while reviving earlier Romantic attempts to associate myth and Christianity. In Tennyson's monologue Demeter is a forerunner of Christ, her grief for Persephone inducing divine sympathy for humankind ("And [I] grieved for man through all my grief for thee" [74]). She also anticipates that "younger kindlier Gods [will] bear us down, / As we bore down the Gods before us" (129–30).

Like Swinburne's "At Eleusis," Tennyson's monologue suggests both a specific occasion and a performative ritual. His poem is also usefully seen in relation to Walter Pater's essay on "The Myth of Demeter and Persephone" in the *Fortnightly Review* (January–February, 1876), which identifies Demeter as a priestess and speculates that the Homeric Hymn might have been ritually recited during the Eleusinian Mysteries. Though Pater ultimately underscores Persephone's alien knowledge derived from her dual habitation in the upper and lower worlds, he also notes that "Demeter cannot but seem the type of divine grief" and that "Persephone is the goddess of death, yet with a promise of life to come."[6] Tennyson could thus claim the authority of a contemporary college don and aesthete in fashioning a more hopeful presentation of the myth than Swinburne.

Whereas Greenwell's Demeter suspects that mortals "perchance ... knew / It was not love for them that drew / Me down to wander" (56–8), Tennyson's Demeter, the monologue's speaker, is a loving universal mother. Most significantly, Tennyson's Demeter withholds crops not out of aggressive vengeance against Olympian gods, as in Swinburne, but because she is so prostrated by grief for her daughter that she can do no more than mourn: "lost in utter grief I failed / To send my life through olive-yard and vine" (107–8). Tennyson closely follows the Homeric Hymn but amends classical tradition by juxtaposing paganism with the loving God of Christianity, who is adumbrated by Demeter and her prophecy of a time when Persephone will

> reap with me,
> Earth-mother, in the harvest hymns of Earth
> The worship which is Love, and see no more
> The Stone, the Wheel, the dimly-glimmering lawns
> Of that Elysium, all the hateful fires
> Of torment, and the shadowy warrior glide
> Along the silent field of Asphodel.   (145–51)

The three Demeter poems have a counterpart in Elizabeth Barrett Browning's "The Dead Pan" (1844), Robert Browning's "Artemis Prologizes" (1855), and Matthew Arnold's *Empedocles on Etna* (1852), which also explore theology and humanity's place in the cosmos. "The Dead Pan" responds to "The Gods of Greece" ("Die Götter Griechenlands" [1788]), by Friedrich Schiller, which lamented the eclipse of sensuous Greek mythology by Christianity. Barrett Browning, in contrast, asserts the absolute superiority of Christian belief and its link to poetry:

> Earth outgrows the mythic fancies
> Sung beside her in her youth
> ...
> God himself is the best Poet,
> And the Real is His song.   (232–3, 248–9)

In "Artemis Prologizes" (1842) Robert Browning more obliquely indicates the superiority of a loving Christian god. The *Hippolytus* of Euripides unfolds the story of Phaedra's lust for her stepson Hippolytus, her suicide when he resists, and Hippolytus' death when his father Theseus believes her posthumous accusation against him. Artemis, the virgin huntress, then appears at the funeral pyre to reveal the innocence of Hippolytus to the horror-stricken father. Virgil's *Aeneid* and Ovid's *Metamorphoses* offered consolatory sequels in which Hippolytus is restored to life, and Browning's prologue follows their precedents. Identifying herself as a loving goddess to woodland creatures and chaste worshipers, among whom Hippolytus was a favorite, Artemis recalls how "I, in a flood of glory visible, / Stood o'er my dying votary and, deed / By deed, revealed, as all took place, the truth" (67–9). The stately blank verse (not a mode readily associated with Browning) is sustained as she recounts the plot of Euripides' drama, then breaks off, "Await[ing], in fitting silence, the event" of the youth's restoration to life (121).

The poem illuminates how the prestige of classical culture could enable poets to treat topics starkly opposed to domestic proprieties (lust, incest, suicide) but also implies a Christian framework of resurrection and redemption – in this case because Browning follows classical precedent so fully, embracing Virgil and Ovid as well as Euripides. Matthew Arnold called "Artemis Prologizes" "One of the very best antique fragments I know."[7] Allusion to multiple classical sources is itself a feature of classical literature,[8] and Arnold no doubt recognized Browning's mustering of multiple sources for the ethical and philosophical frame of his prologue.

Arnold's principal contribution to Victorian adaptations of classical material for philosophical purposes is *Empedocles on Etna* (1852), a verse drama involving Empedocles, the ancient Greek philosopher who commits suicide by leaping into the crater of Mt. Etna; Pausanius, physician to Empedocles; and Callicles (Arnold's invention), a youthful poet whose lyric celebrations of nature and redactions of myth frame and punctuate the poem. The formal choice of dramatic utterance by three characters allows Arnold to juxtapose competing worldviews as he explores the relation of the human mind to the world, self, and nature. Mind has become all-consuming in Empedocles, a plight that clarifies both the integrity of his philosophical quest ("I have loved no darkness, / Sophisticated no truth, / Nursed no delusion" [2.400–3]) and his alienation from the rest of humankind, who seek more than the bleak vision of a "wind-borne, mirroring soul, / [that] A thousand glimpses wins, / And never sees a whole" (1.83–5). Arnold draws upon classical philosophy, history, and myth to probe the modern condition of the alienated intellectual who seeks to live without religious dogma:

>   loth to suffer mute,
> We, peopling the void air,

Make Gods to whom to impute
The ills we ought to bear;
With God and Fate to rail at, suffering easily.   (1.277–81)

Callicles' lyrics, in contrast, embody the responsiveness to natural and aesthetic beauty that Empedocles has lost to age, relentless analysis, and alienating social change, while Pausanius represents lower-order intellects who seek knowledge but require comforting certainties. As Empedocles concludes, "I alone / Am dead to life and joy, therefore I read / In all things my own deadness" (2.320–2). Yet neither is Empedocles willing to spurn analysis and accept the half-truths that propel daily life among the general run of humanity – hence his suicide. The poem was a crucial turning point in Arnold's career. He suppressed *Empedocles* in 1853, commenting in his Preface that whereas poetry should "inspirit and rejoice the reader" and exclude "situations ... in which the suffering finds no vent in action," in *Empedocles* "the dialogue of the mind with itself has commenced."[9] Arnold here acknowledges not only the poem's internal dialogue but his own with classical tradition.

Classical materials in fact readily lent themselves to exploring art's role. George Grote identifies Greek myth as a form of imaginative creation, and Romantic poets had shaped myth into a modern symbolic idiom. Classical literature's endurance also raised questions about Victorian belatedness and impermanence. In *The Four Ages of Poetry* (1820) Thomas Peacock asserts that poetry belongs to an early phase of civilization and declines thereafter (prompting Shelley's retort in the "Defence of Poetry" that "Poets are the unacknowledged legislators of the world").[10] Victorians continued to examine the relevance of poetry to a modern industrial culture and, more specifically, of the past to the present, in works such as Tennyson's "The Lotos-Eaters" (1832, revised 1842) and Barrett Browning's "A Musical Instrument" (*Cornhill Magazine* [July, 1860]).

Tennyson's monologue pits the forward-driving Ulysses – who urges "Courage!" – against weary mariners who seek to remain wrapped in memories and aesthetic delights inspired by their drug of choice, the lotos, rather than undertake the hard task of returning home. A Homeric episode from the *Odyssey* enables Tennyson both to perform the delights of sensuous language –

How sweet it were ...
Eating the Lotos day by day,
To watch the crisping ripples on the beach,
And tender curving lines of creamy spray;
To lend out hearts and spirits wholly
To the influence of mild-minded melancholy   (99, 105–9) –

and to set the delights of aesthetic escape against the demands of creating social order and sustaining communities. The mariners conclude their choric song by pledging, "we will not wander more," but the poem's oscillations between seductive aesthetic delights and troubling memories of suffering unsettle their resolve.

Barrett Browning contributes to dialogues about art by reframing her own in terms of gender. Pan occupies the foreground of "A Musical Instrument," and that of the *Cornhill* illustration that accompanied the poem (Figure 4), as a source of anarchic ruin: "What was he doing, the great god Pan, / Down in the reeds by the river? / Spreading ruin and scattering ban" (1–3). If Pan produces beauty by fashioning a pipe from reeds and blowing "in power by the river[,] / Sweet, sweet, sweet, O Pan! / Piercing sweet by the river!" (30–2), beauty and pain coalesce. For the reed Pan "hacked" and the "pith" he extracts "With his hard bleak steel" are akin to "the heart of a man": "half a beast is the great god Pan, / To laugh as he sits by the river, / Making a poet out of a man" (15, 16, 21, 37–9). As Dorothy Mermin comments, readers familiar with Ovid's *Metamorphoses* would know that the reed was originally the nymph Syrinx, who fled from Pan's lust and was transformed into a reed to escape violation. Here the creation of song is graphically represented in terms of rape, suggesting that female poetry emerges from pain, violation, and sexual knowledge.[11] Through allusion, Barrett Browning boldly asserts a link between female poetics and female sexuality that would have been impossible without classical tradition.

"A Musical Instrument" thus participates in an important Victorian contribution to Anglo-classical tradition: adaptation of classical material to enter debates about gender and sexuality. Even Tennyson's "Tithonus" (*Cornhill Magazine* [February, 1860]) resists conventional masculinity, since it unfolds a scenario of masculine impotence in the present, and sexual receptivity (rather than dominance) in the past, after Aurora, goddess of the dawn, grants her mortal lover's request for immortality but not eternal youth. Now a "white-haired shadow roaming" the portals of dawn with "wrinkled feet" (8, 67), Tithonus recalls the earlier self that

>   lay,
> Mouth, forehead, eyelids, growing dewy-warm
> With kisses balmier than half-opening buds
> Of April, and could hear the lips that kissed
> Whispering I knew not what of wild and sweet.   (57–61)

Gender roles become an overt theme in "Circe" (1870), by Augusta Webster. Whereas Circe is traditionally represented as a seductive witch who betrays

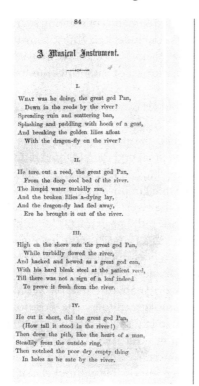

Figure 4   Elizabeth Barrett Browning, "A Musical Instrument," *Cornhill Magazine* (July, 1860), 84–5

men into drinking the potion that transforms them into beasts, Circe's chalice merely reveals their true nature in Webster's monologue. Recoiling in disgust from the beasts who crowd around her with their "piteous fawnings" and "supplicating bleats" (183), she retorts,

> any draught, pure water, natural wine,
> Out of my cup, revealed them to themselves
> And to each other. Change? there was no change;
> Only disguise gone from them unawares:
> And had there been one true right man of them
> He would have drunk the draught as I had drunk,
> And stood unharmed and looked me in the eyes.   (186–92)

Like Amy Levy in "Xantippe," Webster interrogates the transmission of classical tradition by inquiring how situations might look from a female perspective.

A kindred response to classicism and Victorian feminism is Edward Dowden's "Europa," one of five classical monologues grouped as "The Heroines" in his 1876 *Poems*. Europa was carried away by Zeus in the form of a bull, but rather than with fright, Dowden's Europa, the speaker, is filled with exultation, for she recognizes the god beneath the disguise (2–3) and knows him as her destiny. With it comes a "wider orbed … vision of the world" (35) that will free her from a daughter's restricted life, "The daily dictates of my mother's will, / Agenor's [her father's] cherishing hand, and all the ways / Of the calm household" (43–5).

Swinburne adapts classical myth to challenge the very concept of separate sexes in "Hermaphroditus," inspired by an ancient Greek sculpture in the Louvre. Swinburne's four-sonnet sequence represents endless but thwarted desire, whether it is evoked in the gazing observer –

> whosoever hath seen thee, being so fair,
> Two things turn all his life and blood to fire;
> A strong desire begot on great despair,
> A great despair cast out by strong desire   (11–14) –

or in Hermaphroditus –

> Love stands upon thy left hand and thy right,
> Yet by no sunset and by no moonrise
> Shall make thee man and ease a woman's sighs,
> Or make thee woman for a man's delight.   (33–6)

Here a body is denied sexual congress because it is too full of sex. The sonnets conclude by tracing the hermaphrodite's origin to the nymph Salmacis, who desired the beautiful Hermaphroditus, Aphrodite's son, and pleaded for the gods to unite them: "Beneath the woman's and the water's kiss / Thy moist limbs melted into Salmacis," and "all thy boy's breath softened into sighs" (52–3, 55). The poem is technically a form of ekphrasis given its subscription, "*Au Musée du Louvre, Mars 1863*." But it is also designed to trouble and shock; Swinburne suspends heterosexuality and instead insinuates bisexuality or a more unsettled gender ambiguity that cannot be classed.

Victorian Greek studies also opened a space for same-sex desire in poetry, since homosexual relations were an accepted part of ancient Greek life. "Charmides" (1881), by Oscar Wilde, and *Long Ago* (1889), by Michael Field, both appropriate this potential of classical material. Wilde's poem foregrounds fetishism, hubris, and necrophily, since the beautiful youth Charmides sexually assaults the statue of the goddess Athena in her temple and dies in consequence; in turn his beautiful corpse is ravished by a desiring girl. But readers trained in Greek would have recognized Wilde's allusion to Plato's *Charmides*, a dialogue that teaches temperance but also dramatizes Socrates' sexual desire for the beautiful boy Charmides.

Building upon the precedent of Swinburne's "Anactoria," Michael Field deepen the link between Sappho and lesbian desire in *Long Ago*. Most representations of Sappho early in the century invoked the Sappho of Ovid's *Heroides*, who leapt to her death out of unrequited love for the youth Phaon. In 1885 Henry Thornton Wharton issued a memoir and literal translation of Sappho that reintroduced women as the recipients of Sappho's ardent expressions of desire. Illustrations of Sappho appear on the cover and frontispiece of *Long Ago*, and Michael Field preface each lyric with a Greek epigraph drawn from Sappho. Lyric XIV, addressed to Atthis, expresses Sappho's terror when she wakes to find Atthis absent from bed, then recounts how she drew the returning Atthis "down to my breast," vowing that "our very breath / Nor light nor darkness shall divide" (11–14). Swinburne excepted, lesbian love was rarely expressed so directly in serious Victorian poetry. Yet the material resemblance of *Long Ago* to scholarly editions enabled it to enjoy public recognition and positive reviews, and it quickly sold out.

Classical subject matter, then, could be adapted by Victorian poets to explore theology, agnosticism, art, gender, and sexuality. Collectively, these Victorian adaptations extend Anglo-classical poetic tradition and reveal a lively debate over what classicism and its relation to the present signified.

Classical forms

Classicism also bequeathed to Victorians a range of poetic forms that could be used for modern content. One of the most famous results is Tennyson's "Ode on the Death of the Duke of Wellington" (1852), his first significant poem after becoming Poet Laureate in 1850. The choral ode dates back to the Greek poet Pindar (*c.* 520–440 BC) and gave rise to the British irregular ode. Because the ode is inseparable from public occasions and elevated diction and rhetoric, it is an unsurprising choice for Tennyson's tribute to the "Iron Duke": the military hero, who defeated Napoleon at Waterloo in 1815, was briefly prime minister, and became a respected statesman afterward. Bypassing the Romantic odes of Wordsworth and Keats, which treat moments of personal crisis, Tennyson's ode more obviously looks back to older precedents.

Like "Demeter and Persephone," the Wellington ode is another performative poem, calling attention to its public, ritual function as it expresses national sorrow and patriotism. It also steers between the demands of lasting poetry and a specific occasion widely followed by the public in the daily press:

> Bury the Great Duke
>> With an empire's lamentation,
> Let us bury the Great Duke
>> To the noise of the mourning of a mighty nation,
> Mourning when their leaders fall,
> Warriors carry the warrior's pall,
> And sorrow darkens hamlet and hall.   (1–7)

The twin decrees of death and public duty are enforced by imperative voice and the resounding trochees and spondees of lines 1 and 3. Yet the opening also represents the nation's swelling sorrow and unease in the rush of syllables and feminine endings of lines 2 and 4. The entire ritual of burial is recapitulated in the course of the ode, from the initial processional ("let the mournful martial music blow" [17]), to the cathedral service, interment, public eulogy, and ritual of Anglican burial ("Ashes to ashes, dust to dust," "God accept him, Christ receive him" [270, 281]).

Tennyson particularizes the common obsequies of death by recalling the homely detail of the Duke's daily greeting of others "in soldier fashion," recognizing with "lifted hand the gazer in the street," a detail that contrasts meaningfully with his burial "in streaming London's central roar" (21–2, 9). Tennyson briefly alludes to the conservative politics of the Duke (and the Laureate, for that matter) in noting current anxieties about "brainless mobs and lawless Powers" (153) now that a great leader is gone. Above all, Tennyson underscores the inspiration that mourners can derive from one caring "not to be great, / But as he saves or serves the state" (199–200) and for whom "The path of duty was the way to glory" (202, 210, 224). The stateliness, dignity, and rich diction of the ode, a counterpart to the "gorgeous rites" it records (93), thus move beyond a particular moment and public response to a constitutive enactment of British national identity and greatness.

The Wellington Ode immediately acquired such prominence that it became a tacit frame of reference for other odes. Barrett Browning championed the cause of Italian freedom from Austrian rule and was incensed at her country's acquiescence in the status quo. She also diverged from British majority opinion in her attitude toward Napoleon III, who was democratically elected president of the French Republic in 1848 and, after he dissolved parliament and instated universal suffrage in 1852, was ratified as Emperor by a plebiscite. When Napoleon III joined forces with the Italian resistance against Austria, Barrett

Browning appropriated the ode to celebrate him as a champion of freedom in "Napoleon III in Italy" (1860).

As opposed to the equipoise and balance of the Wellington Ode, qualities usually associated with the Latin odes of Horace, Barrett Browning embraces the changeful yet elevated tone of Pindaric odes. It was daring for an Englishwoman to devote an ode to the nephew of Wellington's arch-enemy, especially when her first stanza acknowledges French desire to "renew the line / Broken in a strain of fate / And leagued kings of Waterloo" (7–9). Whereas the Wellington Ode locates its ethical center in duty, "Napoleon III in Italy" lauds the virtue of democracy. Its speaker is no Laureate but one of the "poets of the people, who take part / With elemental justice, natural right" (77–8). She considers Napoleon III to "transcend / All common king-born kings" because "The people's blood runs through him" (296–7, 301) and impels him to aid democracy in Italy.

Barrett Browning's democratic commitments also prompt her fury over Austrian atrocities against Italians ("they wound them / In iron, tortured and flogged them" [207–8]) and her elevation of Italian patriots inspired by Napoleon III: "each man stands with his face in the light / Of his own drawn sword, / Ready to do what a hero can" (181–3). She concludes by exalting revolutionary virtue over duty to the state:

> Courage, courage! happy is he,
>   Of whom (himself among the dead
>   And silent) this word shall be said:
> – That he might have had the world with him,
> But chose to side with suffering men.   (410–14)

Because "Napoleon III in Italy" shares the form and dignity of the Wellington Ode but not its politics, Barrett Browning tacitly draws attention to details that Tennyson omits: leaders were not yet selected by a process of universal suffrage in Britain, and British support of freedoms elsewhere was decidedly uneven.

Rather than resorting, like Tennyson and Barrett Browning, to the irregular Pindaric ode innovated by Abraham Cowley in the seventeenth century, Swinburne adopts the classical Pindaric structure of strophes and antistrophes followed by an epode in "Ode on Proclamation of the French Republic. September 4th, 1870." The Proclamation marked the fall of Napoleon III and imperial rule after his humiliating defeat by Prussia. Swinburne's formal choice evokes an ancient pagan democracy suited to republican hostility to state religion. Pindar's choral odes, moreover, call for lyric rhapsody, Swinburne's special province. Swinburne's ode is celebratory, infused by images of flame, resurrection, and nuptials that symbolize the revived republic. Six strophes contrast France's earlier repudiation of the Revolution under Napoleon III – which he equates with self-murder of the soul – with the resurrection first of liberty, then of France herself, the "many-wounded mother" and now a "Reborn republican" (59, 70). Six antistrophes hail her resurrected soul, which transforms France into the "fairest among women, and a bride" ready to wed "The spirit of man, the bridegroom brighter than the sun!" (145, 147). Just as Christ's relation to the church is often represented in terms of nuptials, Swinburne depicts the newly liberated spirit of man as bridegroom to France. The epode then celebrates the new union that extinguishes slavery and shame:

> This power thou hast, to be,
> Come death or come not, free;
> That in all tongues of time's this praise be chanted of thee,
> That in thy wild worst hour
> This power put in thee power,
> And moved as hope around and hung as heaven above thee.   (272–7)

In stark contrast to Barrett Browning's refrain of "Emperor Evermore," Swinburne celebrates a time when "confounded empire cowers" and the French "crown and crime" are broken "in pieces" (14, 250). Like Tennyson he mentions "lamentations" at the outset (7), but he elevates the principle of "the Republic universal" (215) over British nationhood; he also counters Tennyson's Christian dispensation with the Revolution, "a new sound of a God unknown" (113), which first proclaimed "manhood to mankind" (77). Both Tennyson and Swinburne first published their odes as free-standing pamphlets. This was strategic on Swinburne's part. Not only did this release call for comparison between his and Tennyson's odes, but the heightened artistry demanded by the ode also allowed reviewers to stress Swinburne's craft rather than his politics. As the *Athenaeum* averred, "this poem shows that Mr. Swinburne is more likely than he at one time seemed to be, to do justice to his great natural powers. His conception is clearer, the expression more matured, and his feeling more regulated: in a word, he is more artistic."[12] In Tennyson's hands, then, the Pindaric ode and its British descendant helped memorialize a signal moment in British public life. The well-known Wellington Ode in turn contextualized the odes of Barrett Browning and Swinburne and enabled their very different politics to be enunciated more clearly.

Robert Pattison devotes an entire book to Tennyson's reworking of the idyl,[13] a mobile, highly adaptable lyric form traceable to the Greek poet Theocritus (c. 300–260 BC). Two strands of idyl were particularly important to Victorian poetry: the rural scene or pastoral descending from Virgil's *Eclogues* (37 BC), which also inspired Edmund Spenser's *The Shepherd's Calendar* (1579), and the pastoral elegy extending back to Bion, Moschus, and Theocritus and forward through Milton's "Lycidas" (1638) and Shelley's "Adonais" (1821).

Tennyson's "Audley Court," a classically inspired rural scene grouped with other "English Idyls" in his 1842 *Poems*, is a blank-verse dialogue between Francis Hale, a farmer's son, and a speaker "in the fallow leisure of my life" who has time to talk, sing, and picnic with his friend by the bay at Torquay. For the unscholarly, the poem signals little more than a rural dialogue and singing contest between youths elevated by the scene's beauty. But the speaker tips his hand that something more is afoot by noting that his song was "found ... in a volume, all of songs" and that he "set the words, and added names I knew" (56, 60). Tennyson's Cambridge friends and erudite readers would have recognized his refashioning of the seventh idyl of Theocritus, in which Simichidas sings an earthy, and Lycidas an idealized, song. In setting new words to an inherited song Tennyson at once suggests the timelessness of friendship, art, and pastoral beauty, and attains distance on modern anxieties.

In "Audley Court" a country squire has gone bankrupt and the youths hotly debate the pros and cons of protective tariffs on grain before shaking hands over shared loyalty to the King. Reference to the bay's "latest horn" (10) and the "red granite" (12) over which the friends pass to picnic at Audley Court glances toward geology, but the potentially threatening implications of the fossil record are domesticated to a dish that gives pleasure: "a pasty costly-made, / Where quail and pigeon, lark and leveret lay, / Like fossils of the rock, with golden yolks / Imbedded and injellied" (22–5). Anxiety cannot be wholly displaced, however, even by mockery. Neither youth can find direction in life, and Francis derides those callings on which modern bourgeois society depends, from soldiers and accountants to civil servants and husbands:

> 'Oh! who would fight and march and countermarch,
> Be shot for sixpence in a battle-field,
> And shovelled up into some bloody trench
> Where no one knows? but let me live my life.[']   (39–42)

In Theocritus, Simichidas likewise flouts decorum, contending that for him "the Loves sneezed," and urging Pan to act graciously or else "be bitten and with thy nails scratch thyself" if he doesn't give the dearest friend of Simichidas the boy for whom he burns.[14] Francis's spurning of heterosexual love ("I wooed a woman once, / But she was sharper than an eastern wind" [51–2]) obliquely and safely echoes Theocritus. "Audley Court" updates Theocritus by incorporating modernity's challenges – financial and intellectual instability, potentially purposeless lives – but simultaneously pays tribute to Theocritean form while celebrating friendship and beauty: "the harbour-buoy, / Sole star of phosphorescence in the calm, / With one green sparkle ever and anon / Dipt by itself, and we were glad at heart" (85–8).

Matthew Arnold's "The Scholar-Gipsy" (1853) more overtly infects pastoralism with modern anxieties. "The Scholar-Gipsy" has been termed a pastoral elegy, but the scholar-gipsy lives rather than dies – by escaping from social ambition, anxiety, and merely sensual pleasure into endless wandering amidst a timeless rural landscape. The poem is as indebted to Keats's meditations on mortality and permanence in "Ode to a Nightingale" or "Ode on a Grecian Urn" as to Greek traditions, yet Arnold's opening lines might be taken directly from classical pastoral:

> Go, for they call you, shepherd, from the hill;
>   Go, shepherd, and untie the wattled cotes!
>   No longer leave thy wistful flock unfed,
>   Nor let thy bawling fellows rack their throats,
>   Nor the cropped herbage shoot another head.   (1–5)

The poem's speaker, however, an alienated modern intellectual, cannot inhabit the pastoral scene he observes, which is mediated for him by the book he totes, Joseph Glanvil's *Vanity of Dogmatizing* (1661). In contrast, the scholar of Glanvil's tale finds purpose in life by leaving the university and futile "knocking at preferment's door" (35) to join the gypsies, seeking mastery of their secret hypnotic powers. Seen no more by confrères, he enters into myth, becoming a genius of Oxfordshire perceptible only in unchanging rural tableaux: "Trailing in the cool stream [his] fingers wet" (75) at the ferry crossing, appearing at a stile to offer flowers to country girls ready to dance about the May elm, sitting upon the bank "when hay-time's here / In June, and many a scythe in sunshine flames" (91–2).

After 140 lines devoted to the scholar-gipsy, however, the poem's climax comes in 90 lines detailing the modern ills of "repeated shocks" that "numb the elastic powers" (144, 146), including "languid doubt," "vague resolves," and "divided aims" (164, 175, 204), until the poet cries to the scholar-gipsy to "fly our paths, our feverish contact fly!" (221). Modernity has become a contagious disease. The poem closes with an extended simile of a "Tyrian trader" who flees approaching Greek merchants – "intruders on his ancient home" (232, 240) – sails to the boundaries of the known world, and opens "his corded bales" for "Shy traffickers, the dark Iberians" (249–50). Since the Tyrian sailor, like the Greeks, engages in commerce, a modern preoccupation, this ending seems ambiguous at best. Possibly Arnold intended a framework drawn from classical tradition, since he alludes to Thessaly, the ancient Greek province associated with Achilles and Jason of the Argonauts (115); to Dido, the Carthaginian queen first loved, then abandoned, by Aeneas, founder of Rome (208); and Tyre itself. All were sites alternately free from, then devastated by, imperial conquest. Imperial conquest haunts both the modern and classical frames in Arnold's poem, then; only timeless pastoralism offers any escape. Yet Arnold's wresting the poem from modernity's devastations to the ambiguous Tyrian trader merely suggests how tentative such escape is.

A. Mary F. Robinson's "The Valley" (1901), like Tennyson's and Arnold's pastoral poems, constructs a dialogue between modern and classical perspectives. Coming to pastoral later than they, however, Robinson finds common ground between the ancient and modern worlds by means of geology and anthropology. Gazing upon the green valley of Auvergne, the poet comments, "The farms and forests of this vale of ours, / Are such, methinks, as gods and shepherds love, / And wait the flute of Pan" (10–12). But the impression that this is a vista "unchanged a thousand years" to which Mercury might return "And find, the same Auverne" (13–15) is illusory, for she stands upon a dormant volcano:

> [from] Fire, flood, fierce earthquakes of an elder world,
>   Red flames and smoke of swirling lava streams,
>   Tempests of ash and snow,
>   … the rock I stand upon was hurl'd.   (25–8)

Rather than finding a threat in geological change that overrides nostalgic desires for unchanging pastoral landscape, she finds comfort in primitive natural forces that forged her valley and the humanity that inhabits it: "through a myriad channels … / runs the Force of primitive fire," including "The lives of men who toil, foresee, aspire" and "The growth of grain and vine" (55–60).

Classical pastoralism was also suited to the self-conscious artifice and indifference to verisimilitude that characterized late-century aestheticism. Two poems of the 1880s invoke Latin rather than Greek pastoralism and nod to aestheticism insofar as their relation to Latin poetry becomes part of their subject matter. Robert Browning's "Pan and Luna," published in *Dramatic Idyls: Second Series* (1880), takes its epigraph ("Si credere dignum est") from Virgil's *Georgics*, which Browning immediately translates: "O worthy of belief I hold it was, / Virgil, your legend in those strange three lines!" (1–2). As part of a section on sheep-farming, Virgil tells how Pan "lured and beguiled" the Moon-goddess down to earth with a gift of "Snow-white wool."[15] Delighting in self-referring art, Browning playfully elaborates on Virgil, imagining the moon disrobing and plunging naked to earth, then diving into a cloud out of modesty to hide her nakedness only to be caught in a sticky wool trap set by Pan "by just her attribute / Of unmatched modesty betrayed" (81–2). Browning even explains why he chooses the term "Orbed" to describe the "rounds on rounds" of her "woman-figure" (41–2), eventually retreating to the decorous obliquity of "Say – her consummate circle" (46) as he enumerates its parts. Imagining chaste female purity consenting to Pan's rough advances proves harder. He considers the possibility of an allegorical explanation of lunar eclipses, then reverts to his underlying subject all along, the experience of reading, translating, and transmitting Virgil to a contemporary audience:

> Ha, Virgil? Tell the rest, you! "To the deep
> Of his domain the wildwood, Pan forthwith
> Called her, and so she followed" – in her sleep,
> Surely? – "by no means spurning him." The myth
> Explain who may! Let all else go, I keep
> – As of a ruin just a monolith –
> Thus much, one verse of five words, each a boon:
> Arcadia, night, a cloud, Pan, and the moon.   (97–104)

The title of Tennyson's "Frater ave atque vale" ("Brother Hail and Farewell"), first published in the March, 1883 issue of *Nineteenth Century*, is itself a citation of an elegy by Catullus, the first-century-BC Roman poet. In the text, Tennyson alludes simultaneously to the elegy and to Catullus' poem about the beautiful isle of Sirmio in Lake Garda, which enables him to link natural beauty and ruin, joy and death, past and present. The multiple resonances befit Tennyson's purpose. His brother Charles Tennyson Turner had died the year before Tennyson visited Sirmio, and Tennyson adopts homage to Catullus to utter his own "hopeless woe," restrained by the presence of the elder poet who partially supplies his words:

> Row us out from Desenzano, to your Sirmione row!
> So they rowed, and there we landed – "O venusta Sirmio!"
> There to me through all the groves of olive in the summer glow,
> There beneath the Roman ruin where the purple flowers grow,
> Came that "Ave atque Vale" of the Poet's hopeless woe,
> Tenderest of Roman poets nineteen-hundred years ago,
> "Frater Ave atque Vale" – as we wandered to and fro
> Gazing at the Lydian laughter of the Garda Lake below
> Sweet Catullus's all-but-island, olive-silvery Sirmio!

Like Browning, Tennyson places himself in relation to classical tradition and calls attention to the artifice of his art, but in the process Tennyson also crafts a lyric that brims with elegiac implication.

Pastoral elegy plays a more central role in his *In Memoriam* (1850). Written over a period of seventeen years after the death of Arthur Henry Hallam at age twenty-three, *In Memoriam* serves the function of all elegies of moving the mourner from loss to consolation. Milton had invented means to blend classical pastoral with a Christian framework in "Lycidas" and can aver "Weep no more, woeful shepherds, weep no more, / For Lycidas, your sorrow, is not dead" in the knowledge that Lycidas is translated to heaven "Through the dear might of him that walked the waves" (165–6, 173). The atheist Shelley desired no Christian framework and relied for consolation in his elegy responding to Keats's death on a Platonic conception of the infinite, eternal real that transcends fragmented human perception: "Life, like a dome of many-coloured glass, / Stains the white radiance of Eternity, / Until Death tramples it to fragments" (462–4). Nonetheless, Shelley echoes "Lycidas," declaring that Adonais, too, "is not dead" (343) and that he has "awakened from the dream of life" (344). *In Memoriam* confronts not only the inexplicable death of a rarely gifted, beloved young friend but also new threats to consolation posed by modern science. Tennyson steers a course between Milton's and Shelley's Christian and pagan consolations, reinterpreting the impersonal natural forces of evolutionary process that operate over eons as a gradualist act of divine creation,

> Whereof the man, that with me trod
>   This planet, was a noble type
>   Appearing ere the times were ripe,
> That friend of mine who lives in God,
>
> That God, which ever lives and loves,
>   One God, one law, one element,
>   And one far-off divine event,
> To which the whole creation moves.   (Epilogue, 137–44)

Earlier in the poem Tennyson draws upon the classical conventions of the shepherd poet piping, the Arcadian beauties formerly shared with the shepherd whose death is mourned, and the renewal of nature that at first ironizes loss and later suggests consolatory renewal or permanence. These conventions emerge most prominently when Tennyson considers the function of modern elegiac poetry (Sections 21, 38, 48) or dwells on his companionship with Hallam at Cambridge, where their official studies centered on Greek and Latin (Sections 22–6, 46, 87, 89). Pastoral elegy grants formal distance to Tennyson's meditations on poetry, and seamlessness in form and content to his acts of memorializing.

Section 89 is particularly significant because of its Theocritean context. In Section 87 the speaker revisits Cambridge and recalls his and Hallam's time at university, which prepares for the recurrence of classicism in Section 89 when the poet describes Hallam's later visits to Somersby. Here Hallam leaves behind the "dusty purlieus of the law" for "The sweep of scythe in morning dew" (12, 18). The two men picnic ("banquet in the distant woods," 32), discuss "books to love or hate" (34), explore "Socratic" philosophy (36), and debate politics:

> But if I praised the busy town,
>   He loved to rail against it still,
>   For "round in yonder social mill
> We rub each other's angles down.["]   (37–40)

All the while "the stream beneath us ran, / The wine-flask lying couched in moss" (43–4), until they return at nightfall, when

> brushing ankle-deep in flowers,
>   We heard behind the woodbine veil
>   The milk that bubbled in the pail,
> And buzzings of the honied hours.   (49–52)

The scene and situation closely echo those of "Audley Court" and likewise allude to the seventh idyl of Theocritus. The debate of lines 37–40 even suggests Greek singing contests. Section 89, accordingly, offers at once a consolatory memory, pastoralism's beauty, and the joys of male intimacy, the latter heightened by reference to Theocritean idyl and its associations with same-sex desire. A major achievement of *In Memoriam* is to combine pastoral elegy with elements drawn from other modes, including domestic poetry and amatory sonnet sequences. Tennyson's formal dialogue with classical and Renaissance tradition allows him everywhere to express love for a man without literalizing it in physical embrace and hence to fuse Christian and pagan, divine and natural love into a unifying force of consolation.

Pastoral elegies by two unbelievers shape alternative strategies for negotiating the legacies of classicism, Milton, and Shelley. "Thyrsis" (*Macmillan's Magazine* [April, 1866]), Arnold's elegy on Clough, remains a moving poem suited to the wide audience of a periodical as well as to the erudite, in part because Arnold merges Wordsworthian Romanticism and classical pastoral. The absence of the "signal-elm" (14) from the Oxfordshire landscape through which Clough and Arnold formerly passed so often underscores the sense of radical loss in the opening stanzas: "Now seldom come I, since I came with him. / That single elm tree bright / Against the west – I miss it! is it gone?" (25–7). Similarly, in Wordsworth's Intimations Ode "there's a Tree, of many, one, / A single Field which I have looked upon, / [that] speak[s] of something that is gone" (51–3). The emotional pivot of "Thyrsis" comes when the speaker suddenly rediscovers

"Bare on its lonely ridge, the Tree! the Tree!" (160). His desire to share news of the recovered landmark at first heightens his loss and alienation, since Thyrsis is dead and buried far away in Tuscany. But the impasse is mediated by Arnold's own "Scholar-Gipsy," into which Arnold retroactively inserts Clough: "while [the tree] stood, we said, / Our friend, the Gipsy-Scholar, was not dead" (28–9).

Yet Arnold and Clough developed very different views of poetry, and Clough would not necessarily have welcomed association with his friend's pastoral work. In a slighting review of Arnold's poems in 1853, Clough suggested that Arnold was unlikely to write lasting poetry by "turning and twisting his eyes, in the hope of seeing things as Homer, Sophocles, Virgil, or Milton saw them."[16] Arnold, in turn, does not deem the career of Thyrsis victorious, since social injustices "tasked thy pipe too sore, and tired thy throat – / It failed, and thou wast mute!" (225–6). But neither is his own career successful: "this many a year / My pipe is lost" (36–7). The figure of the scholar-gipsy helps mediate this impasse also, since the gipsy's timeless pursuit of higher mental powers suggests that quests after knowledge and beauty matter regardless of outcome: *"The light we sought is shining still. / Dost thou ask proof? Our tree yet crowns the hill, / Our Scholar travels yet the loved hill-side"* (238–40). The convention of the shepherd's pipe in pastoral elegy, then, as well as his own "Scholar-Gipsy," enable Arnold to avoid insincere tributes because he can abstract Clough's poetry while memorializing their shared past.

For Swinburne in "Ave atque vale" (*Fortnightly Review* [January, 1868]), the question was how to pay tribute to a poet Swinburne admired but had not met. He in fact composed "Ave atque vale" after a premature report of the death of Charles Baudelaire. Pastoral elegy proved useful because its heightened dignity itself suggested that Baudelaire, whose work excited considerable scandal, merited commemoration. The classical convention of shepherds' floral tributes to the dead also provided Swinburne with a seamless method for incorporating multiple references to Baudelaire's *Les fleurs du mal* (*The Flowers of Evil* [1857]) and confirming, as he asserts, that "not death estranges / My spirit from communion of thy song" (104). This is the sole consolation the atheist Swinburne concedes, however:

> not all our songs, O friend,
> Will make death clear or make life durable.
> Howbeit with rose and ivy and wild vine
> And with wild notes about this dust of thine
> At least I fill the place where white dreams dwell
> And wreathe an unseen shrine.   (171–6)

Anthologies frequently reprint Tennyson's classical monologues and Wellington Ode, Arnold's pastorals, and Swinburne's "Ave atque vale." Long poems are more rarely reproduced, yet, as Herbert Tucker claims, the nineteenth-century "canvas fairly swarms with poetical monuments of immense ambition."[17] Some of these long poems are best seen in relation to the novel, but others deliberately position themselves in relation to epic tradition. William Morris is one of the few to do so using classical subject matter. Sixteen of the seventeen books of *The Life and Death of Jason* (1867), written in rhyming couplets, narrate Jason's heroic quest for the golden fleece and the crucial role played by Medea in his successful return. Morris also includes epic conventions of formulaic epithets for the sea ("waters wan"), a catalogue of warriors (Book 3), gods' intervention in human affairs, and funeral games after the usurper King Pelias is killed and Jason is restored to the throne upon his return. Yet Morris challenges classical epic insofar as Medea rather than Jason is the epic's central figure: her ideas and magic make Jason's heroism possible, and if she betrays her father and abandons her homeland she remains a sympathetic figure because she is driven by love whereas her father is murderously greedy. The courageous Jason loves her in turn, and if the book ended with Book 16 Morris's poem would be heroic indeed. But Book 17, set ten years later, represents an abrupt volte-face in tone and subject matter. All the events in it are sanctioned by Morris's classical sources. Yet the postlude introduces medieval and modern elements: the modern note of love's failure, a medieval frame in which Morris pays tribute to the Chaucer of *Troilus and Criseyde* as his "Master," and a tale of adulterous desire, attempted bigamy, and murderous revenge familiar from the vogue of sensation fiction in the 1860s. Morris thus challenges the sway of classical epic by counterposing successive historical forms to it in the last book. Medea destroys first Glauce, the younger woman Jason intends to marry so that he can rule Corinth as well as Thessaly, and then her own sons. Jason realizes too late that he formerly had all he desired but was not content, and he dies ignominiously when he sits under the rotting *Argo* and a falling beam crushes him to death. Classical heroism confronts modern knowledge of love's transience and is undone.

Reviewers readily perceived the epic (as well as Chaucerian) elements of *Jason*, and it was so popular that it went through eight editions in Morris's lifetime. Yet surprisingly few Victorian epics adopted classical subject matter. Pagan myth could be readily adapted to a variety of aims, including Christian teaching, but pagan civilization was a problematic cultural model. The *Athenaeum* concluded its laudatory notice of *Jason* by regretting that Morris had so little interest in creating a Christian framework for the epic that would "bear witness to a living belief, instead of commemorating a dead one."[18] Epic retained its prestige as the highest poetic form and expression of a civilization's ideals, but conflicting conceptions of Homeric epic also made Greek matter problematical for a great imperial power like Britain. In *On Translating Homer* (1861) and *Culture and Anarchy* (1867–8), Arnold insists that Homer's grand style and breadth are correctives to the morbid subjectivity and narrow moralisms of Victorian literature and life. But the German scholar F. A. Wolf theorized in *Prolegomena ad Homerum* (1795) that the *Iliad* and *Odyssey* were products of oral transmission by anonymous bards that were only later written down. Wolf's theory displaced Homer as the founding poet of western tradition, raised similar doubts about biblical authorship, and associated Greek epic with primitive culture – though insofar as British folk tradition could be interpreted as a counterpart to Greek "epic primitivism," this newer theory was welcomed in some quarters.[19]

Roman epic, though still pagan, was another matter. Virgil's historicity and authorship of the *Aeneid* were unquestioned, and growing pride in a British empire that seemed to rival Augustan Rome fueled desire for a Victorian epic that would confirm the cultural prestige of Victoria's realm. In this context it is not surprising that many embraced Tennyson's *Idylls of the King* (1859–85) as the great Victorian epic. Tennyson deals with indigenous legend – the founding of Camelot by King Arthur and its fall – and W. E. Gladstone immediately pronounced Tennyson's subject "national," "Christian," and "universal" in 1859. A decade later the *Spectator* asserted, "the Arthurian idylls have risen from a very exquisite series of cabinet pictures, into a great tragic epic."[20] Though the *Idylls* gave far more attention to the fall of Camelot – and to adultery – than to its glories, Arthur's resemblance to the soul or Christ, against whom the fleshly Guinevere and imperfect knights rebel, provided a satisfyingly Christian meaning to Tennyson's epic, especially after James T. Knowles, founder of the Metaphysical Society, and Henry Alford, Dean of Canterbury and editor of the *Contemporary Review*, advanced this interpretation in lengthy essays.[21] More than a quarter-century earlier, when Tennyson published "Morte d'Arthur" (1842), later refashioned into "The Passing of Arthur" (1869), he prefaced it with "The Epic," in which the poet Everard Hall has written an Arthurian "epic" in "twelve books" but doubts whether "any man" should "Remodel models" or waste time on "faint Homeric echoes, nothingworth" (28, 37–9). After 1869, Tennyson took comparisons of the *Idylls* to classical epic seriously enough to write three more episodes and split "Geraint and Enid" in two so as to have the epic's requisite "twelve books."

The Ring and the Book (1868–9), by Robert Browning, also has twelve books, each a lengthy blank-verse monologue. Two are uttered by the poet, the rest by participants or spectators involved in the seventeenth-century trial of Count

Guido Franceschini for the murder of his wife, Pompilia, who fled from home with the handsome priest Giuseppe Caponsacchi, was captured, and gave birth to a son only two weeks before her husband mortally wounded her in a vicious knife attack. Browning announces the trial's outcome in Book I: when Guido claims benefit of clergy and appeals to the Pope, the Pope decides against him and orders his execution. Yet this leaves undetermined the question of Pompilia's innocence or guilt and where truth begins and ends. Each subsequent monologue provides a different perspective, including the first-hand testimonies of Guido, Pompilia (who survives long enough to be deposed), and Caponsacchi. Telling the same story twelve times over, Browning creates out of historical documents a modern epistemological labyrinth. Victorian commentators most often situated Browning's poem in terms of psychology and the evidentiary complexity of the novel, Shakespearean drama, and history. But the *Saturday Review* noted shortly after the first three books were published that the whole would exceed the *Iliad* in length and asked, "if *Paradise Lost* is to be termed an epic, why not the *Ring and the Book*?" After the whole was published, H. Buxton Forman asserted in the *London Quarterly Review* that this "work of more than twenty-one thousand lines, in twelve psychological monologues, constitutes not only a poem of the highest power and noblest aspiration, but also a great lesson on the adaptability of the strict monologue form for epic uses."[22] If *Idylls of the King* could be embraced as a great Victorian epic because of its aesthetic intricacy and Christian message, Browning's complex psychological epic seemed to verify the march of art and intellect in Victorian England. As Robert Buchanan exclaimed in the *Athenaeum*, "'The Ring and the Book' is beyond all parallel the supremest poetical achievement of our time ... [and] the most precious and profound spiritual treasure that England has produced since the days of Shakespeare."[23] Browning mentions only Herodotus and Faust in his opening book, not Homer or Virgil. From the beginning, however, he determined on a design of twelve books, and it may have been no coincidence that while he was composing *The Ring and the Book* he was also tutoring his son "Pen" in classical literature so that he could gain admission to Balliol College.[24]

Among the epics considered here, only *Aurora Leigh* explicitly aligns itself with epic tradition: "The critics say that epics have died out / With Agamemnon and the goat-nursed gods; / I'll not believe it" (5.139–41). After rejecting chivalric subject matter, contending that "dead ... must be, for the greater part, / The poems made on ... chivalric bones" (5.197–8), Aurora insists that true epic subject matter lies in "this live, throbbing age" (203) and exhorts herself, "Never flinch, / But still, unscrupulously epic, catch / Upon the burning lava of a song / The full-veined, heaving, double-breasted Age"

(5.213–16). Yet critics generally refrained from discussing *Aurora Leigh* in relation to classical epic, and the comment of the *British Quarterly Review* remains unusual: "The conception of the poem as a whole is original, because natural ... Living with broad and genial sympathies in these times, Mrs. Browning ... [fashions] the apparent incongruity of a modern novel in the form of an epic poem."[25] More commonly, critics faulted *Aurora Leigh* for diffuseness and inconsistent realism, sometimes for its unconventional heroine and plot involving rape and an unmarried mother. Epic had long been associated with male authorship, and Barrett Browning's bold assertion of epic stature perhaps inspired some of the same resistance as her plot. Moreover, in keeping with Aurora's repudiation of a-priori rules for art and insistence that a work's inward spirit should determine its form (5.223–36), Barrett Browning crafts a nine-book epic – a number tied to maternal gestation rather than the standard twelve books of martial, masculine epic.

The *Life and Death of Jason*, *Idylls of the King*, *The Ring and the Book*, and *Aurora Leigh* all orient themselves in relation to epic tradition, then, but adopt a range of subject matter and formal methods. Only *Jason* features rhyming couplets, and only *Aurora Leigh* shifts from retrospective narration in Books 1 to 4 to the present-tense narration of diaries and dramatic monologues in Books 5 to 9. Departures from classical conventions enabled Victorian poets to extend epic tradition into the modern era because they "made it new," to borrow Ezra Pound's phrase, even as their differences from each other reveal a lively debate about where cultural ideals, artistic greatness, and conceptual breadth are best located.

Modern European forms

As *Idylls of the King* suggests, classical epic could be reconceived in terms of medieval subject matter, and Thomas Macaulay's *Lays of Ancient Rome* (1842) relied on the assumption of Enlightenment historians that early phases of human civilization produced both folk ballads and epic. The revival of European forms, however, looked to alternative sources from classically inspired precedent, and had a specific historical provenance, especially where the ballad was concerned.

Ballads

In 1765 Thomas Percy published *Reliques of Ancient English Poetry*, a collection of 176 ballads he had discovered in a seventeenth-century folio. Scholars today distinguish among popular ballads, which descend from folk tradition and oral transmission; minstrel ballads, medieval compositions by professional entertainers; and urban broadside ballads (usually topical) that date from the invention of the printing press. Percy had no interest in these last and conceived of all the "ancient," i.e., medieval, ballads as the composition of minstrels ("old rhapsodists"), singling out their qualities of "pleasing simplicity, and many artless graces."[26] The ballad revival quickly became associated with British identity and aesthetic principles of simplicity, directness, and spontaneity; it led to the landmark *Lyrical Ballads* (1798), Wordsworth and Coleridge's attempt to fuse modern lyric with an "ancient" British form. As Wordsworth avers in "Essay, Supplementary to the Preface (1815)," British poetry had "been absolutely redeemed" by the publication of Percy's collection.[27]

Victorian adaptations of the ballad derived from the eighteenth-century ballad revival, British nationalism, and Romanticism, but the significance of ballad form varied. Sometimes ballads' status as national heritage authorized poetic treatment of passion and sexual situations usually excluded from modern subject matter, as with two Victorian ballads that respond to "Child Waters" in Percy's *Reliques*. In Percy's ballad, "Fair Ellen" is pregnant by Child Waters, who ignores her plight and seeks the fairest woman for his bride, forcing Ellen to cross-dress as his page, swim a river, and attend to his horses; eventually the sounds of Ellen moaning in childbirth bring Child Waters to the stable, who after witnessing her croon to her newborn and long for death declares that she shall have both "bridal" and "churching."[28]

Barrett Browning quoted the "ballad-receipt" of "Child Waters" for "making a ladye page – ... 'And you must cut your gown of green / An INCH above the knee'" in sending "The Romaunt of the Page" to Mary Russell Mitford for publication in *Finden's Tableaux* (1839). But as Marjorie Stone notes, Barrett Browning "reverses" the plot of the traditional ballad "by making marriage the beginning and cause of the page's ordeals."[29] The page's father has died avenging the honor of a fellow knight, and her mother, slain by grief, calls on her deathbed for the knight's son to marry their daughter. After a hurried bridal, the new wife has followed her husband to the Crusades disguised as his page and fights alongside him bravely. When the knight hears that his page's "sister" followed her husband to the battlefield thus, the knight haughtily pronounces such a figure "Unwomaned" (196) and vows that, in a like case, he would "forgive, and evermore / Would love her as my servitor, / But little as my wife" (227–9). Hearing Saracens approach, the page tells the "master" to ride on and deliberately invites the death that frees her from desolation while securing the life of her narrow-minded husband. Ballad tradition here makes possible a sympathetic cross-dressing heroine as Barrett Browning yokes traditional female fidelity and aggressive female adventure to craft a bitterly ironic portrait of chivalric masculinity.

D. G. Rossetti's "Stratton Water," written in 1854 but not published until 1870, bears out the contention of Stone that Barrett Browning's ballads influenced Rossetti and other Pre-Raphaelite poets.[30] He, too, draws upon "Child Waters" and reverses some of its situations. If more sexually daring than "The Romaunt of the Page," "Stratton Water" represents romantic love and gender roles far more conventionally. As flood waters rise Lord Sands discovers that his lover Janet is not dead, as his treacherous brother and "false mother" (79) have told him, and quests after her. In contrast to Child Waters or Barrett Browning's chill husband, Lord Sands is both brave and faithful in love, swimming across flood waters to secure a boat and immediately taking Janet, who thought to drown herself as childbirth approached, to church to wed her. The flood is a metaphor of dammed passion suddenly released, and the power of erotic love takes precedence over family ties or conventional religious teaching about sexuality.

Though Christina Rossetti's "Cousin Kate" was published before "Stratton Water," in 1862, it was written after her brother's poem and may reflect acquaintance with it. Along with the ballads "Noble Sisters," "Maude Clare," and "Sister Maude" in her 1862 volume, "Cousin Kate" challenges the sisterly lesson of the title poem, "Goblin Market," by representing betrayals and fierce rivalries for lovers between kinswomen. "Cousin Kate" goes further than the other 1862 ballads in making the speaker's sole triumph over Cousin Kate, by now Lady Kate, consist of

> a gift you have not got,
>   And seem not like to get:
> For all your clothes and wedding-ring
>   I've little doubt you fret.
> My fair-haired son, my shame, my pride,
>   Cling closer, closer yet:
> Your father would give lands for one
>   To wear his coronet.   (41–8)

The speaker's taunt at the bride's infertility and contention that, had she been in Cousin Kate's place, she "would have spit into his face / And not have taken his hand" (39–40) differ strikingly from Rossetti's fallen woman scenarios in other poems, a departure made possible by the ballad's conventions of objective narration and desiring women.

"Romaunt of the Page," "Stratton Water," and "Cousin Kate" all rely on the dialogue, rhyme scheme, and rhythm of traditional ballads, though Barrett

Browning prefaces the ballad quatrain with two trimeter lines in her stanzas. Other Victorian ballads were indebted less to Percy than to *Lyrical Ballads* and, like Coleridge's ballads, accentuated medieval simplicities and modern complexity by juxtaposing them. In Barrett Browning's "The Romaunt of Margret" (*New Monthly Magazine* [July, 1836]) and D. G. Rossetti's "Sister Helen" (1870) that complexity is psychological. Against the backdrop of a beautiful natural scene Margret's shadow, lying quiet on the running river like "a trusting heart / Upon a passing faith" or death's inevitability on life (42–3), detaches and rises to confront her. Her own dark self, rather than a satanic tempter, challenges her to find one who fully reciprocates her love or die. The poem ends with a corpse and a bitterly ironic portrait of domestic relations. Margret, it appears, has forced herself not to know what she knows – that her brother loves his wine more than her, her father his hall – and her attempt to integrate self and knowledge shatters the self.

The sheer length of D. G. Rossetti's "Sister Helen," at nearly 300 lines, signals a literary rather than traditional ballad, yet its force derives from popular ballad's objective narration and dialogue. The dialogue plays out between a naïve child and a young woman racked by rage, murderous determination, triumph, betrayed love, and anguished recognition. The opening stanza plunges directly into this strange mix:

> "Why did you melt your waxen man,
>> Sister Helen?
> To-day is the third since you began."
> "The time was long, yet the time ran,
>> Little brother."
>> (O Mother, Mary Mother,
> Three days to-day, between Hell and Heaven!)   (1–7)

Even Christianity subserves the uncanny. Christ's torture on the cross and three days between death and resurrection are warped into a bridegroom who suffers so painfully on his deathbed that he cannot be shriven and is damned forever:

> "Ah! what white thing at the door has cross'd,
>> Sister Helen?
> Ah! what is this that sighs in the frost?"
> "A soul that's lost as mine is lost,
>> Little brother!"   (288–92)

The rigid patterning, including tag refrains in the second, fifth, sixth, and seventh lines, and a single rhyme in others, is a literary counterpart to the blasphemous ritual that drives the poem to its overdetermined end.

Helen's understatement is another rigid surface feature that deepens the poem's psychological complexity and intensifies the wild emotions it contains.

The most famous Victorian lyrical ballad is "The Lady of Shalott," first published in 1832. Though numerous Victorian paintings extended its fame, readers were entranced from the beginning; and years after the much-revised poem appeared in 1842 George Eliot told Tennyson that she preferred elements of the original.[31] Much in this poem, as in "Sister Helen," depends on key ballad devices, especially direct, objective narration, simple diction, compression, and rhythm. Tennyson, however, artfully adapts the ballad stanza to new effect. Rather than alternating tetrameter and trimeter lines, he caps eight successive iambic tetrameter lines in a culminating trimeter. On either side of "Camelot," moreover, as if to delineate one realm from the other, he allows only one repeating rhyme; yet the rhyme of "Camelot" and "Shalott" – a form of tail-rhyme indebted to medieval romance – unifies the stanza and enriches its sonority. The effect is utterly evocative of the ballad yet nowhere identical with it.

The narrative of the Lady's isolation, magical weaving, mysterious curse, and fatal glimpse of Lancelot in her mirror is also balladic in strategy. Dramatic monologues require an excavation of psychology, while domestic or historical narratives demand realism in motivation and causality. The ballad allows Tennyson to note only, "She has heard a whisper say, / A curse is on her if she stay / To look down to Camelot" (39–41), just as ballad conventions dictate that she accept her condition as a given: "She knows not what the curse may be, / And so she weaveth steadily" (42–3).

Less is indeed more here, and meanings proliferate precisely because they are left unarticulated. The Lady's curse might point to sin, human limits, or (as in Lacanian psychoanalytical readings) a female identity predicated on a lack, while her perception through mirrors raises questions about human access to the real. Her weaving and shift at the end to writing her name invoke an artist figure and linguistic paradigms, while her loneliness and Lancelot's virility introduce erotic themes. The possibilities are such that Kathy Psomiades can trace more than a century of criticism of Victorian poetry through this poem alone.[32]

Supernaturalism is intrinsic to "The Romaunt of Margret," "Sister Helen," and "The Lady of Shalott" but is not an end in itself. Percy included a number of supernatural ballads in *Reliques*, as did Walter Scott in *Minstrelsy of the Scottish Border* (1802), and these, like Gothic fiction, demonstrate the imaginative liberty granted by counterfactual tales. A cluster of *fin de-siècle* ballads depict witches not with horror but with fascination, even sympathy, so that the emphasis shifts to issues of power and freedom more than monstrosity. In contrast to the "Witch of Wokey" in Percy's *Reliques*, for example, who is defined by her bleary eyes and foul, "haggard face,"[33] the quartet of witches in William Bell Scott's "The Witch's Ballad" (1875) are bedizened: "Right braw we were to pass the gate, / Wi' gowden clasps on girdles blue" (9–10). Even dainty at times ("We drew a glove on ilka hand, / We sweetly curtsied, each to each," 33–4), they are also connoisseurs of male flesh, appropriating the power of the gaze usually reserved to men: "All goodly men we singled out, / Waled them well, and singled out" (71–2).

Mary Coleridge, the great-great-niece of the author of *Christabel*, also invests the witch with delicacy in the form of "little white feet" in "The Witch" (1896). Her witch gains ascendancy less through seduction than through exploiting conventional feminine vulnerability and a "voice that women have, / Who plead for their heart's desire" (15–16). "A Ballad of the Were-Wolf" (*Macmillan's Magazine* [September, 1890]), by Graham R. Tomson (later Rosamund Marriott Watson), reconnects monstrosity to the female body. But by day the female were-wolf assumes the guise of a farm wife submissive to the husband against whom the were-wolf faces off as the poem ends. In all three ballads, supernaturalism enables poets to reconfigure traditionally feminine roles in relation to power.

Historical ballads, in contrast to supernatural, were usually conduits of patriotism and British imperialism, though their significance modulated from context to context. Tennyson pays tribute to British glory and manly duty in "The Revenge: A Ballad of the Fleet" (*Nineteenth Century* [March, 1878]) as he recounts the 1591 battle between a solitary pinnace and fifty-three Spanish ships of war. Sir Richard Grenville will not retreat from superior numbers at the price of abandoning sick Englishmen on shore "to Spain, / To the thumbscrew and the stake" (20–1); and he dies avowing, "I have fought for Queen and Faith like a valiant man and true; / I have only done my duty as a man is bound to do" (101–2). Vibrant ballad rhythms and rhyme give the poem the speed and lightness befitting a fleet ship but also suggest a kind of choral patriotic song meant to unify Britons.

In "Casabianca" (*Monthly Magazine* [August, 1826]) Felicia Hemans telescopes the bloody sacrifice of war onto the figure of a young boy who "stood on the burning deck" (1) and refuses to abandon his post until his father, dead below, releases him from prior orders. An explosion blasts the boy apart instead. The boy, too, enacts the highest standards of duty and loyalty, yet he is grotesquely destroyed; more to the point, the boy so mournfully evoked is on the losing French side of the Battle of the Nile (1798), in which Horatio Nelson halted Napoleon's attempts to control Egypt and access India.[34] Heroic victory, duty, and blasted innocence here coalesce, a less self-congratulatory mix than in "The Revenge."

Rudyard Kipling pays tribute to enemy soldiers, but on the condition of a racist epithet in "Fuzzy-Wuzzy" (*Scots Observer* [March 15, 1890]), one of his *Barrack-Room Ballads* (1892). These diverge markedly from the traditional ballad in subject matter but retain its associations with the unlettered folk and musical performance, since the enlisted men speak cockney and adopt the patter and slang of music halls. Given the ballads' topicality and unconventional type fonts that call attention to print as such, they also bring subliterary broadside ballads to mind.

These demotic features are especially effective in the poem first titled "The Queen's Uniform" (*Scots Observer* [March 1, 1890]) but better known as "Tommy." Rather than contrasting black and white soldiers in the Sudan, this ballad sets the competing interests of class difference and national/imperial defense against each other and suggests that enlisted men tend to lose on both sides:

> I went into a public-'ouse to get a pint o' beer,
> The publican 'e up an' sez, "We serve no red-coats here."
> The girls be'ind the bar they laughed an' giggled fit to die,
> I outs into the street again an' to myself sez I:
> O it's Tommy this, an' Tommy that, an' "Tommy, go
>   away";
> But it's "Thank you, Mister Atkins," when the band
>   begins to play –
> The band begins to play, my boys, the band begins to
>   play,
> O it's "Thank you, Mister Atkins," when the band
>   begins to play.   (1–8)

The rhythm and rhyme of the poem conform to the 4/3/4/3, *abcb* pattern of the traditional ballad, but Kipling here musters the lines into fourteeners, which look less like ballads or hymns than the loping lines of broadsides. George Chapman had used the fourteener to translate Homer's *Iliad* in the seventeenth century. Kipling's formal choice elevates the martial context of his speaker but makes it inseparable from an urban, downmarket lexicon that calls into question what is and is not "poetic."

"Tommy" himself is linguistically astute. Rather than being merely the object of poetic language, he keeps his ear cocked to the differing registers his countrymen adopt to gauge whether they are patronizing, exclusive, or reliant on him to protect their own interests. Middle-class patriotism and national duty are here questioned rather than blithely confirmed.

Oscar Wilde evoked the genre of broadside ballad to very different effect in "Ballad of Reading Gaol" (1898), his best-known poem and one of the most significant Victorian ballads. This work is famous partly for its circumstances. Written shortly after Wilde was released from Reading Gaol in May, 1897 after serving two years' hard labor for "criminal indecency with another man," the poem was signed "C.3.3.," Wilde's prison number. Wilde's poem is inseparable from histories of social justice and same-sex desire, but its significance also emerges from ballad tradition. As Wilde commented to his friend and literary executor Robbie Ross, his poem was "divided" in aim and style: "Some is realistic, some is romantic: some poetry, some propaganda."[35] The realism derives from the gritty details of prison routines and Wilde's narrative of the trial, execution, and burial of Charles T. Wooldridge, a member of the Royal Horse Guards who had murdered his wife. The propaganda derives from Wilde's protest against state murder and inhumane treatment of prisoners.

The romantic element is traceable to Coleridge, especially "The Rime of the Ancient Mariner," another narrative of inexplicable crime, guilt, and redemption. Wilde's refrain, "Yet each man kills the thing he loves" (37), parallels the mariner's shooting of the albatross, for both assert innate human capacity for guilt and crime. Wilde also specifically alludes to Coleridge. "[B]y all forgot, we rot and rot" (599) echoes "The very deep did rot" (123) in Coleridge; and the phantoms' ghastly *danse macabre* the night before the hanging (289–324) recalls the animated corpses that encircle the mariner. The poem's ultimate thematic incoherence, according to John Stokes, makes of "Ballad of Reading Gaol" "an unsettled and unsettling poem in which present mercy is threatened by ultimate forgiveness, yet heartless justice meshes with original sin."[36]

Such incoherence has its uses, however. If Wilde echoes Coleridge's lyrical ballad, he alludes by his very subject matter to Victorian street ballads that narrated crimes and executions, often in the voice of the criminal.[37] Kipling, too, gestures toward this urban genre in "Danny Deever" (*Scots Observer* [February 22, 1890]), which recounts another communal response to an inmate's hanging. Street ballads were usually printed in Seven Dials, an area inhabited by Irish immigrants, criminals, and other outsiders. Tellingly, when Wilde considered publishing his ballad in a newspaper, he commented, "I suggest *Reynolds*: it circulates among the lower orders, and the criminal classes, and so ensures me my right audience for sympathy."[38] In "Ballad of Reading Gaol" Wilde writes both as an Irish criminal outsider and as a poet in the high Romantic tradition. The ballad enables Wilde to articulate his dual identity simultaneously.

Insofar as Wilde drew upon the communitarian associations of the ballad while vigorously protesting official policy, he was also working out of a ballad form especially important in the 1840s. After the 1832 Reform Bill failed to remedy the condition of workers, a "People's Charter" demanding rights now taken for granted – e.g., universal suffrage, elimination of property requirements for members of parliament, and the secret ballot – was presented to the House of Commons in 1839 with over a million signatures. Parliament summarily rejected the Charter, but organized efforts continued despite the arrests of leaders and violence against demonstrators. The ballad was an important resource for sustaining momentum and morale.

Though Percy considered each traditional ballad to be the invention of an originating medieval poet, ballads were passed down among the unlettered for centuries, their rhythms, rhymes, and tunes to which they were sung all aiding memory. Moreover, as Thomas Hood's "The Ballad" makes clear, traditional ballads were sold alongside street ballads, both sung aloud on city streets by vendors: "How hard, alas! if ... a farthing short – / To long for 'Chevy Chase'" (17–20). Hymns, another source of communitarian expression in a shared creed, had also widely adapted ballad measure and tunes because these were known to the laity. A Chartist political song, then, could be printed in a Chartist periodical for wide circulation and sung aloud during demonstrations or meetings to deepen solidarity.[39]

"A Chartist Chorus" (*Northern Star* [June 6, 1846]) by Ernest Jones articulates a political aim and political insight into "cotton lords and corn lords" who currently control the means of production:

> Go! treasure well your miser's store
>   With crown, and cross, and sabre!
> Despite you all – we'll break your thrall,
>   And have our land and labour.
> You forge no more – you fold no more
>   Your cankering chains about us;
> We heed you not – we need you not
>   But you can't do without us.[40]

The song climaxes by declaring that "Our lives are not your sheaves to glean" and demanding, "ours shall be THE CHARTER!" (17, 20). Though the song tells no story, unlike the traditional ballad, it entails a vigorous prospective plot that climaxes in political action and rights achieved.

Jones came to the Chartist movement by political conviction rather than class origin and became one of its most prominent poets. In "Leawood Hall" (1855), first published as "The Labourer: A Christmas Carol" (*The Labourer*

[January, 1847]), Jones crafts a literary ballad that revamps both the traditional ballad and Victorian Christmas tale to forceful political effect. In contrast to poverty so blighting that the hearth is cold and the table bare even at Christmas, cottage inmates can see the windows of nearby Leawood Hall blazing at a festive Christmas dinner. Like Barrett Browning and D. G. Rossetti, Jones deepens psychological complexity beyond the traditional ballad; the mother figure, so unlike the Virgin Mary with the infant Jesus, is querulous from illness and famine, while the father, who has "toiled in hope's assurance, / Toiled when hope had changed to fear, / Toiled amid despair's endurance" to no avail, understands the source of her "sharp invective" (34, 41–3).[41]

Jones also taps the medieval associations of traditional and Romantic ballads but denudes them of patriotic nostalgia:

> It was a Norman castle high –
> It was a keep of ages rude,
> When men named murder – *chivalry*
> And robbery was called – *a feud.*   (73–6)

That workers were then also exploited historicizes and makes the present even less bearable. Finally the father rushes to the Hall, is thrown out as a beggar by servants but steals food as he goes, is shot at for his theft, and, after creating a feast for his own family, laughing the while, collapses and dies of the gunshot wound.

Jones ends the poem still resisting sentimental closure:

> Courage now no more dissembled
> Broken strength and baffled will;
> The wistful children stood and trembled,
> And the room grew very still.   (201–4)

The stillness is both an indication of the stilled life of the man and the inadequacy of current poetic tradition or the traditional Christmas narrative, "on earth peace, good will toward men" (Luke 2:14), to articulate a fit end to political and economic inequities.

Jones's poem synthesizes a number of ends to which Victorians adapted ballads. Its strong plot looks back to traditional ballads, yet it is also a lyrical literary ballad that insinuates psychological complexity into a traditional form. It is a polemic, like Wilde's "Ballad of Reading Gaol," that questions the narratives of British identity constructed from a medieval past. And as a song that elicits solidarity among workers, it draws on the longstanding audience for broadside ballads but mobilizes poetry as a political intervention.

Sonnets

To describe a ballad singer yet signal aesthetic distance from this demotic form, Arthur Symons uses a sonnet in "The Street-Singer" (1889). Symons juxtaposes the grinding poverty under which she labors with her pious song:

> She sings a pious ballad wearily;
> Her shivering body creeps on painful feet
> Along the muddy runlets of the street;
> The damp is in her throat: she coughs to free
> The cracked and husky notes that tear her chest.   (1–5)

Lyric is here used to sing ugliness as well as economic oppression. Workers did not require middle-class poets to articulate the conditions of their lives, of course. The last poem of John Clare, son of a thresher who ended his days in an insane asylum in 1864, is a powerful irregular sonnet:

> I feel I am, I only know I am
> And plod upon the earth as dull and void
> Earth's prison chilled my body with its dram
> Of dullness, and my soaring thoughts destroyed.
> I fled to solitudes from passions dream,
> But strife persued – I only know I am.
> I was a being created in the race
> Of men disdaining bounds of place and time –
> A spirit that could travel o'er the space
> Of earth and heaven – like a thought sublime,
> Tracing creation, like my maker, free –
> A soul unshackled like eternity,
> Spurning earth's vain and soul debasing thrall
> But now I only know I am – that's all.

In fourteen lines the poem articulates central philosophical dilemmas associated with Descartes and Heidegger about identity, alienation, and being's relation to the world. It also represents defiance and utter defeat in life. The final colloquial phrase, so modern a touch after the sublime vision that precedes, suggests at once the indignity of being beaten by life, the general plight of puny human knowledge, and approaching death. Significantly, the lines also perform what Victorian critics saw as two hallmarks of the sonnet, its boundedness in form and infinite capacity to express mind, spirit, feeling, nature, and belief.

The sonnet originated in Italy, its name deriving from *sonetto*, for little sound or song. As developed by Dante and Petrarch in the thirteenth and fourteenth centuries, the sonnet consists of two quatrains and two tercets, with two rhymes (*abba abba*) in the octave and three (*cde cde* or some combination) in the sestet. When the sonnet was imported into England in the sixteenth century, the fewer available rhyming words in English promoted an alternative form most closely associated today with Shakespeare: three quatrains in alternating rhymes (*abab cdcd efef*) and a concluding couplet (*gg*). Milton memorably adapted Petrarchan sonnets and elevated language to express the theological significance of martyred Protestants ("On the Late Massacre in Piedmont") and his own blindness ("When I Consider How My Light is Spent"). But afterward the sonnet fell into disuse until revived in the late eighteenth century, for example by Charlotte Smith in her *Elegiac Sonnets* (1784), an important influence on Wordsworth. Victorian commentators uniformly deemed Wordsworth the greatest sonnet-writer in English.

Given the sonnet's association with Shakespeare, Milton, and Wordsworth, but also with Italy, it became another cultural site for articulating British national identity. In this case British heritage was not automatically elevated over Italian precedent, which might have meant rating the sometimes naughty wit of Elizabethan sonnets and their intricate rhymes above the sonnet's originators and the refined expression of spiritualized love in Dante and Petrarch. Instead British national prestige was pegged to literary "correctness," and Victorian critics pronounced the Petrarchan form most authoritative. Not only did the octave–sestet format promote expression of a single idea, but there was, critics argued, an "organic" link between form and expression since a problem or condition posed in the octave was then resolved or answered by the sestet. Critical interest in the sonnet was so lively, and readers so receptive, that discussion spilled across the pages of numerous periodicals and into the introductions of some seventeen Victorian anthologies of sonnets. Nonetheless, as Natalie Houston notes in assessing Victorian debates over the sonnet, practicing poets often departed from the Italianate standard – as do "The Street-Singer" and "I Am."[42] Symons alters the rhyme in his second quatrain and Clare reworks the English sonnet, poignantly using the half rhyme of "dream" and "I am" to underscore his alienation from passion and hope.

The sonnet was well suited to an era of newspapers and magazines, since it required scant time from readers and could easily be wedged into the odd free space. But love sonnets were infrequent. Wordsworth's prestige rested upon poems like "Composed upon Westminster Bridge" and "It is a Beauteous Evening, Calm and Free" rather than amatory lyrics, and more philosophical and descriptive sonnets circulated than the sonnet sequences best known today. Felicia Hemans's "A Remembrance of Grasmere" (*New Monthly Magazine* [September, 1834]), for example, is both a descriptive sonnet and homage to Wordsworth; the speaker remembers his lake in dreamy tranquility and shifts from floating clouds of glory – hues "seem to float / On golden clouds" – to thoughts that lie too deep for tears: "subdue the soul to love, and tears, and prayer" (6–7, 14). The landscape so famously evoked by Wordsworth is sublimated into a metaphor of his poetic mind that absorbs the whole.

"Among the Hebrides" (1876), a descriptive sonnet by Emily Pfeiffer, vividly describes the "bare rock faces and island cones" that "glitter as frost and wind-bleach'd bones" (2–3) against the blue of Loch Carron. The scene is incised on her mind like a cameo made of "Pearl-white coral and sapphire clear" (5), until the intense clarity becomes surreal and suggests "some cove in the long dead moon" (14).[43] The May, 1872 *Cornhill Magazine* praised Wordsworth's sonnets for "the exquisite skill with which the emotions of the mind are associated with the aspects of nature."[44] Hemans and Pfeiffer both extend this tradition while drawing attention to the artifice with which expansive scenes are drawn into the small compass of the sonnet through Hemans's reference to "perfect music" (12) and Pfeiffer's to the "Finely chisell'd" (6) cameo. This self-consciousness, too, is part of Victorian sonnet tradition, since the intricacy of the form means that the sonnet can become a metonym for art itself.

The Victorian sonnet also prompted poets and readers to meditation, since the sonnet's concentrated thought and syntax require effort. Miltonic precedent reinforced the sonnet's suitability for devotions. "The Forest Glade" (1864) by clergyman Charles Tennyson Turner is at first descriptive, telling how a beam of light entered a dark glade and "ran to meet" (3) the poet like a friend. The poet confesses a sad mood interrupted by this "surprise" (7), and the sonnet ends as a form of religious revelation:

> That heavenly guidance humble sorrow hath,
> Had turn'd my feet into that forest-way,
> Just when His morning light came down the path,
> Among the lonely woods at early day.   (11–14)

Tennyson Turner does not hesitate to adopt "impure" form for this pious lyric, however; "The Forest Glade" combines two English quatrains (*abab cdcd*) and an Italian sestet (*efe fef*).

Hardy's "Hap" (1898) is the antiphonal voice of Victorian devotional sonnets, for it is likewise meditative but registers a universe from which God has been ejected and replaced by the impersonal forces of evolution and chance. Within this universe, faith's dark night of the soul would comprise sentimental comfort, since even a "vengeful god" (1) would provide structure and a bracing antagonist. The sestet's pivot dismisses this possibility at once:

But not so. How arrives it joy lies slain,
And why unblooms the best hope ever sown?
– Crass Casualty obstructs the sun and rain,
And dicing Time for gladness casts a moan ...
These purblind Doomsters had as readily strown
Blisses about my pilgrimage as pain.   (9–14)

Sonnet patterns had become so familiar to readers by late-century that Hardy could rely on this knowledge to enact his sonnet's theme. Up to Time's "moan" the sonnet conforms exactly to the Shakespearean pattern. Then Hardy casts the dice and turns up a rhyme for "moan" instead of the concluding couplet readers expect, subjecting readers to the experience of chance as well.

Though they are lesser known works today, meditative Victorian sonnets illuminate the challenge that erotic sonnet sequences posed to poets and critics. For women poets the challenge was even greater because women were usually the objects of desire in sonnet sequences, and merely reversing the genders – praising the man's attractions or tracing the throes of desire suffered in looking upon him – would have feminized the man and (according to middle-class standards) unsexed the woman. Barrett Browning composed her sequence during her courtship and did not show them to Robert Browning until three years after their marriage, when he was grieving over his mother's death. Even after he convinced her that she should publish the sequence, she insisted on titling it as if it were a translation (*from the Portuguese*) rather than original work.

Alison Chapman usefully offers the metaphor of translation to identify Barrett Browning's larger poetic task in the sequence: reworking inherited tradition so that a female poet can express erotic love.[45] To do so Barrett Browning reinvents the sonnet-sequence plot. Rather than depicting a first sight of the beloved that preludes acquaintance, desire, love's obstacles, eventual declarations, and union, she scripts a contest between herself and the force of love in the first third of the sequence, celebrates the avowal of love and desire in the middle, then sublimates physical passion into more spiritualized love in the final third.

In *Pamphilia to Amphilanthus* (1621) by Mary Wroth, the first sonnet sequence in English by a woman, the poet begins with the martyring of her heart to Love (Eros) at Venus's bidding, so that when she capitulates, she does so to personified Love rather than to an embodied lover. Barrett Browning follows a similar poetic strategy to inaugurate her sequence. When "a mystic Shape did move / Behind me, and drew me backward by the hair," the speaker guesses that the mastering power is Death. But "The silver answer rang, – 'Not Death, but Love'" (1.14). Representing a woman who considers herself pledged to death quells any implication of unruly desire and sets up a second plot strand wherein the male beloved is an agent of God who helps her to reaffirm and rejoin life. In Sonnet XVI she capitulates to love: her conquering lover is "more noble and like a king" (2) and she yields not as a ravished woman but "as a vanquished soldier yields his sword / To one who lifts him from the bloody earth" (9–10). As conqueror he elevates rather than crushes her, and she glances back toward her earlier contest with love while praising her lover's magnanimity. The sonnet also tacitly establishes their shared vocations, since the pen and sword are related metaphors.

In this context the female poet can avow erotic love, exchanging locks with her beloved in Sonnets XVIII and XIX, reveling in the declaration of love in XXI ("Say over again, and yet once over again, / That thou dost love me" [1–2]), and affirming that the claims of spiritual love do not invalidate physical love in XXII ("Let us stay / Rather on earth, Belovèd" [9–10]). Sonnet XXIX is in fact highly erotic. Though the governing concept is that she prefers her lover to her thoughts and poems about him, the images of vine and palm suggest a clinging woman and man in a state of phallic readiness:

> I think of thee! – my thoughts do twine and bud
> About thee, as wild vines, about a tree,
> Put out broad leaves, and soon there's nought to see
> Except the straggling green which hides the wood.
> Yet, O my palm-tree, be it understood
> I will not have my thoughts instead of thee
> Who are dearer, better! Rather, instantly
> Renew thy presence; as a strong tree should,
> Rustle thy boughs and set thy trunk all bare,
> And let these bands of greenery which insphere thee
> Drop heavily down, – burst, shattered, everywhere!
> Because, in this deep joy to see and hear thee
> And breathe within thy shadow a new air,
> I do not think of thee – I am too near thee.

From this point in the sequence, however, Barrett Browning pursues a neo-platonic plot, never repudiating earthly love but repositioning it as a conduit of spiritual love, especially by revamping the earlier images of her lover as princely court poet, merciful conqueror, and burgeoning tree. In Sonnet XXXI he is a type of the biblical Holy Spirit, descending in the guise of a dove who ministers to her amidst her doubts: "when my fears would rise, / With thy broad heart serenely interpose: / Brood down with thy divine sufficiencies" (10–12).

In the sequence's final sonnets Barrett Browning synthesizes the elevated tone and imagery of the meditative sonnet and her "translation" of the amatory sequence tradition. Sonnet XLII glances back to the burgeoning greenery of XXIX yet sublimates it into a spiritual symbol, for she alludes to the Tannhäuser myth in which God's mercy to a pilgrim is expressed when the Pope's bare staff miraculously blooms. As well, this sonnet caps the sequence's motif of ministering angels, for her soul's guardian angel and her earthly lover have merged:

> "My future will not copy fair my past" –
> I wrote that once; and thinking at my side
> My ministering life-angel justified
> The word by his appealing look upcast
> To the white throne of God, I turned at last,
> And there, instead, saw thee, not unallied
> To angels in thy soul! Then I, long tried
> By natural ills, received the comfort fast,
> While budding, at thy sight, my pilgrim's staff
> Gave out green leaves with morning dews impearled.
> I seek no copy now of life's first half:
> Leave here the pages with long musing curled,
> And write me new my future's epigraph,
> New angel mine, unhoped for in the world!

As their swords equalized them in XVI, so their pens – hers as poet, his as recording angel who creates a new future for her – do here. At once deeply personal and broadly allusive, allied to the traditions of amatory and meditative sonnets alike, this sonnet is a fit overture to the familiar climax of the sequence, in which the poet numbers over the many ways she loves. By revising the amatory plot of Elizabethan sonnet sequences and incorporating elements of the meditative Victorian sonnet, Barrett Browning retains poetic authority while also recounting a love relationship that culminates in happy union.

Unlike Barrett Browning, Christina Rossetti wrote *Monna Innominata: A Sonnet of Sonnets* (1881) with publication in mind. Mary Wroth had included "A Crown of Sonnets Dedicated to Love" in *Pamphilia to Amphilanthus* – fourteen sonnets in which the end of one sonnet forms the first line of the next – but Rossetti's immediate sources of inspiration are the sonnet sequences of Dante, Petrarch, and Barrett Browning, as well as Francis Hueffer's *The Troubadours* (1878), which identified fourteen "Lady Troubadours" among twelfth-century minstrels.[46] As her preface makes clear, Rossetti reworks poetic tradition in three ways. She inserts into the Victorian historical imagination a woman troubadour "sharing her lover's poetic aptitude"; counters *Sonnets from the Portuguese* by representing a woman poet whose love culminates in separation rather than marriage; and fashions a woman more "attractive" to her own imagination than Dante's and Petrarch's idealized figures of Beatrice and Laura.

As with Barrett Browning, who alludes to Theocritus in her opening lines, Rossetti's scholarly credentials form part of her work's matrix, but Rossetti's expertise is modern Italian rather than classical literature. Thus to each sonnet she affixes an untranslated epigraph (one line each) from Dante and Petrarch, making doubly legible her "translation" of sonnet tradition. The attention she lavishes on paratext, i.e., material framing the text, and her self-referential structure of fourteen sonnets alike shift attention to literary performance. This, too, revises poetic tradition, since her pronounced distance from autobiographical expression upends the poetess tradition that so closely associated women's lives with their poems – an assumption enforced by Barrett Browning's intensely private sonnets.

Rossetti also inverts Barrett Browning's plot: *Monna Innominata* begins with the desiring woman poet and ends with her "Youth gone, and beauty gone" and a renunciatory subsiding into the "Silence of love that cannot sing again" (14.1, 14). The point seems less to displace Barrett Browning than to suggest an alternative relation between amatory and spiritual love. When chided by her lover, Rossetti's speaker avows that she "Would lose not Him, but you, must one be lost" (6.3). She looks only to the afterlife for perfect love: "life reborn annuls / Loss and decay and death, and all is love" (10.13–14). And she similarly commends her lover to God, "Whose love [alone] your love's capacity can fill" (13.14). If the Lady Troubadour silences herself as a singer of love songs in the last line, the texts remain. Yopie Prins has pointed to the ironic tendency of most Victorian resuscitations of Sappho to imply spontaneous immediacy while relying on a posthumous voice of Sappho caught in the act of leaping to death.[47] Rossetti revises this tradition of the poetess as well; her words announce the erasure of a fictional speaker's songs in a text that preserves them.

Rossetti opened her 1881 volume with a sonnet dedicated "To my first Love, my Mother" ("Sonnets are Full of Love" [5]) and sent a copy to poet Augusta Webster, whose work she admired. Possibly Webster took inspiration from the dedicatory sonnet. Webster's posthumous *Mother and Daughter: An Uncompleted Sonnet Sequence* (1895) reshapes sonnet tradition by delineating maternal rather than erotic love. "Love's Mourner," Sonnet XI, in fact treats the "dear patient madness ... men call woman's love" as a misnomer: "Naming for love that grief which *does* remain" (6–8). The amatory sonnet's desiring gaze is likewise reconfigured within the context of mother and daughter. The mother glories in her daughter's beauty but does not seek to possess it: "Child, I'd needs love thy beauty stranger-wise: / And oh the beauty of it, being thou!" (II.13–14). The daughter in turn refuses to admit signs of age ("on my brow the thin lines [that] write good-byes") in the mother, for "Loverlike to me, / She with her happy gaze finds all that's best" (XVI.3, 9–10). Though her sonnets express profound love, Webster contains sentimentality from the beginning. To a poet-mother, there is pain in knowing that the beloved infant daughter's sweet spring of life "Too soon" (I.10–12) will give way to "sister womanhoods," when the daughter will be "dearer" but no longer physically close (XX.9–10). The incomplete sequence testifies to another vulnerability in mother–daughter love, since in most cases mothers die before daughters and never know the end of the life stories they begin.

If the gender relations of Renaissance amatory sonnet sequences required women poets actively to negotiate tradition, George Meredith and D. G. Rossetti also reworked sonnet tradition in notable ways. Meredith's *Modern Love* (1862) depicts an unraveling marriage rather than courtship, and he similarly undoes "correct" sonnet structure. To register complex, sometimes excessive emotion and analysis, his sonnets burst the form's ostensible bounds and overflow into two extra lines. The resulting sixteen lines are organized into four Petrarchan quatrains, each beginning with a new rhyme scheme (*abba cddc effe ghhg*), as if even in rhyme, as in the marriage, continuity cannot be maintained. The marriage founders because it is too empty, too diminished in passion and intimacy, and yet, like the sixteen-line sonnet, too full – of unsated desires, jealousy, and secrets, as the opening sonnet establishes:

> By this he knew she wept with waking eyes:
> That, at his hand's light quiver by her head,
> The strange low sobs that shook their common bed,
> Were called into her with a sharp surprise,
> And strangled mute, like little gaping snakes,
> Dreadfully venomous to him.   (I.1–6)

Alienated within "their common bed," the couple resemble "sculptured effigies ... / Upon their marriage-tomb, the sword between" (I.14–15).

Despite this emotionally intense, vivid beginning, *Modern Love* can no more be read in transparent biographical terms than Christina Rossetti's *Monna Innominata*. Not only do the intricate syntax and unconventional imagery call attention to themselves, but the point of view is also unstable, alternating between "he" and "I" as if the genre oscillated between narrative vignettes and dramatic monologues. Yet the heightened artifice is in keeping with the husband's tortured self-consciousness and sense of alienation.

Gender roles, too, are radically revised in this sequence. The husband suspects his wife of an affair; if he becomes fiercely jealous, threatening to play the role of

Othello (who strangles his wife under similar suspicions), he is also feminized, merely reacting to the active sexual role she has appropriated. It is ultimately unclear whether she is guilty of adultery or not, and the deliberate ambiguity is itself innovative. In striking contrast to Tennyson's King Arthur, who terms "that man the worst of public foes / Who either for his own or children's sake ... lets the wife / Whom he knows false, abide and rule the house" ("Guinevere" [1859], 509–12), Meredith's speaker avers, "I see no sin: / The wrong is mixed. In tragic life, God wot, / No villain need be!" (XLIII.13–15).

Similarly, while Barrett Browning and Christina Rossetti ground the transcendent meaning of love in divine love, evolutionary cosmology underlies Meredith's grim plot. Humans are "First, animals; and next / Intelligences at a leap" (XXX.1–2); if "Intelligence and instinct" (8) unite in erotic love, "Swift doth young Love flee, / And we stand wakened, shivering from our dream" (11–12), newly aware of the impermanence decreed by natural law. Violently yoking this insight with poetic tradition, Sonnet XXX concludes, "Lady, this is my sonnet to your eyes" (16), a bitterly ironic meditation on the revised significance of women's beauty and love under modern conditions.

D. G. Rossetti's *House of Life* is modern, paradoxically, by virtue of its medievalism. The title refers to the first of twelve "houses" in medieval astrology, and the whole is deeply influenced by Dante's *Vita nuovo*, which Rossetti translated in the 1840s and first published as *The New Life* in 1861. Dante's *New Life* is an autobiographical account in mixed prose and verse of his love for Beatrice from his first sight of her to her early death and its aftermath. Dante ends by noting a "very wonderful vision" and expressing the "hope that I shall yet write concerning her what hath not before been written of any woman," a reference (according to Rossetti's note) to the *Divine Comedy*.[48] In form *The New Life* is highly self-referential; most sonnets, which tend to be highly metaphoric, abstract, and indirect, are preceded or followed by Dante's prose exegesis of their structure and symbolism. Writing-in-process, self-referentiality, and abstraction, similarly, are crucial features of Rossetti's sequence.

The second section of Rossetti's 1870 *Poems*, comprising fifty sonnets and eleven songs, was entitled "Sonnets and Songs, towards a Work to Be Called 'The House of Life.'" Like Dante's *New Life*, the 1870 *House of Life* was thus a hybrid genre that gestured toward a larger work to come. *The House of Life: A Sonnet-Sequence*, in *Ballads and Sonnets* (1881), then realized the promise of his 1870 work. Asterisks in the 1881 table of contents designated sonnets from 1870, to which over forty additional sonnets were added, the whole rearranged into two parts: "I. Youth and Change" and "II. Change and Fate." In both structure and generic consistency the 1881 work is far more unified, and the new "Introductory Sonnet" has become a defining text in British sonnet tradition:

> A Sonnet is a moment's monument, –
> Memorial from the Soul's eternity
> To one dead deathless hour. Look that it be,
> Whether for lustral rite or dire portent,
> Of its own arduous fulness reverent:
> Carve it in ivory or in ebony,
> As Day or Night may rule; and let Time see
> Its flowering crest impearled and orient.
>
> A Sonnet is a coin: its face reveals
> The soul, – its converse, to what Power 'tis due: –
> Whether for tribute to the august appeals
> Of Life, or dower in Love's high retinue,
> It serve; or, 'mid the dark wharf's cavernous breath,
> In Charon's palm it pay the toll to Death.

One of many Victorian sonnets on the sonnet, the introductory lyric enfolds an intricate set of paradoxes: the sonnet as monument emphasizes a tribute to the dead and what Matthew Arnold calls *Architectonicè* in his 1853 Preface, an informing principle of design; the sonnet as double-sided coin indicates a medium of exchange between life and art, life and death, art and commerce; the sonnet depends on the transient moments it memorializes yet the "Soul's eternity" transforms the moment into a deathless "hour"; the sonnet is a transparent window onto the soul yet opaque, for its motivating force is hidden on the other side that, like the moon's, is forever inaccessible. Obviously self-referential, the sonnet itself, like the coin it figures, points in two directions, ahead to the new sequence yet also back to the 1870 "House of Life" sonnets, which now attain retrospective exegesis and memorialization as a "past" moment of art.

In *The New Life*, as noted earlier, Dante provides both retrospective and introductory auto-exegesis of sonnets; Rossetti's Introductory Sonnet is thus also a performative tribute to his medieval predecessor, an act of revival as well as a new invention. Such calling attention to art as art, though sanctioned by medieval precedent, makes *The House of Life* the most modern of Victorian sonnet sequences. In foregrounding its own artifice, it shares a defining feature of *fin-de-siècle* aestheticism and suggests, as Walter Pater and Wilde were to argue more explicitly, that art exists for its own sake rather than in service to moral or social purpose. As Jerome McGann suggests, such exposure of the means of art's coming into form, or its "inner standing point," also registers cognitive process in response to, and as, sensuous, embodied perception.[49]

Rossetti also effects an innovation upon the amatory plot of sonnet sequences. Part I focuses on passionate erotic love but, as Sonnet XXXVI makes clear, the speaker responds both to old love (the "waste remembrance and forlorn surmise" of "heart-beats" and "fire-heats long ago" [6, 11]) and a new beloved (who "yields thee life that vivifies / What else were sorrow's servant and death's thrall" [3–4]). His sonnets idealize love but not a sole predestined lover; love itself is a permanent force, but its embodied manifestation is transient. Rather than building toward union, accordingly, Part I begins with consummated love (Sonnets VI and VII), then modulates to severance (Sonnet XL) and a vision of the dead beloved in the Willowwood sequence (Sonnets XLIX to LII). Whether the consummation and loss concern the first love, the second, or both remains unclear. Part II, "Change and Fate," then unfolds in the context of loss and mortality and reflects on time and art as well as the ambiguous significance of life's pilgrimage.

More emphatically than *Sonnets from the Portuguese* or *Monna Innominata*, then, *The House of Life* merges amatory and meditative traditions. As Rossetti commented of his larger aim in 1870, "I should wish to deal in poetry chiefly with personified emotions; and in carrying out my scheme of the 'House of Life' (if ever I do so) shall try to put in action a complete dramatis personae of the soul."[50] The completed sequence achieves this detached, impersonal treatment of highly personal subject matter, and its themes of love, life, death, and art sustain the high seriousness of Dantean precedent. Yet the ambiguity, pessimism, and shifting love objects of the sequence also indicate that transcendent divinity – so important a foundation for eternal love in Dante, Barrett Browning, and Christina Rossetti – is no longer an operative force. Just as Sonnet LXXVII asserts a lifelong pilgrimage to "Lady Beauty" (9), so *The House of Life* pays its devoirs most consistently to art rather than to transient or transcendent love.

Fixed forms

If the medieval revival intensified interest in ballads and sonnets, it also led to aestheticism by another channel. Here, too, D. G. Rossetti played a crucial role. Along with the intermediary version of *The House of Life*, his 1870 *Poems* included translations from the medieval French poet, priest, and thief, François Villon, beginning with "A Ballad of Dead Ladies." Each of the eight-line stanzas asks where famous women from Héloise to Cleopatra and Joan of Arc have gone, only to rejoin, "But where are the snows of yester-year?" The poem then ends in a four-line envoy. Rossetti was not translating a folk or literary ballad but a *ballade*, one of several fixed verse forms developed in medieval France, and his evocative lyric helped inspire further interest in French fixed verse forms including the *sestina, villanelle,* and *rondeau.*

This development denotes increased literary cosmopolitanism as well as emergent preoccupation with form as such. Hitherto anti-Gallic prejudice, especially after the Napoleonic wars, had limited influences migrating from France. Matthew Arnold's critical essays in the 1860s, however, resolutely held French literature up as a needed counterexample to English literature. In "The Function of Criticism at the Present Time" (*National Review* [November, 1864]), Arnold asked, "How much of current English literature comes into this 'best that is known and thought in the world'? Not very much, I fear; certainly less, at this moment, than of the current literature of France or Germany."[51] Since contemporary French "*Parnassiens*" such as Théodore de Banville were reviving the fixed verse forms of Villon, Charles d'Orléans, and Pierre de Ronsard and composing modern counterparts, Arnold helped open a conduit to this revival in England.

Swinburne discovered Villon before Rossetti, and "A Ballad of Burdens," not strictly a *ballade* but inspired by Villon, appeared in *Poems and Ballads* (1866). Its refrain, "This is the end of every man's desire," alluded to "fair women," "bought kisses," "long living," "dead faces," and more. The waste laid to all sweet things was recapitulated in the closing envoy:

> Princes, and ye whom pleasure quickeneth,
>   Heed well this rhyme before your pleasure tire;
> For life is sweet, but after life is death.
>   This is the end of every man's desire.   (73–6)

Public recoil from a volume that also included "Anactoria," "Dolores," and "Fragoletta," however, deflected attention from this early revival of Villon.

The principal impetus for reviving fixed forms came from Andrew Lang's volume of translations, *Ballads and Lyrics of Old France* (1872), and a range of British commentary in periodicals and books by Edmund Gosse, Austin Dobson, George Saintsbury, Lang, and others. These English "Parnassians" led unexceptional lives by middle-class standards – Gosse and Dobson worked for the Board of Trade – and their poems never affronted middle-class tastes. Indeed, Gosse himself argued in "A Plea for Certain Exotic Forms of Verse" (*Cornhill Magazine* [July, 1877]) that renewed dedication to form was a healthy antidote to the emotional excesses and diffuse forms of Spasmodic poets who had outraged critical sensibilities in the 1850s.

That the new interest in form would have some unexpected consequences is clear from Tennyson's "To the Queen," affixed to *Idylls of the King* in 1873.

Among "signs of storm" threatening the nation, Tennyson identifies "Art with poisonous honey stolen from France" (49, 56). Tennyson most likely was glancing toward Swinburne, whose "Memorial Verses" in memory of Théophile Gautier appeared in the January, 1873 *Fortnightly Review*; a footnote referenced Gautier's *Mademoiselle de Maupin*. Swinburne's privately printed "Sonnet (with a Copy of 'Mademoiselle de Maupin')," published the same year, describes this tale of bisexuality, cross-dressing, and libertinism as a "golden book of spirit and sense, / The holy writ of beauty" (1–2). The French revival of fixed forms had itself been filtered through Gautier, as James K. Robinson notes: "Banville's theories rested on Gautier's assumption that form, not subject matter, was of first importance."[52] Rossetti and Swinburne cared very much about the matter of their poems. The English Parnassians' interest in form as an end in itself nourished poems that announced their devotion to art through the weightlessness of their matter; unintentionally, they furthered assumptions that (since form rather than content defines art) art is amoral.

An example of English Parnassianism is Edmund Gosse's "Sestina," a form in which the unrhymed end words of the first stanza are recapitulated in variant orders in five more stanzas and a concluding tercet. Gosse's "subject" is the history of the *sestina* itself:

> In fair Provence, the land of lute and rose,
> Arnaut, great master of the lore of love,
> First wrought sestines to win his lady's heart,
> Since she was deaf when simpler staves he sang,
> And for her sake he broke the bonds of rhyme,
> And in this subtler measure hid his woe.   (1–6)

Gosse's poem, like many others associated with the revival, was ephemeral, yet in "Ballade of Dead Actors" (*Magazine of Art* [1886]) Henley uses the obtrusive repetitions and artifice of the *ballade* to fine effect, memorializing theatrical workers while underscoring their repetitive performances and the artifice shared by the theatrical and poetic arts:

> Where are the braveries, fresh or frayed?
> The plumes, the armours – friend and foe?
> The cloth of gold, the rare brocade,
> The mantles glittering to and fro?
> The pomp, the pride, the royal show?
> The cries of war and festival?
> The youth, the grace, the charm, the glow?
> Into the night go one and all.   (9–16)

Henley is here also writing specifically urban verse, another mode to which fixed forms were well suited because indifference to content empowered poets to capture brief impressions of the city rather than intoning the permanent beauties of nature or the soul. In Henley's *rondeau* "In Rotten Row" (*London* [September 1, 1877]), for example, the poet smokes a cigarette and watches sweethearts as well as passersby on horse or foot.

Rondeaux consist of a quintet, quatrain, and sestet governed by two rhymes and a refrain derived from words in the first line. Austin Dobson also uses the form to announce an urban poetics in "On London Stones" (1876):

> On London stones I sometimes sigh
> For wider green and bluer sky; –
>   Too oft the trembling note is drowned
>   In this huge city's varied sound; –
> "Pure song is country-born," – I cry.
>
> Then comes the spring, – the months go by,
> The last stray swallows seaward fly;
>   And I – I too! – no more am found
>   On London stones!
>
> In vain! the woods, the fields deny
> That clearer strain I fain would try;
>   Mine is an urban Muse, and bound
>   By some strange law to paven ground;
> Abroad she pouts; – she is not shy
>   On London stones!

The lyric is gossamer-light, a self-conscious trifle. Yet Amy Levy found it memorable enough to adopt lines 12 to 13 for the epigraph to *A London Plane-Tree and Other Verse* (1889).

Indeed, women also participated in the vogue of fixed verse forms even though its principals were men centered at the Board of Trade (fittingly, since fixed forms could be repeatedly manufactured). One of the wittiest interventions is by May Probyn, who taps the *ballade*'s association with poignant nostalgia – especially for long-dead ladies – only to domesticate it to a grandmother whose querulous refrain that times have "altered" since her youth rebukes her fashion-conscious, rather fast granddaughter: "Maids should learn at their elders' knee – / But things have altered since I was young" (27–8).[53] Probyn pays tribute to newly-available female freedoms while gently mocking the usual masculine erotics of ballades by contemporaries.

Both Probyn and Graham R. Tomson also make shrewd use of the *villanelle*, five tercets and a quatrain governed by two rhymes and repetition of the first and third lines in variant order throughout. Probyn uses the form to represent the obsessive search for a single face on city streets: "I watch the shadows in the crowded street – / Each passing face I follow one by one – / In every sound I think I hear her feet" ("Villanelle," 4–6). Tomson uses the form's repetitions ironically, to register surprise that "Love would stay" when she "deemed him but a passing guest, / Yet here he lingers many a day" ("Villanelle," 1–3).[54]

Gleeson White's edition of *Ballades and Rondeaus* (1887), in which many of these poems were gathered, effectively marked the end of the revival since reviews were dismissive. Short-lived as a movement, the resuscitation of fixed forms nonetheless had long-lasting effects. Not only did this dialogue with modern European forms help propel aestheticism, but it also helped make cosmopolitanism and fixed verse forms available to twentieth-century poets. Ezra Pound's "Sestina: Altaforte" or the *villanelles* of Dylan Thomas and Elizabeth Bishop, "Do not Go Gentle into That Good Night" and "One Art," far supersede the preceding examples from the Victorian revival but descend from it. That an Anglo-Gallic medieval revival in the later nineteenth century could usher in key elements of modernism is a reminder of why study of poetic tradition is so useful, and why Victorian dialogues with poetic tradition as well as Victorian experimentalism extended poetic tradition and inform it today.

Chapter 3

The impress of print: poems, periodicals, novels

Our chain on silence clanks.
Time leers between, above his twiddling thumbs.
Am I quite well? Most excellent in health!
The journals, too, I diligently peruse.
Vesuvius is expected to give news:
Niagara is no noisier. By stealth
Our eyes dart scrutinizing snakes.

George Meredith, *Modern Love* (1862)

We talked modern books
And daily papers, Spanish marriage-schemes
And English climate – was't so cold last year?
And will the wind change by to-morrow morn?
Can Guizot stand? is London full? is trade
Competitive? has Dickens turned his hinge
A-pinch upon the fingers of the great?

Elizabeth Barrett Browning, *Aurora Leigh* (1856)

In *Modern Love* and *Aurora Leigh* periodicals and contemporary fiction are commonplace features of a quotidian world within which modern erotic relationships unfold. Poetry, too, as prior chapters indicate, routinely appeared in newspapers and magazines, where it was read alongside fiction, news, and other prose forms. If *Aurora Leigh* cites Dickens and draws on *Jane Eyre* for its plot, novelists likewise incorporated contemporary poetry into their creations, suggesting why it is important to look at these multiple print forms together.

Two of the most widely anthologized Victorian theories of poetry today are "On Some of the Characteristics of Modern Poetry," by Arthur Henry Hallam, first published in *Englishman's Magazine* (August, 1831), and "What is

Poetry?" by John Stuart Mill, published under the pseudonym "Antiquus" in the *Monthly Repository* (January, 1833). Hallam argues that "Whenever the mind of the artist suffers itself to be occupied, during its periods of creation, by any other predominant motive than the desire of beauty, the result is false in art."[1] Mill circumscribes poetry even more narrowly, explicitly defining poetry against public discourse and the novel, which he aligns with the primitive impetus to storytelling and mere "incident":

> the faculty of the poet and the faculty of the novelist are as distinct as any other two faculties ... for the [novel] is derived from *incident*, the other from the representation of *feeling* ... [The novelist] has to describe outward things, not the inward man.
>
> ...
>
> Poetry and eloquence are both alike the expression or uttering forth of feeling. But ... eloquence is *heard*, poetry is *over*heard. Eloquence supposes an audience; the peculiarity of poetry appears to us to lie in the poet's utter unconsciousness of a listener.[2]

If Hallam identifies poetry with art for art's sake three decades before aestheticism emerged as a significant force, Mill defines poetry in terms of privacy and against rhetoric. These theories, however, were minority views of poetry and its function until late in the nineteenth century.

Periodicals and poetry

The entanglement of poetry, periodicals, and fiction in print culture affected not only Victorian reading practices but also the conceptualization of poetry. As David Masson, Professor of English at the University of London and eventual editor of *Macmillan's Magazine*, asserted in the August, 1853 *North British Review*, "We cannot open a magazine or a review without finding something new said about our friend 'The Poet,' as distinguished from our other friend, 'The Prophet,' and the like."[3] With Hallam and Mill, Masson insists that poetry is set apart from the ordinary world, and he rejects explicit didactic or persuasive purpose as the proper aim of poetry. Citing Goethe, he also agrees with Mill that poems give form to the poet's successive moods.

But he views poetry's relation to other genres and the public realm in far more fluid terms. Following Francis Bacon and Coleridge, Masson identifies poetry with the creation of fully imagined, hence vivid and concrete, alternative worlds; and given this emphasis on fiction, Masson freely moves between poetry and novels before singling out imagery and meter as poetry's distinguishing features. He also insists (1) that poetic creation is an "intellectual process of producing a new or artificial concrete [*sic*]," (2) that "these ... morsels of imagined concrete ... are as truly the poet's *thoughts* about life as any seven scientific definitions would be the thoughts of the physiologist or physician," (3) that "every thought of his in the interest of this world is an excursion into *that*," and, as a result of the poet's intellectual engagement, (4) that "in almost every poem there is much present besides the pure poetry." He instances Shakespeare, whose creativity and breadth of intellect might suggest a poet into whose "mind poetical in *form*, there had been poured also all the *matter* that existed in the mind of his contemporary Bacon."[4] Masson's model of poetic creation places a premium on imagination and poetry's artifice but also configures poetry as conducting a ceaseless interchange with the world.

E. S. Dallas, whose treatise on *Poetics* (1852) is under review in Masson's essay, further connects poetry to a wide rather than private audience in his 1866 study of poetry's psychological appeal: "Great poetry was ever meant, and to the end of time must be adapted, not to the curious student, but for the multitude who read while they run – for the crowd in the street, for the boards of huge theatres, and for the choirs of vast cathedrals, for an army marching tumultuous to the battle, and for an assembled nation silent over the tomb of its mightiest."[5] Within such a critical context, as well as proliferating print culture, it is not surprising that poetry was often presupposed to be in dialogue with periodicals and contemporary fiction.

Book publication always remained the goal of Victorian poetry. Though periodicals might be bound into volumes and set alongside other books in personal libraries, they were ephemera profoundly at odds with poetic aspiration toward lasting fame. Critics also denigrated poetry too closely linked to serials. As the *Leader* dourly commented in its April 7, 1855 issue, "Magazine poetry is seldom the poetry which 'repays perusal.' Out of one's teens, one assiduously avoids it."[6]

Because so many poems first found their publics, however, in the pages of periodicals that circulated more widely than books of verse, it is important to consider how periodicals shaped Victorian poetry. They did so by the pressure they exerted on length and content, their timing, and their reviews. Only established poets or those with literary connections could hope to publish longer works in periodicals, as with Tennyson's "Sea-Dreams" in *Macmillan's Magazine* (January, 1860), or the serialization of *Lawrence Bloomfield in Ireland*, by William Allingham, in twelve monthly parts in *Fraser's Magazine* (November, 1862–November, 1863). Short, immediately accessible poems were most likely to find berths in magazines. To make an impact, they also needed to be memorable, since periodical readers did not necessarily pick up a magazine or newspaper to read poetry but might be led to do so. Dramatic incident or pictorial qualities that might inspire an editor to commission an illustration helped secure readers' attention, as did lyrics that tapped patriotic sentiment, or moved readers to tears or a welcome state of piety. Brevity also increased a poem's chances of success because it could be easily memorized in an era of recitation; poems committed to memory moved beyond the ephemeral periodical page and could be shared with others, extending their circulation.

Editors who found short work useful for rounding out issues or filling a blank spot, however, also screened, and sometimes censored, content. Thackeray famously barred "Lord Walter's Wife" from the *Cornhill* even though he had solicited a poem from Barrett Browning. Conceding that the "moral" of her poem – about a married woman who disdains coyness and flirts back with her husband's friend to unmask his hypocrisy and misogyny – was "most chaste pure and right," Thackeray pronounced his readership "too squeamish" for an "account of unlawful passion."[7] *Blackwood's* printed Barrett Browning's "Cry of the Children" in 1843 but rejected Part I of *Casa Guidi Windows* in 1848, though whether on grounds of politics, length, or form is unclear.[8] In the 1870s Leslie Stephen refused the free-verse portions of Henley's *In Hospital* for the *Cornhill*; and the *Month*, which published Newman's *The Dream of Gerontius* and poems by Wilde, refused Hopkins's "The Wreck of the Deutschland." Poems that too directly challenged norms of technique or ideology were firmly shut out by editorial gatekeepers.

On the other hand, Hopkins's desire to place his greatest poem in a periodical is telling. Alice Meynell recalled the impact of reading Henley's "Hospital Outlines" in *Cornhill Magazine* (July, 1875) when she reviewed *A Book of Verses* thirteen years later, and the poetry of D. G. Rossetti received its first review in response to the sixteen *House of Life* sonnets published under the title "Of Life, Love, and Death" in the *Fortnightly Review* (March, 1869).[9] Periodical publication could thus also support experimentalism, particularly in upmarket or niche titles whose readers welcomed such work. Since a periodical poem was always a one-off publication amidst other fare, unconventional poems could also be inserted in mainstream magazines. Though Swinburne's "Faustine" was censured along with rest of the notorious *Poems and Ballads* in 1866, this poem occasioned no outcry when it appeared in the May 31, 1862 *Spectator*, a widely read weekly whose literary editor was the eminently respectable Richard Holt Hutton.

The rapidity with which a poem could be printed and elicit public response also attracted poets to periodicals. Indeed, publishing one or two poems in advance of a volume's release was an effective means of promoting new work. Since any periodical poem was also swept up in the news cycle in which the entire issue, not just the poem, participated, poems could also win intensified attention, even fame, by virtue of their timing. When Thomas Hood's "Song of the Shirt" appeared in a special Christmas issue of *Punch* (December 16, 1843), the surrounding Christmas contents and the season itself, with its emphasis on benevolence and compassion, intensified the impact of his poem.

"Song of the Shirt" succeeded a series of articles in *The Times* on sweated labor, but Hood's ceaselessly laboring yet starving seamstress engaged readers in ways that the articles had not, thanks to the poetic force of Hood's compression and stark drama. Published anonymously, his poem tripled the circulation of *Punch* just when the paper was in danger of failing. Newspapers immediately reprinted the poem, extending its reach, and Hood even heard his poem sung by poor seamstresses to music of their own devising on city streets.[10] Periodical publication, then, helped secure lasting as well as immediate fame for "Song of the Shirt."

Tennyson's "The Charge of the Light Brigade" itself responded to an article in *The Times*, from whence originated his memorable phrase, "Someone had blundered." The poem appeared in the December 9, 1854 *Examiner* and immediately reached an audience of 5,000 readers just when interest in the incident was highest. So famous did the poem become that when Tennyson tried to alter the poem, removing "Someone had blundered" in *Maud and Other Poems* (1855), he was forced to reverse himself because readers demanded a phrase that had already entered cultural memory.

Though the culture of reviewing was hardly new to the Victorian era, its influence widened after 1830 with the emergence of the *Athenaeum*, a weekly review notable for its disinterested assessments rather than ties to political parties. Numerous periodicals followed suit, though the *Athenaeum* remained a premier critical voice late into the century. Tennyson's "Hendecasyllabics" (*Cornhill Magazine* [December, 1863]), addressed to "indolent reviewers," registers the effects of such critical scrutiny, coyly pleading in its eleven-syllable lines,

> O blatant Magazines, regard me rather –
> Since I blush to belaud myself a moment –
> As some rare little rose, a piece of inmost
> Horticultural art, or half coquette-like
> Maiden, not to be greeted unbenignly.   (17–21)

In "The Ballad of Imitation" (*Belgravia* [March, 1878]), Austin Dobson similarly registers the power of critics, who can "whisper your Epic –'Sir Éperon d'Or'– / Is nothing but Tennyson thinly arrayed / In a tissue that's taken from Morris's store" (17–20). But he tucks a mocking riposte into the envoy:

> And you, whom we all so adore,
> Dear Critics, whose verdicts are always so new!–

> One word in your ear. There were Critics before ...
> And the man who plants cabbages imitates, too!   (25–8)

As long as reviews did not explode poems' claims to merit altogether, poets and reviewers enjoyed a productive commercial symbiosis: reviewers had copy for pay, and poets received free advertising, especially in longer essay-reviews that liberally quoted extracts. Periodical readers also benefited because they could acquaint themselves with the newest poetry by purchasing (or borrowing) an inexpensive journal rather than a high-priced book. A striking instance occurs in Christina Rossetti's 1863 letter to Dora Greenwell on New Year's Eve: "What think you of Jean Ingelow, the wonderful poet? I have not yet read the volume, but reviews with copious extracts have made me aware of a new eminent name having risen among us."[11]

Hostile reviews, however, could silence a budding poet forever. "A weekly – no, an ev'ryday / Reviewer takes my fame away, / and I am all undone!" (4–6), Hood's lackluster poet bewails in the comic "Ode" ("J[ERDA]N, farewell!"). When Tennyson's friend John Sterling asserted in a review that "Morte d'Arthur" (1842) "does not come very near to us," Tennyson abandoned his plan to complete the Arthurian epic and, as Edgar Shannon remarks, that decision "changed the whole pattern of his literary career and may well have affected seriously the position he is to hold in English letters."[12]

Though exhortations to write a specific kind of poem exerted minimal force, two important critical controversies demonstrate the power of periodical reviews to mold poetic creation and reading practices. The first involved the "Spasmodic" poets, a group first lauded by leading intellectuals and critics, then blasted from cultural memory by a single critical review that started a chain reaction of condemnation. As Herbert Tucker explains, Spasmodism was a continuation of Romantic epic born of a desire to articulate the universe by plumbing the mind, sensibility, and imagination of the sole mortal empowered to comprehend it: the poet.[13] Intensity of reaction and profuse imagery proved the poet's sensitivity to the cosmos, and because there was nothing the mind could not take in and little action besides the poet-protagonist's creation of poetry, poems expanded radically. Philip James Bailey's *Festus*, for example, grew from some 8,000 lines in the first edition (1839) to 40,000 lines in 1901.

If "Spasmodic" poetry embodied high literary aspirations, it also suggested radicalism – since cosmic poets recognize no barriers to thought and expression – and elicited class anxieties after Alexander Smith, son of a Glaswegian textile designer who entered the trade at age ten, was hailed in the *Eclectic Review* as a new genius by George Gilfillan, a progressive critic and Presbyterian minister. Through Gilfillan's sponsorship, Smith began to serialize *A Life Drama* in a weekly paper entitled the *Critic*. The enormous power "Spasmodics" attributed to poetry is evident in this passage detailing Chaucer's effect on poet Walter and his mentor:

Breezes are blowing in old Chaucer's verse,
'Twas here we drank them. Here for hours we hung

O'er the fine pants and trembles of a line.
Oft, standing on a hill's green head, we felt
Breezes of love, and joy, and melody,
Blow through us, as the winds blow through the sky.
Oft with our souls in our eyes all day we fed
On summer landscapes, silver-vein'd with streams,
O'er which the air hung silent in its joy;
With a great city lying in its smoke,
A monster sleeping in its own thick breath.[14]

George Henry Lewes was so impressed by Smith that he drew readers' attention to the "exuberant fragments of this young poet," asserting that "there is no mistaking the fact – and it is a 'great fact' to be recorded of any one – that he is a born Singer, a poet by divine right."[15]

But W. E. Aytoun, poet, critic, and Edinburgh professor, remained hostile. Aytoun coined the term "Spasmodic" to discredit the movement in his March, 1854 *Blackwood's* review of Smith, and struck more forcefully still when he pretended to review *Firmilian* by "T. Percy Jones," making up the passages he censured. He then completed a full-length parody, *Firmilian; or, The Student of Badajoz: A Spasmodic Tragedy*, in July, 1854, which ridiculed Gilfillan, Smith, and other contemporaries in recognizable caricatures.[16] In essence, the Spasmodic school was laughed to death. But the controversy also affected better-known poets. Matthew Arnold's censure of the mind in dialogue with itself in the 1853 Preface to his *Poems* was one reaction. Richard Cronin points to another: "Tennyson's *Maud* was identified as soon as it was published as a Spasmodic poem, and in particular as a poem in which Tennyson, the Poet Laureate, had indecorously yielded to the influence of a 23-year-old Glasgow factory worker."[17] "Spasmodism" had become a disciplinary whip wielded in periodicals to keep poets in line.

A second critical controversy initiated by poet Robert Buchanan in "The Fleshly School of Poetry: Mr. D. G. Rossetti" (*Contemporary Review* [October, 1871]) showed the lingering influence of the Spasmodic controversy as well as hostile reaction to Swinburne's *Poems and Ballads* (1866). Buchanan asserted that "the fleshly school ... in spite of its spasmodic ramifications in the erotic direction, is merely one of the many sub-Tennysonian schools expanded to supernatural dimensions." Buchanan hence associated Rossetti with a discredited school from the 1850s and simultaneously belittled him as a mere imitator of Tennyson. Buchanan also cleverly insulted Swinburne while using him against Rossetti, asserting that Swinburne "was only a little mad boy letting off squibs" of naughtiness. But Rossetti was "a grown man ... of actual experience," who deliberately chose to elevate poetic expression over content, body over soul, and expose in "shameless nakedness" the "most secret mysteries of sexual connection" in "Nuptial Sleep."[18] In contrast, Buchanan praised Tennyson's handling of sensuality in "Vivien" (1859), one of the *Idylls of the King*, because its sensuality was balanced by a strong intellectual and moral framework. Clearly Buchanan hoped to snuff out the reputation of Rossetti, whose *Poems* had attained a fifth edition, just as Aytoun extinguished the vogue of Spasmodism.

But Buchanan did not publish the attack under his own name. When the *Athenaeum* disclosed Buchanan's authorship, Rossetti quickly followed up with a *signed* essay, "The Stealthy School of Criticism," slating Buchanan for the cowardly pseudonym, refuting the charge of indebtedness to Buchanan – whose poetry failed to interest him – and underscoring the attention to soul in his sonnet sequence.[19] Buchanan, then, did not quash Rossetti's poetry. But he nearly snuffed out the poet: his attack was one of several factors in Rossetti's 1872 suicide attempt. If Buchanan's poetic reputation, not Rossetti's, has suffered in the long run, Rossetti still removed "Nuptial Sleep" from the completed *House of Life* (1881), and it remained suppressed for thirty years. In this instance, poet and reviewer had alike been hurt by controversy. The periodical press was thus two-edged. It helped make poetry a pervasive presence in Victorian culture, but it also affected what poets were inclined to write, and inhibited access to poets and poems that too blatantly challenged mainstream conventions.

Poetry and Victorian novels

From 1814 to 1846 the number of new fiction titles roughly doubled those of poetry and drama; from 1870–1919, 23 percent of all new books were novels, and only 6 to 7 percent were poems or dramas.[20] Poets were keenly aware that Victorian poetry successively lost ground to the novel in the literary marketplace. As Clough observed in an 1853 review,

> there is no question, it is plain and patent enough, that people much prefer Vanity Fair and Bleak House. Why so? ... is it, that to be widely popular, to gain the ear of multitudes, to shake the hearts of men, poetry should deal more than at present it usually does, with general wants,

ordinary feelings, the obvious rather than the rare facts of human nature? ... The modern novel is preferred to the modern poem, because we do here feel an attempt to include ... these positive matters of fact, which people, who are not verse-writers, are obliged to have to do with.[21]

Some poets simply withdrew from competition with the novel and embraced poetry's marginal status, as Austin Dobson does in "The Ballad of Prose and Rhyme" – published in the same issue of *Belgravia* as the first installment of Thomas Hardy's *The Return of the Native* (January, 1878). Dobson's opening stanza alludes to the workaday world of the Board of Trade and, in common with the first paragraph of Hardy's novel, to drear November weather, only to emphasize poetry's distance from both:

> When the ways are heavy with mire and rut,
>   In November fogs, in December snows,
> When the North Wind howls, and the doors are shut,–
>   There is place and enough for the pains of prose;
>   But whenever a scent from the whitethorn blows,
> And the jasmine-stars at the casement climb,
>   And a Rosalind-face at the lattice shows,
> Then hey!– for the ripple of laughing rhyme!   (1–8)

Poetry is here positioned as an occasional indulgence, a lightsome escape from enveloping dankness and a diversion from omnipresent prose.

Another response to the novel's dominance, however, was to reconceive poetry in terms of the novel, producing a novel-in-verse or, in M. M. Bakhtin's phrase, a novelized poem.[22] *Aurora Leigh* (1856) remains the most prominent example today. As early as 1845 Barrett Browning, a voracious reader of George Sand and other novelists, conceptualized a hybrid poetics along the lines Clough endorsed in his 1853 review. As she wrote to Robert Browning,

> my chief <u>intention</u> just now is the writing of a sort of novel-poem – a poem as completely modern as "Geraldine's Courtship," running into the midst of our conventions, & rushing into drawingrooms and the like "where angels fear to tread"; & so, meeting face to face & without mask, the Humanity of the age, & speaking the truth as I conceive of it out plainly.[23]

The beginning of *Aurora Leigh* realizes that aim, plumping readers into a domestic drawing room from whence they hear the sounds of the nursery above:

>   still I catch my mother at her post
> Beside the nursery door, with finger up,

> "Hush, hush – here's too much noise!" while her sweet eyes
> Leap forward, taking part against her word
> In the child's riot. Still I sit and feel
> My father's slow hand, when she had left us both,
> Stroke out my childish curls across his knee.   (1.15–21)

If the poem begins in the midst of action (*in medias res*) as befits an epic and echoes Wordsworth's Intimations Ode in noting the child's journey from "the coasts of life / ... inward" (1.10–11), its beginning also calls to mind the reformed Mr. Dombey in *Dombey and Son*, smoothing away the curls of his beloved granddaughter from her forehead, or the domestic intimacies of *David Copperfield*. If the work's larger purpose is to delineate the poet's growth and poetry's central role in reforming the world, furthermore, it proceeds by means of a courtship plot drawn partly from contemporary fiction.

Eight years prior to *Aurora Leigh*, Clough published *The Bothie of Tober-na-Vuolich*, itself a novel-poem in nine books that incorporates elements of epic. (Originally entitled *The Bothie of Toper-na-fuosich* after an actual highland hut in which Clough had stayed, the poem was privately retitled by Clough after he learned that the Erse name of the hut, or bothie, signified an obscene toast to "the bearded well"; after his death the new title became standard.) The form and content of *The Bothie* explicitly set elements of epic and fiction in dialogue with each other while also glancing toward contemporary poems. Clough's adoption of dactylic hexameter, the meter of classical epic, was prompted by reading Longfellow's *Evangeline* in 1848. His opening, in which Oxford undergraduates and their tutor observe Highland games and attend a feast at which aristocrats, students, and rustics mingle, echoes the opening scene of Tennyson's *The Princess* (1847). If *The Bothie*'s meter, concentrated language, and sources are firmly embedded in a poetic matrix, however, its realist detail, some of its language, and its plot – a cross-class romance between Philip Hewson, poet and "radical hot, hating lords and scorning ladies" (1.131), and Elspie Mackaye, a Highland peasant's daughter – are as firmly tied to the Victorian novel.

Philip is no romantic hero, nor Elspie a conventional heroine destined to love at first sight. His theories of labor's aesthetic beauty merge with sexual desire to make him first think he loves Katie, the lassie who enjoys flirtations, then the beauteous Lady Maria, whom he turns to in a reactionary fit. Wrong twice, this flawed lover gradually develops profound feelings for Elspie. She, unlike the docile Marian Erle in *Aurora Leigh*, rivets Philip's attention through her piercing glance of superior knowledge and judgment when he walks with Katie. She herself is deeply suspicious of a gentleman's love and spurns the prospect of assimilation to genteel life. When, moreover, Philip suggests that women's natural gifts are the antidote to men's intellectual lives and that at most she will require that he read *to* her, she explodes his sentimental nonsense and reveals her bookishness (8.114–24). Yet she also frankly acknowledges desire and acts on it, sometimes unwillingly: she is no pasteboard figure of rectitude.

If recurring lyrical passages invoke pastoral tradition, pastoralism and epic elevation are deliberately juxtaposed to quotidian detail. Book 2, for example, opens with a Virgilian epigraph (in Latin) and an epic formula for dawn ("Morn, in yellow and white came broadening out from the mountains"), then settles down to the mundane matter of what men eat for breakfast, just as novels glimpse many a sideboard:

> Tea and coffee was there; a jug of water for Hewson;
> Tea and coffee; and four cold grouse upon the sideboard;
> Cranberry-jam was reserved for tea, and for festive occasions:
> Gaily they talked, as they sat, some late and lazy at breakfast,
> Some professing a book, some smoking outside at the window.   (2.9–13)

The juxtaposed epic and novelistic features interrogate each other to create a formal corollary to the competing claims of inherited ideals and complex contemporary realities in the poem. In describing the debate between a Tory and an empirical student –"He to the great might-have-been upsoaring, sublime and idéal, / He to the merest it-was restricting, diminishing, dwarfing" (3.156–7) – Clough is also articulating his poetics, as he does more movingly when Elspie accepts betrothal to Philip:

> I feel much more as if I, as well as you, were,
> Somewhere, a leaf on the one great tree, that up from old time
> Growing, contains in itself the whole of the virtue and life of
> Bygone days, drawing now to itself all kindreds and nations,
> And must have for itself the whole world for its root and branches.
> (8.89–93)

Elspie's branching syntax mirrors the tree and registers the way her passion makes her feel a vibrant part of the whole world. Poetically Elspie is finding a way to insert a cross-class marriage into history despite few precedents. Metapoetically, Clough is articulating his indebtedness to past poetic tradition while extending poetics to the contemporary world claimed by the novel, one defined by its complex diversity and earthliness.

Clough's continuous tie to poetic tradition is secured by his dactylic hexameters, but he gradually drops the epic or mock-epic invocations that in early books precede realist narration. Books 7 to 9 instead open in the direct utterance of the novel, and the end (unlike *Aurora Leigh*) draws no elevated conclusion, bids farewell to no muse. Like a novel, it instead narrates the later life of the wedded couple in New Zealand, where they do not change the world (significantly, the Maori are never mentioned) but merely continue it through children and their life's work. Along the way Clough even draws language from the novel, adapting slang from Dickens's *Old Curiosity Shop* ("mazy," "rosy," in 3.96–7) and *Pickwick Papers* (Mr. Jingle's "singular, very" and "beautiful, very" in 4.141, 5.23).[24]

The influence of the novel, however, can be overstated relative to the proliferation of long Victorian poems, narrative poetry, realist detail, and direct language. All were legacies of Romantic poetry as well. Wordsworth insists in his 1802 Preface that the poet is one "man" speaking to another, and even denies the distinction between the language of prose and poetry, while the long poetic narratives of Scott, Southey, and Byron overshadowed the novel until Scott's Waverley novels began to shift the balance. William St. Clair, moreover, points out that the earliest canonical Romantic poems were the historical narratives of Scott and Byron, with the romantic lyrics of Wordsworth, Coleridge, Shelley, and Keats belatedly gaining recognition among Victorians.[25] As well, more democratic conceptions of human nature influenced by Enlightenment philosophers gave new interest and dignity to humble or outcast figures. Romantic poetry in its earliest sense, then, designated long narrative poems, a practice sustained in the 1820s by Hemans and Landon.

In contrast to Mill's contention that the poet speaks principally to himself, revealing his inner being to an audience that overhears, Coleridge, Shelley, and Thomas Carlyle viewed the poet as a form of prophet empowered by imagination to perceive cosmic process; such views gave added weight to poetry's role in an uncertain time.[26] To the degree that poets were encouraged to continue speaking to "men" about the world at hand or to come, not only the novel and Romantic precedent but also internal logic drove the Victorian long poem. Brief lyrics and narratives were insufficient to articulate social and natural realms that changed daily in the face of rapid technological, industrial, legal, and scientific reforms. As Philip writes to his tutor in *The Bothie*, he can discern no clear hero or battle to follow, "Only infinite jumble and mess and dislocation" (9.94). He solves his personal dilemma by marrying Elspie and attempting a new life in a distant colony. Indeed, Matthew Reynolds argues that marriage functions in the long poems of Clough, Barrett Browning, Tennyson, and Robert Browning as a poetic trope of political and aesthetic unity that welds poetry to evolving national, international, and gender relations – even if the marriage plot was also a defining feature of the Victorian novel.[27]

A strong and pervasive historical sense likewise drove the need to write at length. William Morris's *The Earthly Paradise*, published in three installments from 1868 to 1870 and running to over 40,000 lines, is on the face of it an attempt to escape from modernity. The Apology terms the poet an "idle singer of an empty day" rather than a prophet: "Of Heaven or Hell I have no power to sing" (1.7). And the "Prologue" adjures readers to "Forget six counties over-hung with smoke, / Forget the snorting steam and piston stroke" (1–2) and retreat with the poet instead to Chaucer's time.

The governing plot recounts the familiar, and futile, attempt to escape mortality. Young Norsemen fleeing the plague quest after an earthly paradise free from death; but the only paradise available is the realm of art, which cannot vanquish death but creates a circumscribed space within which experience is rich and beautiful. So the men discover in their thirty-year journey, which ends on an isle of Greek descendants with whom they share their respective cultural hoards of stories. The narrative proper begins in spring and ends in winter, each of twelve books recounting one classical and one medieval verse tale headed by a month lyric. Storytelling becomes its own end in the poem, and reviewers most often praised Morris's work – which was widely read and enjoyed – for the smoothness and delight of the narrative stream upon which readers could happily float. For all these reasons *The Earthly Paradise* is a key document in aestheticism.

Yet in another sense the poem is deeply contemporary, the product of a self-consciously historical era that saw itself as heir to all preceding ages and cultures whose artifacts were increasingly stored in grand and systematized museums. The narrative desire to contain so much of the past, to serve as a compendium of culturally diverse stories preserved in a distinctly modern edifice, also propels the expansive length of Morris's poem.

The multiplicity of long Victorian poems, then, had multiple sources in addition to the novel. And poems continued to overshadow novels in literary prestige until late in the century. As Joanne Shattock observes, "What was crucial to the reviewing of poetry up to the end of the nineteenth century was the underlying assumption of poetry's central position in literary culture."[28] This point is clear in a series of lectures on the novel given by David Masson to the Philosophical Institution of Edinburgh in 1858. To establish the novel's worth, Masson begins by aligning it with poetry:

> If we adopt the common division of Literature, into History,
> Philosophical Literature, and Poetry or the Literature of Imagination,
> then the Novel, or Prose-Fiction, as the name itself indicates, belongs to
> the department of Poetry. It is poetry inasmuch as it consists of matter of
> imagination ... The prose counterpart to Lyric Poetry or Song is Oratory,

or, at least, a conceivable species of oratory, which might be called the Prose Ode, or Rhapsody. The prose counterpart to the metrical Drama is, of course, the Drama in prose. There thus remains, as the prose counterpart to Narrative Poetry, the Romance or Novel. The Novel, at its highest, is a prose Epic; and the capabilities of the Novel, as a form of literature, are the capabilities of Narrative Poetry universally, excepting in as far as the use of prose, instead of verse, may involve necessary differences.[29]

Understanding Victorian print culture, then, requires looking at ways in which poetry influenced or left an imprint on the novel as well as the impact of the novel on poems.

A particularly clear instance is sensation fiction, a publishing vogue launched in late November, 1859 by Wilkie Collins's *The Woman in White* in *All the Year Round*, edited by Charles Dickens. Sensation fiction merged melodrama, crime fiction, and copy from newspaper crime or divorce reports with domestic fiction. Short, weekly installments heightened suspense and delivered doses of voyeuristic thrills. In the April, 1863 *Quarterly Review*, H. L. Mansel famously associated sensation fiction with "preaching to the nerves" and the "perpetual cravings of the dram-drinker." He also asserted that "The sensation novel is the counterpart of the spasmodic poem." Mansel thus grants to Spasmodic poetry the responsibility for breaking down prior limits on appropriate subject matter and intensifying vivid literary effects, developments that led to the new school of fiction.[30]

Nor was this the only poetic influence on sensation fiction. Tennyson's first installment of *Idylls of the King* appeared in July, 1859; on September 10, 1859 "Queen Guinevere," a poem by Mary Elizabeth Braddon under the pseudonym Mary Seton, appeared in the *Brighton Herald*:[31]

> I wear a crown of gems upon my brow,
>> Bright gems drop down upon my yellow hair,
> And none can tell beneath their grandeur, how
>> My brain is racked with care:
>>> ...
> Oh, fatal passion, that absorbs my life!
>> Oh, dreadful madness, that consumes my soul!
> A queen, aye, worse; oh, misery, a wife!
>> God give me self-control!   (1–4, 37–40)[32]

Braddon's emphasis on Guinevere's golden hair and scandalous secret come directly from Tennyson's "Guinevere": "O golden hair, with which I used to play / Not knowing," Arthur laments to his crouching wife (544–5).

Braddon's Guinevere would soon metamorphose into Lady Audley, another blonde who epitomizes feminine standards of beauty while harboring scandalous sexual secrets in the best-selling *Lady Audley's Secret* (1862). Braddon's intense response to Tennyson's queen suggests the profound impact of his poem on her imagination and the importance of his having opened the topic of adultery to drawing rooms under the aegis of poetry's cultural authority and the Queen's Laureate – though divorce court newspaper reports preceded Tennyson in publicizing adultery after passage of the 1857 divorce law. Swinburne explicitly linked these print forms in his riposte to "The Fleshly School of Poetry" in *Under the Microscope* (1872), asserting that in the *Idylls* Tennyson had "reduce[ed] Arthur to the level of a wittol, Guenevere to the level of a woman of intrigue, and Launcelot to the level of a 'co-respondent.' Treated as he has treated it, the story is rather a case for the divorce-court than for poetry ... as mean an instance as any day can show in its newspaper reports of a common woman's common sin."[33]

Another Braddon novel likewise seems conceptually as well as textually indebted to Tennyson's poetry. *John Marchmont's Legacy* (*Temple Bar* [December, 1862–January, 1864]), set largely in Tennyson's Lincolnshire, involves the forced sequestration of Mary Marchmont and her babe. Mary is manipulated into thinking that her husband Edward Arundel is dead rather than seriously injured following a train wreck, and that her marriage and her husband's love are alike shams. Braddon makes her indebtedness to Tennyson's "Mariana" explicit in placing a "dismal pool of black water" next to Marchmont Towers in Lincolnshire (Chapter 5) and having Paul Marchmont, the story's villain, complain that "the place is dreary as Tennyson's Moated Grange" (Chapter 12). Later still, when Paul has been unmasked, he hears "strange noises in the empty rooms as he passe[s] by their open doors, weird creaking sounds and melancholy moanings in the wide chimneys" (Chapter 42), just as "within the dreamy house, / The doors upon their hinges creak'd" amidst Mariana's maddening solitude (61–2).

Braddon also taps Lincolnshire for its association with the "Spasmodic" *Maud* (1855) and its scenes of rivalry, violence, morbidity, and despair, especially in characterizing Olivia Arundel. At first Olivia is a Mariana figure trapped in the stultifying life of a dutiful clergyman's daughter with no outlet for intellect or passion. Just as Tennyson's Mariana laments, "I am aweary, aweary" (11, 23ff.) and "most ... loathed the hour" of sunset (77), so Braddon's Olivia "was weary of her life ... The slow round of duty was loathsome to her" (Chapter 7). Olivia's unrequited passion for her cousin Edward unhinges her mind and propels her first into morbid obsession, then into plots against her cousin's wife. Braddon quotes *Maud* (1.247) in noting that griffins and gargoyles "keep watch and ward" (1:226) over the dreary mansion (Chapter 5); the role of griffin is later transferred to Olivia: "Olivia Marchmont kept watch and ward over Edward and Mary" (Chapter 13).

Rather than drawing plots or governing metaphors from poetry, Victorian novels more typically quoted contemporary poetry at strategic points. In part the impetus was to align the novel with the higher art form of poetry; by this means Braddon could spread a patina of refinement and grace over commercial fiction. For George Eliot, in contrast, chapter epigraphs drawn from contemporaries (as well as Shakespeare, Milton, and her own compositions) helped signal that her fiction was itself high art. In *Felix Holt*, the first novel in which Eliot systematically followed Scott's precedent of "mottoes" affixed to chapter beginnings, Sonnet VI ("Go from me") from *Sonnets from the Portuguese* prefaces Chapter 32 and adumbrates Esther Lyon's perception that soon Felix Holt "would be gone, and that they should be farther on their way, not towards meeting, but parting." In Chapter 43, an epigraph concocted from Sections 85 and 129 of *In Memoriam* again signals Esther's fidelity to Felix ("loved the most when most I feel / There is a lower and a higher!" [129.3–4]) even though she is now a woman of property and he an imprisoned radical. In fact, Chapter 43 is suffused with references to poetry, including Barrett Browning's "Lady Geraldine's Courtship," Tennyson's "The Lord of Burleigh," and Byron's *Giaour*. The multiple references not only position poetry as an expected frame of reference but function as all skillful allusion does, to signify complex meanings economically.

At other times citing poetry solidified a novelist's bond with an audience, which is one reason that Victorian fiction abounds in allusions to Tennyson: his work seeped into popular as well as literary awareness to become something of a common property. The same was true of Keble's *The Christian Year*, upon which Thackeray drew to establish a date – "The *Christian Year* was a book which appeared about that time" – in Chapter 3 of *Pendennis* (November, 1848–December, 1850). In Eliot's *The Mill on the Floss* (1860) the kindly clergyman of St. Ogg's, Dr. Kenn, also quotes Keble when he witnesses Maggie Tulliver's struggle against her attraction to Stephen Guest in Chapter 9, Book VI ("The Great Temptation"): "The souls by nature pitched too high, / By suffering plunged too low" ("St. Philip and St. James," 45–6).

In contrast, Gaskell and Hardy staked out specific cultural alliances through their citation of contemporary poems. Shortly after *Aurora Leigh* appeared, Elizabeth Gaskell selected an epigraph drawn from Book 5 for the title page of her *Life of Charlotte Brontë*:

> "Oh my God,
>   Thou hast knowledge, only Thou,

How dreary 'tis for women to sit still
On winter nights by solitary fires
And hear the nations praising them far off."

                                AURORA LEIGH. [5.434, 438–41]

Not only does this citation forecast Gaskell's portrait of Brontë as a writer struggling onward despite the successive deaths of her siblings and radical loneliness, but the grouping of Brontë, Gaskell, and Barrett Browning on the title page also registers a network of powerful women authors all of whom had been attacked for impropriety in *Jane Eyre* (1847), *Ruth* (1853), and *Aurora Leigh* respectively.

Thomas Hardy quotes *In Memoriam* (33:5–8) when Angel Clare decides not to disturb Tess's confused religious ideas in *Tess of the d'Urbervilles* (Chapter 25), first serialized in the *Graphic* (July 4–December 26, 1891); far more interesting are his quotations from Swinburne's *Atalanta in Calydon* (Chapter 35) and, more daringly, "Fragoletta" (Chapter 42) in the same novel. By this means Hardy aligns himself with avant garde art and tacitly supports the cause of sexual candor even in the pages of a popular family paper that forced him to suppress chapters depicting Tess's seduction by Alec d'Urberville and baptizing of her illegitimate newborn child.

Lines from Swinburne had earlier appeared in Chapter 40 of *The Woodlanders* (*Macmillan's Magazine* [May, 1886–April, 1887]), as well as fourteen lines from "Two Points of View" by Hardy's close friend Edmund Gosse when the newly married Grace Melbury hails Giles Winterbourne, who has long loved her (Chapter 25). Gosse's lyric contrasts a speaker who finds it impossible to forget with a faithless lover: "If I forget – / The salt creek may forget the ocean"; "You still are [queen], I still am slave – / Though you forget" (15–16, 27–8). If "Two Points of View" exactly suits Hardy's scene, the long excerpt functions equally to circulate part of Gosse's recently published *Firdausi in Exile and Other Poems* (1885) to a wider set of readers.

The consequences of recurring citations were the increased circulation of poetry through the pages of widely purchased and widely consumed contemporary fiction, and the implied assumption that readers did or ought to read poetry. This was so even when not a line was quoted – as when Thackeray drew a chapter vignette illustrating "The Lady of Shalott" and placed it at the head of Chapter 48 of *Pendennis*. Novels thus testify to the prominence of Victorian poetry generally and of individual authors specifically, which explains the scant references to Robert Browning until the 1870s. After *The Ring and the Book* established Browning as the most intellectually distinguished poet of the age, Eliot affixed a generous quotation from *Paracelsus* (1835) to Chapter 50 of

Daniel Deronda (February–September, 1876) and Hardy quoted from *Pippa Passes* (1841), *Easter-Day* (1850), and "By the Fireside" (1855) in various chapters of *Tess*.

The novel forcibly shaped elements of Victorian poetry, then, and poetry in turn exerted influence on novels' conceptualization, modes, and linguistic texture. Their generic relation is best understood as mutually interactive – a circumstance that makes Clough's *Bothie*, *Amours de Voyage*, and *Dipsychus* paradigmatic Victorian texts in their dialogue between high poetic tradition and the novel. A similar dialogue is evident in the course charted by sensation fiction. If Tennyson and the "Spasmodics" helped spark the emergence of sensation fiction, the resulting fiction market dominated by tales of violence and passion that "preached to the nerves" made Swinburne's *Poems and Ballads* (1866) a less surprising development than it is if viewed only in relation to other poems. In a notice of *Songs before Sunrise* the 1871 *Edinburgh Review* explicitly identified Swinburne as an adherent of the "sensational school":

> The writers of this school appear to delight in extreme physical experiences – ecstasies and horrors – for their own sake … One of the worst but most inevitable results of this sensational literature is, indeed, to be found in the diseased appetite for artificial mental stimulants it produces … Hence the rage for sensational novels and sensational literature, and hence too, we fear, the appearance of a sensational poet.
>
> In all the main features of his poetry Mr. Swinburne is faithful to the school.[34]

The interactive sensationalism of fiction and poetry is also legible in poems warmly embraced by critics and readers. Tennyson was a dedicated reader of Mary Elizabeth Braddon's novels (not surprisingly, given the frequency with which he met his poems in her pages), and the immensely popular *Enoch Arden* (1865) adapts the bigamy plot that was closely associated with Braddon's sensation fiction. Tennyson spiritualizes bigamy by having Annie consult the Bible when trying to determine whether her sailor husband Enoch is dead before she accepts his old rival's proposal of marriage. And Enoch's heroic act of repression when he returns to England long after surviving shipwreck and glimpses Annie, his children, and Annie's new husband and baby through the window is treated as a form of sacrifice tantamount to emotional crucifixion. Still, the situation remains bigamy; and Tennyson's indebtedness to popular fiction as well as his customary hovering amidst multiple perspectives may inform the odd mix of heroism and crass commercialism in his closing lines: "So past the strong heroic soul away. / And when they buried him the little port / Had seldom seen a costlier funeral" (909–11).

Contemporaries also discerned a link between Robert Browning's twelve testimonials concerning wife-murder in *The Ring and the Book* (November, 1868–February, 1869) and the violent incident and multiple narrators of Wilkie Collins's *The Woman in White* (*All the Year Round* [November 26, 1859–August 25, 1860]) and *The Moonstone* (*All the Year Round* [January 4–August 8, 1868]). As comic poet Mortimer Collins acidly remarked in the stanza devoted to Browning and "His last and longest poem" in *A Letter to the Right Hon. Benjamin Disraeli, M.P.* (1869), "He tells a tale whose actors would delight / Charles Reade or Wilkie Collins, men of might" (148–50).[35] Browning had of course preceded Collins in probing criminal psychology and tying truth claims to a particular rather than universal point of view.

Though most reviews of *The Ring and the Book* made no mention of Collins and instead compared Browning's achievement to Miltonic epic or Shakespearean psychology, a minority of skeptical reviewers asserted, like the Catholic *Month*, that his diction was "downright prose." The Nonconformist *British Quarterly Review* more waspishly asserted, "The effect produced upon the mind resembles that which results from reading through a long trial in the newspapers – evidence *in extenso* … and the subsequent comments of a dozen different journals … It is the newspaper in blank verse." (Not coincidentally, Mortimer Collins also penned this anonymous review.)[36] The strict division between praise that ignored all links to fiction and attacks that underscored them (since sensation fiction was often termed the newspaper novel) suggests critical anxiety in 1869 to separate great Victorian poems from fiction – in stark contrast to Clough's 1853 advocacy of their convergence. Only after Henry James had retheorized the novel as a high art form that, similar to Browning's massive poem, demanded readers' active participation and the crafting of action from a unifying point of view, could Browning's poetry and fiction comfortably be named in relation to each other – as they were in James's 1912 address in honor of Browning's centenary, "The Novel in 'The Ring and the Book.'"[37]

Poetry and fiction converged in a number of other shared Victorian modes. If early in the century Scott and Robert Burns used Scots dialect to racy effect in their novels and poems, Thomas Hardy's fiction and William Barnes's poems later adopted Dorset dialect to strengthen literary realism and regional rather than national historical identity. The provincial novel and provincial poem likewise intersected among readerships. *Scenes of Clerical Life* (*Blackwood's Magazine* [January–November, 1857]) was Eliot's earliest provincial fiction, and *Adam Bede* (1859), itself deeply indebted to Wordsworth, elevated the provincial novel to major status and paved the way for Hardy's fiction. Poetic counterparts include Tennyson's "Dora" (1842), Jean Ingelow's "Supper at the

Mill" (1863), and A. E. Housman's collection of lyrics entitled *A Shropshire Lad* (1896). Similarly, Linda Peterson traces the flourishing of domestic poetry, (e.g., Hemans's "Homes of England") in the 1830s, 1840s, and 1850s, when domestic novels such as *Dombey and Son*, *David Copperfield*, *Vanity Fair*, *Pendennis*, and *Jane Eyre* dominated fiction.[38]

At the opposite extreme of homely, quotidian domestic literature was *unheimlich* (Freud's term for the uncanny) supernaturalism. As editor, Dickens interwove stories by Collins, Gaskell, George Augustus Sala, Hesba Stretton, and himself with a long narrative poem by Adelaide Procter for his first Extra Christmas Number of *All the Year Round* called *The Haunted House* (1859). Procter's contribution, later titled "A Legend of Provence," narrates the ambiguous tale of a devout nun seduced by the wounded knight she tends. She elopes with him, then ends up a prostitute after he abandons her. When she seeks refuge in the convent after repenting, she discovers that the Virgin Mary has kept her place in her guise, and the sexually experienced woman resumes her old role without penalty. Whether readers saw in Procter's poem a Christmas tale of mercy and forgiveness or an indication that vigorous female sexuality and holiness were compatible, the point is that Dickens, rather than conceiving of poetry as a category apart, constructed the same sort of narrative bridge between Procter's poem and Sala's and Collins's stories as he used between prose tales. Only this bridge led into and away from heroic couplets rather than columns of prose.

At the *fin de siècle* fraught sexuality and psychological extremes were more deliberately woven into supernatural poems and fiction. "The New Medusa" (1882) by Eugene Lee-Hamilton is a disturbing dramatic monologue set in the early seventeenth century. The speaker confesses to a priest how a woman saved from the sea, her "black, wet, rope-like locks … backward cast" (70), became his lover. When, one night, a nightmare of strangulation awoke him, he struggled to consciousness to find her long locks wrapped about his neck and arms; wakeful another night, he reached out to her and encountered, instead of hair, the cold, writhing forms of snakes. Fleeing, he returned another night, drawn by her beauteous face; when moonlight disclosed a twining mass of snakes where hair should be, he beheaded her – and now is tortured by doubt whether he was an avenger against monstrous evil or only a murderer driven to crime by madness.

The poem is usefully read in tandem with the story "Prince Alberic and the Snake Lady" (*Yellow Book* [July, 1896]) by Lee-Hamilton's half-sister Vernon Lee, set roughly in the same time period. The female of the story alternately appears as the young prince's secret godmother at night and, by day, as the small green pet snake he keeps in his room. When the prince refuses to marry the wealthy bride selected for him by his grandfather, the latter scents a mistress; and when his men search the room and find the snake they kill it. The prince soon dies and the disfigured body of a woman is found in the room. Both siblings' tales, then, approach the uncanny in psychological more than ghostly terms.

A decade later poetry and fiction representing the uncanny included poems such as John Barlas's "The Cat-Lady" (1889) and Michael Field's "La Gioconda" (1892) and of course the paradigmatic *Dracula* (1897) by Bram Stoker. There is less psychological ambiguity on the surface in these works, but in their shared preoccupation with shape shifters they touch on matters familiar from Freud: the strange interweaving of eros and the death wish, fear of the "other," and the profound alienation resulting from a sense that the conscious "I" is indissolubly tied to a set of inchoate animal drives that emerge unpredictably.

Poetry and fiction converged most intimately in the careers of several Victorian poet-novelists. The first publication of the Brontë sisters was their poems of 1846 rather than a novel, and George Eliot's first publication was the poem "Knowing that Shortly I Must Put off This Tabernacle" in the *Christian Observer* (January, 1840). After Eliot became a distinguished novelist she returned to poetry, most notably in *The Spanish Gipsy* (1868) but also in a series of poems in *Macmillan's Magazine* and *Blackwood's* (as well as in the epigraphs she composed for her novels). If Hardy abandoned fiction after *Jude the Obscure* to focus solely on poetry, numerous figures from Bulwer Lytton and George Meredith to Amy Levy and E. Nesbit practiced both forms simultaneously. Caroline Norton even issued several collections of tales "in Prose and Verse," evidently finding it as unproblematical to interchange genres as Dickens did in his 1859 Extra Christmas Number. And most novelists tried their hands at occasional poems, including Thackeray, who as editor placed his own "*Vanitas vanitatum*: A Poem" in the July, 1860 issue of *Cornhill*.

Conclusion

Part II of this study examines a range of issues from religion or science to empire and democratic movements, on which poets, novelists, critics, and journalists all spoke out in newspapers, magazines, and books. The interactive exchange among genres within mass print culture is of course a major premise of this study. How and why the rich interchange of serious poetry with periodicals and fiction – and the wide readership of poetry – gave way to a more segmented literary scene is a complicated development that can only be suggested here. Four factors in particular affected poetry's place in popular media. Though poetry did not disappear from widely circulating periodicals at the century's end, the increasing syndication of fiction and a desire to capture readers who had only the minimal five years' education required by the 1870 Education Act inclined editors to fill the space formerly occupied by poetry with exciting short stories and "tit-bits." Such fare was to be found earlier in the century, of course, but when poetry still commanded literary prestige and retained its longstanding associations with piety, it could elevate a magazine's status and appeal to readers' "higher" sentiments.

The prestige of poetry continued to sanction poems associated with aestheticism and decadence in upmarket *fin-de-siècle* periodicals targeted at progressive, well-educated audiences. But once Wilde – a byword for aestheticism – was convicted of gross indecency with another man, art for its own sake became suddenly suspect. Meantime the novel, which had always sold better than poetry, was commanding recognition as a "high" art form and no longer needed to invoke or quote poetry for validation. Simultaneously, academic English studies at Cambridge and Oxford tacitly moved poetry out of the public domain and into privileged institutional spaces; these institutions, moreover, had reason to emphasize poetry's intellectual challenge to justify academic credit for what every literate Briton could read. All these factors were in place when, in addition, modernist poets began to emphasize innovative styles that were the reverse of E. S. Dallas's axiom that "Great poetry was ever meant ... for the multitude."

Great poetry remains more widely read today than is sometimes assumed, but Victorian assumptions that poetry was an expected part of every reader's experience have largely been lost. Nonetheless, comprehending Victorian print culture in even rudimentary terms means finding a place for poetry as an essential component.

Part II

The rhetoric of Victorian poetry

Introduction to Part II

> This world's no blot for us,
> Nor blank; it means intensely, and means good:
> To find its meaning is my meat and drink.
> "Ay, but you don't so instigate to prayer!"
> Strikes in the Prior: "when your meaning's plain
> It does not say to folk – remember matins,
> Or, mind you fast next Friday!" Why, for this
> What need of art at all?   Robert Browning, "Fra Lippo Lippi" (1855)

W. B. Yeats famously asserted of Victorian poetry, "My generation, because it disliked Victorian rhetorical moral fervour, came to dislike all rhetoric. In France, where there was a similar movement, a poet had written, 'Take rhetoric and wring its neck.'"[1] Yeats had some grounds for associating Victorian poetry with rhetoric. For example, "Dover Beach" (1867), Matthew Arnold's famous meditation on the relation of erotic love to human mortality and uncertainty, has seemed forced to some readers. Walt Whitman objected to Arnold as a "dude of literature,"[2] and the poem's diction has seemed unnecessarily fine to others. In this context "rhetoric" signifies inflated language and unearned ponderousness. Having contrasted the waves' constant breaking on shore to a steadily ebbing "sea of faith" in prior stanzas, Arnold's speaker concludes,

> Ah, love, let us be true
> To one another! for the world, which seems
> To lie before us like a land of dreams,
> So various, so beautiful, so new,
> Hath really neither joy, nor love, nor light,
> Nor certitude, nor peace, nor help for pain;
> And we are here as on a darkling plain
> Swept with confused alarms of struggle and flight,
> Where ignorant armies clash by night.   (29–37)

The night-time war scene, drawn from the Battle of Epipolae in Thucydides' history of the Peloponnesian War, is movingly powerful, but more readers than American poet Anthony Hecht, author of "The Dover Bitch: A Criticism of

113

Life," have found the invocation of love against this backdrop hollow, the "Ah, love" and "Hath really neither" spuriously elevated in the context of chaos.

Insincerity is a psychological and cosmic problem in Hardy's "Her Dilemma" (1898), which likewise concerns love and impermanence:

> The two were silent in a sunless church,
> Whose mildewed walls, uneven paving-stones,
> And wasted carvings passed antique research;
> And nothing broke the clock's dull monotones.
>
> Leaning against a wormy poppy-head,
> So wan and worn that he could scarcely stand,
> – For he was soon to die,– he softly said,
> "Tell me you love me!" – holding long her hand.
>
> She would have given a world to breathe "yes" truly,
> So much his life seemed hanging on her mind,
> And hence she lied, her heart persuaded throughly
> 'Twas worth her soul to be a moment kind.
>
> But the sad need thereof, his nearing death,
> So mocked humanity that she shamed to prize
> A world conditioned thus, or care for breath
> Where Nature such dilemmas could devise.

The deliberately plain diction avoids varnishing death – vividly conveyed through the carved "wormy poppy-head." Though here, too, a conclusion is drawn about humanity and nature, the woman keeps the thought to herself instead of apostrophizing her suitor; and the poem so roots these declarations in a psychological moment (the woman's compelled choice between truth and kindness, her apprehension of cosmic blight) that they seem intrinsic to the scene rather than uttered from a poetic platform. Faith has decayed here too, but the point is signaled directly in images of a "sunless" church with "mildewed walls," not stated abstractly. Finally, Hardy's poem, though equally a product of its time, has notably cut the tie to contemporary debates whereas Arnold's poem suggests a poet struggling with his age and arguing both with it and himself, able neither to dispense with consolation nor affirm faith.

There is another sense of "rhetoric," however, than the pejorative one adopted by Yeats. Rhetoric can also signify persuasive public discourse grounded in civic virtue and truth-seeking, a mode long given an honored place in poetic tradition. As Horace argues in *Ars poetica* (*c.* 19 BC), the role of poetry is both to delight and instruct (*delectare et docere*), an aim also evident in Virgil's *Aeneid* (30–19 BC), which fosters patriotism by constructing an epic account of Rome's founding. Such aims also underlie much satiric and political poetry in Britain. In the *Critique of Judgment* (1790), however, Enlightenment philosopher Immanuel Kant famously sundered poetry from rhetoric, identifying poetry with the free play of the mind and elevating it above rhetoric, which in being tied to particulars gives less access to understanding than does imagination.[3]

Though Kant's views have profoundly influenced European and Anglophone literary tradition, rhetoric in its positive guise has never been set aside by poets. Shelley asserts poets' power both to apprehend universal truth and to effect public good when he terms them "unacknowledged legislators of the world" in "A Defence of Poetry." Blake's "London" in *Songs of Experience* (1794) pushes toward the universal in articulating the subjectivity of oppressed human beings under the allied forces of church, state, and commerce ("mind-forged manacles"); but his lyric also stages a powerful political protest. So does Yeats's "Easter 1916," which at once commemorates and models patriotic sacrifice on behalf of a free Ireland against British rule. For that matter, Yeats decried "Victorian rhetoric" in a BBC broadcast delivered to a public audience of thousands, perhaps hundreds of thousands, of listeners. Though Yeats argued from conviction, his talk on "Modern Poetry" was hardly innocent of persuasive design, since it aimed to consolidate the prestige and style of modernist poetry. If no sham, Yeats's talk itself depended on rhetoric.

Aristotle identifies three principal means of persuasion: *logos* (logic), *pathos* (appeals to feeling), and *ethos* (the rhetor's character). Logic encompasses dialectic, or disputation proceeding by question and answer, as well as evidentiary argument. The latter has little place in poetry, since prose is so much more efficient in marshaling evidence and deriving a conclusion from premises. But an impulse to question, answer, question anew, and engage readers' emotions characterizes much of the finest poetry. As Paul Ricoeur asserts,

> the poet does not argue, *stricto sensu*, even if his characters argue ...
> Conversion of the *imaginary* is the central aim of poetics. With it, poetics
> stirs up the sedimented universe of conventional ideas which are the
> premises of rhetorical argumentation. At the same time, this same
> breakthrough of the imaginary shakes up the order of persuasion, from
> the moment it becomes less a matter of settling a controversy than of
> generating a new conviction.[4]

This honorific rhetoric, as well as "rhetoric" in Yeats's invidious sense, are both germane to Robert Browning's "Fra Lippo Lippi." In lines 316–18 the Prior insists that art should manipulate its audience, seducing them to act in accordance with a powerful institution's dictates, to which Fra Lippo responds, "What need of art at all?" (320). Lippo advocates instead a Kantian free play of the mind: "my head being crammed, the walls a blank, / Never was such prompt disemburdening" (143–4). Yet the poem also clearly participates in ongoing Victorian debates about the true aims and subject matter of poetry. Like Clough in his 1853 *North American Review* essay (cited in Chapter 3), Fra Lippo argues that realism elevates human consciousness rather than lowering it:

> we're made so that we love
> First when we see them painted, things we have passed
> Perhaps a hundred times nor cared to see;
> And so they are better, painted – better to us,
> Which is the same thing. Art was given for that;
> God uses us to help each other so,
> Lending our minds out.   (300–6)

Browning himself creates a realist portrait of a monk whose exuberance and genius coexist with lechery, hypocrisy, and wheedling. Insofar as "Fra Lippo Lippi" formally enacts the aesthetic doctrine its speaker advocates, the poem takes a side in a contemporary debate. Yet it does so on behalf of truth-seeking and untrammeled imaginative free play.

The dialectic of Victorian poetry was intensified by the omnipresence of print culture, which multiplied voices and viewpoints and even dialogized lyrics within periodicals. Poem challenged poem, and, as the preceding chapter demonstrates, verse was in conversation with periodicals and fiction. As an esteemed public literary form, poetry was also in conversation with public events, and succeeding chapters accordingly examine the "rhetoric" of Victorian poetry in Ricoeur's sense, as poets attempted to open new perspectives and generate convictions in an era of profound cultural change by moving readers and prompting new questions. Of course, many poets did write, as it were, under the aegis of Browning's prior, as Martin Tupper demonstrates in these lines on workers versus the wealthy from his immensely popular *Proverbial Philosophy*:

> The poor man rejoiceth at his toil, and his daily bread is sweet to him:
> Content with present good, he looketh not for evil to the future:
> The rich man languisheth with sloth, and findeth pleasure in nothing,
> He locketh up care with his gold, and feareth the fickleness of fortune.
> Can a cup contain within itself the measure of a bucket?[5]

Such lines quell the legitimacy of the Chartist movement and instead affirm class inequities under the guise of a moral rebuke to the rich. And though Tupper adopts a form of free verse, there is nothing radical about his message.

The best Victorian poetry, in contrast, confronted emergent change and cultural anxiety and, moreover, did so through poetic form, activating dialectic in poetic terms rather than delivering lessons with "rhetorical moral fervour." By means of the dramatic monologue, for example, Browning evades *ex cathedra* pronouncements on aesthetics or moral purpose in "Fra Lippo Lippi," instead modeling art and knowledge alike as processes rather than fixed apothegms. Even as the poem affirms realism it opens questions that it refuses to settle. Does Fra Lippo always mean what he says? Can principles of transcendent art be best conveyed by an artist who breaks vows and revels with prostitutes?

The poem also engages the revival of the Catholic see of Westminster in 1850 and the doctrine of celibacy for priests: if the body and its drives are not to be despised in art, should they be in life or religious teachings? While, in Ricoeur's words, using "the imaginary in order to shake up the very order of persuasion" and help "generat[e] ... new conviction[s]," Browning in "Fra Lippo Lippi" also fashions poetic form and multiple voices to set elusive, mobile positions in play on a range of public issues. In this he exemplifies in its best sense the rhetoric of Victorian poetry.

Chapter 4

Poetry, technology, science

Those hells upon earth, since the Steam King's birth
    Have scatter'd around despair;
For the human mind for heav'n design'd,
    With the body, is murdered there.
Edward P. Mead, "The Steam King"[1]

A sad astrology, the boundless plan
That makes you tyrants in your iron skies,
Innumerable, pitiless, passionless eyes,
Cold fires, yet with power to burn and brand
His nothingness into man.   Tennyson, *Maud* (1855), 1.634–8

From coupler-flange to spindle-guide I see Thy Hand, O God –
    Rudyard Kipling, "McAndrew's Hymn" (*Scribner's Magazine*
    [December, 1894]), 3

Marshall Berman's characterization of modernity aptly encapsulates the Victorian experience of confronting rapid technological development and scientific breakthroughs: "To be modern is to find ourselves in an environment that promises us adventure, power, joy, growth, transformation of ourselves and the world – and, at the same time, that threatens to destroy everything we have, everything we know, everything we are."[2] For engineers, capitalists, and middle-class employees, technology was an engine of profit; new machines also benefited writers and readers, distributing print nationwide in mere hours and lowering printing costs until anyone with a penny could purchase hours of reading. McAndrew, the Scottish engineer and servant of empire in Kipling's "Hymn," even sees God's providence in his steamship's machinery. But to workers harnessed to and sometimes mauled by machines, whose wages were kept low by the same economic system that spurred development, new technologies were a harrowing source of misery.

Science posed another cultural paradox. "Natural philosophy," as science was once termed, approached universal laws identified by scientists as testimony to God's greatness, a view most famously articulated in William Paley's metaphor of watch and watch-maker in *Natural Theology* (1802): "suppose I had found a *watch* upon the ground, and it should be inquired how the watch happened to be in that place ... [T]he inference, we think, is inevitable, that the watch must have had a maker."[3] But numerous nineteenth-century scientific developments conspired to displace God and the humanity supposedly created in His image from the center of the cosmos, as the speaker of *Maud* laments in confronting "A sad astrology" (1.633). New geological and evolutionary theories revised creation into an infinitesimally slow (rather than instantaneous) act governed by impersonal forces of erosion, uplift, and natural selection rather than a personal deity.

The nebular hypothesis first articulated in 1796 by Pierre-Simon Laplace, which argued that the solar system gradually formed from a gaseous nebula, posited a secular heavenly analogue to terrestrial geology. Nor could even heavenly bodies be deemed eternal. After James Joule had formulated the first law of thermodynamics, the conservation of energy, by the 1840s Lord Kelvin and James Maxwell had established the second law known as entropy, the inevitable dissipation of heat and resulting tendency toward disorder. The implication was clear: the sun, source of life and light on earth, was doomed one day to expend its energy and die out.

Discomfiting as such theories might be to those who believed in an eternal creator and creation, the radical overturning of received dogmas by scientific innovation also suggested the power of the human mind to craft new solutions to longstanding problems from disease to poverty. And the prospect of getting closer to the truths of the physical universe could be liberating. When Archbishop Samuel Wilberforce mockingly inquired during a June, 1860 Oxford debate whether his opponent, biologist Thomas Henry Huxley, was descended from an ape on his grandfather's or grandmother's side, Huxley rejoined that the shame lay in misusing intellectual gifts to "distract" an audience with "eloquent digressions, and skilled appeals to religious prejudice," whereas there was no shame in owning an ape for an ancestor.[4] Science and technological innovation in turn provided new metaphors to poets and writers – in this respect an unqualified boon – while also spurring the invention of new conceptual and formal frames that could articulate humanity's relation to the physical universe.

Technology and social justice

By memorably representing workers' conditions and inspiring heightened emotions conducive to action, poetry had a powerful role to play in Chartism and related social reforms. Edward P. Mead's principal technique for achieving these goals in "The Steam King" – a poem cited by Friedrich Engels in *The Condition of the Working Class in England* (1845) – is biblical allusion. The literal meaning of "Moloch" (Hebrew for "king") and Old Testament depictions of Moloch as a pagan god demanding the sacrificial burning of children allow Mead to invoke political, moral, and religious frames of reference as he associates the factory system with unjust, unnatural, unchristian tyranny.

This king has only one arm made of "iron," an allusion to the endlessly moving crankshafts of power looms driven by the coal-generated steam Mead terms "living fire." But this king is also unnatural because "children are his food" (5–6, 11–12), a reference to children routinely employed as cheap labor in excessively hot mills.[5] An unnatural king also implies unnatural subordinates who carry out his behests, the mill owners:

> His priesthood are a hungry band
>   Blood-thirsty, proud, and bold;
> 'Tis they direct his giant hand,
>   In turning blood to gold.   (13–16)

In this context, both Christian duty and British patriotism demand the expulsion of a pagan foreign king if the nation is to survive:

> Then down with the King, the Moloch King,
>   Ye working millions all;
> O chain his hand, or our native land
>   Is destin'd by him to fall.   (29–32)

When Mead in his penultimate stanza explicitly names the People's Charter – "Then your charter gain and the power will be vain" (39) – the poem's forceful governing trope gives way to awkward literalism. Yet Mead's ethical logic demands a call to action that can remedy the ontological, moral, and political states represented in prior stanzas.

When the Chartist movement dissipated after 1848, shifting political and rhetorical situations required alternative poetic strategies. Rather than urging solidarity in political action, working-class poets and activists generated "new convictions" (in Ricoeur's sense) by exposing structural economic and class distinctions. The two quatrains of "'Get Up!'" (1872) by Joseph Skipsey, a poet whom D. G. Rossetti admired, use habitual present tense to suggest numbing routine; the first-person utterance and dialect establish a participant's rather than observer's perspective; and the surprise of the last line indicates that for miners, as for many other industrial workers, potential death is as routine as work itself:

> "Get up!" the caller calls, "Get up!"
>   And in the dead of night,
> To win the bairns their bite and sup,
>   I rise a weary wight.
>
> My flannel dudden donn'd, thrice o'er
>   My birds are kiss'd, and then
> I with a whistle shut the door
>   I may not ope again.[6]

Ellen Johnston, "The Factory Girl," combines a dramatic monologue and balladic refrain ("What care some gentry if they're weel though a' the puir wad dee!") in "The Last Sark" (1867), which unfolds the consequences of low wages and unemployment on workers' wives.[7] Having pawned everything else, the family have nothing but John's "auld blue sark" (shirt) to pawn when he comes home without finding work (1–2). But the real drama is the social conditioning of discourse itself by starvation wages. In the first stanza the wife comments that her "head is rinnin' roon about far lichter than a flee" (3), and by the end she is fainting with hunger: "The bairn is faen' aff my knee – oh! John, catch haud o' him, / You ken I hinna tasted meat for days far mair than three" (22–3).

Adopting the rhetoric of pathos, the poem emphasizes the gulf between genteel prosperity and workers' starvation, but "The Last Sark" also makes subtly ironic use of the refrain. Its generic reference to gentry and formulaic utterance contrast starkly with the specific representations of bodily sensation and economic crisis suffered by John and his wife. The gentry can abide suffering in their midst because they themselves lump the poor into a category of indifferent interest; even in the shared practice of stereotyping an entire class, a gulf opens between the gentry's and a starving wife's power to work harm to others.

Poetry by workers not only addressed shifting political and social conditions but also challenged poems on similar topics by middle-class poets, who enjoyed wider access to readerships and never faced the worst effects of the factory system. In "The Factory" (1835), for example, Letitia Landon adopts the balladic measure and trope of Moloch also featured in "The Steam King":

> We read of Moloch's sacrifice,
>   We sicken at the name,

> And seem to hear the infant cries –
>   And yet we do the same; –
>
> And worse – 'twas but a moment's pain
>   The heathen altar gave,
> But we give years, – our idol, Gain,
>   Demands a living grave!   (21–8)

Like Mead, Landon censures exploitative child labor and the elevation of commercial profit over humane policy. But Landon strategically adopts the pose of poetess and maternal sentimentality to arouse sympathy for the children's plight: "such should childhood ever be, / The fairy well" (45–6).

This stance enjoyed wide appeal and was also consistent with Christian morality. However, rather than advocating the overthrow of King Moloch and the people's right to a Charter, like Mead, Landon merely incites awareness of injustice: "O England! ... / While those small children pine like slaves, / There is a curse on thee!" (89, 91–2). "The Factory" skirts the matter of workers' capacity to remedy their own plight, instead underscoring children's passivity under a tyrannous factory system – "A thousand children are resign'd / To sicken and to die!" (19–20) – and suppressing mention of adult workers or the social injustice of mill owners. Her poem strategically adapts the poetess role to public issues of social justice, then, but seeks no public authority or outlet in public action.

In *A Voice from the Factories* (1836), published anonymously, Caroline Norton assumes the public voice that Landon forgoes. Norton approaches social justice and factory work from an aristocratic, governmental perspective, dedicating her poem to Lord Ashley, the Tory MP who helped pass the 1833 Factory Act limiting hours for women and children, and mentioning "Commissioners" and "printed Reports" in her dedicatory epistle. She also defends the legitimacy of applying "serious poetry to the passing events of the day," concluding that "reasonings dressed in the garb of poetry" are appropriate since "poetry is the language of feeling [and] should be the language of the multitude; since all men can feel, while comparatively few can reason acutely."[8] Whereas Landon invokes ballad tradition and conventional femininity, Norton complements her elevated social position by turning to high poetic tradition, adopting Spenserian stanzas and alluding to Milton's *Paradise Lost* in the opening line ("When fallen man from Paradise was driven").

Like Landon, however, Norton works from within the status quo, conceding that the poor must labor to survive (stanzas 21, 52) and repudiating workers' political agitation. If "Men rarely set Authority at naught" and the peasant, "from his cradle taught / That some must *own*, while some must *till* the land, /

Rebels not" (stanza 54), she nonetheless warns that when disparities between laws for the wealthy and for the poor are too blatant, "discontent" ensues; and "Where there is strength, *REVOLT* his standard rears" (stanza 56). Rather than eliciting sympathy for victims, like Landon, or solidarity with workers, like Mead, Norton fosters a view of children conducive to reform that will benefit England in the long run: "Untaught, unchecked, they yield as vice invites: / With all around them cramped, confined, impure, / Fast spreads the moral plague which nothing new shall cure" (stanza 14). These were concerns also expressed in publications such as *The Manufacturing Population of England* by Peter Gaskell (1833), who emphasized the harmful effects on families when women and children worked in factories.

Having conceded so much, Norton can then challenge her audience and its complacent premises. Noting the longstanding association of Britain with liberty, she assails British statesmen who defend childhood labor as a cost-saving measure, attacking both their morality ("[in] defence / Of the unalienable *RIGHT OF GAIN*," these men "Upheld the cause of torture and of pain" [stanza 17]) and their rhetoric: "Proud of each shallow argument they stand, / And prostitute their utmost powers of tongue / Feebly to justify this great and glaring wrong" (stanza 16). Writing anonymously and so unsexing herself to obtain a hearing, Norton charges that the statesmen unsex themselves in prostituting their gifts. Shrewd allusion to Felicia Hemans's famous "Homes of England" – "'The happy homes of England!' ... / A source of triumph, and a theme for song" (stanza 32) – likewise enables Norton to deflate paternalistic presumption. In a seeming flourish of patriotism inspired by Hemans, Norton crafts a seven-stanza vignette of sentimental middle-class domesticity in which the father returns home after a day's work to his wife and happy children. Then the poet abruptly asks: "Which of these little precious ones shall go / ... To that receptacle for dreary woe, / The Factory Mill?" (stanza 39). Self-congratulatory middle-class domesticity suddenly modulates into the public accusation that law makers condone one law for their families, another for workers.

Herself ineligible for parliamentary service, though closely acquainted with many of its powerful agents, Norton thus crafts a mobile poetic rhetoric that engages the perspectives of rulers and workers, women and men. Her skill helps explain the poem's longevity beyond its immediate political and rhetorical situation. Commenting that "little pent-up wretches" work "Where the air thick and close and stagnant grows, / And the low whirring of the incessant wheel / Dizzies the head, and makes the senses reel" (stanza 10), she was providing imagery for Barrett Browning in stanza 7 of "The Cry of the Children" (*Blackwood's Magazine* [August, 1843]), published when the 1844 Factory Act was being debated in parliament and the press.

Technology and poetic mobility

If industrial machines could oppress workers while enriching owners and managers, new technologies of communication and transport altered human perception of time and space. Distance shrank when foreign scenes were accessible by steamship and train, or reported via telegraph, which linked towns and cities throughout Great Britain and, after undersea cables were laid in the 1860s, Britain with Europe and America in an information network. New sensations of speed and power over the natural world arrived with intercity trains and, in the last third of the century, with urban transport, when underground trains catapulted passengers from one end of the city to the other at speeds previously unthinkable. For poets, new technologies provided new metaphors, sensory tableaux, and terms on which an audience could be imagined.

Not all poets were pleased. The prospect of a railroad running through his beloved Lake District prompted Wordsworth – the first Poet Laureate appointed by Queen Victoria – to turn polemicist with an 1844 sonnet decrying this "rash assault" on beauty ("On the Projected Kendal and Windermere Railway" [2]). (For good measure Wordsworth excoriated the visual technologies that brought distant or imagined scenes to readers as a "vile abuse of pictured page!" in "Illustrated Books and Newspapers" [12], his sonnet of 1846.) Wordsworth was implicitly challenging the young poet who would succeed him as Laureate, for in 1842 Tennyson embraced the railroad as a new metaphor of progress, not merely alluding to new technology but forming a modern poetic idiom upon it.

The speaker of "Locksley Hall" oscillates between bitter disillusionment and idealism after being jilted by his cousin Amy for a wealthier suitor. If he harks back to a youthful "Vision of the world" wherein air travel and commerce would usher in a utopian age (120–8), he is stranded in a rueful present: "So I triumphed ere my passion sweeping through me left me dry, / Left me with the palsied heart, and left me with the jaundiced eye" (131–2). Momentarily recoiling from modernity, he considers retreating to a tropical paradise where "would be enjoyment more than in this march of mind, / In the steamship, in the railway, in the thoughts that shake mankind" (165–6) – and where nubile women of color would grant sexual favors: "I will take some savage woman, she shall rear my dusky race" (168). But the privileged Briton triumphs, spurning "the gray barbarian" who, the speaker claims, ranks "lower than the Christian child" (174). The poem concludes when the spurned lover recommits himself to modern progress envisioned as a rushing train: "Not in vain the distance beacons [*sic*]. Forward, forward let us range, / Let the great world spin for ever down the ringing grooves of change" (181–2).

If "Locksley Hall" provided Victorian audiences with fresh rhythms and images of British dominance, its crude racism and uncritical imperialism are untenable today. Even for many Victorians the speaker's hierarchies of race must have looked odd next to his association of modernity with worldwide brotherhood (128–30) and cross-class solidarity: "Men, my brothers, men the workers, ever reaping something new" (117). "Locksley Hall" is usefully read alongside Ernest Jones's "The Factory Town," published two years later in *The Labourer*, which Jones coedited. In contrast to the "bloated trader" driven in "his golden chariot" on a road down which "rush the masses, / Crushed beneath his stubborn will" (65–72), Jones asserts of the workers:

> There they lie – the withered corses,
>   With not one regretful thought,
> Trampled by thy fierce steam-horses,
>   England's mighty *Juggernaut*. (77–80)[9]

Jones not only recapitulates Tennyson's meter (slightly disguised by breaking one trochaic octameter catalectic line in two) but also upends the careful separation in "Locksley Hall" between Britain and the "Orient" by adopting the trope of the Juggernaut, in Hindu myth an enormous car beneath which people are crushed amidst the progress of Krishna. By invoking the "steam-horse" Jones explicitly references trains as well as industrial machinery and exposes Tennyson's train as a Juggernaut that demands the sacrifice of Orientalized workers to concepts of British superiority.

Imperialism, mobility, and poetic innovation also meet in "McAndrew's Hymn." Kipling follows Tennyson in crafting a metaphor of progress from machinery when his speaker, a "dour Scots engineer" (115), contrasts current with older technology:

> Ten pound was all the pressure then – Eh! Eh! – a man wad drive;
> An' here, our workin' gauges give one hunder sixty-five!
> We're creepin' on wi' each new rig – less weight an' larger power:
> There'll be the loco-boiler next an' thirty miles an hour! (27–30)

McAndrew similarly associates the tropics with sexually accommodating women. As a young man on his first voyage he momentarily succumbed to temptation and, rather than his mother's stern Christian God, temporarily worshiped a pagan life force: "the Leevin' God, / That does not kipper souls for sport or break a life in jest, / But swells the ripenin' cocoanuts an' ripes the woman's breast" (68–70). Imperialist assumptions are in fact more pervasive in "McAndrew's Hymn" than in "Locksley Hall" but are also more subtly evoked, for example, in the casual ease with which the globe is mapped in relation to Britain at the center: "Or make Kerguelen [between Africa, Antarctica, and Australia] under sail – three jiggers burned wi' smoke! / An' home again – the Rio run" (101–2). More tellingly, the theology McAndrew hears in engine parts working in unison is the code of empire and imperial rule: "'Law, Orrder [*sic*], Duty an' Restraint, Obedience, Discipline!'" (167).

Kipling's poem is ultimately inspired more by Robert Burns and "Holy Willie's Prayer" than by "Locksley Hall," however, as McAndrew's reference to Burns during his Calvinist confession of sin and faith makes clear:

> Romance! Those first-class passengers they like it very well,
> Printed an' bound in little books; but why don't poets tell?
> I'm sick of all their quirks an' turns – the loves an' doves they dream –
> Lord, send a man like Robbie Burns to sing the Song o' Steam!
> To match wi' Scotia's noblest speech yon orchestra sublime
> Whaurto – uplifted like the Just – the tail-rods mark the time.   (148–53)

Kipling extracts a symphony from mechanical acoustics just as McAndrew extracts theology from steam, renewing poetic rhythm and diction in the process. For example, Kipling halts, then restores iambs to register a rod returning to *its* rhythm: "Till – hear that note? – the rod's return whings glimmerin' through the guides" (157). The line is at once lyrical, making skilful use of assonance and alliteration, and highly technical: steam engine "guides" are "the rods on which the cross-head of the piston slides" (*OED*). The latest technology and poetic tradition also merged in the poem's first publication in a transatlantic publication, *Scribner's Magazine*, which featured a Kipling letter and Howard Pyle's lavish illustrations on the cover (Figure 5).

William Allingham, in "Express (*From Liverpool, Southwards.*)," has more modest aims than Tennyson in "Locksley Hall" or Kipling in "McAndrew's Hymn," but more fully represents the altered human sensorium ushered in by machine-driven speed as he describes what a passenger on an express train sees through the window:

> By orchards, kine in pleasant leas,
>   A hamlet-lane, a spire, a pond,
> Long hedgerows, counter-changing trees,
>   With blue and steady hills beyond;
>   (House, platform, post,
>   Flash – and are lost!) (13–18)[10]

Objects swiftly rushing by give the poet no time to narrate a scene, only to name them as they pass. Each stanza's concluding couplet intensifies metrical speed in response, shifting from tetrameter to trimeter.

SCRIBNER'S MAGAZINE

Vol. XVI   DECEMBER 1894   No. 6

MCANDREWS' HYMN

By Rudyard Kipling

ILLUSTRATIONS BY HOWARD PYLE

. . . *and the night we got in, sat up from twelve
to four with the Chief Engineer who could not get
to sleep either. . . said that the engines made
him feel quite poetical at times, and told me things
about his past life   He seems a pious old bird ; but
I wish I had known him earlier in the voyage.*

—*Extract from private letter.*

Figure 5   Rudyard Kipling, "McAndrew's Hymn," *Scribner's Magazine*
(December, 1894), cover

"Express" begins and ends at railway terminals, when amidst "Brick mazes,
fiery furnace-blasts, / Walls, wagons," the train's "ponderous rank /
Glides in [or out] with hiss and clank" (33–6); and Allingham concludes by moralizing
on British greatness:

> So have we sped our wondrous course
> Amid a peaceful busy land,

    Subdued by long and painful force
    Of planning head and plodding hand.
      How much by labour can
      The feeble race of man! (37–42)

In between, however, Allingham writes as an impressionist poet and inventively clips syntax to complement the visual snapshots of his quatrains. In the middle – during the ride, so to speak – he participates in the avant garde impressionism of *fin-de-siècle* poets who crafted a poetics of transience and mobility to represent new human perceptions made possible by new technologies of speed.[11]

Science and the crisis of new epistemologies

Tennyson's telescope and microscope can still be glimpsed at Farringford, his home in the Isle of Wight, a material trace of Tennyson's interest in science and technologies of vision. In *In Memoriam* (1850), *Maud* (1855), and "Lucretius" (*Macmillan's Magazine* [May, 1868]), he fashioned from physics, astronomy, geology, and biology metaphors and a subtle rhetoric attesting that even if newer scientific epistemologies challenged religious teachings and human significance, science was amenable to human thought, feeling, and meaning. It was for this "argument" more than any specific tenets that Tennyson served as a key Victorian mediator between science and the public.

    In Memoriam, which appeared nine years prior to *On the Origin of Species* (1859), makes no mention of natural selection, Darwin's mechanism for relentless biological change and his key contribution to the theory of evolution. But the new geology formulated by Lyell had already established the impermanence of species in the fossil record. In facing the incomprehensible death of a gifted young friend, Tennyson is driven to consider evidence that the individual has scant significance to nature – "of fifty seeds / She often brings but one to bear" (55.11–12) – since even species are transient: "A thousand types are gone: / I care for nothing, all shall go" (56.3–4). Some of the poem's most famous lines directly express the opposition of scientific theory to traditional solace offered by the Bible to humanity,

    Who trusted God was love indeed
      And love Creation's final law –
      Though Nature, red in tooth and claw
    With ravine, shrieked against [t]his creed. (56.13–16)

The impassioned questioning in Section 56 bespeaks the anguish and uncertainty that scientific epistemology could inspire; nor does the poem discount the scientific model that Tennyson confronts intellectually and emotionally. To the final question of Section 56, "What hope of answer, or redress?" (27), the only available response is uncertainty: "Behind the veil, behind the veil" (28).

But Tennyson stages a key intervention at this point. Section 57 exemplifies the conditions of impasse and retreat, yet also, crucially, represents a mourner who can go on in the face of scientific knowledge and sustain a relation to the dead: "Peace; come away ... / we do him wrong / To sing so wildly: let us go" (1.3–4). Seventy-five sections later the poet offers a spiritualized, consolatory version of evolution indebted to Arthur Henry Hallam's own theological writings, whereby God is reimagined as a process, an embodiment of cosmic evolution moving toward perfection: "one far-off divine event, / To which the whole creation moves" (Epilogue, 143–4). This solace is patently a poetic creation, for it is neither scientific nor theological but metaphoric, literally a "transfer" (from the Greek root of "metaphor") from one epistemology to another. In effecting that transfer, Tennyson fashions a new narrative of evolution to which divinity, eternal love, and human significance are crucial.

As Barri Gold points out, *In Memoriam* is also profoundly interwoven with the first and second laws of thermodynamics propounded in the nineteenth century; yet again the poem anticipates scientific principles "in the air" though not yet fully formulated by Kelvin and Maxwell. Gold reciprocally argues that poetry influenced physics since science too relies on metaphorical thought, positioning the individual life and cosmos as analogous if differently scaled systems that participate in the second law of entropy and heat death. "Metaphor" and "entropy," Gold points out, even derive from the same root and similarly posit transformation, difference, and diffusion within a larger conservation, whether of meaning or energy. Second-law thermodynamics predominate in the poem's early sections, as Tennyson envisions nature, like the dead body of Hallam, deprived of heat, light, and energy: "From out waste places comes a cry, / And murmurs from the dying sun" (3.7–8). But as the poem proceeds Tennyson situates loss of life and heat within a larger first-law conservation of energy, until death signifies a transformation of energy and form but not loss, and "waste" modulates into the etymologically related "vastness": "My love involves the love before; / My love is vaster passion now; / Though mixed with God and Nature thou" (130.9–11).[12] The *In Memoriam* stanza, an iambic tetrameter quatrain rhyming *abba*, reinforces Tennyson's mediation of contemporary physics. The stanza is a constant conserved throughout this long poem; yet the emotion and mood of one section are dissipated and metamorphosed by succeeding sections; similarly, the outer rhyme provides a stable reference point to which the stanza always returns, but only via dynamically transformed sonic effects in the inner couplet.

Because *Maud* filters all perception through the unstable, fragile sensibility of its speaker – who breaks down completely after he kills Maud's brother in a duel – and because its controversial treatment of the Crimean War elicited negative reviews, this work's response to science never had the impact of *In Memoriam*. Nonetheless here, too, Tennyson tacitly urges the compatibility of feeling and knowing, poetry and science, by representing the human meanings that science could elicit or acquire. The transience of humankind within geological time helps fuel the speaker's bitter cynicism prompted by his father's business failure and probable suicide, and the prosperity of his former partner, Maud's father:

> A monstrous eft was of old the Lord and Master of Earth,
> For him did his high sun flame, and his river billowing ran,
> And he felt himself in his force to be Nature's crowning race ...
> So many a million of ages have gone to the making of man:
> He now is first, but is he the last? is he not too base?   (1.132–4, 136–7)

Astronomy, as does physics in *In Memoriam*, functions to represent the power of love after the speaker and Maud share a "long loving kiss" (1.656). In contrast to the "sad astrology" that underscores human insignificance, (1.634–8), the stars now "crown a happy day / Go in and out as if at merry play" for the speaker, "Who am no more so all forlorn" (1.628–30).

The rhetoric of "Lucretius" is more complicated. The poem is experimental insofar as Tennyson renders the phantasmagoria of an ascetic Latin philosopher under the influence of an aphrodisiac, and covertly polemical insofar as the pagan's monologue is an implicit brief against materialist philosophy and for immortality. But the historical Lucretius was both a poet and scientist who in *De rerum natura* (first century BC) articulated atomic theory in terms that long remained influential. Early in the nineteenth century, chemist John Dalton updated Greek atomic theory, establishing atomic weights and principles of combination in *A New System of Chemical Philosophy* (1808–10). Since Tennyson informally studied chemistry after leaving Cambridge in 1831, he may have known this modern reworking of Lucretian philosophy; certainly he takes care to give the poem a chemical context, noting that the love potion given to Lucretius by his wife "Confused the chemic labor of the blood" (20). In the poem Lucretius awakens after a surreal dream of atomic theory in which relentless combination is indistinguishable from anarchy and dissolution:

> it seemed
> A void was made in Nature; all her bonds
> Cracked; and I saw the flaring atom-streams
> And torrents of her myriad universe,

Ruining along the illimitable inane,
Fly on to clash together again, and make
Another and another frame of things
For ever.   (36–43)

Lucretius finds no solace for his nightmare since "If all be atoms, how then should the Gods / Being atomic not be dissoluble?" (114–15). Deprived of his one pleasure, the ability to order words and thoughts into poems (223–5), Lucretius ultimately determines to take his life and allow "Great Nature" to "forc[e] far apart / Those blind beginnings that have made me man, / Dash them anew together at her will" (244–6). If in *In Memoriam* scientific knowledge threatens the poet who retreats from a vision of nature "red in tooth and claw," in "Lucretius" the scientist cannot suffice without the poet or a belief in immortality. Tennyson privately commented in 1866 of a man who committed suicide by "covering his face with a chloroformed handkerchief[,] 'That's what I should do ... if I thought there was no future life.'"[13] As public discourse "Lucretius" is important for urging the crucial role of poetry, which conjoins knowledge and feeling, in an increasingly scientific age.

A love philtre "tickl[es] the brute brain within the man's" (21) in "Lucretius"; Robert Browning dramatizes the brute brain itself in "Caliban on Setebos; or, Natural Theology in the Island" (1864). If Browning's subtitle is topical, glancing toward Darwin's recent challenge to William Paley's *Natural Theology*, his title designates the poem's literary status as a delightful supplement to *The Tempest*. Browning takes up Caliban and imagines this "savage" (as Shakespeare calls him) creating a primitive's version of Paley during a moment of leisure. Browning's intertextuality and topicality tacitly argue, like "Lucretius," that poetry, science, and public debate are integrally related. Caliban may echo Kant in averring that his creative efforts with turfs and dead animal parts have "No use at all" and are done "for work's sole sake" (198). And Browning's bursts of lyricism, as when a frigid "rock-stream" running into a tropical sea is termed "A crystal spike 'twixt two warm walls of wave" (34, 37), similarly suggests aesthetic delight as an end in itself. Yet autotelic art is continuously in dialogue with contemporary debate.

The poem also sets several religious traditions in dialogue with each other, with Browning maintaining a free play of mind amidst all and refusing to declare allegiances. The poem's epigraph, "'Thou thoughtest that I was altogether such a one as thyself'" (Psalms 50:21), clearly points to Caliban's fashioning in his own image a capricious, savage god who delights equally in "Making and marring" (97). But Caliban's theology also suggests Calvinism when he imagines himself a god electing some creatures to grace, others to torment

(100–8). Similarly, the poem incorporates paganism insofar as Caliban conceives the overthrow of one god by another – "the something over Setebos / That made Him, or He, may be, found and fought, / Worsted, drove off and did to nothing, perchance" (129–31) – just as Hesiod narrates the overthrow of Cronos by Zeus in the *Theogony*; that Caliban's deity "lessoned [man] he was ... merely clay" and must send up burnt offerings (94.271–4) also recalls the gods of Homer and Greek tragedians. Yet the poem simultaneously glances toward the Higher Criticism recently introduced into England in the controversial *Essays and Reviews* (1860), a collection of essays by biblical scholars that applied historical methods to the Bible rather than treating the text as divinely inspired. In 1862 Bishop Colenso began to issue several volumes that dismissed the veracity of the Pentateuch and book of Joshua as history, implying that these early books of the Bible were (like Caliban's own god) a product of human imagination instead.

The gamut of religious reference comprises not only a dialogue but also a tacit chronology, from totemism to paganism to Calvinism to the skeptical Higher Criticism. This sequence suggests another emergent Victorian science, anthropology. Though E. B. Tylor would not publish "The Religion of Savages" in the *Fortnightly Review* until 1866, his tenet of primitive animism, or the savage projection of spirits glimpsed in dreams into natural phenomena, and his later thesis of primitive survivals in modern civilization were already evident in "Wild Men and Beast-Children," published in the debut issue of *Anthropological Review* in May, 1863. Here Tylor insisted that "The native Australian and the Andaman Islander" were *not* "little removed from ... the lower animals" as many assumed, but were "the same in kind as ... more advanced races," and that "among ignorant or superstitious men the step is easily made from an abstract belief ... to the application of them to particular persons."[14] In representing a "savage mind" that nonetheless takes joy in creativity and interest in theology, like many modern Europeans, Browning not only anticipated Tylor but also was highly topical once again.

Ironically, however, Caliban also resembles a Darwinian naturalist in his vivid observations of animal behavior:

> Yon auk, one fire-eye in a ball of foam,
> That floats and feeds; a certain badger brown
> He hath watched hunt with that slant white-wedge eye
> By moonlight; and the pie with the long tongue
> That pricks deep into oakwarts for a worm,
> And says a plain word when she finds her prize,
> But will not eat the ants; the ants themselves

That build a wall of seeds and settled stalks
About their hole – He made all these and more.   (47–55)

Compare the observations of Darwin himself in the *Origin*:

> I have often watched a tyrant flycatcher (Saurophagus sulphuratus) in
> South America, hovering over one spot and then proceeding to another,
> like a kestrel, and at other times standing stationary on the margin of
> water, and then dashing like a kingfisher at a fish. In our own country the
> larger titmouse (Parus major) may be seen climbing branches, almost like
> a creeper; it often, like a shrike, kills small birds by blows on the head; and
> I have many times seen and heard it hammering the seeds of the yew on a
> branch, and thus breaking them like a nuthatch.[15]

Nor is it irrelevant that Darwin's major insights, like Caliban's, occurred on
an island setting, the Galápagos. Like Darwin too, Caliban comments on the
fossil record, having "Dug up a newt … turned to stone, shut up inside a stone"
(214–15), and on adaptation, though in Caliban's mind it is Setebos, not
impersonal forces of nature, that threaten creatures in their struggle for existence: "discover how [to elude extermination] or die! / All need not die, for of the
things o' the isle / Some flee afar, some dive, some run up trees" (218–20).
Caliban crudely grasps even that lower forms, including perhaps Setebos himself,
evolve into higher: "If He surprise not even the Quiet's self / Some strange day, –
or, suppose, grow into it / As grubs grow butterflies" (246–8).

   But what is the point? Is it that Caliban forms a primitive counterpart to
the sophisticated intellection of Darwin (and, in religion, of Calvin or Paley)? Is
it that premier scientists never fully transcend their own primitivism? One of
Caliban's least endearing traits is his deliberate cruelty to lower creatures such
as the "sea-beast, lumpish, which he snared, / Blinded the eyes of … / And split
its toe-webs" – though his cruelty is clearly a form of self-loathing: "pens the
drudge / In a hole o' the rock and calls him Caliban" (163–6). Is Caliban's
deliberate, creative cruelty so different from some scientific work? In his late
section on oceanic islands Darwin notes that "land-shells are easily killed by
sea-water," as he knows from experimentally putting their eggs into it, which
immediately sink and die; he then recounts immersing a hardy species in the
sea for fourteen, then twenty days at a stretch, no disturbing prospect to a
human being but surely adverse to the land-shell.[16] Because the precise
direction of Browning's poetic sympathies remains unfixed, only in Kantian
terms – the free play of an inventive creative mind on the topic – is the poem's
aim certain. The Shakespearean framework forms another constant, but so
does the tacit argument that poetry is a fit lens through which the newest
scientific debates could be filtered.

Huxleyan poetics

If Tennyson and Browning registered the shockwaves when long-familiar paradigms of religion and science were challenged at mid-century, several younger poets who had never fully embraced traditional Christianity found Darwin's theories deeply exciting, especially since they freed poets' imaginations to conceive of alternative perspectives on humanity and the universe. May Kendall's allusion to Huxley in "Lay of the Trilobite" (*Punch* [January 24, 1885]) indicates her poem's allegiance, just as her humor registers a sensibility so unthreatened by evolution that it turns key concepts into satiric barbs against human pretense. When the poem's arrogant speaker, convinced of his own "mighty mind" (4), chances upon a trilobite fossil millions of years old, he expounds upon the wonder of a "providential plan, / That he should be a Trilobite, / And I should be a Man!" (13–16). The monologue becomes a dialogue when, to the speaker's surprise, the trilobite talks back.

In contrast to the pompously certain speaker, the lowly trilobite is an agnostic, a term coined by Huxley in 1869 to indicate rigorous refusal to believe what lacks compelling evidence. As the trilobite asserts, "I don't know how the thing was done, / Although I cannot doubt it; / But Huxley – he if anyone / Can tell you all about it" (21–4). Citing Huxley, the trilobite contends that worshiped deities are "ghosts and dreams" (25) and that humanity developed from lower forms, including "Jelly-fish and Trilobites / By Natural Selection" (31–2). But the poem's real thrust is to question whether humanity is a higher form at all:

> You've Kant to make your brains go round,
> > Hegel you have to clear them,
> You've Mr. Browning to confound,
> > And Mr. Punch to cheer them!
> The native of an alien land
> > You call a man and brother,
> And greet with hymn-book in one hand
> > And pistol in the other!
> > ...
> You've cannon and you've dynamite
> > To give the nations rest.   (33–40, 43–4)

Higher development, it seems, produces lies and large-scale destruction, in contrast to the trilobite that, having no brain at all, was "gentle" and "didn't grumble, didn't steal" (49, 53). As the proud speaker ruefully concludes, "I wish our skulls were thicker, / I wish that Evolution could / Have stopped a little quicker" (66–8).

Despite its potentially risible title, "Men and Monkeys" (1884), by A. Mary F. Robinson, gives serious consideration to the descent of man. On an exquisite spring day awash in delicate scents and color forms, a poet-aesthete is disturbed by figures far removed from her in class and sensibility, an Italian organ-grinder, a "peasant-lass" (23), and a monkey. The stolid humans, overborne by heat and fatigue, are deaf to the nightingale's song:

> They only saw the dust that they
> Raised in their dismal trudging on.
> They did not even stop to hear
> The rare sweet call of the nightingale;
> The hurdy-gurdy's squeak and yell
> Was too accustomed to their ear.   (43–8)

In contrast,

> suddenly I heard
> The monkey mimic the singing-bird,
> And snatch a trail of the flowering may.
>
> And down the road I saw him still
> Catching and clutching the blossom white,
> Waving his long, black arms in delight,
> Until they passed over the brow of the hill.   (50–6)

The thrust of Robinson's poem, like that of "Caliban upon Setebos," remains ambiguous. The inertness of the "Italian vagrants" (22) may result from class oppression, from the female aesthete's presumption of class and racial superiority, or from degeneration, since humans descended from apes have become inferior to the one they have in tow. Whether Robinson intends in the final stanza to equalize poet and monkey as allied aesthetes and hence ironize her earlier sense of superiority, represent the monkey's ascent on the evolutionary scale as it discovers beauty and mimesis as ends in themselves, or simply record a memorable sense impression is equally unclear. "Men and Monkeys" minimally asserts that the highest human faculties are grounded in the natural world, not opposed to them; the "Archangels tall" of the second quatrain are not transcendent heavenly beings but the herbs less euphoniously known as dead-nettle or black horehound, whose flowers offer up their pollen to bees in a process of ecological symbiosis.

Of all the poets considered here, George Meredith articulates Huxleyan poetics most fully in "The Woods of Westermain" (1883). Images drawn from the woods abound and are sometimes as detailed as naturalists' observations: "Cumbered by dry twig and cone, / Shredded husks of seedlings flown,

/ Mine of mole and spotted flint" (3.5–7). But the poem is addressed to the mind and imagination as much as to the eye and invites readers to a new way of seeing the world. Rising to the challenge requires dropping the egoism at which Kendall scoffs in "Lay of the Trilobite" and using the evolutionary development of higher intellect to understand that humanity is one with an interrelated natural world, not above or beyond it. To realize this vision is to create a new song that "In subduing does not slay" (3.87) but instead

> through measured grave accord,
> Hears the heart of wildness beat
> Like a centaur's hoof on sward.
> Drink the sense the notes infuse,
> You a larger self will find:
> Sweetest fellowship ensues
> With the creatures of your kind.   (3.90–6)

A residual threat persists, hence the poem's refrain: "Enter these enchanted woods, / You who dare" (1.12–13). But the threat comes from human egoism, an evolutionary throwback to days when the struggle for scarce resources inspired grasping selfishness and a monster "all maw" who, "growling o'er his bone, / Sharpened he for mine and thine" (4.67, 71–2).

Leaving this "dragon" behind and embracing one's embeddedness in nature augments rather than diminishes the self: "You with others, gathering more, / Glad of more, till you reject / Your proud title of elect" (4.30–2). The poem never underestimates the difficulty of repudiating human supremacy over nature but insists that this radically new epistemology benefits humanity, in part by realizing the promise of human reason:

> You must love the light so well
> That no darkness will seem fell.
>   ...
> Light to light sees little strange,
> Only features heavenly new;
> Then you touch the nerve of Change,
> Then of Earth you have the clue.   (4.1–2, 11–14)

More, those who are simultaneously in and see the whole of nature perceive a "Beauty ... past amaze" (4.142–4).

Ultimately Meredith enunciates a new theology in which body and eros are not opposed to spirit but interconnected with it and intellect, in part because the evolved human being is capable of imagining such a complex construct, but also because sexual union, natural law perceptible to reason, and imagination are interconnected in the physical universe:

Pleasures that through blood run sane,
Quickening spirit from the brain.
Each of each in sequent birth,
Blood and brain and spirit, three
(Say the deepest gnomes of Earth),
Join for true felicity.

...

Earth that Triad is: she hides
Joy from him who that divides;
Showers it when the three are one
Glassing her in union.   (4.167–72, 177–80)

If "The Woods of Westermain" is indebted to Darwin and Huxley on one hand and the Christian trinity on the other, its rhetorical creation of new experiences as a means of generating new convictions is always intrinsically poetic. The harmony that is Meredith's "argument" is also the defining element of "song," hence the poem's highly self-conscious references to musicality throughout.

Both "The Woods of Westermain" and *The Ascent of Man* (1889), an epic poem by Mathilde Blind, present an evolving world from which a transcendent God is absent; both consider selfishness (which Blind figures as hunger) the principal enemy to humanity; both construct a new theology rooted in the physical universe. But Blind situates her theology in maternity rather than a revisionary trinity. Her maternal principle is a female counterpart to Coleridge's "ABSOLUTE" or God, in which is found "the absolute identity of subject and object, which it calls nature, and which in its highest power is nothing else but self-conscious will or intelligence."[17] If Coleridge's creator contemplates itself in the world it also creates, Blind's maternal principle creates through the physical act of birth, then contemplates and yearns toward both an aspect of self *and* another independent being in the form of her child. Hence the maternal life principle at the center of the universe also unifies physicality, spirituality (i.e., love), and evolutionary process – since the new life to which she gives birth is an essential step toward human development and change. Blind's poem, accordingly, is structured by recurring acts of birth. Once oceans have formed, "lo, from the womb of the waters, upheaved in volcanic convulsion, / Ribbed and ravaged and rent there rose bald peaks," the mountains in turn becoming "the broad-bosomed mothers of torrents and rivers perennial." The advent of poetry, the highest human achievement because it creates and orders forms of reality while liberating spirit from body to embrace the cosmos, is imaged in the birth of Phoebus Apollo and Diana by their mother Leto, both a goddess and a "woman lying / And in spasms of anguish crying, / Shuddering through her mortal frame." At a cosmic level the birth of new stars and planetary systems recapitulates the birth process of earth itself: "Light more light on each far-circling earth, / Till life stirred crepuscular seas, and mountains / Heaved convulsive with the throes of birth."[18]

Blind's epic also departs from Meredith in devoting far more attention to the history of civilization and social conditions, and presents a dourer outlook in consequence. From pre-history through the French Revolution and its aftermath, the result is always the same: "Though [man] can stay the flood and bind the waters, / His hand he shall not stay / That bids him sack and slay."[19] Hence there is no "ascent," only recapitulation of prior development. Blind's 1870 lecture on Shelley illuminates her own aim in her epic: "[he] fully believed in his power of making a breach in the solid rampart of custom" – in Blind's case, customary uncritical embrace of commerce and competition.[20] Murderous violence as a result of competition for scarce resources in nature – "The drip of blood, the hoarse death-rattle, / The roar of rage, the shriek of pain" – has modulated into greed and violence in the "imperial city" in which the wealthy exploit workers, and the poor, "human rubbish, gaunt and squalid," suffer hunger that drives them to domestic violence in turn: "Howls of babes, the drunken father's damning, / Counter-cursing of the shrill-tongued wife."[21]

Like the speaker of *Maud*, Blind assails the tacit "war" incited by predatory capitalism as less honest than open war; like Edward Mead and Ernest Jones, she denounces the structural inequities that sacrifice workers to greed. But she differs from all in directly connecting these conditions to a human nature that is itself red in tooth and claw as a result of evolutionary process:

> Peace ye call this? Call this justice, meted
> Equally to rich and poor alike?
> Better than this peace the battle's heated
> Cannon-balls that ask not whom they strike!
> Better than this masquerade of culture
> Hiding strange hyæna appetites,
> The frank ravening of the raw-necked vulture
> As its beak the senseless carrion smites.
>
> What of men in bondage, toiling blunted
> In the roaring factory's lurid gloom?
> What of cradled infants starved and stunted?
> What of woman's nameless martyrdom?
> The all-seeing sun shines on unheeding,
> Shines by night the calm, unruffled moon,
> Though the human myriads, preying, bleeding,
> Put creation harshly out of tune.[22]

The concluding pages announce that "Ascent" is still possible if humanity will act on the higher powers developed during evolution and transfigure the earth by choosing physical, emotional, and spiritual love over grasping acquisitiveness. But *Ascent of Man* is more important for synthesizing responses to technology and science and by seeking principles that underlie and potentially mediate both. Quicksilver in its own shifting rhythms and auditory effects as if to mirror in poetry the manifold variations of species within nature, epic in its ambitions and historical scope, *Ascent of Man* is at once scientific and political (as well as highly imaginative) in representing both the promise and potentially overdetermined effects of the origin of the human species.

Chapter 5

Poetry and religion

With Christians, a poetical view of things is a duty – we are bid to colour all things with hues of faith, to see a Divine meaning in every event and a super-human tendency.

John Henry Newman, review of *The Theatre of the Greeks*[1]

The poet may imagine opinions, doctrines, heresies, cogitations, debates, expositions – there is no limit to his traffic with the moral any more than with the sensuous appearances of the universe; only, as a poet, he deals with all these as concrete things, existing in the objective air, and from which his own soul stands royally disentangled.

[David Masson], "Theories of Poetry and a New Poet" (1853)[2]

For the power of Christianity has been in the immense emotion which it has excited; in its engaging, for the government of man's conduct, the mighty forces of love, reverence, gratitude, hope, pity, and awe, – all that host of allies which Wordsworth includes under the one name of *imagination*.

Matthew Arnold, Preface, in *God and the Bible* (1875)[3]

Secular and sacred models of poetry have competed for primacy at least since Aristotle and Plato: Aristotle emphasizes poetry's imitative function and psychological effects in the *Poetics*; Plato's Socrates underscores poetry's link to divine inspiration in *Ion*. Nineteenth-century poetry has largely been conceptualized in secular terms, whether in Wordsworth's democratic conception of the poet as a man speaking to men in a state of heightened feeling, Kant's autotelic aesthetics, or John Stuart Mill's mediate position that poetry expresses feeling but the poet speaks only to himself. Barrett Browning, Christina Rossetti, Patmore, Hopkins, and a majority of poetry readers, however, took for granted that poetry was intimately related to religious faith. This widespread view affected how poetry was produced, read, and understood in its own time and helped shape the rhetoric of many poems circulating in print culture.

140

Victorian poetry's link to religion derives from biblical tradition (especially David's authorship of the Psalms), Dantesque and Miltonic epic, English hymnody, and a line of British poets extending from Langland through George Herbert, William Cowper, and the mature Wordsworth among others. Poetry's sacred function was also profoundly influenced by the Oxford (or Tractarian) Movement, an attempt to revivify faith and its ancient foundations in the face of secular modernity. Most historians date its inception to the July 14, 1833 sermon preached by John Keble on the theme of national apostasy after parliament suppressed ten Irish bishoprics and implicitly elevated temporal over spiritual authority. Leaders of the Oxford Movement, including Keble and Newman, positioned the Anglican Church as an upholder of unbroken Christian tradition because it was a *via media*, or middle way, between corrupt Roman Catholic "superstitions" (e.g., saints' intercessions) and Calvinist repudiation of apostolic succession.

Both Keble and Newman, however, were also poets who positioned poetry and worship as mutually constitutive forms in their Tractarian poetics (discussed below). Keble's *The Christian Year*, first published in 1827, had gone through 158 editions by the time copyright expired in 1873, which G. B. Tennyson calculates as amounting to one copy for every sixty Britons. Keble's artistry was admired by Wordsworth, Arnold, George Eliot, George Saintsbury, and A. E. Housman, and exerted profound influence on Christina Rossetti; *The Christian Year* was also read alongside the English *Book of Common Prayer* and the Bible by families throughout Britain on Sundays.[4] It was thus simultaneously a major Victorian poem and a medium of worship.

The Christian Year was not the sole religious best-seller of the Victorian era: religious books outsold all other categories from 1814 to 1846.[5] Additionally, popular religious magazines like *Good Words* (begun the same year as *Cornhill* and typically outselling it) and pious verses and religious news printed in countless papers and magazines swelled the presence of religion and poetry in print. As the prior chapter demonstrates, even poetic response to the factory system or scientific theory readily ventured into religious matters as well.

Religion necessarily entails rhetoric insofar as worship services include interpretation of scriptures, religious teaching, and moral exhortation – in Christianity a branch of rhetoric termed "homiletics." "Homily" itself derives from a Greek term (ὁμιλία) for discourse or conversation, an interchange of feeling and thought through language – a not inapt definition of poetry. Newman went further, however. When organizing devotional poems to be published in *British Magazine* from 1833 to 1836 under the running title *Lyra apostolica* (collected into a book in 1836), Newman commented, "Do not stirring times bring out poets? Do they not give opportunity for the rhetoric of poetry and the persuasion?"[6]

Newman shocked Britons and abruptly halted the Oxford Movement when he converted to Roman Catholicism in 1845, inspiring rhetoric of another sort in the press. Theological dispute, in fact, pervaded Victorian culture in a way not seen since (though clashing faiths that impinge on politics, daily lives, and media reports are familiar realities today). This chapter examines poetry and religion in the contexts implied by its epigraphs: poems on a continuum with religious practice, poems representing religious scenes, and poems registering doubts about the efficacy of religious faith. All intersected in an ongoing dialogue characteristic of Victorian poetry and the context in which it was received.

Poetry and worship

Any discussion of Victorian poetry's interchange with religious worship must begin with *The Christian Year*. Keble's poetics were inseparable from the Tractarian doctrines of Reserve and Analogy. Because finite mortal minds were incapable of apprehending an infinite God directly, indirection – so crucial to poetry – was also crucial to faith and worship. Poetry in turn suggested that if the created world were "read" as a poem pregnant in meaning, the world-as-text could divulge hints or glimpses of divinity. If Reserve was the underlying condition of God's revelation to humanity, Analogy was the means. Just as similes in poetry allowed the otherwise unsayable to be indirectly articulated, so in nature surface phenomena could be studied for their resemblance to God in His wrath, mercy, love, sacrifice, and power. Similarly, the religious poet could discover fitting analogies in verse that then demanded (as the world did of believers) active interpretation. This conception of religious poetry entailed that the poet be sincere, self-effacing, and expressive, and that the poem worked to strengthen readers' faith. Because, for Keble, an act of imagination was also a religious act, the poet might be said to be divinely inspired, as Plato averred; and even non-religious or pagan poetry could convey indirect religious truths through God's grace and Reserve.

Since Keble's Tractarian poetics inclined him toward nature poetry, *The Christian Year* is often discussed in the context of Wordsworth. "Fifteenth Sunday after Trinity," prefaced by an epigraph from Matthew 6:28 ("Consider the lilies of the field, how they grow"), indicates why. The opening octet not only addresses a field of lilies, just as Wordsworth contemplated a field of daffodils in "I Wandered Lonely as a Cloud," but also surveys life's "downward" progression reminiscent of the narrowing prison house in "Ode: Intimations of Immortality":

> Sweet nurslings of the vernal skies,
>> Bath'd in soft airs, and fed with dew,
> What more than magic in you lies,

> To fill the heart's fond view?
> In childhood's sports, companions gay,
> In sorrow, on Life's downward way,
> How soothing! in our last decay
>   Memorials prompt and true.   (1–8)

Keble next suggests that the lilies are "Relics ... of Eden's bowers" (9) that have retained their unstained purity and alike share our "mirth" or "dwell" along "Our paths of sin, our homes of sorrow" (25–6, 28). The lilies also "could draw th' admiring gaze / Of Him," both God and man, "who worlds and hearts surveys" and "taught" the lilies' "silent lessons" (37–8, 40, 35). The poet ends by reading the lilies' lesson for humankind directly:

> Alas! of thousand bosoms kind,
>   That daily court you and caress,
> How few the happy secret find
>   Of your calm loveliness!
> "Live for to-day! to-morrow's light
> To-morrow's cares shall bring to sight,
> Go sleep like closing flowers at night,
>   And Heaven thy morn will bless."   (49–56)

The lyric is direct and accessible, its message of hope and consolation clear even to unpracticed readers of poetry. Yet just as the lily is a site of Reserve, "more than magic" (3) lying behind its appearance, so is the lyric, which harbors shifting perspectives and juxtapositions that enact complex religious meaning. In moving from the lilies as remnants of Eden to the object of Christ's gaze and blessing, Keble restages the transit from the Old Covenant of the Old Testament to the New, Christ's sacrifice and redemption of fallen humanity. In recovering Christ's gaze and pronouncement upon the lilies the poet also enacts the role of priest, revivifying Christ's message in the present and modeling the arduous effort required to unpack sacred meaning available in the world to the "few" possessed of its "happy secret" (51). The reader who attends carefully can recognize and likewise enact a new dispensation.

Most discussion of *The Christian Year* also emphasizes its self-effacing simplicity and intense personal expression, qualities able to touch readers deeply in private perusals. But like Victorian sermons, *The Christian Year* also had a public dimension and a public rhetoric. *The Christian Year*, for example, is profoundly intertextual. Each lyric is preceded by an epigraph, usually drawn from scriptural readings assigned for the Sunday identified in the title; and numerous footnotes cite biblical passages as well as works of history, exegesis, travel, biography, philosophy, and poetry – Milton, Herbert,

Cowper, Burns, Gray, Aeschylus, and (unexpectedly, given its homoeroticism), the Greek Anthology. Everywhere *The Christian Year* announces that it is a text to be *read with* others, opening onto the public world of letters rather than retiring into privacy.

Above all, *The Christian Year* functions as supplement to and exegesis of the *Book of Common Prayer*, both following the same church calendar. As G. B. Tennyson observes, *The Christian Year*

> directed attention to the Church itself as a visible body, for it was the Church that was the source and keeper of the ecclesiastical year and of its observance through the Prayer Book. *The Christian Year* thus exercised a gentle polemic in favor of the visible Church and her formularies ... By creating a mirror-effect of influence on and subordination to the Prayer Book, *The Christian Year* benefited from the authority of the Prayer Book while also reinforcing that authority.[7]

This rhetorical dimension of Keble's text helps to explain the numerous lyrics addressed to priests even while it complicates his status as poet. For in lyrics such as "Fifth Sunday after Trinity," addressed to "fishers" of men's souls who can become downcast over repeatedly empty nets, Keble is both lyric speaker and a member of the priestly audience, originating poet and religious communicant.

Keble rehearses his poetics in "Septuagesima Sunday" (the ninth before Easter, still seventy days ahead), which is rendered in accessible ballad stanzas:

> There is a book, who runs may read,
>   Which heavenly truth imparts,
> And all the lore its scholars need,
>   Pure eyes and Christian hearts.
> The works of God above, below,
>   Within us and around,
> Are pages in that book, to show
>   How God Himself is found.   (1–8)

Keble then suggests a number of analogies. The sky "embracing all / Is like the Maker's love" (9–10); "The saints above are stars in Heaven" (21); "The dew of Heaven is like Thy grace, / It steals in silence down" (29–30).

But the surface simplicities of "Septuagesima Sunday," as in "Fifteenth Sunday after Trinity," cloak underlying complexity. In the last two stanzas Keble renders all interpretation provisional and tacitly implies that his own lyrics may need to be probed and reread:

> Two worlds are ours: 'tis only Sin
>   Forbids us to descry

> The mystic heaven and earth within,
>   Plain as the sea and sky.
> Thou, who hast given me eyes to see
>   And love this sight so fair,
> Give me a heart to find out Thee,
>   And read Thee everywhere.   (41–8)

Since all mortals are sinful, all confront veiled meaning: transparent reading is retroactively rewritten as opacity, interpretation as contingent process rather than hoarded nugget. The consistency with which Keble's individual lyrics enact his poetics and theology extends the theological poetics of Reserve and the function of *The Christian Year* as a performative ritual. For Keble tacitly calls upon skilled readers to look beyond simple surface messages that soothe or console and to become active interpreters who in discerning underlying poetic structures participate in complex religious meaning and, simultaneously, in a faith community.

If *The Christian Year* combines humble personal lyrics into a whole that enacts theology, consolidates ecclesiastical authority, and facilitates communal worship, the hymn was another religious genre that elicited communal response through the voice of an individual. Newman's "Lead, Kindly Light" was first published as "Faith" in the serialized *Lyra apostolica* in *British Magazine* (February, 1834) and later retitled "The Pillar of the Cloud." Newman never intended "Lead, Kindly Light' as a hymn and may never have heard it sung. Instead he wrote a lyric during a sea voyage following serious illness, subscribing "At Sea. June 16, 1833" to three stanzas that memorably image human vulnerability and willed surrender to God's guidance. The ocean setting, which positions a fragile, manmade craft amidst the sea's immensity, intensifies the human condition of a man "far from home" (3) unable to see his way. Having realized the folly of reliance on human agency, he now prays to be led by God: "I do not ask to see / The distant scene, – one step enough for me" (5–6).

The paradox of willed surrender is conveyed by counterpointing the speaker's humble prayer with the poet's active shaping of form, including predominantly pentameter sestets intersected by dimeters in the second and fourth lines, a refrain, and subtle metrical variants. The speaker's plight is almost always rendered in regular iambs, but to represent God's divine agency Newman adopts spondees: "Léad Thóu me ón." The opening line invoking divine agency similarly uses a spondee ("Léad, Kíndly Líght, amíd the encírcling glóom"). Only in looking back to a time of sin, when "Príde rúled my wíll" (12), does a line devoted to the speaker imitate the spondees reserved for divinity – an indirect poetic means of representing human error. Like all prayers, Newman's poem includes another paradox: human pleas to the divine are customarily expressed in the imperative rather than interrogative mode. The third stanza, however, drops the imperative voice, since restored faith resulting from God's active presence within signals that the prayer has been answered:

> So long Thy power hath blest me, sure it still
>   Will lead me on,
> O'er moor and fen, o'er crag and torrent, till
>   The night is gone;
> And with the morn those angel faces smile
> Which I have loved long since, and lost awhile.   (13–18)

Though "Lead, Kindly Light" is memorable as art, Newman always claimed that he was more interested in rhetoric than poetics. "My object was *not* poetry but to bring out *ideas*," he wrote to F. W. Faber in 1850; and he called the entire *Lyra apostolica* in which "Lead, Kindly Light" first appeared a "ballad ... undertaken with a view of catching people when unguarded."[8] His poem did "catch people," but not quite as he intended, nor in the form he approved. The same year that Newman converted to Catholicism his poem (not yet identified as his) was included in the *Bible Hymn Book* by a Presbyterian compiler; in 1870 Edward Henry Bickersteth included "Lead, Kindly Light" in an evangelical hymn book entitled *The Hymnal Companion to the Book of Common Prayer* and added a fourth stanza suitable for funerals ("Lead, Saviour, lead me home in childlike faith, / Home to my God," etc.), which transformed Newman's lyric into a beloved popular work sung by members of heterogeneous classes and sects.[9] The rhetorical and rhythmic force of the communal hymn, however, illuminates elements in the lyric poem that secular scholarship is likely to downplay: the promise of divine light amidst human doubt and threat of death, the comfort of losing the self in divinity or a congregation, the old story of the sinner redeemed, and the pleasure of being carried along on a wave of rhythm and harmony provided by musical accompaniment.

Three other famous Victorian hymns were by women, a reminder of the authorizing agency women writers could find in religion. Newman and Keble were sanctioned by their university educations and ordinations to address worshipers, but they defined poetry in terms that might apply to aspirants innocent of Latin. Keble's "Palm Sunday" lyric in *The Christian Year*, for example, begins by calling poets "Heirs of more than royal race, / Fram'd by Heaven's peculiar grace, / God's own work to do on earth" (3–5). After conceding that poets could appropriate their gifts to idols or "vilest using" (35, 38), the lyric concludes on a humbler note:

> Childlike though the voices be,
>> And untunable the parts,
> Thou wilt own the minstrelsy,
>> If it flow from childlike hearts.   (45–8)

The poetess, so often deemed childlike in her spontaneous expression, could appropriate Keble's last stanza as readily as priests and in doing so lay claim "God's own work to do on earth."

If women's hymns typically praised the greatness of God and affirmed religious duty, they also tacitly asserted women's right to speak as poets in both private and communal settings. And they were widely heard, since hymns were sung on street corners and in parlors as well as at meetings or worship services. "Nearer, My God, to Thee" (1841) was written by the political radical, Unitarian, and friend of Robert Browning, Sarah Flower Adams – a reminder that Christian piety could authorize political resistance as well as women's public agency. Simpler than Newman's "Lead, Kindly Light," Adams's hymn succeeds because it is at once a fervent, reiterated prayer ("Nearer, my God, to Thee, / Nearer to Thee!) and self-exhortation to follow God closely in pain or joy, awake or in sleep.[10]

Cecil Frances Alexander's "All Things Bright and Beautiful," first published in *Hymns for Little Children* in 1848, was Tractarian, teaching children to look at the created world as a text everywhere revealing God:

> Each little flower that opens,
>> Each little bird that sings,
> He made their glowing colours,
>> He made their tiny wings.   (5–8)

In contrast to Adams, the Anglo-Irish Alexander had a vested interest in the status quo and, in a stanza deleted from most hymnals, treated class difference as part of God's plan as natural as the birds, mountains or meadows:

> The rich man in his castle,
>> The poor man at his gate,
> God made them, high or lowly,
>> And order'd their estate.   (9–12)

It is rather as a nature poem that Alexander's hymn compels, extending Christian charity to animals who share the earth, and teaching, like Keble (to whom she dedicated another volume of hymns), that God "gave us eyes to see" how God "has made all things well" (25, 28).[11]

The title of Frances Ridley Havergal's "Consecration Hymn" ("Take my life, and let it be"), first published in 1878, does not refer to a bishop's ordination, as it might in a Tractarian work. Rather, it announces an evangelical, personal consecration of self to Christ and the authorizing of religious practice outside an all-male church hierarchy – even if Havergal wrote elsewhere, "a true woman's submission is inseparable from deep love."[12] Havergal always asserted that every word of her immensely popular hymns came to her directly from God; but she seemed to recognize the power she wielded: "I never before realized the high privilege of writing for 'the great congregation.'"[13]

"Take my life," still part of the Anglican hymn book, turns the imperative mode of prayer into an act of giving rather than asking and follows a freshly conceived internal logic. First beseeching God to possess all the worshiper's "moments and my days," the speaker next offers up bodily extremities ("Take my hands, and let them move / At the impulse of Thy love," 5–6), then the more intimate voice and lips that will endlessly sing praise and convey God's "messages" (12). Next she cedes what the world recognizes as gifts, her "silver" and "gold" and "intellect" (13, 15), followed by possessions visible only to God: her will, heart, and love, all poured out at the feet of God as a "treasure-store" (22). Thus when she concludes, "Take myself, and I will be / Ever, *only* ALL for Thee" (23–4), the totality is vivid and realized rather than abstract.[14] That the hymn writer's language could so easily be adopted as the worshiper's own, so easily remembered through anaphora and simple but not trite language, imparts to "Consecration Hymn" the qualities of all successful hymns. And because it, like "Nearer, My God" and "All Things Bright and Beautiful," was repeatedly sung in congregations across Britain and North America, women's hymns played an important public role in communal worship despite women's exclusion from church offices.

Given the influential poetic theories of J. S. Mill or Kant and the appeal of individual versus communal identity, poems that can be read as private lyrics are most familiar today. Both Patmore's "The Toys" (*Pall Mall Gazette* [November 30, 1876]) and Tennyson's "Crossing the Bar" (1889) denote acts of prayer within resolutely private contexts. In "The Toys," Patmore's persona is self-doubting, vulnerable, for its starting point is an act of domestic violence:

> My little Son, who look'd from thoughtful eyes
> And moved and spoke in quiet grown-up wise,
> Having my law the seventh time disobey'd,
> I struck him, and dismiss'd
> With hard words and unkiss'd,
> His Mother, who was patient, being dead.   (1–6)

The sixth line at once judges the father and suggests why he is so harried and ill-tempered. The repentant father weeps when he later checks on his son in bed and sees tears on the boy's lashes.

But he is moved most by the toys the child has arranged to bring solace in lieu of the absent father and mother, including "A piece of glass abraded by the beach / And six or seven shells, / A bottle with bluebells" (17–19). In praying that night, the father not only understands his own limits – "Thou rememberest of what toys / We made our joys" (26–7) – but learns from them to imagine a Godly father more patient and loving than himself. In his own death, he hopes, God will "leave Thy wrath, and say, / 'I will be sorry for their childishness'" (32–3). Patmore's lesson of human error and God's mercy is embedded in a personal poem notable for subtle psychology and metrical deftness, as in the stark irregularity and absent rhyme of line 3, which sonically enacts the lawlessness father and son share.

If Patmore was a practicing Roman Catholic, Tennyson avoided formal creeds altogether yet insisted on personal immortality. "Crossing the Bar" is an agnostic's prayer, addressed as much to the poet's survivors as to a personal God:

> Sunset and evening star,
>   And one clear call for me!
> And may there be no moaning of the bar,
>   When I put out to sea.
>
> But such a tide as moving seems asleep,
>   Too full for sound and foam,
> When that which drew from out the boundless deep
>   Turns again home.   (1–8)

The "call" of death is clear but not the issuer, and Tennyson invokes the afterlife in natural rather than Christian terms. Moreover, rather than biblical texts, Tennyson echoes his own, since variants of "boundless deep" appear in "The Ancient Sage" and above all in the "Coming" and "Passing of Arthur": "From the great deep to the great deep he goes." If "The Toys" reinforces the common practice of family prayers and Christian doctrines of sin and forgiveness, Tennyson's "prayer" recalls the Metaphysical Society (1869–80), of which he was a founding member, which brought together churchmen, scientists, and agnostics to discuss the grounds of belief, but foundered, according to Tennyson, "because after ten years of strenuous effort no one had succeeded in even defining the term 'Metaphysics.'"[15] "Crossing the Bar" affirms belief in the afterlife and a personal relationship with the creator but never quite settles what either might be.

Emily Brontë's faith is more certain, radical, and private in "No coward soul is mine," "the last lines [of poetry]," according to Charlotte, "my sister Emily ever wrote."[16] Rather than adopting the usual feminine stance of humility, Brontë claims identity with godhead itself:

No coward soul is mine
No trembler in the world's storm troubled sphere
I see Heaven's glories shine
And Faith shines equal arming me from Fear

O God within my breast
Almighty ever-present Deity
Life, that in me hast rest
As I, – Undying Life, have power in thee   (1–8)

To Keble or Patmore the poem would presumably signal hubris, but if, as this clergyman's daughter argues, God indeed resides within, a sense of unbounded power and certainty are theological correlates rather than prideful assertion. Such views could develop only apart from formal religious instruction, about which Brontë is also unconventionally dismissive: "Vain are the thousand creeds / That move men's hearts, unutterably vain, / Worthless as withered weeds" (9–11). In Brontë's lyric, then, depth of religious faith, unsparing critique of organized religion, and unconventional femininity merge as they rarely if ever do in other poems of the period.

Christina Rossetti is Brontë's counterpart: she too writes intensely private, deeply original devotional lyrics but does so within strict Anglican parameters. She was particularly influenced by Tractarian poetics and Keble's *The Christian Year*, spending enough time with her copy to illustrate all 109 lyrics with original designs. Keble's principles of Reserve and Analogy, as well as his metrical and stanzaic variations, shaped her poetics; B. M. Lott in fact terms Keble "the chief stanzaic experimenter in the age until the appearance of Christina Rossetti."[17] Though Rossetti could not directly influence public worship as Keble did, she separated "Devotional Pieces" from other poems in her 1862 and 1866 volumes, cordoning off a poetic space to which readers could bring a worshipful orientation.

Two "Devotional Pieces" in *Goblin Market and Other Poems* indicate her debt to Keble as well as her distinctive innovations. But for the unruly violence of its imagination, "Symbols" might take a place in *The Christian Year*. Explicitly Tractarian, her lyric adopts simple diction and scenes from natural and domestic life to disclose deeper religious significance, in this case humanity's impotent will and fallen state. The speaker anxiously tends a rosebud and nest of "speckled eggs" (9), only to see the flower drop soon after blooming and parent birds flee before the eggs hatch. In fury the speaker breaks the bough and "crushed the eggs," demanding "vengeance" (13, 16, 18). She then hears voices from the eggs and "dead branch" (19) – resonant symbols of birth and rebirth since the cross is sometimes termed a dead tree – asking, "what if God, / Who waiteth for thy fruits in vain, / Should also take the rod?" (22–4).

Keble rarely represents human depravity so directly. He intensifies religious mystery in "Holy Communion," for example, through compressed juxtaposition, observing "That man, His foe, by whom He bled, / May take Him for his daily bread" (11–12), fusing the murderers of God and beneficiaries of His grace into a single identity. Rossetti unleashes the Old Adam more disruptively. And while Keble often used sestets in *The Christian Year,* as Rossetti does here, she alters his usual pattern (two sets of tetrameter lines followed by a trimeter in, for example, "First Sunday after Easter") by adopting a trimeter only in the final line, thereby reinforcing the theme of fallenness with a sonic falling effect.

"A Better Resurrection" shifts away from Tractarian meditation on nature to prayer, each octet ending with an invocation to Jesus. The lyric is deliberately abstract at the outset: "I have no wit, no words, no tears; / My heart within me like a stone" (1–2). Stanza 1 thus concludes, "O Jesus, quicken me." That "quickening" is evident in stanza 2, which erupts in a flurry of Tractarian analogies: "My life is like a faded leaf, / My harvest dwindled to a husk"; "My life is like a frozen thing" (9–10, 13). In her newly quickened state, she can foresee that "rise it shall – the sap of Spring" (15) and so prays, "O Jesus, rise in me," beseeching Christ's inward presence and her own enactment of the Resurrection. Her final stanza then stages a transfiguration not only of the speaker but also of conventional Christian imagery:

> My life is like a broken bowl,
>   A broken bowl that cannot hold
> One drop of water for my soul
>   Or cordial in the searching cold;
> Cast in the fire the perished thing,
>   Melt and remould it, till it be
> A royal cup for Him my King:
>   O Jesus, drink of me.   (17–24)

Actively seeking death and resurrection, announcing total surrender to Christ, the poet also imagines herself in the role of Christ, asking Him to drink of her as the communicant drinks of His blood in the Eucharist. Like Brontë in "No coward soul is mine," Rossetti has daringly realized the concept of Christ within and in so doing reworks the imagery of Christianity's central ritual of communion. "Don't be original" was one of Keble's watchwords to ensure that poetry served God rather than human needs and pride.[18] Though extending his performative poetics, Rossetti breaks Keble's rule in "A Better Resurrection" as surely as the poem's broken bowl is destroyed to become a "royal cup." As devotional poet she is both dutiful and rebellious daughter, "Goblin Market"'s Lizzie and Laura at once.

Hopkins presents a double paradox. Like Keble, he fuses poetry with worship, priest with poet, and finds the natural world "charged with the grandeur of God" ("God's Grandeur" [1]). He literally followed Newman, moreover, into the Catholic Church, converting from High Anglicanism in 1866. Yet his devotional impulse fostered radical poetic originality rather than Keble's communal poetics, and in his poems Christ bursts into souls rather than holding Himself in reserve. More than Rossetti, Hopkins developed a divided response to Tractarian poetics, and it is more difficult to situate his work in terms of public versus private worship. "Spring and Fall" and "The Wreck of the *Deutschland*" resemble *The Christian Year* in their priestly aims. The latter was prompted by his rector's comment that nuns who fled religious persecution in Germany only to drown in shipwreck in the mouth of the Thames merited a poem, and in submitting this work to a Catholic periodical Hopkins clearly envisioned his meditation on martyrdom as part of a public faith community. But publishers' resistance to his formal innovations meant that his poetry functioned as private devotions until posthumous selections appeared in *The Poets and the Poetry of the Century* (1893).[19]

The life and death cycle of spring and fall is a longstanding Christian theme, as in Keble's "Twenty-Third Sunday after Trinity": "the calm leaves float ... / How like decaying life they seem to glide! / And yet no second spring have they in store" (7, 9–10). Keble contrasts the leaves' uncomplaining descent into "oblivion" (17) with humanity's laggard embrace of the chance to "rise again" (21). Keble thus offers religious instruction alongside Tractarian analysis of a November scene. In Hopkins's "Spring and Fall" (1893) the poet-priest catechizes a young girl whose springtime innocence is reflected in her name, designating a "daisy." Saddened by the desolation of autumn gold as leaves fall ("grieving / Over Goldengrove unleaving" [1–2]), Margaret is taught along with the reader:

> Sorrow's springs are the same.
> Nor mouth had, no nor mind, expressed
> What héart héard of, ghóst guéssed:
> It is the blight man was born for,
> It is Margaret you mourn for.   (11–15)

Even the gentle Margaret is part of fallen humanity, as she grasps spiritually ("ghóst guéssed") what adults recognize through reason. If the homiletic thrust of the Keble and Hopkins poems is similar, marking their work off from Brontë's and Rossetti's, Hopkins creates greater intensity through a more intimate exchange between priest and worshiper; the final line's explosive insight; and language and rhythm that require mobile, alert readers who encounter, like Margaret, hitherto unknown signifiers.

In "The Wreck of the *Deutschland*" the priest is himself brought to a powerful revelation of martyrdom's meaning by Christ, the martyred nun, and the act of writing. Trace elements of Tractarian Reserve and Analogy are evident in stanza 5, in which the poet-priest perceives God "under the world's splendour and wonder" (38), and stanza 8, which analogizes a "lush-kept plush-capped sloe / ... mouthed to flesh-burst" and flooding inward "being" (59–61) to Christ's sacrifice and a worshiper's sudden comprehension of it. Hopkins thus fuses residual Tractarianism with innovative diction and rhythm; and in alternating, then mixing scenes of private devotion and martyrology, he also fuses meditation and homily, subjective and external revelation, author-priest and transfigured believer, to reconceive religious verse.

"Part the First" recalls the poet's moment of conversion and meditates on Christ's nature – no gentle Christ, as so often in Keble. Rather, Hopkins's Christ works through "lightning and lashed rod" (10), "fire" (16, 74), "terror" (12), and wrenching intimacy that is at once excruciating and exquisite:

> Thou hast bound bones and veins in me, fastened me flesh,
> And after it álmost únmade, what with dread,
> > Thy doing: and dost thou touch me afresh?
> Over again I feel thy finger and find theé.   (5–8)

Just as Rossetti and Brontë rework the gender roles of devout women in their devotional lyrics, so Hopkins opens a space for homoeroticism within religious asceticism,[20] in part by adapting the longstanding association of religious and erotic experience (as in Bernini's sculpture of a swooning St. Teresa) to male experience of Christ.

In formal terms these lines reinforce Hopkins's incarnational theology and prepare for "Part the Second." Fully to realize Christ means realizing His descent into human form and His astonishing bodily suffering on the cross to redeem fallen humanity. The *imitatio Christi* (imitation of Christ) urged upon believers and the literal partaking of Christ's body and blood in the Catholic Eucharist both signified an entering of Christ into the body and participation in His sacrifice as well as love and mercy. In this context the sloe-plum of stanza 8 is also the human soul pierced by Christ that then bursts to blessed effect or awareness of sin within "the man, the being" (61) who is Jesus. Christ's revelation is thus shattering, painful, infinitely intense, and merciful; and it must be continually renewed if the believer is to avoid reversion to a fallen state. Part of the poem's drama, accordingly, is the speaker's struggle fully to realize Christian sacrifice in the martyred nun and their shared "King" (80) – hence, too, the difficulty of the verse, which can effect a triggering "revelation" of meaning in readers as well.

"Part the Second" begins as poetic narration, seeming to shift from the poet-priest's private devotions to public homily about the nun's Christian example. Hopkins's account, based on newspaper reports, is stirring and vivid, recreating the fearsome storm into which the ship sailed and the terror, sounds, and sensations experienced by "Two hundred souls" (92). Among them is a brave man who enacts merely mortal redemption and sacrifice; trying to rescue women, he is "pitched to his death at a blow," then "dandled ... to and fro" as a corpse from the rope he relied on for security (124, 126). Then "a lioness arose breasting the babble, / A prophetess towered in the tumult, a virginal tongue told" (135–6). At this pivotal moment the poet disrupts the narrative homily with his subjective response to the scene composed of "tears" (142) and unexpected "glee" (144):

> Ah, touched in your bower of bone
> Are you! turned for an exquisite smart,
> Have you! make words break from me here all alone,
> Do you! – mother of being in me, heart.   (137–40)

The lines echo stanza 1 and can refer to the nun as readily as to the poet. By simultaneously rupturing narrative and fastening the link of Parts I and II, Hopkins indicates the necessity of entering into what the worshiper contemplates in devotion.

He similarly conjoins poet and nun in stanza 24, the climax of the poem. While he was safely housed in Wales she was realizing martyrdom and incarnational theology, calling out not for mortal safety but rather "calling 'O Christ, Christ, come quickly': / The cross to her she calls Christ to her, christens her wild-worst Best" (191–2). Eleven additional stanzas are required for the poet to realize the meaning of her martyrdom. His self-doubt in the process – "But how shall I ... [sic] make me room there: / Reach me a ... Fancy, come faster" (217–18) – models for readers the struggle needed to locate religious meaning in the world's sights, events, and narratives. Yet as the poem demonstrates, Christ's incarnational agency makes such meaning available.

Hopkins concludes with a prayer that is at once communal and an expression of the poet-priest's achieved identification with the nun: "Let him easter in us, be a dayspring to the dimness of us, be a crimson-cresseted east" (277). In Hopkins's best-known work, poetic participation in faith forms a continuum with communal worship and Victorian devotional poetry yet fully corresponds to neither. The totality of poems discussed in this section, then, represent a complex, ongoing conversation among religious poets and their works' intersection with religious institutions, contemporary events, and the public world.

Woman poets and biblical scenes

Barrett Browning takes up the dilemma of finite beings' attempt to perceive infinitude in "The Seraphim" (1838) but affords it very different treatment from Tractarian verse. As Jewish poet Grace Aguilar was doing the same year, and as Amy Levy would later, Barrett Browning intervened in Victorian religion by reimagining a key biblical scene, here the Crucifixion. God has ordered all angels to earth to observe Christ's woe on the cross, but brother angels Ador and Zerah, momentarily stunned by an emotion foreign to heaven, linger behind and provide an oblique glimpse of God:

> *Ador.* There the Shadow from the throne
> Formless with infinity
> Hovers o'er the crystal sea
>   Awfuller than light derived,
> And red with those primæval heats
>   Whereby all life has lived. (11–16)

Since angels, too, lack infinitude, Ador wonders if his momentary prostration results from God's "Bearing to my finite essence / Incapacious of their presence, / Infinite imaginings" (55–7) and warns Zerah not to gaze directly on God's love, which would strike him with "ecstatic pain" (80) so that "ever, ever, wouldst thou be / Amid the general chorus dumb, / God-stricken to seraphic agony" (85–7). In an epilogue the poet wonders, "what am I / To counterfeit, with faculty earth-darkened, / Seraphic brows of light / And seraph language never used nor hearkened?" (1020–3).

In conceding mortal limits but adopting a heavenly perspective nonetheless, Barrett Browning registers more allegiance to poetic tradition than to a church, just as, in her 1838 Preface, she links "The Seraphim" to Greek drama rather than the Bible: "I thought, that had Æschylus lived after the incarnation ... he might have turned ... to the sublimer meekness of the Taster of death for every man ... to HIS more awful silence, when the agony stood dumb before the love!"[21] Romantic imagination understood as a faculty instinct with the infinite is even more relevant to the poem. If Keats and Shelley refashioned Greek myth to represent eternal beings, Barrett Browning restages Christian myth, taking the cosmic significance of Christ's Atonement for granted and pouring her energies into creating an original scenario consistent with but not in the Bible. She thus performs the role indicated by David Masson: "The poet may imagine opinions, doctrines, heresies, cogitations, debates, expositions – there is no limit to his traffic with the moral any more than with the sensuous appearances of the universe."

Like "The Seraphim," "A Drama of Exile" (1844) also reimagines biblical scenes. In fact they are paired poems demonstrating the inseparability of the Fall from Christ's redemption and the power of love both divine and human. At the end of "The Seraphim," the earth reports that "Adam dead four thousand years, / ... Starts with sudden life and hears" (972, 983).

"A Drama of Exile" is the "prequel" to "The Seraphim," opening with Lucifer's exulting song of ruin before Eden's closed gates and his encounter with Gabriel, who hints at future redemption: "God is more ... / And capable of saving" (199, 200). That promise is sustained when Christ appears to Eden's exiles, inspiring Adam to prophesy that Eve will be "sole bearer of the Seed / Whereby sin dieth" (1838–9), and Christ pronounces,

> Look on me!
> As I shall be uplifted on a cross
> In darkness of eclipse and anguish dread,
> So shall I lift up in my piercèd hands,
> Not into dark, but light – not unto death,
> But life, – beyond the reach of guilt and grief,
> The whole creation. Henceforth in my name
> Take courage, O thou woman, – man, take hope!   (1980–7)

Eve, the protagonist of the poem, is wracked by guilt and despair at having not merely defied God but also condemned Adam to death. Yet Adam is sustained by his love for Eve:

> God! I render back
> Strong benediction and perpetual praise
>   ...
> That thou, in striking my benumbèd hands,
> And forcing them to drop all other boons
> Of beauty and dominion and delight, –
> Hast left this well-belovèd Eve, this life
> Within life, this best gift between their palms,
> In gracious compensation!   (464–5, 468–73)

Adam teaches Eve to value herself, while she teaches him humility and a new model of love born of her realization through sin and guilt that "Only my gentleness shall make me great, / My humbleness exalt me" (1278–9). These traits will be realized in motherhood, though she is aghast at having condemned the unborn generations she will bring into being to death. A vision of Christ and His praise of His mother, to whom "An angel fresh from looking upon God" will "Descend" (1960–1), enable Eve to go forward, modeling in her painful birth and nurturance the suffering and love of Christ's sacrifice.

To align Eve as mother with Christ was an innovation indeed. As Barrett Browning comments in her 1844 Preface, her focus in the poem is "Eve's allotted grief, which, considering that self-sacrifice belonged to her womanhood, and the consciousness of originating the Fall to her offence, – appeared to me imperfectly apprehended hitherto, and more expressible by a woman than a man."[22] The Preface also reveals her sense of competing with Milton, equally bold for a woman poet. As well as looking back to Milton, her poem anticipates Marian Erle in *Aurora Leigh*, who is likewise redeemed and sanctified by motherhood. Implicitly, Barrett Browning is arguing in both poems that a fallen woman can be reclaimed just as fallen humanity was redeemed by Christ. Indeed, another of Barrett Browning's innovations in representing Eve is to mix biblical discourse with language drawn from the novel's fallen woman:

> Alas, – peace foregone,
> Love wronged, and virtue forfeit, and tears wept
> Upon all, vainly! Alas, me! alas,
> Who have undone myself, from all that best,
> Fairest and sweetest, to this wretchedest
> Saddest and most defiled – cast out, cast down.   (1286–91)

Yet Barrett Browning was resolutely traditional in one respect. As Cynthia Scheinberg observes, Victorian poetry was specifically aligned with Christianity; the hermeneutics of typology, whereby Old Testament events were read as foreshadowing Christian revelation, meant that Jewish tradition was accorded only relative value, as in "The Seraphim" and "A Drama in Exile."[23] The pre-eminence of Christianity clarifies why displacing it from poetry was so challenging and why dissident poets typically underscored their repudiation rather than (as in more recent verse) ejecting Christian content without comment. But the matter was more complicated for Jewish poets, who were exiled from both the homeland and mainstream cultural identities, who shared a range of reference with Christian poets but understood it differently, and who risked losing a wide audience if they overtly elevated Jewish themes.

Amy Levy's "Captivity" (*Cambridge Review* [1885]) is a powerful New Woman poem in its implied correlation between women culturally conditioned to accept their subordination and a caged bird that, if released after long captivity, "would come back at evening, heartbroken, / A captive for aye" because "There was wrought what is stronger than iron / In fetter and bar" (19–20, 23–4).[24] But Levy pairs the bird with a "lion in chains" that "strains … at the fetter, / In impotent rage" (2, 5–6), and that cannot return home even if released: "Shall he traverse the pitiless mountain, / Or swim through the foam?" (13, 15–16).

Since the lion is an emblem for Jews through their founding ancestor, the Lion of Judah (Genesis 49:8–9), and since captivity in Egypt (Exodus 1–40) is a defining episode in Judaism, "Captivity" articulates not just women's condition but, as Scheinberg suggests, the vexing issues of assimilation and the Jewish homeland.[25] Long captive in England, assimilated Jews might well lament, "I cannot remember my country, / The land whence I came" (25–6) and question whether they might, once free, "wander in vain" (37). This coding of religious identity is covert, however, because it overlaps with Christian reference. In Revelation 5:5 and typological Christian tradition the Lion of Judah refers to Jesus (hence the lion-savior in *Chronicles of Narnia*, by C. S. Lewis); and Keble devotes a number of lyrics in *The Christian Year* to Aaron, who induced Jewish tribes to worship the golden calf while they wandered in the desert. "Captivity" might evoke but also baffles Christian interpretation in terms of Jesus or Aaron as a type of false priest. Levy crafts a poem that can find a general audience responsive to themes of slavery and captivity, a narrower audience of New Woman readers committed to women's rights, a specifically Jewish audience, and perhaps an audience of Jewish women in particular, since she merges the noble lion and caged bird with a crucial Jewish narrative. Levy's "Captivity" is secular, sacred, Jewish, and feminist all at once.

"The Wanderers" (1838), by Grace Aguilar, is similarly complex and culturally resonant. Aguilar's narrative, subtitled with the biblical passage it represents ("Genesis, xxi.14–20"), fuses themes of the above poems by Barrett Browning and Levy: exile, wandering, motherhood, and fallen women. Aguilar's choice of Hagar and Ishmael underscores Jewish tradition and racial difference in ways quite different from "Captivity," however. Ishmael is conceived when Sarah, the aged wife of Abraham, gives her handmaid, the Egyptian-born Hagar, to Abraham so that he can father a child. When Ishmael is seventeen, Sarah miraculously gives birth to Isaac, at which point God orders Abraham to expel Ishmael. Abraham does not wish to spurn his son but follows God's commands, just as he will later obey when told to sacrifice Isaac.

As with the Lion of Judah, Hagar and Ishmael are appropriated to Christian meaning in the New Testament when Paul asserts that descendants of Ishmael and the slave Hagar represent those in bondage to the old faith while the freeborn Isaac represents the New Covenant of Christianity (Galatians 4:21–31). Both Christian and Jewish readers would recognize themes of exile in Aguilar's poem, but contending Jewish and Christian hermeneutics enable Aguilar to articulate a specific Jewish identity through Hagar. According to Daniel A. Harris, who reprints the poem, Aguilar, a Sephardic Jew, is simultaneously representing the recurring experience of Diaspora for Jews while contesting women's subordination within the Jewish community.[26]

Aguilar adopts ballad meter arranged as fourteeners to narrate the story of Abraham's obedience, Hagar's anguish over sustaining her son's life in the desert, and Ishmael's blithe hope and delight in freedom. When Ishmael suddenly asks Hagar to "lay me down" when "something cold and rushing seems thro' all my limbs to steal" (29–30), she flees, determined not to see her child die, only to hear "a still small voice" (44) that commands her to "trust in thy Maker's word," promises that "I will of [Ishmael] a nation make" (44, 46, 48), and opens Hagar's eyes to a well amidst desert sand that saves her son's life. As Harris notes, "the still, small voice" echoes the phrasing of God's manifestation to the prophet Elijah, imparting heroic status to the mother whom Christians might denigrate as a concubine, racial other, and outcast, and asserting within the Jewish community that women are worthy of prophetic status and "theophany."[27]

Aguilar's achievement is to merge this representation of Jewish tradition and womanhood with poetess verse. Hemans, the pre-eminent poetess, had died only three years before "The Wanderers" was published; Aguilar's poem, like much of Hemans's work, is marked by direct narration, piety, and sentimental elevation of motherhood as in this concluding stanza:

> She held him to her throbbing breast, she gazed upon his face –
> The beaming features, one by one, in silent love to trace.
> She bade him kneel to bless the Hand that saved him in the wild –
> But oh! few words her lips could speak, save these – "My child,
>   my child!"   (57–60)

Aguilar departs from Hemans, however, in articulating a dissident national identity and a model of racial difference within nations, just as she departs from Barrett Browning's adaptation of the Bible to high Romantic tradition or Levy's reliance on biblical narrative and cultural coding to enact multiple cultural identities.

Reimagined biblical scenes or texts occur in numerous other poems: the raising of Lazarus in Robert Browning's "An Epistle Containing the Strange Medical Experience of Karshish, the Arab Physician" (1855); "Eden Bower" (1870), by D. G. Rossetti; "Adam and Eve" (1888), by A. Mary F. Robinson. Those by Barrett Browning, Levy, and Aguilar, however, clarify the particular appeal of this form of religious verse for women poets as well as the range of their poetic strategies. Though women poets were automatically excluded from religious vocations by virtue of sex, religious poetry was quite another matter. Through it women could respond to the pervasive association of poetry with religion, yet intervene in religious and cultural tradition to affirm the validity and power of the female imagination and, in the case of Levy and Aguilar, Jewish identity.

Poetry and religious dispute

In *Das Leben Jesu kritisch bearbeitet* (1835), David Friedrich Strauss systematically analyzed miraculous events in the New Testament, concluding that they were not revelation or authentic history but myths seized upon by early Christian writers to identify Jesus with the Messiah. In 1846 Mary Ann Evans, later George Eliot, published her translation of Strauss's book, *The Life of Jesus Critically Examined*, and so made this skeptical critique available throughout England. The blow to devout Christians is discernible in "The 'Higher Criticism'" (1864), a sonnet by Charles Tennyson Turner, who avers that Higher Criticism "Strikes its small penknife through the covenants / Both old and new, and, in a trice, supplants / Without replacing, all we love and need" (6–8).

If Christianity was under assault from without, it was also marked by disputes from within, some dating back to the sixteenth-century break with the Roman Catholic Church, others to the seventeenth-century clash between Puritans and advocates of a unified church and state. Most poets discussed in the opening section of this chapter derive from Anglo-Catholic, or High Church, tradition, which emphasized the Anglican Church's commonality with Roman Catholicism since both claimed descent from the primitive church. Though jealously guarding against Catholic encroachments on the faithful in Britain and dismissive of Catholic "superstition," Anglo-Catholics embraced ancient traditions including ritual, priestly vestments, and saints' days, as well as church hierarchy and apostolic succession. In some dioceses High Anglicans even instated Anglican Sisterhoods (one of which Maria Rossetti, sister to Christina and D. G., joined in 1873).

Broad Church Anglicanism looked forward rather than back, arguing that the church should accommodate modern discoveries rather than fighting rearguard actions against them. Tennyson's *In Memoriam* functions as a Broad Church poem in this sense, for he resolves the threat of evolutionary theory by reinterpreting it in ways consistent with an afterlife and the divinity of Christ, whom the poet addresses in the prologue's opening line: "Strong Son of God, immortal Love" (1). Evangelical Anglicanism, in contrast, emphasized original sin, personal commitment to God, the literal truth of the Bible, and rigorous observation of the Sabbath; to these Anglicans, High Church ritual smacked of papist superstition and intervened between the worshiper and God.

Outside the Anglican Church stood dissenters, who refused allegiance to the state church. They were highly diverse, ranging from highly intellectual Unitarians such as Florence Nightingale and James Martineau (Harriet's brother), or Congregationalists like the young Elizabeth Barrett Barrett, to a mix of Baptist, Methodist, Moravian, and Independent chapels that catered to a cross-section of classes and locales.

All the poems considered below represent the repositioning of faith after the emergence of Higher Criticism and new scientific theory, and two involve dissenters. A particularly influential repositioning of religion in the nineteenth century, at least for poetry, was led by Matthew Arnold, who argued that a moribund Christianity should be supplanted by the timeless verities of art. In *God and the Bible* (1875), in fact, Arnold simply reassigned what he termed the highest qualities of religion to poetic imagination. Appropriating religion's function to literature proved to be enormously influential not only for literary history but also for higher education, since English Studies could be justified on the grounds of representing the "best that has been thought and said," not just a philological research method. Significantly, all three poems discussed below reject religious certitude and foreground the medium and hermeneutics of poetry over religious texts.

Robert Browning's *Christmas-Eve and Easter Day* (1850), the only new work published between his marriage in 1846 and *Men and Women* in 1855, bears the clear impress of Higher Criticism: one section of "Christmas-Eve" is set in a University of Göttingen lecture hall over which an exponent of the new scholarship presides. Written shortly after the death of Browning's mother, a dissenter, the work also devotes an extended passage to the fictional "Mount Zion" chapel situated in a poor section of London, plus a brief side trip to St. Peter's Basilica. "Christmas-Eve" thus immerses readers in religious difference and competing orientations as a condition of reading the poem. "Easter Day" is a colloquy between its speaker, who maintains "How very hard it is to be / A Christian!" (1–2), and a complacent believer. Despite shifts between the two parts in scene, speaker, meter, and rhyme scheme, *Christmas-Eve and Easter Day* is unified by its consistently approaching religion as a question, not a source of certain answers.

Browning's formal choices reinforce this orientation. His title suggests, on one hand, a faith paradigm of birth and resurrection; yet as terminal points of Jesus's earthly life the paired Christmas-Eve and Easter also suggest some form of *Das Leben Jesu*. The frame of reference in "Christmas-Eve" is similarly self-evident and in question. Browning's vivid scenes in a dissenter's chapel, St. Peter's basilica, and a German lecture hall emphasize the roles of "brain and heart" (294) in religion. The Mount Zion preacher offends by his "immense stupidity" as he "hug[s] the book of books to pieces," serving up to his uneducated flock "a patchwork of chapters and texts in severance" (144, 156–7). If the chapel also offends by sheer ugliness – it is filled with an ill-dressed, ill-washed congregation with here a "greasy cuff" and there a "horrible wen" on view (141, 178) – the Roman Catholic Christmas-Eve service seems designed to arouse suspicion through its aesthetic gorgeousness. Yet the speaker claims that "above / The scope of error" he can "see the love" of God (647–8) that motivates worshipers.

The Göttingen lecture hall stifles "heart" entirely, offering only intellect; Higher Criticism "Pumps out with ruthless ingenuity" all air from faith and leaves only "vacuity" (912–13). Three orientations to Jesus thus confront each other and contend for supremacy but find none, for the speaker sees merit and flaws in each and contends that all preach to confirm, not incite, belief:

> Each method abundantly convincing,
> As I say, to those convinced before,
>   But scarce to be swallowed without wincing
> By the not-as-yet-convinced.   (268–71)

But in fact there are four perspectives, not three. As in Browning's other poems utterance is mediated by a socially situated speaker. A tendency toward snobbery and self-congratulation mark this speaker as no more reliable than other Browning monologists: he visibly recoils from dirty traces of labor in the chapel and later applauds his own enlightened tolerance. Despite criticizing the practice in others, he, too, seeks to confirm what he already believes. His "church" in which "faith sprang first" (273) was Wordsworthian: "In youth I looked to these very skies, / And probing their immensities, / I found God there," both in his "power" and "his love" (279–81, 284). When, after re-professing his faith (288–374), a miraculous lunar rainbow appears, he considers it a direct revelation "shown me, there and then, – / Me, one out of a world of men," until, "gazing / With upturned eyes, I felt my brain / Glutted with the glory" (405–6, 420–2). A more direct theophany follows when Jesus Himself appears and, like the ghosts of Christmas past, present, and yet to come in Dickens's *Christmas Carol*, transports the speaker to other sites before returning him to his starting place.

In the process the speaker learns that neither his original "church" nor revelatory lunar rainbow (perhaps just moonshine after all?) suffices. For after witnessing the Göttingen lecture he suddenly seems abandoned by Jesus and asks, "Have I been sure, this Christmas-Eve, / God's own hand did the rainbow weave?" (1203–4). When he literally makes a leap of faith to catch hold of Jesus' hem once more, he finds himself back in the chapel. Abandoning superciliousness, he now chooses the chapel over his earlier "church" and meekly joins in the congregational hymn and "doxology" at the poem's end (1341–59). But is the airborne Jesus more real than the revelation of the lunar rainbow, especially since chapel worshipers eye the speaker disapprovingly as if he had fallen asleep? The poem refuses to make a revelation of its own and leaves the question unsettled.

The speaker of "Easter Day," whose social proclivities are less vividly indicated, converses with a Christian who trusts in the verities of the human heart (185–9) and clings to the "safe side" (269) of comfort and commitment. Whether the dialogue is imaginary or real, transactional or inward, is never clarified. The speaker insists on faith's arduousness, it turns out, because three years ago on Easter-Eve he experienced the beginning of Judgment Day – "On every side / Caught past escape, the earth was lit" with fire (534–5) – and chose the world rather than eternal salvation (552–5). When he tried to assure himself it had been a dream, "HE stood there" (640) and pronounced the speaker forever "shut / Out of the heaven of spirit" (696–7). Trying to justify his choice, the speaker affirmed natural beauty, then learning, then art, then mind, repeatedly choosing the finite over the infinite until he chose love and threw himself on God's mercy:

> And I cowered deprecatingly –
> "Thou Love of God! Or let me die,
> Or grant what shall seem heaven almost!
> Let me not know that all is lost,
> Though lost it be – leave me not tied
> To this despair, this corpse-like bride!
>
> ...
>
> Only let me go on, go on,
> Still hoping ever and anon
> To reach one eve the Better Land!"   (991–6, 1001–3)

God immediately embraced the speaker, who awakened at dawn on Easter Day. But even the immediate experience of God and judgment failed to secure certitude; the speaker remains unsure whether he experienced a vision and, if so, whether it was "False or true" (1010). Sometimes he even doubts whether he has been saved (1030–8) and so concludes, fittingly, with joyous assertions that fade into a question: "Easter-Day breaks! But / Christ rises! Mercy every way / Is infinite, – and who can say?" (1038–40).

Browning's poetic obliquity, which demands that readers exercise their minds, itself implies endorsement of ardent struggle rather than easy certainty, of texts that divulge neither fixed nor haphazard meaning but offer contingent significance obtained through indirect hints. An implied corollary, perhaps, is that no sect or person can legitimately derive authority by claiming direct revelation of God but must continue humbly to seek the divine alongside others. If truth glimpsed through oblique hints recalls the doctrine of Tractarian Reserve, the demand for critical engagement with theological narrative is post-Straussian.

In Matthew Arnold's "Stanzas from the Grande Chartreuse" (*Fraser's Magazine* [April, 1855]), faith has melted away in the face of new knowledge and Arnold's speaker is left "Wandering between two worlds, one dead, / The other powerless to be born, / With nowhere yet to rest my head" (85–7). The poem issues from the Continent, where so much skeptical philosophy and method originated in the nineteenth century, but the Arnoldian persona is doubly deracinated because he speaks from a Carthusian monastery where medieval practices persist. As a tour guide directs travelers upward (an insertion of modernity's commodified tourism into the Alpine scene), ghostly images accumulate in keeping with the monastery as medieval remnant and the merely spectral existence of its once-assured faith (11–13, 16, 22, 35–6). Rather than being alienated from the Carthusian monks after "rigorous teachers seized my youth, / And purged its faith, and trimmed its fire" (67–8), the speaker identifies with them because his very grief over loss of faith makes him likewise anachronistic.

Arnold explicitly speaks as a poet when his "I" modulates to an "us" (108) who comprise the "Last of the race of them who grieve" (110) and who have themselves been martyred to modernity. "What helps it now," he asks, "that Byron bore" across this same Continent "The pageant of his bleeding heart" (133, 136) or that Shelley's "lovely wail" has been carried off by the Italian breeze (139–40)? To situate poets as martyrs is to enforce the displacement of religion by secular modernity in favor of poetry. The conclusion's extended simile likewise foregrounds literariness, recalling Homeric simile and metaphysical conceit while fusing medievalism, alienation, and melancholy. As the poet avers, "We are like children reared" in the "shade" of "some old-world abbey wall" who glimpse distant soldiers marching under banners on an unknown mission, or hunters bent on pleasure; but the children resist calls to action because they cannot flourish "in other ground" than "cloistral" "reverie" and "prayer" (169–210).

Into "A Ballad in Blank Verse on the Making of a Poet" (1894), John Davidson compresses the matter of Victorian devotional lyrics, hymns, and

Swinburnean paganism. Though partly autobiographical, the poem's focus is less the painful dissonance between evangelical parents and their free-thinking literary son than the clash of irreconcilable belief systems and the unconscious drives that impel them. It offers a proto-Freudian, tragic vision of humanity and the harm humans do to each other because they cannot transcend their impetus toward totalizing systems. The striking modernity of Davidson's framework indicates how far avant garde intellectuals had traveled from Christianity in the wake of Darwin and Strauss, as does the son's characterization of Christian theology: "so dull a God, / A useless Hell, a jewel-huckster's Heaven!" (359–60). Unlike Arnold, Davidson does not posit literature as a privileged alternative to religion. Instead the cult of literature is simply that – one more cult, and the son briefly glimpses the mechanism underlying both imaginative creativity and successive religions that incite bloodshed: "Some thought imprisons us; we set about / To bring the world within the woven spell" (421–2). A corollary is the derivation of "Our ruthless creeds" from "The petrifaction of a metaphor" (423, 425). The subtitle ("on the Making of a Poet"), then, is partly ironic: this is no paean to literature and its liberating triumph. The poet is no better than other believers.

Davidson foregrounds the fashioning of literature in his title – the self-evident contradiction of a "ballad" in "blank verse" when these signify different forms – and so adopts a literary medium yet underscores its contingency. A ballad simultaneously implies the hymn measure of the son's evangelical parents, a striking narrative involving passion and violence, traditional folk materials, and a refrain. There are actually two refrains in Davidson's poem, one designating Scotland as a site where old and new ideas clash and "savage" (141, 357) creeds cause pain or kill outright, the other reconfiguring Scotland as a site of poetic beauty and tradition.

Blank verse evokes tragedy and epic magnitude as well as the novel in verse. Fittingly, Davidson's story anticipates elements of Samuel Butler's *The Way of All Flesh* (1903). The son's visits to the firth elicit visions of natural splendor ("shores that fringe the velvet tides / With heavy bullion and with golden lace," 18–19) as well as the music of mermaids (194–200). In contrast, all associated with his parents' ascetic faith is gnarled, cramped, and ugly, from his father's "pinch-beck cross" (51) and mother's "wrinkled eyelids, mortised hands" (93) to the smirking "children in the gallery" at church (185). Kicking over the traces within which his parents would confine him, even if it means visiting prostitutes on occasion ("the outcast Aphrodite[s]" found "in the dark streets of a noisome port" [144, 146]), enables the son to access beauty and exercise the mind that his father deliberately "closed and barred" (51).

Insofar as blank verse is the medium of English epic and Shakespearean tragedy, it is partly ironized. Literature's prestige confirms to the son the high importance of his vocation, but on its strength he only "broke his mother's tender heart, / Until she died in anguish for his sins" (131–2). Literature, so to speak, kills as surely as "savage creeds," and the son deludes himself as surely as the father. After his mother's death he can see that literature, even "the noblest," amounts to "lies" (152) and decides that "I'll have no creed" (214) – only to form a new one: "I am God: this Self, / That all the universe combines to quell, / Is greater than the universe" (227–9). Even after momentarily comprehending human propensity to belief systems, the son slips back into the old mode, declaring that he will become "The first of men to understand himself …" (445).

Davidson, like Browning, also embeds epistemological uncertainty into the scaffolding of his poem. It is not clear, as the son assumes, that the father dies in thrall to his God. The son has momentarily converted to Christianity to ease his guilt over his mother's death and comfort his dying father. When the father realizes that his son's conversion is bogus, he is aghast but then declares, "If I may, my son – / If it be God's will, I shall go to hell / To be beside you" (280–2). Though the dying father deems belief in predestination blasphemous, since it turns God into "An impotent spectator!" (329), he gasps out at the moment of death a predestinarian credo (331–52) complete with a vision of the New Jerusalem that rivals in shimmering beauty the pagan landscapes envisioned by his son. The credo might be sincere. But if it is a performance, the father gives up what is dearest to his heart, firm faith in God, to be with his son in hell, a form of sacrificial love rivaling Christian models.

Since the son cannot even conceive that his father might give a false performance equivalent to his own faked conversion, the question is who the real poet of the title is: the son, or the father capable of imagining such a loving gesture on behalf of his son. No matter which, the net effect is loss. The sheer waste of love and life ensuing from protagonists' attempts to follow the noblest beliefs of which they are capable, and the human condition on which these attempts are predicated, render the poem profoundly tragic. In this sense, the medium of blank verse is fully commensurate to Davidson's matter.

As this chapter indicates, poetry's intersection with faith, religious institutions, and religious debate was intense and wide-ranging. Theology as well as secular forces (including print culture) intensified poetic dialogues with religion. Yet in the most interesting Victorian poems, rhetoric addressing issues of faith was embedded in, not imposed upon, poetic form itself.

Chapter 6

Poetry and the heart's affections

These three made unity so sweet,
My frozen heart began to beat,
Remembering its ancient heat.
                    Alfred Tennyson, "The Two Voices" (1842)

I've bedewed it with tears, and embalmed it with sighs.
'Tis bound by a thousand bands to my heart.
    Eliza Cook, "The Old Arm-Chair"   (*Weekly Dispatch* [May, 1837])

I run, I run, I am gathered to thy heart.
                    Alice Meynell, "Renouncement" (1893)

At century's end Oscar Wilde brilliantly dismantled Victorian sentiment in *The Importance of Being Earnest* (1895). If sentimentality remains one of the least-liked features of Victorian literature today, its appeals to the heart and preoccupation with emotion are more legible when approached in the context of Victorian religion, domestic ideology, and material conditions. The poetic prestige of Wordsworth and Keble, and the value that both placed on hearts receptive to being moved, helped legitimize appeals to the heart in poetry. Poetry had long been considered the preserve of pathos in any case through its link to song, and secular concepts of sympathy reinforced appeals to the responsive heart associated with Victorian piety. As Isobel Armstrong notes, sympathy had both a moral and aesthetic function since imaginatively identifying with another furthered moral judgment as well as one's ability to read post-Romantic lyrics and the psychologically intricate dramatic monologue.[1] The heart in this sense was at once an organ of piety, secular morality, intellection, and aesthetic experience.

Victorian domestic ideology also had a profound effect on poetry's appeal to sentiment. Though "separate spheres" ideology was a middle-class construct, it affected all classes, in part through Victorian legislation aimed at preserving the home as a bulwark against laissez-faire capitalism, which required competition rather than sympathy and was indifferent to moral considerations because it was driven by what Adam Smith termed in *The Wealth of Nations* (1776) an "invisible hand" of market forces.[2] The middle-class home was conceived as a refuge presided over by a morally pure, emotionally nurturing woman, to whom husbands and fathers brutalized by the marketplace could resort for spiritual and emotional sustenance, and under whose benign influence children could be shielded from moral, economic, and sexual taint until they reached adulthood.

Of course such a home was a fiction. As Louis Althusser asserts, "Ideology represents the imaginary relationship of individuals to their real conditions of existence."[3] Working-class women could not and aristocratic women did not devote themselves wholly to housekeeping – nor did middle-class women, who also shopped, traveled, and visited. Indeed, the absorbing plots of Victorian realist fiction would have been impossible had its characters lived as women were enjoined to do: Jane Eyre escapes a bigamous marriage by a hair's breadth because she works as a governess; Becky Sharp gives the lie to domestic ideology altogether, both in her brief social triumphs and her masquerade as a pious churchwoman at the novel's end. Nonetheless, home became ratified as a sacred place in literature, the press, and social institutions, and poetry participated in this larger elevation of home and domestic affections, whether in the conclusion to Tennyson's "The Two Voices" (1842) or Coventry Patmore's *The Angel in the House* (1854–63).

Even when families were torn by strife or could not afford embellishments that imparted grace to daily living, home might still become a sacred space through death. Infant mortality rates remained high; this was particularly so in impoverished districts, but the death of children and women in childbirth was a common experience in an era preceding antibiotics or sterile medical instruments. This era also preceded nursing homes or removal of the seriously ill to large-scale hospitals that medicalized death and raised a barrier between this universal human fate and daily life. Victorians of all ages died at home and were usually prepared for burial there as well. The convergence of domestic ideals and the common domestic experience of death intensified society's focus on mourning and the need to articulate emotional response. If death has always been one of the great themes of poetry, Victorian poems such as Tennyson's *In Memoriam* and Eliza Cook's immensely popular "The Old Arm-Chair" filtered loss through domesticity.

The heart, however, has also long functioned as a synonym for erotic love, another central theme of poetry across time and cultures. Erotic desire was at once a preoccupation of Victorian culture, which popularized St. Valentine's Day, and a source of unease. For erotic passion could undermine middle-class manhood, which was defined in terms of emotional and economic self-discipline,[4] or ruin the purity of women. Alice Meynell's ecstatic dream of erotic union, significantly, occurs in a sonnet entitled "Renouncement" (1893). Nonetheless, female desire is central to poems such as Tennyson's *The Princess* (1847) and Barrett Browning's *Aurora Leigh* (1856), in which erotic plots are coupled with social critique. As well, erotic love could become an occasion for philosophy, as in "Dover Beach," a reminder that the heart is often used to figure the mind as well as the emotions, as when we determine to get to the heart of a matter.

Poetic representation of the heart was also inseparable from the literary marketplace. Printing brief sentimental lyrics in periodicals and newspapers enabled publishers to assure audiences that they kept domestic sanctities in mind while producing ephemeral commodities purchased for information or entertainment. Thousands of inches of newspaper columns and pages of magazines were thus devoted to emotional expression and designs on readers' heartstrings. The vogue of literary annuals in the second quarter of the century helped make the mournful poetess a drawing room staple – and professional success. Sentiment, then, could be a commercial strategy as well as conduit of piety, sympathy, affection, mourning, desire, and philosophy. Sometimes these motives jostled and challenged each other within single poems, at other times in contrasting poems gathered into periodicals or books. In its totality this work composed a dialogue within Victorian culture about what mattered in life, how to shape domestic and social conduct, and how to understand the human condition.

Poetess verse

Rather than being dismissed as a cliché who wrote clichés, the poetess has been reclaimed as an object of serious study because of the complex currents woven into this figure – as might be assumed from the very fact that women ostensibly dedicated to stereotypic femininity were professional writers who attracted wide readerships. Isobel Armstrong traces poetesses' registration of emotional pangs not merely to religion and social codes but also to David Hume's philosophy, which asserted the primacy of sense impressions over ideas. As well, Armstrong suggests that in relentlessly conforming to expectations of women's spontaneous invention, emotions, and tears, the poetess called convention into question through violent exaggeration that suggested pathology or parody.[5] Jerome McGann, alternatively, contrasts poetry inspired by Locke, whose philosophy instigated new interest in "sensibility" ("the mind within the body") and a re-examination of the complex relation of mind and body, with poetry inspired by the literary marketplace, which encouraged sentimentality ("the body in the mind") and generated a second-order, overdetermined poetry designed to elicit readers' sympathy and participation. Poetess verse, according to McGann, thus performs an allegory of its commercialization rather than reaching toward some larger aesthetic end.[6] Both the poetess's potential challenges to convention and her commercialization are central to understanding her work.

As earlier discussion of "Properzia Rossi" (Chapter 1) and "Casabianca" (Chapter 2) indicate, Felicia Hemans readily challenged assumptions that women poets wrote directly from the heart or that sacrificial death in war was always ennobling. *Records of Women* (1828), in which "Properzia Rossi" appeared, was also a great commercial success, going through four editions in five years and earning Hemans and her publisher substantial profits.[7] "The Land of Dreams," first published in the December, 1829 *Blackwood's Edinburgh Magazine* and then in *Songs of the Affections* (1830), occupies an intermediate position between aesthetic and commercial allegiances: Hemans asserts poetic authority by exploring dreams, a traditional site of poetic imagination, but also accommodates the poetess conventions of pure affections and piety.

She prefaces her poem with an epigraph from Byron ("The Dream" [1816]) and compares dream visions to "a wizard's magic glass" (5), an ancient city, and the shoaling sea that is both "A realm of treasures, [and] a realm of graves!" (18). But she narrowly constricts the meaning they have for her – "for *me*, O thou picture-land of sleep! / Thou art all one world of affections deep" – from which she is sundered since "All the beloved of my soul are there!" (21–2, 26). Underscoring the poignancy of a woman who revisits the dead in vibrant dreams only to wake to loneliness, the poem cries for dreams that show the future rather than past – "And oh! with the loved, whom no more I see, / Show me my home, as it yet may be!" – so that "my soul" may "bear on through the long, long day, / Till I go where the beautiful melts not away!" (51–2, 55–6). "The Land of Dreams" pays homage to the legacy of Byron and his poem ending in domestic misery (a risky affiliation for a woman poet in 1829) but is also admirably suited to a mass market: Hemans looks to eternity but is generically pious rather than asserting a specific religious allegiance; she is mournful and elicits sympathetic emotional response but is not too sad; she is decidedly feminine but does not exclude men who might have experienced grief or loneliness.

"Italian Girl's Hymn to the Virgin," also published in *Songs of the Affections*, similarly tugs at and validates dominant norms. The Latin epigraph from the *Sicilian Mariner's Hymn* registers Hemans's erudition, the act of prayer, and a Roman Catholic setting that for Protestants would condemn yet also explain the poem's address to a female divinity and mixing of eroticism with religion. In alternating lines of trimeter and pentameter that restlessly shift among iambs, trochees, and dactyls to suggest the speaker's restive heart, the girl prays to Mary to preserve her lover even while confessing that she needs saving from him because of "excess" passion and "wild idolatry" that "scarce leav[e] Heaven a part" (26, 36, 30). Perhaps Tennyson's "Mariana in the South" (1832), which depicts a similar scene, was partly prompted by Hemans, who was his mother's favorite poet. Moreover Tennyson, Richard Cronin asserts, carried out his poetic apprenticeship by learning to write "as a woman." But Tennyson's insistent sensuality (for example, "From brow and bosom slowly down / Through rosy taper fingers [she] drew / Her streaming curls of deepest brown" [14–16]) and vividly realized landscape highlight by contrast the safe confines within which Hemans stages her poem.[8]

Letitia Landon (L. E. L.), who first won notice through her poems in the *Literary Gazette*, was, like Hemans, immensely popular: *The Improvisatrice* (1824) went through six editions in a single year. Landon's performance as poetess challenged the unwavering respectability of "*Mrs.* Hemans," as she was known. If passionate, transgressive women surface in Hemans, they are the staple of "L. E. L." Rather than abstractly describing passion, Landon transmutes it into physical sensation, as in "The Charmed Cup," an interpolated tale of seduction, abandonment, and accidental murder in *The Improvisatrice*:

> And fondly round his neck she clung;
> Her long black tresses round him flung, –
> Love chains, which would not let him part;
> And he could feel her beating heart,
> The pulses of her small white hand.   (532–6)

Ida's beating heart can be felt because her breasts press so closely upon her lover. If rendering passion as physicality dates back to Sappho, one of the authorizing figures behind "L. E. L.," Landon's sensational details and oriental narratives prompted reviewers to term her "a female Byron." And just as audiences came to identify Byron's poetic daring with the poet's personal scandals, rumors of sexual liaisons circulated about Landon, leading John Forster, Dickens's good friend, to break his engagement with her in 1834 – rumors recently supported by new evidence of three illegitimate children raised in France, fathered by William Jerdan, editor of the *Literary Gazette*.[9]

Yet despite such daring in fiction and fact Landon's work remained sufficiently acceptable to be popular. Her very focus on love, after all, reinforced assumptions that women are defined by emotion. Moreover, her passionate heroines typically die, not only imitating the Ovidian Sappho but also paying a socially sanctioned penalty for their transgressive desire. And her poems ultimately uphold key conventions of the poetess and women's domestic roles. Both the unnamed Improvisatrice and Eulalie in *A History of the Lyre* (1828) claim nothing less than genius and are admired for their talent like the heroine on whom they are modeled, Corinne in Madame de Staël's eponymous novel of 1807, the metrical odes of which Landon translated in 1833. Yet Landon's Improvisatrice acknowledges only relative power ("but a woman's" [25]) and asserts the direct transfer of her heart's emotions into verse: "I poured my full and burning heart / In song" (28–9). Eulalie, moreover, considers the pure lily of the valley the fit "emblem" of woman, "she whose smile / Should only make the loveliness of home – / Who seeks support and shelter from man's heart" (186–8), compared to which she herself is an "Eastern tulip" of "radiant colours" that, too much in the sunshine, has "begun to wither" at noon (194–5, 197–8). Both these fictional poetesses die, one from too much and the other from too little experience of passion.

Looked at another way, however, Landon's plots suggest that marriage is as threatening to women as genius or passion while offering less freedom and power. Lorenzo flees from the Improvisatrice because he is already pledged to Ianthe, a pure, meek heiress whom he marries out of honor; Ianthe is too weak to live, and after a respectful pause at her grave Lorenzo returns to his true love. If she, too, dies, she outlasts her rival long enough to share one passionate kiss. The narrator's obedient bride in *A History of the Lyre* wanes after three years of marriage and must be taken to Italy, where her husband again seeks out the company of Eulalie. Since Landon adopts a male narrator in *A History of the Lyre*, moreover, this poem does not comprise a poetess's spontaneous outpourings but a carefully crafted narrative.

Both poems, finally, are structured according to the movements and experiences of independent career women rather than domestic protagonists. Readers access their narratives by seeing what the women see in galleries, salons, moonlit streets, gardens, and palaces. Only when the Improvisatrice is dying is the scene set in her home. Landon states a poetess credo, then, but enables readers to experience vicariously the public life and independence of the literary professional behind the poem. Such a public female poet does not surface again until *Aurora Leigh*, for which *The Improvisatrice* and *A History of the Lyre* are precursor poems.[10] As wielded by Hemans and Landon, the poetess pays lip service to contemporary domestic manuals and critical standards even while crafting a less overt rhetorical poetics that enlarges the imagined poetic space within which a middle-class woman could move.

Domestic affections

Tennyson's Greek epigraph announces his link to Sappho in "Fatima" (1832), but his orientalism and opening lines suggest indebtedness as well to L. E. L., then at the height of her fame: "O Love, Love, Love! O withering might! / O sun, that from thy noonday height / Shudderest when I strain my sight" (1–3). "Mariana" and "The Lady of Shalott" aside, it was not by female portraits that Tennyson made his mark, however, but by dramatic monologues, philosophical poems, and domestic verse. "The Two Voices," originally entitled "Thoughts of a Suicide," combined elements of all three. Centered in the mind of a man who despairs of religious faith yet fears death, the poem enacts the speaker's "divided will" (106) through its dialogue between the voices of hope and cynical despair. The voluble voice of hope speaks in predictable clichés about man's "Dominion" over the world (21), human progress, and youthful ambition to engage the battle of life ("Waiting to strive a happy strife, / To war with falsehood to the knife" [130–1]), and thus is repeatedly trounced by the more incisive, less bombastic voice of despair.

Tennyson also reverses expectations by assigning a "still small voice" (1) not to God, as in the Bible (or poems by Keble and Aguilar), but to doubt and temptation, underscoring the epistemological impasse of a mind no longer able to sort out which voice works toward good or ill. Only turning away from the mind to the heart helps shift the balance from despair to the voice of hope, which drops pat phrases to speak more haltingly:

> Moreover, something is or seems,
> That touches me with mystic gleams,
> Like glimpses of forgotten dreams –
>
> Of something felt, like something here;
> Of something done, I know not where;
> Such as no language may declare.   (379–84)

Tennyson's rhymed tercets suggest formally what is soon revealed, that there is a third perspective, which comes when the doubter opens the window and sees amidst those walking to church a Victorian family:

> One walked between his wife and child,
> With measured footfall firm and mild,
> And now and then he gravely smiled.

The prudent partner of his blood
Leaned on him, faithful, gentle, good,
Wearing the rose of womanhood.

And in their double love secure,
The little maiden walked demure,
Pacing with downward eyelids pure.   (412–20)

If this vignette is another cliché, it does serviceable work in the poem. At the sight the doubter's "frozen heart began to beat" and he blesses them (422–4), now finding within a "silver-clear" (428) voice that bids him "'Rejoice! Rejoice!'" (462). In "First Sunday in Lent" Keble positions domestic "joys that crowd the household nook, / The haunt of all affections pure" (51–2) as a potential distraction from a focus on ascent to God. Tennyson suggests that domestic affections are a surer bulwark against despair than traditional theology, which too easily breaks up amidst the changed conditions of modern life.

Tennyson's family vignette, as well as the high regard in which "The Two Voices" was held, indicated that high poetic seriousness and philosophy could consort with domestic affections, which hence were appropriate for male as well as female poets. Coventry Patmore's *The Angel in the House*, like "The Two Voices," came to define a Victorian domestic ideal that revolved around a dependent wife. Patmore's was a serial poem, its first three volumes, *The Betrothal*, *The Espousals*, and *Faithful For Ever*, appearing in 1854, 1856, and 1860, and its last, *Victories of Love*, serialized in *Macmillan's Magazine* (October–December 1861) prior to book publication in 1863. Its slow unfolding over time was crucial to its theme that married love is not an end point gained but a process of growth and maturation. This flies in the face of love poetry that glories in first love and consummation but usually falls silent about how two beings maintain concord or passion ever after. Patmore emphasizes his innovation in the Prologue (1854), claiming that he "The first of themes, sung last of all. / In green and undiscover'd ground, / Yet near where many others sing" (32–4). Married love also enables Patmore to decant passion and lust from love poetry; mature married love suggests domestic affection instead.

The Roman Catholic Patmore never forgets that marriage is a sacrament, and rather like Keble he emphasizes that mundane marital details are a medium through which to glimpse the underlying divine love that marriage figures and is founded upon. Each of Patmore's cantos in the *Betrothal* and *Espousals* pairs an elevated prelude with a mundane, novelistic narration of courtship and marriage. This hybrid design everywhere enacts Patmore's premise that knowing both God and a spouse relies on wedding earthly to spiritual, material to transcendent being:

> This little germ of nuptial love,
>   Which springs so simply from the sod,
> The root is, as my song shall prove,
>   Of all our love to man and God.   (*The Betrothal*, 537–40)

The courtship narrative forms a strong tonal contrast, as when Felix and Honoria "laugh'd and talk'd, / And praised the Flower-show and the Ball" (450–1) or experience temporary separation when "The bell rang, and, with shrieks like death, / Link catching link," the train sweeps her away for a month's visit (835–6).

Even Patmore's rhymes conveying these trite events become symbolic of marriage's union of the physical and spiritual, fittingly, since rhyme emerges from the linking of material sign with impalpable but audible sound and breath. The poet makes this poetic design explicit in the preludial "Paragon" when he refers to his "hymn" to arouse "these song-sleepy times / With rhapsodies of perfect words, / Ruled by returning kiss of rhymes" (238–40). Rhymes figure both the sacred ("hymn") and marriage's physical consummation ("kiss").

Victorian and later readers have been struck less by Patmore's poetics than by his relentless idealization of marriage and representation of womanhood. In the first edition of *The Betrothal* Patmore acknowledged women's intellectual agency – "Her privilege, not impotence/ Exempts her from the work of man" – and instanced Jeanne d'Arc, the prophets Miriam and Anna, Deborah the judge, and Queen Victoria herself ("The full-grown Lion's power and pride / Led by the soft hands of a Queen").[11] But he dropped this stanza from later editions while continuing to position the husband as authoritative speaker and the wife as silent listener and ministering angel: "when we knelt, she seem'd to be / An angel teaching me to pray" (875–6). Over time Patmore's poem became a metonym for domestic ideology itself, ceasing to matter as a poem once the cultural and theological forces that brought it into being faded into the background.

Even his contemporaries challenged Patmore's view of marriage and women. Richard Holt Hutton disliked the "prudish" Honoria and noted Patmore's

> exaggerated view of women's natural graces, and a very depreciating view of their capacities for growth … he treats them as if they had no more capacity for moral and intellectual growth than a flower or bird; and, in his very fine "parallel" between men and women, assigns all the gradual progress to those, and attributes an involuntary blossoming to these.[12]

Poets as well as critics contested Patmore's marriage philosophy. Published the same year as *The Espousals*, *Aurora Leigh* features a bridegroom who sees, like Patmore's, that "the love of wedded souls, / ... still presents" the "counterpart" to God's love, but Romney has learned to prize a wife who will "work for two, / As I, though thus restrained, for two, shall love!" And Romney cedes poetic vision to Aurora: "Now press the clarion on thy woman's lip" (9.882–2, 911–12, 929).

Gerald Massey's riposte to *The Angel in the House* is especially deft in "My Love" (1861). The lyric matches the long poem in lilting musicality, domestic affection, and fond endearments. But Massey, the self-taught son of a canal boatman who himself went to work at eight, could appreciate a wife who is "no light Dreamer" but "a brave life-sea swimmer, / With footing found in Home" (10, 12–13), and he explicitly rejects Patmore's angelic wife:

> My winsome Wife, she's bright without,
>   And beautiful within;
> But – I would not say quite without
>   The least wee touch of sin.
>
> My Love is not an Angel
>   In one or two small things;
> But just a wifely woman
>   With other wants than wings.
> You have some little leaven
>   Of earth, you darling dear!
> If you were fit for Heaven,
>   You might not nestle here.   (14–24)

Massey demonstrates the constrained femininity of *The Angel in the House* not by rejecting married love but by embracing women's humanity and companionship.

Young children and babies also inspired domestic rhapsodies to the point that Anthony Trollope ridiculed them in "Baby Worship," the title of Chapter 16 of *Barchester Towers* (1857). A popular late-century lyric indicates a representative tone:

> Oh, baby, baby, baby dear,
> We lie alone together here;
> The snowy gown and cap and sheet
> With lavender are fresh and sweet;
> Through half-closed blinds the roses peer
> To see and love you, baby dear.[13]

This lyric is more interesting than many others, however, because it forms only one tonal register in *The Moat House* by New Woman poet E. Nesbit.

In her narrative poem the lullaby is sung by a former nun who renounces
religion and marriage to form a free union with her lover. Nesbit thus simultaneously articulates maternal love for a child and questions the social footing
on which it is predicated.

Ellen Johnston, the "Factory Girl" poet, likewise links maternal passion
to sexual nonconformity in "A Mother's Love" (1867). The lyric intensifies the
wrench of a mother's separation from her six-year-old daughter by repeating
initial ("I love thee, I love thee") and terminal ("Mary Achin") phrases in each
quatrain, a performative validation of the mother-poet's insistence that "I
love thee, I love thee, is ever my lay, / I sigh it by night and I sing it by day"
(25–6).[14] Johnston pairs expression of devoted love with frank admission of
the child's illegitimacy, which paradoxically dignifies the child and counterbalances the mother's ostensible social pathology with normative maternity:

> I love thee, I love thee, and six years hath now fled
> Since first on my bosom I pillow'd thy head;
> Since I first did behold thee in sorrow and sin,
> Thou sweet offspring of false love – my Mary Achin.   (5–8)

In Nesbit and Johnston, then, maternal sentiment veers away from sentimentality because it is in dialogue with both simple domestic ideals and complex
social conditions.

That Nesbit is best-known today as a children's writer is a reminder that
the Victorian era was the first to develop a mass print culture specifically
targeted at children, both in books and in children's periodicals such as *Boy's
Own Magazine* (1855–74) and *Girl's Own Paper* (1880–1908). It is in this
context that two volumes of Victorian children's verse have emerged as
classics: Christina Rossetti's *Sing-Song: A Nursery Rhyme Book* (1872) and
Robert Louis Stevenson's *A Child's Garden of Verses* (1885). The former
opens with baby worship by way of dedication –

> Angels at the foot,
>   And Angels at the head,
> And like a curly little lamb
>   My pretty babe in bed   (1–4) –

but also includes the fun of "If a pig wore a wig" and Rossetti's memorable lines
on the wind:

> Who has seen the wind?
>   Neither you nor I:
> But when the trees bow down their heads
>   The wind is passing by.   (5–8)

Though Stevenson, unlike Rossetti, excludes death from his volume, he makes room for childhood fear and illness, transforming the latter into adventure with the help of toy soldiers in "The Land of Counterpane," until the boy speaker concludes,

> I was the giant great and still
> That sits upon the pillow-hill,
> And sees before him, dale and plain,
> The pleasant land of counterpane.   (13–16)

Such work, full of whimsy and charm, is made possible by Romanticism's elevation of the child and the two-spheres ideology that insisted on middle-class homes presided over by loving mothers who carefully nurtured innocence. Because this social framework set childhood apart from commerce and sexual taint, it could function as an intensely imaginative, rich emotional site congenial to poetry. Eliza Ogilvy's "A Natal Address to My Child, March 19th 1844" (1856) manages to combine the fun of children's verse with maternal love and adult skepticism. The mother who only shortly before moaned in childbirth addresses the baby now "screaming in the Nurse's lap" (4) and like many a mother carefully scrutinizes the newborn's body to make sure all is sound and whole. But she refuses to idealize what she sees:

> No locks thy tender cranium boasteth,
> No lashes veil thy gummy eye
> And, like some steak gridiron toasteth,
> Thy skin is red and crisp and dry.   (5–8)[15]

The wry maternal voice concludes by turning the humor on itself as the baby continues to wail: "Oh! how she squalls! – she can't bear rhyme!" (28). Victorian domestic poetry, then, often is sentimental and has ideological designs on readers. But its expression of domestic affection is multivocal, not uniform, and often grounded in vibrant poetic form.

Death and mourning

The daughter celebrated in Ogilvy's poem died the following year, and Ogilvy joined a host of Victorian domestic mourners. The second stanza of Eliza Cook's "The Old Arm-Chair" reverses the direction of baby worship but not its sentimentality, detailing the child's love for the mother, who dispensed "gentle words" and "taught me to lisp my earliest prayer" from the "hallowed seat" near which the child "lingered" with "listening ear"

(9–15). The first stanza, more subtly, indicates the speaker's inability to let go of her mother or of grief through an uneasy metaphor, since the chair so clearly stands in for the mother's dead body:

> I Love it, I love it; and who shall dare
> To chide me for loving that old Arm-chair?
> I've treasured it long as a sainted prize;
> I've bedewed it with tears, and embalmed it with sighs.
> 'Tis bound by a thousand bands to my heart.   (1–5)

If the popularity of "The Old Arm-Chair" indicates the desire for sentimentality among mass readerships, the poem also registers the physical proximity of death to daily life and suggests some cultural means by which Victorians mediated such unwanted intimacy.

As noted earlier, Tennyson wove into his confrontation with first and last things in *In Memoriam* recurring domestic scenes, picturing a father, mother, and fiancée at home not knowing that the distant soldier, sailor, or suitor they fondly contemplate lies dead (6.9–44). In another section he compares himself to a "widower" – which the bereaved Queen Victoria altered to "widow" in her copy of the poem – vainly grasping for the "late-lost form that sleep reveals" (13.1–2). Like Cook, Tennyson also represents a parent's death within domestic walls, contrasting servants' pragmatic action with the children who sit "by the hearth," "Cold in that atmosphere of Death, / And scarce endure to draw the breath" (20.13–15). By articulating loss in the imagery and language of domestic grief, Tennyson opened up his private experience to contemporaries just as his adaptation of elegy and pastoral positioned the work within wider poetic tradition. In her response the queen was representative rather than exceptional. Samantha Matthews instances an old man who treated the poem as a kind of churchyard and assigned different sections to late friends, aided by editions like the first that began each section on a new page with the effect of successive headstones.[16]

Death and mourning were sometimes appropriated to social protest by poets, as in Caroline Norton's "The Creole Girl" (1840). On one hand eliciting sympathy for the beautiful, innocent Creole girl who dies, Norton's narrative also pillories moral cowardice and hypocrisy among those purporting to sustain the sanctity of the home. Along the way she opens a rare vantage onto racial hybridity and sexual license in British society. The title character is "the child of Passion, and of Shame" of her father "of noble birth" and, "too obscure for good or evil fame, / Her unknown mother" (1.5–8).[17] Norton's overt target is social prejudice against illegitimacy, which causes neighbors and potential suitors to shun the girl after she comes to live with her father.

But "Creole" could designate a European or African descendant born in the West Indies, and slavery seems a tacit reference for the girl's mother since slavery had been outlawed in the British empire only seven years before Norton's poem appeared. Though the girl is termed "fair" (1.9, 13) she seems racially marked, "The languid lustre of her speaking eye, / The indolent smile of that bewitching mouth" seeming above all to "betray" her "natal sky" (1.37–9). And the poem's conclusion that in heaven "There shall thy soul its chains of slavery burst" (2.77) deepens the oblique hints introduced earlier. Norton thus disrupts boundaries between "home" and "abroad," "noble" and "enslaved," "black" and "white" while recounting others' attempts to impose them: "'moral England,' striking down the weak, / And smiling at the vices of the strong, / On her, poor child! her parent's guilt would wreak" (1.25–7).

The sentimental tone in these and other lines identifies "The Creole Girl" as poetess verse, especially in the opening lines that announce the girl's death and tilt the poem toward mournful sympathy. The title character's racial otherness also recalls the tragic "Hindoo" and "Moorish" beauties of L. E. L.'s *Improvisatrice* and much other poetess verse in literary annuals. Part II, however, reveals that the narrator is not, as Part I seems to imply, a poetess, but the physician called "To 'minister unto a mind diseased,' – / When on her heart's faint sickness all things pall'd" (2.6–7). The poem thus structurally enforces what it narrates, the unreliable relation of surface appearance to inward identity and the danger of quick judgments. This narrative strategy also widens Norton's framework beyond poetess verse, for "The Creole Girl" is less a tale of love and death than of social illness that needs physicking. The physician understands his patient's malady only when he comes upon her reading "Coralie," a "tale of one, whose fate had been / Too like her own" (2.34, 36–7). "The Creole Girl" likewise offers both a diagnosis of social ill and an implied cure through the medium of sympathetic grief for the death of a lovely young woman.

Poetic response to grief most often took the form of religious consolation, as in "Sleeping and Watching" (1844), by Barrett Browning. Its three stanzas represent a woman watching over a sleeping child ("Little head and little foot / Heavy laid for pleasure" [9–10]), whose sweetness contrasts with the sleepless mother. She is ill and will soon bring sorrow to the babe ("keep smiling, little child, / Ere the sorrow neareth" [21–2]), though sleep will bring her release from pain and a different form of awakening:

> [I] Sleeping shall be colder,
> And in waking presently,
> Brighter to beholder:

Differing in this beside –
   (Sleeper, have you heard me?
Do you move, and open wide
   Eyes of wonder toward me?) –
That while you I thus recall
   From your sleep, I solely,
Me from mine an angel shall,
   With reveillie holy. (42–52)

Little studied today, the poem was praised by Edgar Allan Poe as a "sweet piece of mingled imagination and nature," while the reviewer in *League*, the official journal of the Anti-Corn Law League, indicates a popular, less literary response: "There is a music of divine melancholy in the following little piece, entitled 'Sleeping and Watching,' relieved throughout by the hope that is full of futurity, which wins its way to the soul, and finds its place in memory for ever."[18]

Two of the lyrics on death most highly regarded today resist Victorian sentiment by stemming tears and even repudiating human ties. In contrast to Section 1 of *In Memoriam*, in which the speaker prefers "To dance with death, to beat the ground" (12) rather than relinquish grief, Tennyson's "Break, break, break" (1842) paradoxically expresses suppressed grief: "I would that my tongue could utter / The thoughts that arise in me" (3–4). Rather than through words, the poem registers grief obliquely through rhythm and image: "Break, break, break, / On thy cold gray stones, O Sea!" (1–2). The spondees and caesuras of the first line, as well as the rough plosives of repeated 'b's and 'k's, enact the halting words of which the speaker shortly complains, while its repetitions bespeak successive waves not only of the sea but also of loss that induces numbness. Like the mourner's grief, moreover, the sea is self-contained, disgorging only itself in its endlessly breaking waves, yet compelled by a momentous force held at a remove (the barren moon paralleling death). In the second quatrain the mourner deliberately turns away from the domestic ties and earnest labor that mark normative daily life, his heart so full that it is cold to others. The speaker can see that it is "well for the fisherman's boy, / That he shouts with his sister at play!" (5–6) but is outside their magic circle. Only an inanimate thing that evokes ideas of touching and reunion can release the grief within:

And the stately ships go on
To their haven under the hill;
But O for the touch of a vanished hand,
And the sound of a voice that is still! (9–12)

The lyric ends with muted release, repeating with a difference the opening lines and partly identifying what the speaker mourns: "But the tender grace of a day that is dead / Will never come back to me" (15–16). Even now the speaker cannot state who is dead or even what day he references, only the fragile luminousness of a day that is dead. Direct loss of a loved human being remains unstated, but the speaker's grief has become like the moon to the sea, an invisible force with power to move what lies outside itself.

Christina Rossetti's "When I am dead, my dearest" forms a remarkable contrast to poetess verse and her own devotional lyrics. She adopts apostrophe and an endearment only to erase human relationships, sweetly singing a song of alienation wherein raindrops and dew remain literal rather than metaphors for grief:

> When I am dead, my dearest,
>   Sing no sad songs for me;
> Plant thou no roses at my head,
>   Nor shady cypress tree.
> Be the green grass above me
>   With showers and dewdrops wet;
> And if thou wilt, remember,
>   And if thou wilt, forget.   (1–8)

More surprising still is the lyric's agnosticism, its refusal of recourse to eternity for consolation or hope as in Barrett Browning's "Sleeping and Watching." Rossetti's speaker contemplates with equanimity the posthumous dreams that frightened Hamlet from suicide and foresees no encounter with God or angels. She is radically indifferent to what she will leave behind, equally inclined to accept chance remembrance or the happiness of remembering nothing:

> I shall not see the shadows,
>   I shall not feel the rain;
> I shall not hear the nightingale
>   Sing on as if in pain.
> And dreaming through the twilight
>   That doth not rise nor set,
> Haply I may remember,
>   And haply may forget.   (9–16)

The immanence of the unsaid in Rossetti's and Tennyson's lyrics of thwarted grief is a key to their power and longevity with audiences that today are more "at home" with poems focused on alienation, not sentiment; on the individual, not daily domestic ties; on depression, not the outpourings of grief. Understanding Victorian poetry in its larger context, however, requires attention to poems written in service to as well as against the heart.

Erotic love and courtship

In Charles Dickens's autobiographical novel, David Copperfield comes to deem his marriage to Dora Spenlow a "first mistaken impulse of an undisciplined heart."[19] David articulates dangers that could lurk for men in erotic love, luring them into marriages with women unworthy of devotion or motherhood. For middle-class women the stakes were higher yet, since few career alternatives to marriage were available and spinsterhood lacked the attractions of comfortable bachelorhood. Above all erotic love posed sexual danger to women: one false step could ruin all prospects of marriage and social acceptance. Even avowing love too soon was dangerous, leading to "that mock to woman's pride – / A wretch that loves unwoo'd, and loves in vain" (Norton, "The Creole Girl," 1.127–8).

Alice Meynell's "Renouncement" (1893), inspired by love for the priest who inducted Meynell into Catholicism, also responds to a culture that defined women in relation to the heart but forbade them to act on it. The sonnet, however, is subtler than the domestic ideology it seems to ratify – D. G. Rossetti in fact considered it one of the finest poems ever written by a woman.[20] The title deliberately miscues, for the lyric intensifies erotic desire rather than denying it. The first six words enjoin repression on the speaker – "I must not think of thee" – but "The thought of thee" reappears in line 3 as an appositive for "all delight" (2); "the thought of thee," now "hidden yet bright," invades line 6; and the phrase, now clipped to "thee" since "I must stop short of thee the whole day long," concludes the octet. If the repeated "thee" indicates desire, Meynell's interruptive punctuation and semantics ("I must not," "I shun," "it must never, never come in sight," "I must stop") register the forces of repression. The octet is thus more performative than declamatory: desire and repression contest each other's sway as equal antagonists, a far cry from demure renunciation. The sestet abandons caesuras (except to prolong release in the final line) and merely pauses at line endings as the speaker rehearses her deliberate preparations for sleep. But the instant her "will as raiment [is] laid away" (10), leaving her naked to desire, the sonnet's sole enjambment unlooses passion that is all the more forceful for prior restraints: "With the first dream that comes with the first sleep / I run, I run, I am gathered to thy heart" (13–14). Meynell encircles her poem with prohibition only to enact indulgence within.

Prohibition of sexuality was far less uniform than L. E. L.'s doomed lovers or Meynell's sonnet might imply. At mid-century two long poems validated intense female desire by demonstrating its compatibility with marriage. In *The Princess*, Ida enters marriage only when she surrenders state power, and her reward is a partner of very moderate virility. Still, in contrast to Honoria in *The Angel in the House*, whose physicality is insisted upon yet strangely muted, Ida is the erotic equal of the prince, whom she comes to care for in the feminine service of nursing him. When he asks for a kiss, she is both sympathetic and sexual, especially in the first edition:

> She stooped; and with a great shock of the heart
> Our mouths met: out of languor leapt a cry,
> Passion from the brinks of death and up
> Along the shuddering senses struck the soul,
> And closed on fire with Ida's at the lips.[21]

When the prince reawakens during the night, he hears her reading aloud the deeply erotic "Now sleeps the crimson petal, now the white." Inspired by the Persian *ghazal*, the lyric renders sexual consummation from a female perspective, evoking naked receptiveness through allusion to Danaë (whom Jove impregnated while taking the form of a golden shower) and delicately suggesting the act of taking another within:

> Now lies the Earth all Danaë to the stars,
> And all thy heart lies open unto me.
> Now slides the silent meteor on, and leaves
> A shining furrow, as thy thoughts in me.
> Now folds the lily all her sweetness up,
> And slips into the bosom of the lake:
> So fold thyself, my dearest, thou, and slip
> Into my bosom and be lost in me.   (VII.167–74)

She next reads "Come down, O maid, from yonder mountain heights," which completes her capitulation to love and marriage; but the poem traces that normative shift to the arousal of female desire.

If Aurora Leigh also capitulates to love and marriage, she keeps her agency and career; yet Barrett Browning and Tennyson concur in assigning intense erotic desire to their heroines. After Aurora sobs out, "and I love you so, / I love you, Romney" (9.713–14) she cannot be sure

> which of our two large explosive hearts
> So shook me[.] That, I know not. There were words
> That broke in utterance ... melted, in the fire, –

Embrace, that was convulsion, … then a kiss
As long and silent as the ecstatic night,
And deep, deep, shuddering breaths, which meant beyond
Whatever could be told by word or kiss.　(9.718–24)

Meg Tasker astutely notes that "For men as well as women, sexual matters were much easier to write about in verse" compared to Victorian novels, which were often read aloud in drawing rooms. "Not only may sexual desire or activity be described indirectly, through metaphor and allusion (this, after all, is possible in prose), but they could be more freely employed as metaphor in poetry."[22] There is a metaphoric "meant beyond" in the above passage, but Barrett Browning also insists on female desire as such.

At other times poets approached love through the medium of philosophy, participating in a venerable tradition extending back to Plato's *Symposium* and more recently to Shelley in *Epipsychidion* (1821).Not surprisingly, given Shelley's influence on him, Robert Browning follows his Romantic precursor in approaching love as a cosmic force through which two human beings realize their capacities and relation to the infinite. "Love among the Ruins" (1855) weighs the claims of pastoral love in the present against past glory. and both against mortality. Relative to the growls and rough music of other Browning poems, "Love among the Ruins" is unusually lyric, its very medium coming down on the side of harmony and sweetness, while the counterpoint of long and short trochaic lines suggests plenitude versus brevity in life as well as art. Each stanza also pits a feminine landscape of undulating verdant hills ("slopes of verdure, certain rills / From the hills / Intersect and give a name to" [15–17]) against a martial, masculine city:

Where the domed and daring palace shot its spires
　　Up like fires
O'er the hundred-gated circuit of a wall
　　Bounding all,
Made of marble, men might march on nor be pressed,
　　Twelve abreast.　(19–24)

The former empire has been overtaken by the grass, and all that is left of glory impelled by "gold / Bought and sold" (35–6) is a turret where "a girl with eager eyes and yellow hair / Waits me there" (55–6). At this point, in anticipation of the lovers' embrace (69–72), feminine and masculine forms begin to meet and mingle: the phallic turret is inhabited by a woman, and the girl passively waiting also appropriates the masculine energy of "eager eyes" where once "the king looked" (59), directing them to love rather than imperial greed and glory. That two of the poem's binaries begin to break down may suggest that the present is also less cut off from the past than it purports. Yet the chiming rhymes and vibrancy of love in the present muffle lurking irony. Reminiscent of Sappho's fragment devoted to Anactoria, in which not armed horsemen or ships are the loveliest sight in life but the one desired, "Love among the Ruins" addresses an audience familiar with "gold" and imperial glory, and asserts that "Love is best" (84).

Browning's philosophy is clearer still, and more daring, in another poem from *Men and Women* (1855), "The Statue and the Bust." Here a Florentine duke and woman about to marry look upon each other for the first time and realize themselves:

> And lo, a blade for a knight's emprise
> Filled the fine empty sheath of a man, –
> The Duke grew straightway brave and wise.
> He looked at her, as a lover can;
> She looked at him, as one who awakes:
> The past was a sleep, and her life began.   (25–30)

But they do not act on the revelation, and once having bowed to prudence and social expectations they cannot break the habit. Their failure is underscored, not remedied, by art, and the statue and bust they commission to memorialize their love – cold simulacra of living forms – are all they leave behind. The poet breaks in at the end to address readers, warning that the story applies to them (250). Contending that, even had the Florentine lovers committed adultery, "a crime will do / As well, I reply, to serve for a test" (227–8), the poet concludes that the sole "sin I impute to each frustrate ghost / Is – the unlit lamp and the ungirt loin" (246–7). Only by acting on love, the poem implies, is the good life possible.

Browning's elopement with the former Elizabeth Barrett Barrett was a warrant for such views. But several contemporaries challenged his erotic philosophy on the grounds of ontology, the very nature of being and the world in which love unfolds. Adelaide Procter's "Philip and Mildred" (1858) narrates a long engagement that ends successfully in marriage yet leads to heartbreak rather than fulfillment owing to the effects of time and circumstance on human relations. Procter reworks two scenarios familiar from Tennyson's *In Memoriam*. In Section 60 Tennyson compares himself to a village girl "whose heart is set / On one whose rank exceeds her own" (3–4) and who, cut off from "his proper sphere" (5), "sighs amid her narrow days, / Moving about the household ways" (10–11). Four sections later (Section 64) Tennyson compares Hallam to "some divinely gifted man, / Whose life in low estate began / And on a simple village green" (2–4), who "breaks his birth's invidious bar" (5) to take a place on "Fortune's crowning slope" (14). Procter's Philip is "the genius of the village, who was born for something great" (32). Pledged to Mildred before he leaves for London, he succeeds – and remains true – against the odds.

Procter borrows not only a scenario of Tennyson's but also his trochaic octameter from "Locksley Hall," which Elizabeth Barrett Barrett also adopted in "Lady Geraldine's Courtship." These famous monologues respectively linking progress to spurned love and successful love to cross-class relations underscore Procter's singularity in mixing progress, class mobility, and marriage with bitter disappointment. All is foreshadowed in the first and last words of the opening line, "Lingering fade the rays of daylight, and the listening air is chilly." It is the day on which Philip and Mildred are to wed. But a "learnèd Traveller" (33) in the village secures a post for the self-taught Philip, who vows that in London Mildred's voice, "Like a guardian spirit by me" (50), will "murmur thoughts of home, and love" (52) and "charm my peaceful leisure, sanctify my daily toiling" (53) – a clear articulation of domestic ideology that the subsequent poem brings into question. Philip also asks Mildred to keep next to her heart the ring intended for their wedding.

But as months extend to years, the ring becomes an emblem not of eternal love but of Mildred's narrow life and her inability to transcend her limits and locale:

> And she turned aside, half fearing that fresh thoughts were fickle
> changes –
> That she *must* stay as he left her on that farewell summer night.
> …
> Yet why blame her? it had needed greater strength than she was given
> To have gone against the current that so calmly flowed along;
> Nothing fresh came near the village save the rain and dew of heaven,
> And her nature was too passive, and her love perhaps too strong.
>
> (99–100, 105–8)

When, years later, Philip attains distinction and sufficient wealth to marry, he returns for her. But his intellectual work is now so habitual that "He would give her words of kindness" (161), then "turn with eager pleasure to his writing, reading, dreaming" (163). Mildred comes to see that in marriage "she only held the casket, with the gem no longer there" (144) – an oblique image as well of the empty womb resulting from her late marriage and Philip's stunted desire. She welcomes early death, and the poem ends as "the cold, blue rays of moonlight" shine on "the Ring upon her finger" and on the corpse's "sweet smile" as if "some angel" were "lingering near her" (187–90). Unobtrusively, Procter has ringed the poem with the "lingering" and "chill" found in the opening line.

The final scene is sentimental, the poem's feminist politics hopeful when Procter adjures women, "love, if thou willest; but, thine own soul still possessing, / Live thy life: not a reflection or a shadow of his own" (93–4). Yet these elements are enwound with a less optimistic philosophy: "to grasp the thing we long for, and, with sorrow sick and dreary, / *Then* to find how it can fail us, is the saddest pain of all" (147–8). Were Philip selfish or brutal "Philip and Mildred" would indeed be a feminist critique, just as the work would be merely sentimental if Philip or Mildred had died before marrying. Procter, however, takes care to emphasize Philip's virtue, his "grieving truly, with a tender care and sorrow" (181), as his wife fades. In this poem, living according to the age's highest domestic and chivalric codes is not enough to overcome the defeat of human intention by time, change, and determinism.

"Dover Beach" (1867), recirculated to twenty-first-century audiences in the novel *Saturday* (2005), by Ian McEwan, has rarely been paired with Procter's poem. Yet "Philip and Mildred" illuminates and is illuminated by Arnold's best-known work. Anthony Hecht's "The Dover Bitch" (1967) critiques "Dover Beach" for turning a wedding night into an occasion for melancholy philosophy: "To have been brought / All the way down from London, and then be addressed / As sort of a mournful cosmic last resort / Is really tough on a girl, and she was pretty."[23] Read in the context of "Philip and Mildred," "Dover Beach" looks less idiosyncratic, more symptomatic of pessimism underlying mid-century self-confidence and the booming capitalism of an imperial world power. Like Procter, Arnold finds the world fundamentally antagonistic to human joy and fulfillment, and the poem advocates love not because, as in Browning, it is a liberating cosmic force, but because it is the best refuge available in an alien world:

> Ah, love, let us be true
> To one another! for the world, which seems
> To lie before us like a land of dreams,
> So various, so beautiful, so new,
> Hath really neither joy, nor love, nor light,
> Nor certitude, nor peace, nor help for pain.   (29–34)

Arnold in turn highlights the piety of Procter's last line – "For on earth so much is needed, but in Heaven Love is all!" (192) – and her recourse to narrative to broach philosophical issues. In contrast, Arnold shapes an overtly philosophical poem. To the cliffs of Dover, so substantial by day but strangely evanescent in moonlight, he opposes the "eternal note of sadness" (14) discerned in "the grating roar / Of pebbles which the waves draw back, and fling, / At their return, up the high strand" (9–11). Suggestive of paltry human beings flung about by larger forces, the pebbles will transmute into the ignorant armies of the closing lines like so many seeds of Cadmus. More than Procter, too, Arnold makes the philosophy and the poem of a piece, systematically exploring a narrowing sense of human possibility by looking back to the tragic vision of Sophocles (15–20), then forward to the collapse of Christian certitude in the nineteenth century, and relating all to the sea imagery that unifies the poem. Since this is a night scene, when little is clear, Arnold privileges sonic rather than visual imagery to represent the devastating recession of faith (in contrast to the bright visual image of faith's sway), extending aural effects through enjambment and syntax:

> But now I only hear
> Its melancholy, long, withdrawing roar,
> Retreating, to the breath
> Of the night-wind, down the vast edges drear
> And naked shingles of the world.   (24–8)

If Procter's work cannot rival the fame or force of Arnold's poem, it anticipates the Hecht parody and clarifies the tenuousness with which Arnold conjoins love and philosophy in his poem by drawing out the effects on a woman of a husband who would rather think than be with her.

Hardy synthesizes, as it were, the concerns of Procter and Arnold in "Neutral Tones" (1898). God is as absent from this world as in "Dover Beach," but his speaker is focused on a lover and as vulnerable to the effects of changing affections as Mildred is. Like both Procter and Arnold, Hardy also represents love as the impulse of puny beings dwarfed by a hostile world. The "tones" of Hardy's title designate both the colorless winter setting – "We stood by a pond that winter day, / And the sun was white, as though chidden of God, / And a few leaves lay on the starving sod" (1–3) – and love's former passion now decayed into indifference:

> Your eyes on me were as eyes that rove
> Over tedious riddles solved years ago;
> And some words played between us to and fro –
>   On which lost the more by our love.   (5–8)

Hardy strips away narrative elements, leaving only the hard-edged imagery and human situation. If this technique aligns "Neutral Tones" with modernist verse, it is also an expressive strategy, for by now the speaker is too wearied of the matter ("tedious riddles") to bother specifying details. The final stanza is also in part expressive, indicating how the speaker's memory encodes past pain in clustered images. But its stark confrontation with repeated disillusionment, pessimism, and a godless world amount to a philosophical world view:

> Since then, keen lessons that love deceives,
> And wrings with wrong, have shaped to me
> Your face, and the God-curst sun, and a tree,
>   And a pond edged with grayish leaves.   (13–16)

The heart and its knowledge remain the frame of reference in "Neutral Tones," yet it announces no expectation of sympathy or piety, much less the inauguration of happy, fecund domesticity. It is instead the recognizable world of the alienated modern individual.

Victorian poetry of the heart's affections ranges across sentimentality and sexuality, death and faith, complacency and pessimism, sincerity and profit-taking. It is not the product of a naïve culture but of a complex mix of poetic tradition, theology, ideology, and material conditions. The resulting poetry, happily, cannot be easily summed up. Understanding the historical underpinnings of this large body of work and the intricate cross-currents within it helps to reveal its heterogeneity, liveliness, and capacity to form a complex rhetoric.

Chapter 7

Poetry and empire

The loyal to their crown
Are loyal to their own far sons, who love
Our ocean-empire with her boundless homes
For ever-broadening England, and her throne
In our vast Orient.   Alfred Tennyson, "To the Queen" (1873)

We took our chanst among the Kyber 'ills,
     The Boers knocked us silly at a mile,
The Burman give us Irriwaddy chills,
     An' a Zulu *impi* dished us up in style:
But all we ever got from such as they
     Was pop to what the Fuzzy made us swaller.
     Rudyard Kipling, "Fuzzy-Wuzzy," *Scots Observer* (March 15, 1890)

     But those who slay
Are fathers. Theirs are armies. Death is theirs –
The death of innocences and despairs;
The dying of the golden and the grey.
The sentence, when these speak it, has no Nay.
And she who slays is she who bears, who bears.
                    Alice Meynell, "Parentage" (1896)

The Albert Memorial across from the Royal Albert Hall in London was built between 1863 and 1872 to memorialize Queen Victoria's husband after his death in 1861, but it is also a serviceable metaphor of poetry's relation to empire. The Gothic Revival design selected by architect George Gilbert Scott is meant to suggest unbroken national tradition stretching back to the Middle

Ages. Sculptures on the monument designate crucial components of the nation Albert served. One group, for example, lauds British manufacturing and engineering. Four other groups represent the continents but offer imperial as well as geography lessons. In contrast to the crowned figures representing Europe, the Asian and African groupings include a half-naked Indian woman and nearly naked African youth, anti-sartorial signifiers of primitivism and therefore of peoples suited to oversight by a great Christian nation. The entire base of the monument is then surrounded by a sculpted "Frieze of Parnassus" representing 169 architects, composers, painters, sculptors, and poets. The fundamental connection of art and empire could nowhere be more clearly articulated. Today, of course, for Londoners strolling in Hyde Park or hurrying to find a place at a "Prom" concert the memorial is part of the background barely registered. In that respect, too, the Albert Memorial figures the relation of empire and poetry, since the empire was so taken for granted that it became a usually unobtrusive yet palpable presence in the landscape of Victorian poetry.

As noted in Chapter 4, "McAndrew's Hymn" represents the discovery of God in a machine by a Scottish engineer in service (in all senses) to the empire. Since the prospect of missionaries bringing "heathen" peoples to Christ could serve as cover for economic and military incursions, it is not surprising that imperial discourse sometimes inhabited religious poetry. "Monday in Whitsun-Week" in Keble's *The Christian Year*, for example, asserts that faithful Christians "mayst share / With Christ His Father's throne, and wear / The world's imperial wreath" (82–4), while "Tuesday in Whitsun-Week" enlists Christian soldiers:

> And wheresoe'er in earth's wide field,
> Ye lift, for Him, the red-cross shield,
> Be this your song, your joy and pride –
> "Our Champion went before and died."   (73–6)

Likewise the poetess sometimes worked alongside the soldier. Between the initial publication of "The Homes of England" in *Blackwood's Edinburgh Magazine* (April, 1827) and *Records of Woman* (1828), Hemans shifted her epigraph from Joanna Baillie's *Ethwald* ("– A land of peace, / Where yellow fields unspoiled, and pastures green, / … smile gladly") to Sir Walter Scott's *Marmion* ("Where's the coward that would not dare / To fight for such a land?"). Entrée to the poem thus shifted from a drama that elevated family loyalty over political ambition to a poem that celebrated military valor and British unity, from women's influence and the virtues of peaceful insularity to the masculine martial values needed to fight foreign foes. The poem's wish that "hearts of native proof [may] be rear'd, / To guard each hallow'd wall!" (35–6) of English homes acquires new emphasis in relation to *Marmion*, suggesting a glance toward soldiers far away who could be rallied, and remembered, through the personal and ideological resonances of "home."

Yet poetry did not merely ratify but also intervened in imperial discourse. Celebrations of national heritage such as Tennyson's 1852 "Ode on the Death of the Duke of Wellington" or Arthur Conan Doyle's 1898 "The Song of the Bow" ("The men were bred in England: / The bowmen – the yeomen")[1] were forced to compete for readers with poems that fractured British identity back into its constituent parts. In *The Star of Attéghéi* (1844), a long narrative by Frances Browne about the tragic love of a Circassian princess who fights alongside her Polish lover against the Russians, the Irish narrator comments "How well my wearied country knows / The power that dwells in strangers' gold."[2] "Speranza" (Lady Wilde) was even more direct in "A Lament for the Potato" (1864): "Woe for Lorc's ancient kingdom, sunk in slavery and grief; / Plundered, ruined, are our gentry, our people, and their Chief" (5–6).[3] Mathilde Blind demonstrated the rapacity and barbarity of late-eighteenth-century Highland Clearances in Scotland following the 1745 uprising in *The Heather on Fire* (1886), another long narrative that, like Sir Walter Scott's poetic narratives, offered historical documentation in footnotes, only to different political effect.

Nor were the British Isles always the predominant frame of reference in poetry. Edwin Arnold's *The Light of Asia* (1879), which unfolded the life and teachings of Buddha in eight blank-verse books, was so popular that it went through sixty editions in England and drew the ire of William Wilkinson, author of *Edwin Arnold as Poetizer and Paganizer* (1884), because Arnold made an alternative to Christianity so attractive. In 1882 Edmund Gosse oversaw the posthumous publication of *Ancient Ballads and Legends of Hindustan* by Indian poet Toru Dutt, which included Dutt's translations of Sanskrit into English verse and miscellaneous poems such as "The Casuarina Tree" that vividly rendered Indian natural and domestic scenes. Such work not only resisted an exclusively British world outlook but also paved the way for W. B. Yeats's efforts to secure the publication of Rabindranath Tagore's *Gitanjali* (1912) in England, for which Yeats wrote the introduction.

Three imperial events, the Great Exhibition of 1851, the Indian "Mutiny," and the scramble for Africa, are useful co-ordinates for mapping the contested domain of Victorian poetry and empire. Much imperial poetry was shamelessly jingoistic and bloodthirsty – rhetoric in the worst sense. But as the examples of Tennyson, Kipling, and Meynell might suggest in "To the Queen," "Fuzzy-Wuzzy," and "Parentage," poets did not speak with one voice; single poems, moreover, often registered deep ambivalence and contending views about Britain's imperial mission. The very challenge of crafting poems that could contain divided impulses within aesthetically satisfying structures, paradoxically, could lead to poems generated by empire but surviving Britain's imperial moment.

1851 and the Great Exhibition

The cult of empire may have quickened after Queen Victoria assumed the title "Empress of India" in 1876, but "The sun never sets on the British empire" was a saying in use as early as 1841.[4] A decade later the Great Exhibition, sponsored by Prince Albert, opened at the Crystal Palace in Hyde Park on May 1, 1851. Its purpose was to showcase British scientific, agricultural, and industrial production alongside that of other nations in keeping with Albert's view that history tended toward the unifying of humanity. But this unity was located in Britain's imperial center, not across international boundaries. As Elizabeth Barrett Browning tartly commented in *Casa Guidi Windows* (1851),

> Imperial England draws
> The flowing ends of the earth from Fez, Canton,
> Delhi, and Stockholm, Athens and Madrid,
> The Russias and the vast Americas,
> As if a queen drew in her robes amid
> Her golden cincture, – isles, peninsulas,
> Capes, continents, far inland countries.   (2.578–84)

The British exhibits began with hundreds of items from India, which inspired *The Times* to enthuse over the empire's benevolence: "We have ransacked that territory not after the fashion of ordinary conquerors but with a just appreciation of those hidden sources of labour and springs of commerce which, in the end, are more remunerative than mines of silver or gold."[5] Colonial exhibits from Canada, Australia, and the West Indies were also included, as well as a cornucopia of domestic products separated from the imperial artifacts by British sculpture on one end and Augustus Pugin's medieval court on the other. Imperialism informed even the domestic industrial exhibits, however. A work honoring Lord Ellenborough, Governor-General of India from 1841 to 1844, depicted Asia placing a laurel wreath on Britannia's head and a British soldier domineering over African and Chinese captives.[6]

Tennyson was appointed Poet Laureate in November, 1850 and presented to Victoria in March, 1851, too late for him to participate in the Exhibition's opening ceremonies. Instead his earliest Laureate verse was "To the Queen," which paid his courtly devoirs by linking Victoria to progress ("you that hold / A nobler office" than "warrior kings of old" [1–4]), domestic affections ("A thousand claims to reverence closed / In her as Mother, Wife, and Queen" [27–8]), and empire ("your greatness, and the care / That yokes with empire" [9–10]). Tennyson immediately affixed the dedication to his seventh edition of *Poems* and thereafter to all his collected poems, textually linking them to empire.

He was still given a chance to celebrate the Great Exhibition when its tenth anniversary prompted plans for an International Exhibition on the site now occupied by the Natural History Museum in South Kensington. By the time it opened the prince so closely associated with it had died, and Tennyson added memorial lines ("Mourned in this golden hour of jubilee, / For this, for all, we weep our thanks to thee!" [8–9]) to "Ode Sung at the Opening of the International Exhibition" (*Fraser's Magazine* [1862]). The ode, sung by 4,000 voices, was a ringing tribute to Albert and the Crystal Palace:

> The world-compelling plan was thine, –
> And, lo! the long laborious miles
> Of Palace; lo! the giant aisles,
> Rich in model and design;
> Harvest-tool and husbandry,
> Loom and wheel and enginery,
> Secrets of the sullen mine,
> Steel and gold, and corn and wine,
> Fabric rough, or fairy-fine,
> Sunny tokens of the Line,
> Polar marvels, and a feast
> Of wonder, out of West and East,
> And shapes and hues of Art divine!   (10–22)

The piling-up of phrases answered to the lavish displays of the Great Exhibition, but it was merely an occasional poem that saluted a now ghostly figure.

Gerald Massey, the worker poet closely associated with Chartism, presented a very different sense of internationalism and British power in 1851. "Kings Are but Giants because We Kneel" draws on Massey's political activism to enunciate the systemic forces that perpetuate adverse wages and working conditions for laborers. More radically, the poem's first stanza identifies a military–industrial alliance that diverts workers from seeking justice at home to fighting wars against their counterparts in other countries. In contrast to celebrations of monarchs, empires, and industrial profits in the year of the Great Exhibition, Massey overturns their claims to fealty:

> Good People, put no faith in Kings, nor merchant-princes trust,
> Who grind your hearts in Mammon's press – your faces in the dust –
> Trust to your own true thought! to break the Tyrant's dark dark ban;
> If yet one spark of freedom lives, let man be true to man.
> We'll never fight again, Boys! with the Yankee, Pole, or Russ.
> We love the French as Brothers, and the fervid French love us!
> We'll league to crush the fiends who kill, all love and liberty,
> They are but Giants because we kneel, one leap, and up go we!   (1–8)

Though, like Tennyson's, his song was fit to be sung by a crowd, Massey hails an altogether different "noble brotherhood" and international unity.

After the outbreak of the Crimean War in 1854, however, when British soldiers were dying at the hands of Russians, Massey relinquished the stanza and his original title. In 1854 he reissued the poem as "They Are but Giants while We Kneel" and pared the text down from five stanzas to four, removing his salute to international workers.[7] Russia's attempt to gain a seaport on the Mediterranean in 1854 threatened Britain's sea routes and, moreover, its crucial overland routes to India. A war instigated by Russian aggression and British imperial interests thus overtook Massey's fierce protest of empire and commerce in the very teeth of the Great Exhibition in 1851. His erasures register the power of empire to leave its impress on poetry and print culture.

The Indian Mutiny

On May 10, 1857 sepoys – Indians employed as soldiers by the East India Company – began an insurrection prompted by a technological innovation: the new Enfield rifle, which required them to bite off ends of greased cartridges to load the rifle with shot. British officials saw only the technical advantage of more accurate firearms and ignored concerns among Hindu and Muslim soldiers that the cartridges were greased with cow- or pig-fat in violation of their religious observances. Once the revolt began in Meerut it spread to nearby Delhi as well as Lucknow, Cawnpore (Kanpur), and Agra, and was not officially ended until more than a year later. Rebels routinely shot the British commanders they overthrew, and at Cawnpore women and children originally promised safe passage were killed and their bodies tossed into a well. Once Britons learned the news, response was immediate, profound, and violent. Not only had the attack come from supposedly loyal soldiers in territory considered quite safe, but it had also erupted into atrocity. Worse, the bodies of British mothers had been violated, and rumors of rape and other degradations at the hands of "natives" swirled.

The effects on the public imagination can be gauged from the first and last stanzas of Martin Tupper's "The Indian Martyrs," which reached half-a-million people through the pages of the *London Journal*:

> Ah, who shall comfort England for her daughters and her sons,
> Her gentle, and her generous, her own heroic ones!
> Polluted, tortured, murdered – intolerable fate,
> To be the sport of demons in their lust and in their hate!
>
> ...
>
> England swears to set her mark upon that traitor land!
>
> Her mark, the hand of justice, the Cross – a cross of flame
> Where Englishwomen perished in unutterable shame:
> Her mark, the Cross of Mercy too above those martyred good,
> A marble cross on that burnt spot where once proud Delhi stood![8]

Tupper's violent prophecy was only too readily realized in brutal reprisals against rebels and, in some instances, even the shooting of Indians out of British cannons.

Women poets were no more pacific in the aftermath of the Mutiny than Tupper. Mary Elizabeth Braddon paused amidst her fledgling acting career to pen "Delhi," published in the September 26, 1857 *Beverley Recorder and General*:

> Down to the ground! Scattered be every stone!
> Annihilation be thy mildest fate;
> And be thine epitaph, these words alone:
> "Here lie the bones of fiends infuriate –
> "Here rot the carcases of a million slaves;
> "And here, *free* Britain's unstained banner waves!"[9]

Using printed marks on the page, Tupper and Braddon imaginatively project British marks upon Indian ground and rewrite momentary Indian victory into British power and vengeance.

Christina Rossetti also responded to news reports of the violence. Though Delhi was a major center of the uprising and Cawnpore sparked the fiercest publicity, a group of British soldiers and their families, including Captain and Mrs. Skene, were also killed by rebels at Jhansi after being promised safe passage. As the *Illustrated London News* reported, Mrs. Skene assisted her husband by loading guns so that he and his men could shoot Indians scaling the tower in which they had taken refuge, but "Skene then saw that it was no use going on any more, so he kissed his wife, shot her, and then himself." Jan Marsh, who reprints the account, observes the convergence of "love, fear and death" in the poem and Rossetti's representation of "female heroism" that results from giving voice to a military wife.[10]

Rossetti's response to the Mutiny, like Braddon's, was first published in a periodical, though *Once a Week* bungled her signature by assigning "The Round Tower at Jhansi. – June 8, 1857" to "Caroline G. Rossetti." Unlike Braddon's and Tupper's verses, her poem forgoes imagined vengeance to focus on the paradoxical expression that married love might take in a horrific situation. Relying on readers' familiarity with current events and the uprising's associations with sexual violation to remain customarily elliptical, Rossetti neither named Skene nor visualized his actions. But the dehumanized terms in which she portrayed Indian rebels was clear:

> A HUNDRED, a thousand to one; even so;
>   Not a hope in the world remained;
> The swarming, howling wretches below
>   Gained, and gained, and gained.
>
> S – look'd at his pale young wife: –
>   "Is the time come?" "The time *is* come."
> Young, strong, and so full of life;
>   The agony struck them dumb.
>
> "Will it hurt much?" "No, mine own:
>   I wish I could bear the pang for both."
> "I wish I could bear the pang alone:
>   Courage, dear! I am not loth."
>
> Kiss and kiss: "It is not pain
>   Thus to kiss and die.
> One kiss more." "And yet one again."
>   "Goodbye." "Goodbye."[11]

Like other poetess verse, the poem invited affective response to domestic affection and personal sacrifice on behalf of patriotism and purity – though not piety. Rossetti represented murder-suicide without comment, emphasizing the extremity of threat and the couple's certain death to sidestep the matter.

When Rossetti reprinted the poem in *Goblin Market and Other Poems* (1862), she inserted a new, third stanza that fleshed out the action and introduced a prayer that God would be merciful:

> Close his arm about her now,
>   Close her cheek to his,
> Close the pistol to her brow –
>   God forgive them this!   (9–12)

She also appended a note acknowledging that, as with many other early reports from India, her dramatic scenario was not true (since Skene and his wife were killed after surrendering): "I retain this little poem, not as historically accurate, but as written and published before I heard the supposed facts of its first verse contradicted." Not only did she retain the poem, but she also placed it directly after "Goblin Market," the title poem, highlighting it into prominence. Significantly, the Jhansi rebel leader was also a woman, the Rani of Jhansi, who had deeply resented British annexation of her territory when her husband died without an heir. In the end she met the same fate as Mrs. Skene (if by very different means): after demonstrating courage and intrepid action, she was shot while fleeing her military attackers. Readers who recalled this detail might discern in the Jhansi poem another pair of women besides Lizzie and Laura who resemble yet contrast with each other simultaneously. At the very least Rossetti's positioning of "In the Round Tower of Jhansi" next to "Goblin Market" calls attention to the imagined scene of rape in both. Reading the two together suggests that in addition to the connection "Goblin Market" bore to the commodity markets celebrated in the Great Exhibition, her goblins also nudged against the borders of empire.

Alfred Lyall fought as a magistrate-turned-volunteer during the 1857 uprising, narrowly escaping with his life when his horse was shot out from under him near Meerut, and died at Tennyson's Farringford home in 1911. As a high-level Indian administrator and, in retirement, author of a critical book on Tennyson, Lyall might be expected to sound strident imperialist themes in his poems. Yet Lyall's reflective turn, detailed knowledge of India, and deeply ironic sensibility resulted in complex imaginative responses to the 1857 uprising. Though he could never be claimed as an Indian advocate, he was able to do what almost no other poet did: imagine the revolt from an Indian point of view.

In "Rajpoot Rebels" (1889), purportedly written in 1858, the poem's frame sets the scene of wounded rebels driven to the heights of Nepal and underscores their doom. When their leader rises to speak he concedes that the English have "'driven us surely and slowly, / 'They have crushed us blow on blow'" (55–6). But the mobility and aesthetic distance intrinsic to dramatic utterance enable Lyall to describe hardships suffered by Indians on behalf of their own loyalties and ideals and to fashion a rebel speaker who articulates the injustice and littleness of life imposed on Indians by British rule:

> 'They have burnt every roof in the village,
> 'They have slain the best of my kin,
> 'They have ruined and burnt and pillaged,
> [']And yet we had done no sin;
>
> ...

'When the army has slain its fill,
'When they bid the hangman cease;
'They will beckon us down from the desert hill
'To go to our homes in peace.

...

'At the sight of an English face [to]
'Loyally bow the head,
'And cringe like slaves to the surly race
'For pay and a morsel of bread;

'Toil like an ox or a mule
'To earn the stranger his fee –
'Our sons may brook the Feringhee's rule,
'There is no more life for me!'   (29–32, 57–60, 65–72)

The insistent quotation marks remind readers that the poet does not speak in his own voice, but the lines nonetheless register a rare note of sympathy for Indian rebels.

"Theology in Extremis; or, A Soliloquy that May Have Been Delivered in India, June, 1857" (*Cornhill Magazine* [September, 1868]) is a British counterpart to "Rajpoot Rebels." As its headnote drawn from an Indian newspaper indicates, an English prisoner is about to be executed if he refuses to "profess Mahometanism," and the outcome is signaled in the Latin cue, "MORITURUS LOQUITUR," we who are about to die speak. In "The Indian Martyrs" Tupper opposes Christian martyrs to vicious "demons," but Lyall infuses complex irony into his poem by choosing as speaker an honest doubter unsure of what lies beyond death: "I could be silent and cheerfully die, / If I were only sure God cared" (63–4).

The poem begins ironically too, as the doomed man, "bred to [an] easy-chair" (18), thinks back to how he used to read tales about similar situations for amusement, indirectly acknowledging that brutality and torture are indigenous to the West: "They were my fathers, the men of yore, / Little they recked of a cruel death; / They would dip their hands in a heretic's gore" (19–21). In the end Lyall sounds a note of patriotism – "for the honour of English race, / May I not live or endure disgrace" (113–14) – but ironizes it by having the speaker consider holding onto life, then realize that he "must be gone to the crowd untold" of "martyrs who die like me, / Just for the pride of the old countree" (121, 125–6). The deliberate archaism of "countree" ties the speaker's death not only to the cruel fathers of yore (mirror images of the present "Mahometans") but also to past martyrs who died for a faith that offers no comfort or security to this dying man.

Equally complex is Lyall's response to the aftermath of 1857, direct British rule of India and, in 1876, Victoria's assumption of the title "Empress of India."

"Studies at Delhi, 1876" contrasts the interior monologues of a "Hindu Ascetic" as the pageantry of the British Raj passes by, and of a British veteran of 1857 during a pacific game of "Badminton" at a garden party. More than imperial snapshots, "Studies" is an ironic, pessimistic contemplation of imperial might and its future dissolution. The Hindu wonders, "Is it a god or a king that comes?" when his meditation is interrupted by "legions, rank on rank, / And the cannon roar, and the bayonets" (3–4). The poem obliquely hints at the hubris of titles and majesty in which the British wrap themselves, and the final stanza asserts the Raj's transience through the lens of Hindu theology:

> When shall these phantoms flicker away?
> Like the smoke of the guns on the wind-swept hill,
> Like the sounds and colours of yesterday:
> And the soul have rest, and the air be still.   (13–16)

"Badminton," like the shuttlecock it evokes, darts between male and female, peace and war, surface pleasantries and underlying past, its very perspective insisting on the complexity that India comprises. The British speaker outwardly conforms to gentility and its decorative pastimes ("Lightly the demoiselles tittered and leapt" [5]), but within he harks back to 1857:

> Hardly a shot from the gate we stormed,
> Under the Moree battlement's shade;
> Close to the glacis our game was formed,
> There had the fight been, and there we played.   (1–4)

The lightsome merriment of the afternoon's game has been purchased by violence and gore; and a reference to the "saviour of Delhi," John Nicholson, who was shot while leading the storming of the city, is merged with pastoralism as well: "North, was the garden where Nicholson slept" (7). The pacific note struck in the final quatrain is similarly delusive, and culminates in a curse suggesting uncertainty about the empire's permanence:

> Near me a Musalmán, civil and mild,
> Watched as the shuttlecocks rose and fell;
> And he said, as he counted his beads and smiled,
> "God smite their souls to the depths of hell."   (9–12)

In all three poems by Lyall one perspective counters another, a textual means of resisting assumptions of monolithic imperial power or British superiority. Lyall thus achieves intratextually the effect his work has when placed alongside poems representing Indians by Tupper, Braddon, and Rossetti, which suppress the sympathetic imagination usually operative in their poems and in Victorian poetics.

The Scramble for Africa

In the 1870s the United States was rebounding after its Civil War and Germany was a rising power under Otto von Bismarck. Even as it was forced to compete with the USA and European rivals for global markets, Britain was also struggling, like the rest of Europe, under the first real economic depression since the industrial boom began. In this context Africa offered an enticing prospect of raw materials and new markets for European goods, and the 1880s witnessed a fierce competition known as the "Scramble for Africa" as European powers sought to claim territory. By this point post-Darwinian notions that equated European pre-eminence with the "survival of the fittest" and pre-industrial Africa with unvarying "primitivism" outside the dynamic sphere of modern progress accompanied the drive toward annexations, which could be represented in terms of British destiny and the inevitable triumph of civilization over savagery.

Unsurprisingly, Africans saw no benign purpose in European incursions and offered fierce resistance, leading to a series of wars in the century's last two decades. In the north, British interests centered on the Nile and the Suez Canal, which offered a more direct route by sea to India. In 1875 Britain purchased a large share in the canal and attempted to maximize control over the area. British troops were an occupying force along the Nile by 1882, around the time that the Mahdi, a charismatic religious leader in Sudan intent on expelling corrupt officials and renewing the observance of Islam, gained ascendancy. General Charles Gordon, an earlier Governor-General of Sudan famous for his military exploits in China, was reappointed Governor-General in 1884, and sent to Khartoum to relieve Egyptian forces under threat by the Mahdi. But in January, 1885 the unthinkable happened when the Mahdi's forces overtook Khartoum and slew Gordon and his followers. Tennyson's epitaph on Gordon appeared in *The Times* on May 7, 1885 and represented public shock and sorrow over a hero many thought invincible:

> Warrior of God, man's friend, and tyrant's foe,
> Now somewhere dead far in the waste Soudan,
> Thou livest in all hearts, for all men know
> This earth has never borne a nobler man.

From humiliating defeat Tennyson wrested an undying exemplar of empire. Britain thereafter desisted from further attempts to quell the Sudan and focused attention on Egypt, operating a virtual protectorate from 1883 to 1907.

In the south of Africa, Britain acquired the Cape Colony at the beginning of the nineteenth century and annexed the formerly independent Transvaal in

1877, renaming it the South African Republic. This precipitated a war with the Zulu in 1879, and with the Boers, descendants of Dutch colonists pushed out by the British, in 1880. Though Prime Minister Gladstone signed a peace treaty with the Boers in 1881, a second war erupted in 1899, exacerbated by the imperial ambitions of colony Prime Minister Cecil Rhodes and the high economic stakes posed by the area's gold and diamond mines. Though Britain eventually defeated the Boers in 1902, it was a hard-fought war between white Boers, who resorted to guerilla warfare, and supposedly superior British forces. The cult of imperialism was called into question by the deaths of so many young men in their prime far from home and by sordid accounts of disease, missteps, inefficiency, and, on occasion, resounding defeats.

Africa thus became a textual as well as territorial crossroads, eliciting discrepant responses from late-Victorian poets. Two offer divergent views of what it meant for white British soldiers to fight against black in the Zulu War and the campaign against the Mahdi. In "The Fight at Rorke's Drift. January 23rd, 1879" (1882) Emily Pfeiffer, despite customary sensitivity to injustices faced by women, adopts an apparently untroubled assumption of British superiority over Zulu "savagery."[12] The fight at Rorke's Drift has remained in cultural memory, less because of Pfeiffer's poem than the film *Zulu* (1964), starring Stanley Baker and the young Michael Caine. Both the film and the narrative poem recount how a large Zulu force, having wiped out some 800 British soldiers at Isandhlwana, moved on to Rorke's Drift, where only 80 Britons and 30 to 40 soldiers in hospital held the fortification. They were attacked by 4,000 Zulu but held them off despite repeated onslaughts, until the Zulu withdrew. It had indeed been a remarkable feat of courage and endurance. But the film and poem do not call into question the imperial enterprise that instigated the fight. Nor does Pfeiffer in any way temper British heroism; in the film, in contrast, Lieutenant John Chard, later awarded the Victoria Cross, cynically comments on the questionable heroism of cutting down row after row of Zulu with British guns.

Pfeiffer's predominantly iambic heptameter helps drive the action onward, with end-stopped or enjambed lines alternately retarding or enforcing speed. Pfeiffer's principal image of a dark ocean wave that repeatedly attempts to swamp an island of pale faces underscores race and contrasts the overwhelming force of the Zulu with the puniness of young soldiers defending the station, whom she repeatedly refers to as "lads" (9, 12), "boys" (14), and "youngsters" (18). As Pfeiffer says of their achievement, "Those lads contemned Canute, and shamed the lesson that he read, – / For them the hungry waves withdrew, the howling ocean fled" (71–2) – an allusion to the tenth-century king who instanced the impossibility of holding back waves from the shore to demonstrate the limits of kingship. "[F]airer" (63) Europeans have triumphed over "savage faces" (29), and Pfeiffer ends by glorifying the island state from whence they come:

> Britannia, rule Britannia! while thy sons resemble thee,
> And are islanders, true islanders, wherever they may be;
> Islands fortified like this, manned with islanders like these,
> Will keep thee Lady of thy Land, and Sovereign of all Seas.   (73–6)[13]

Like Pfeiffer's narrative, the title of Kipling's "Fuzzy-Wuzzy," subtitled "(Soudan Expeditionary Force)," marks off racial difference in demeaning terms, and its chorus of soldiers tends to clump all but the Sudanese into an undifferentiated mass of racial Others:

> We took our chanst among the Kyber 'ills,
>   The Boers knocked us silly at a mile,
> The Burman give us Irriwaddy chills,
>   An' a Zulu *impi* dished us up in style:
> But all we ever got from such as they
>   Was pop to what the Fuzzy made us swaller.   (13–18)

If these battles map the British empire's reach from Burma and Afghanistan to South Africa, however, Kipling's soldiers, unlike the Pfeiffer persona, also narrate casualties inflicted by black soldiers on the British. Since they adopt hybrid language to do so, mixing not only the registers of heroic ballad and music hall's demotic slang but also English and foreign terms (*impi* is Zulu for army or detachment), the poem's linguistic texture also represents the ability of blacks to impose cultural markers on whites.

The poem in fact pays tribute to soldiers identified simultaneously as heathen and equals, sung by soldiers who do what official Britain will not, attest to the Sudanese men's skill and valor: "'E 'asn't got no medals nor rewards, / So *we* must certify the skill 'e's shown" (26–7). In a double sense the Sudanese thus exceed the reach of British imperialism and open a space beyond its physical and ideological force:

> 'E's a daisy, 'e's a ducky, 'e's a lamb!
>   'E's a injia-rubber idiot on the spree,
> 'E's the on'y thing that doesn't give a damn
>   For a Regiment o' British Infantree!
>   So 'ere's *to* you, Fuzzy-Wuzzy, at your 'ome in the Soudan;
>   You're a pore benighted 'eathen but a first-class fightin' man;
>   An' 'ere's *to* you, Fuzzy-Wuzzy, with your 'ayrick 'ead of 'air–
>   You big black boundin' beggar – for you broke a British square!
>   (41–8)

The entire passage is a welter of racism, imperialism, and admiration for social equals and military superiors. These contending forces are the poem's principal message: if racism compromises its transnational act of sympathetic identification, the identification itself saps the foundations of racial superiority on which late-Victorian imperialism rested.

Kipling's "Loot" (*Scots Observer* [March 29, 1890]) similarly cracks open the veneer of imperial ideology, this time to expose the rapaciousness and unheroic acts that marked Britain's imperial enterprise. The poem recounts a series of brutal acts committed by common soldiers, from murder and torture of natives to shaking them down for valuables, and the refrain's equation of "dogs an' men," and adjuration to "Tear 'im, puppy!" indicate the tawdry inhumanity at issue. If "Loot" attests to anarchic hooligans enlisted among British forces, their greed encounters no check but "mostly" collusion from "a Sergint an' a Quartermaster too" (49); and by the time they wish "good-luck to those that wears the Widow's clo'es," i.e., the Queen's uniform, "An' the Devil send 'em all they want o' loot!" (56–7), the chorus become paradigmatic rather than particular, exposing the greed and exploitation that infect empire from top to bottom. The music hall technique of rowdy chorus and punctuated horn toots also punctures the genteel surface of empire usually displayed in the press and public ceremony:

> But the service rules are 'ard, an' from such we are debarred,
> > For the same with English morals does not suit.
> > (*Cornet*: Toot! toot!)
> Why, they call a man a robber if 'e stuffs 'is marchin' clobber
> > With the –
> (*Chorus*)   Loo! loo! Lulu! lulu! Loo! loo! Lulu! Loot! loot! loot!
> > Ow the loot!
> > Bloomin' loot!
> > That's the thing to make the boys git up an' shoot!   (5–13)

Significantly, poet Robert Buchanan launched an attack on Kipling's *Barrack-Room Ballads* (which include "Fuzzy-Wuzzy" and "Loot") in 1899, after the second Boer War had erupted, complaining that Kipling celebrated "hooliganism" and "cockney ignorance."[14] It was an indication of how unsettling Kipling's work could be even as it entrenched the presence of empire in poetry.

On the eve of the Boer War two contrary voices anticipated the self-divisions the conflict would elicit at home. Henry Newbolt created a chant of empire and militant masculinity in "Vitaï lampada" (the torch of life), first published in 1897. Newbolt concisely limns two vivid tableaux, a cricket game and distant battle, connecting a quintessentially British game to British valor and honor. The cheering touch of a team captain who rouses a player when odds are against them – "But his Captain's hand on his shoulder smote – / 'Play up! play up! and play the game!'" (7–8) – finds its counterpart in a desperate desert scene when (as in "Fuzzy-Wuzzy") the square has been broken, "The Gatling's jammed and the Colonel dead" (11), and "the voice of a schoolboy rallies the ranks: / 'Play up! play up! and play the game!'" (15–16). Newbolt's poem entered cultural memory because of its concision, nostalgia, and adaptability to schoolrooms, not its subtlety, and the third stanza overtly teaches the moral:

> This is the word that year by year,
> While in her place the School is set,
> Every one of her sons must hear,
> And none that hears it dare forget.   (17–20)[15]

Newbolt's assertively homosocial tableaux are contested by a poem of greater conciseness published the prior year, Alice Meynell's "Parentage." In twelve lines Meynell provides a systemic feminist critique of empire, connects female acquiescence to complicity in oppression, and models female resistance by talking back to the historical source that forms her epigraph:

> *"When Augustus Caesar legislated against the unmarried citizens of Rome, he declared them to be, in some sort, slayers of the people."*
>
> Ah! no, not these!
> These, who were childless, are not they who gave
> So many dead unto the journeying wave,
> The helpless nurslings of the cradling seas;
> Not they who doomed by infallible decrees
> Unnumbered man to the innumerable grave.
>
> But those who slay
> Are fathers. Theirs are armies. Death is theirs –
> The death of innocences and despairs;
> The dying of the golden and the grey.
> The sentence, when these speak it, has no Nay.
> And she who slays is she who bears, who bears.

When government is exclusively masculine, as it was prior to women's suffrage, the moral responsibility for state-sanctioned slaughter is theirs, and the cradles women once rocked give way to young men's passive corpses that are "nurslings" tossed by "cradling" seas. In *Women and Labour* (1911) Olive Schreiner declared that dead soldiers were a horrific war tax on the unenfranchised women who gave birth to them. Meynell makes the point lyrically a decade-and-a-half earlier.

The rhetoric of Meynell's poem is as direct and teachable as Newbolt's until the last line, when the repeated "who bears" simultaneously indicates the sheer numbers of children born to die in war and women who "bear with" or endure the rule of men, until their compliant wombs come to resemble the sea that devours war casualties. Passive acquiescence in the status quo also obliquely connects mothers to their sons' inert corpses. In contrast to this unifying passivity, the play of language in Meynell's last line requires mobile minds, so that the most powerful effect of Meynell's poetic rhetoric occurs off the page in the minds of alert readers.

Thomas Hardy's poems on the Boer War, begun October 11, 1899, include some of his best-known, especially "Drummer Hodge" (1901), about a dead Wessex soldier whose bones will disintegrate beneath alien skies. "The Departure. (Southampton Docks: October 1899)," later renamed "The Embarcation" (1901), appeared in the October 25, 1899 *Daily Chronicle* just two weeks after war had been declared. Rather than asserting or critiquing empire, Hardy historicizes it, evoking in the first three lines as many different empires that had entered or left Britain through the same port: Vespasian's, which like Britain in late-nineteenth-century Africa annexed new territory in a distant colony from the south to the Scottish highlands; the Saxons, who under Cerdic extended into Wessex; and Henry V, whose naval invasion of France began at Southampton and was capped by the historic triumph at Agincourt. The allusion to Henry and, by association, his patriotic oration in Shakespeare's *Henry V* ("Once more unto the breech ... for Harry, England, and Saint George!" [III.i.1, 34]) sets up a framework for patriotism that Hardy then proceeds to undo.

For in the context of prior empires the current, "Vaster battalions press[ing] for further strands" (5) testifies only to the absence of progress in human nature, despite its enhanced technology and institutions. Victoria's troops, like Vespasian's almost 2,000 years earlier on the same spot, merely "argue in the selfsame bloody mode / Which this late age of thought, and pact, and code, / Still fails to mend" (6–8). Looking ahead, the poet foresees no triumph or defeat, only "the tragical To-be" (11). The sole certainty of war is that people will die – hence the encapsulation of life and death in the simile he fashions for soldiers marching past: "Yellow as autumn leaves, alive as spring" (9). The "To-be" is also tragic because of its very repetitiveness; as in Meynell's poem, human obtuseness allows young soldiers to embark "None dubious of the cause, none murmuring" (12). Hardy ends with the families, the feminized bystanders who illustrate the human capacity to see yet not see at the same time: "Wives, sisters, parents, wave white hands and smile, / As if they knew not that they weep the while" (13–14).

Hardy's choice of the sonnet evokes love, here of country and sons, and philosophically poses the questions the young soldiers do not and cannot ask.

Hardy's most powerful technique, however, is setting the young soldiers' departure against the historical backdrop of millennia, giving the lie to the dogma of European progress on which exploitation of Africa was based. Newbolt's spirited comrades here become tools used by the state, as in Meynell, and like Meynell Hardy hints at the harmful effect of women's acquiescence in state policy. But his historical distancing enables him to pull back and comment as well on the tragedy of human existence itself, which outlasts the war at hand.

Imperial obliquity

D. G. Rossetti and Tennyson also turned to history to consider empires and their meaning. Rossetti's "The Burden of Nineveh," first published in the August, 1856 *Oxford and Cambridge Magazine*, then substantially revised in his 1870 *Poems*, meditates on successive waves of lives, empires, faiths, and art from within the British Museum as the Assyrian winged bull-gods excavated by A. H. Layard in the 1840s arrive for installation. The complex situation is signaled by the title, which refers simultaneously to the literal load, or burden, of the ancient relics shipped to the museum; the significance of the past bearing upon the present; the tragic fate of all empires; and, since "burden" can designate both a poetic refrain and motif, the poem's theme and potential secondariness as merely recurring words. Lest readers miss these resonances Rossetti affixed a headnote to the magazine version of the poem: "'*Burden.* Heavy calamity; the chorus of a song.' – *Dictionary.*"

Like the imperial state, the imperial museum is empowered to wrest tributes from antiquity or enfeebled states and interpret their meaning. Since the Great Exhibition of 1851 had included a court devoted to Nineveh because of public interest in Layard's work, the poem tacitly gestures toward that earlier imperial landmark as well, and to the commerce undergirding empire – an association more evident in Rossetti's references to "cold-pinch'd clerks" (servants of commerce), and the print commodities of "'Layard's Nineveh'" and *Punch* in the 1856 text (1856: 66, 70, 74).[16]

The principal "burden" of Rossetti's poem is transience – the disappearance of Nineveh beneath the dust of centuries until Layard arrived; the similar disappearance of the great civilizations of "Greece, Egypt, Rome" (1870: 86); the eclipse of gods once worshiped in earnest; and the likelihood that Britain, too, one day will lapse:

> That future of the best or worst
> When some may question which was first,

Of London or of Nineveh.
For as that Bull-god once did stand
And watched the burial-clouds of sand,
Till these at last without a hand
Rose o'er his eyes, another land,
And blinded him with destiny: –
So may he stand again; till now,
In ships of unknown sail and prow,
Some tribe of the Australian plough
Bear him afar, – a relic now
Of London, not of Nineveh!   (1870: 168–80)

The echo of Shelley's "Ozymandias," which represents the shattered statue of an ancient king inscribed with his assertion of invincible power, obliquely suggests the similar hubris of the British empire. As the poet imagines later eras confronting this relic of Victorian London and assuming that the race of Britons "walked not in Christ's lowly ways, / But bowed its pride and vowed its praise / Unto the God of Nineveh" (1870: 188–90), the bull-god (semantically linked to that figure of Englishness, John Bull) becomes a trope of British empire in its aspiration, power, and ultimate futility. In all these respects Rossetti's poem, like Hardy's "The Departure," takes a specific imperial moment in the present, juxtaposes it to an ancient past, and thereby suggests the empire's inevitable demise.

Unlike Hardy, Rossetti also shifts the ground of his poem toward myth, especially in moving from the 1856 to the 1870 version. The 1856 poem opens with the jumble of cities and museums that makes it difficult to see larger patterns of significance: "I have no taste for polyglot: / At the Museum 'twas my lot, / Just once, to jot and blot and rot" (1856: 1–3). This was replaced in 1870 with a glance toward the museum's Elgin Marbles and, by association, Keats's encounter with Grecian relics in "Ode on a Grecian Urn":

In our Museum galleries
To-day I lingered o'er the prize
Dead Greece vouchsafes to living eyes, –
Her Art for ever in fresh wise
From hour to hour rejoicing me.
Sighing I turned at last to win
Once more the London dirt and din.   (1870: 1–7)

Here urban dailiness is less the object of critique than the antithesis of art, which can transcend time. If the anxious glance toward Keats again suggests worrisome belatedness, it also alerts readers to the possibility that Rossetti's own song aspires to myth that can absorb and transmute the jumble of quotidian London and museum display cases into lasting statement. Indeed, his text becomes a literary museum through its multiple echoes of Keats, Shelley, Byron, the Bible, and the "mythic chain of verse" (1870: 82) he imagines sung before the winged bull-god in Assyrian Nineveh. Rivaling the bricks and mortar of the museum in its ability to encompass diverse "relics" (1870: 107), the poem also serves as a textual Rosetta (or Rossetti) Stone more accurately interpreting British culture to future generations than its material artifacts. The attainment of "Burden of Nineveh" to myth is dubious, but in its shift toward myth – which is repetitive, polyglot, yet able to live beyond the civilization that generates it – Rossetti fashioned a key strategy for poetic response to the British empire.

Perhaps the exemplary poem of empire, in both regressive and positive senses, is *Idylls of the King*, issued in parts from 1859 to 1885 but first begun in 1842 with "Morte d'Arthur" and "The Epic." The completed *Idylls* is literally framed by empire. The 1861 "Dedication" terms Prince Albert "Scarce other than my king's ideal knight" (6) and pays tribute to Albert's role in the Great Exhibition: "Far-sighted summoner of War and Waste / To fruitful strifes and rivalries of peace" (36–7). "To the Queen," added to the 1873 Library Edition of Tennyson's works, expressly states an imperial code of conduct for all citizens:

> The loyal to their crown
> Are loyal to their own far sons, who love
> Our ocean-empire with her boundless homes
> For ever-broadening England, and her throne
> In our vast Orient.   (27–31)

The symbolic patterning that emerged in the 1869 *Idylls*, moreover, spurred some commentators to identify Tennyson's achievement with British cultural greatness. James T. Knowles, Tennyson's friend and personal architect, analyzed the poem's symbolism in a letter to the editor of the *Spectator*: "King Arthur ... stands ... for ... the 'King within us' – our highest nature, by whatsoever name it may be called – conscience; spirit; the moral soul; the religious sense; the noble resolve. His story and adventures become the story of the battle and preeminence of the soul and of the perpetual warfare between the spirit and the flesh." Simultaneously Knowles asserted the Englishness of the poem, comparing its gradual growth over time to the formation of a Gothic cathedral such as Canterbury.[17] *Victoria Magazine*, similarly, contended that "it is a distinction of glory, both of the poet, and of the nineteenth century, in which he writes, that he has made his prime hero to be a man of pure and lofty character, and his goodness to be of such a type, so gracious, and so chivalrous, as to win for it the love and enthusiastic reverence of all who read of it."[18]

The poem overtly rehearses imperial themes, moreover. The earliest act of the mythic British king is to consolidate an empire, drawing "many a petty king" under his dominion, clearing "great tracts of wilderness," and defeating the "heathen horde" ("Coming of Arthur," 5, 10, 36). "Wolf-like men" who inhabit uncivilized wildernesses and heathens who "on the spike that split the mother's heart / Spitt[ed] the child" ("Coming of Arthur," 32, 38–9) suggest both evolutionary primitives and the atrocities of mutinous Indians who require the firm governance of a Christian king. Finally, the emphasis on Arthur's fair skin and blue eyes ("Coming of Arthur," 329; "Passing of Arthur," 337) introduces racial politics into the poem, unmistakably associating Arthur with Anglo-Saxon Englishmen rather than Celts or dark heathens. Downplaying their own links to Celticism to celebrate empire, the 1860 *Dublin University Magazine* and *Blackwood's Edinburgh Magazine* compared Arthurian knights to British soldiers in India or the Crimea.[19]

Indirectly, too, the poem acts to consolidate Britain's imperial power. As Herbert Tucker notes, in requiring readers to condemn Guinevere for an adulterous (hence treasonous) act that is never narrated, the poem models the consensual process of the state, requiring citizens' assent to what they have not fully examined or even accessed.[20] Several elements consolidate the imperial foundations of *Idylls of the King*: the parallels between Arthur and Christ, which prompted William Gladstone to declare in the 1859 *Quarterly Review* that Tennyson's subject is "national: it is Christian ... [and] though highly national, it is universal";[21] the work's recruitment of domestic affections and ideology into imperial service, so that Guinevere's placing desire above domestic duty threatens the hierarchy on which "orderly" marriage and empire depend; and the association of technology with a thriving empire, since Merlin is an engineer and scientist as well as artist and statesman ("Merlin and Vivien," 165–7).

But Tennyson's allegiance to imagination and myth as well as to empire leads him everywhere to question and subvert the empire he also upholds. Alongside the symbolic design of Arthur as a type of Christ, for example, Tennyson integrates a recurring cycle of seasons. Insofar as spring suggests life resurrected out of wintry death the seasonal cycle enforces Christian meaning. But in shifting toward purely natural description it also suggests the pagan vegetation gods soon to be documented by anthropologist James Frazer in *The Golden Bough* (1890). If the seasonal motif suggests lives and kingdoms that flourish and pass it also invokes historicism and, as in Rossetti's and Hardy's imperial poems, the inevitable fall rather than enduring greatness of the British empire. The overdetermined patterning of "The

Coming" and "The Passing of Arthur" likewise impart inevitability to Arthur's fall, loosening the mediating force of individual faith or betrayal and subordinating moral and political tragedy to impersonal forces that oddly resemble the materialist philosophy of Tristram in "The Last Tournament," whose armor "all in forest green, whereon / There tript a hundred tiny silver deer, / And ... holly-spray for crest, / With ever-scattering berries" ("The Last Tournament," 170–2) signifies the vagaries of Darwinian survival. In "The Passing of Arthur" the dying king repeats the credo of his advent, "The old order changeth, yielding place to new" ("Coming of Arthur," 508; "Passing of Arthur," 408), now adding, "And God fulfils himself in many ways, / Lest one good custom should corrupt the world" ("Passing of Arthur," 409–10). The logic of Tennyson's mythic design and literary sources demands this echo. But if even a "good custom" can "corrupt" a world and will fall apart like others before it, no empire can claim exceptional status. Nor can a doctrine of progress be tenable.

Proliferating echoes and doublings in Tennyson's Arthuriad likewise undermine unitary imperial meaning. Pelleas, who comes to a court past its prime, counterbalances Gareth, who arrives during its springtime and fairly romps to victory over a series of brothers impersonating day, noon, evening, and death – the very life span that at the end of the poem so threatens the realm and Arthur's lasting achievement. Gareth, though disguised as a kitchen-knave, wins a noblewoman, for in these early days faith and meritocracy prevail over all challenges.

Pelleas is as innocent and idealistic as Gareth, as willing as Arthur to look for good in people. But when he devotes himself to Ettarre as his lady love and Gawain as brother knight, then is callously betrayed by both, he is unhinged by the disillusionment and becomes Arthur's dark counterpart, the Red Knight of the North who wars against the king he once reverenced and resembled. Arthur's defeat of the Red Knight is pyrrhic, for the barbaric slaughter of the rebels by Arthur's unseasoned troops is indistinguishable from heathen atrocities that earlier marked off his Christian realm from pagans:

> [Arthur's knights] slimed themselves:
> Nor heard the King for their own cries, but sprang
> Through open doors, and swording right and left
> Men, women, on their sodden faces, hurled
> The tables over and the wines, and slew
> Till all the rafters rang with woman-yells,
> And all the pavement streamed with massacre.
>
> ("The Last Tournament," 470–6)

"Massacre," that word so strongly associated with the 1857 Indian uprising, is here applied to the troops of the king who, in Gladstone's words, was eminently "national" and "Christian." The scene in fact recalls British excesses after Delhi was stormed. Tennyson's imagination thus takes him well beyond imperial borders into the irreducible contradictions of human psychology that refuse to settle neatly within ideological parameters.

Even the length at which Tennyson plumbs the realm's undoing in contrast to the brevity of its efflorescence testifies to a pessimistic, tragic vision at odds with staunch patriotism and unreflecting imperial duty. Like the Indian poems of his fellow poet and friendly critic Alfred Lyall, Tennyson created a profoundly contrapuntal, divided perspective on empire that questioned what it affirmed, undid what it ratified. By resorting to myth, not history, Tennyson also created a poem that enjoyed a wide readership even after critical opinion shifted away from it at the century's end. The *Idylls* thus exemplies the doubts inspired by empire as well as its aspirations. "To the Queen" may state an imperial code of conduct, but Tennyson arrives at that message by way of narrating a lapse of imperial duty (from the suggestions that Canada be relinquished). And its closing lines raise spectres that were more likely to dim than propel celebrations of British power in 1873:

> some are scared, who mark,
> Or wisely or unwisely, signs of storm,
> Waverings of every vane with every wind,
> And wordy trucklings to the transient hour,
> And fierce or careless looseners of the faith,
> And Softness breeding scorn of simple life,
> Or Cowardice, the child of lust for gold,
> Or Labour, with a groan and not a voice,
> Or Art with poisonous honey stolen from France,
> And that which knows, but careful for itself,
> And that which knows not, ruling that which knows
> To its own harm: the goal of this great world
> Lies beyond sight: yet – if our slowly-grown
> And crowned Republic's crowning common-sense,
> That saved her many times, not fail – their fears
> Are morning shadows huger than the shapes
> That cast them, not those gloomier which forego
> The darkness of that battle in the West,
> Where all of high and holy dies away.   (48–66)

Even in the presence of his queen the demise of empire gets the last word and best line, an encapsulation of the vexed relation of poetry and empire.

Chapter 8

Poetic liberties

But the arm of the elders is broken, their strength is unbound and undone.

> A. C. Swinburne, "A Song in Time of Revolution. 1860."
> (*Spectator* [June 28, 1862])

I read a score of books on womanhood
To prove, if women do not think at all,
They may teach thinking.

> Elizabeth Barrett Browning, *Aurora Leigh*, Book 1 (1856)

I am that thing
Called half a dozen dainty names, and none
Dainty enough to serve the turn and hide
The one coarse English worst that lurks beneath.

> Augusta Webster, "A Castaway" (1870)

Expressing solidarity with foreign revolution could indirectly critique British tyranny and shore up the cause of liberty at home, as in Swinburne's "A Song in Time of Revolution. 1860," written in response to the Italian uprising against Austrian rule. Earlier Ernest Jones had celebrated the outbreak of revolutions from Italy and Poland to Paris in the 1848 *Labourer*: "The nations are all calling, / To and fro, from strand to strand; / Uniting in one army."[1] When he gave a speech that advocated flying a Chartist flag over parliament, however, Jones was arrested and spent two years in solitary confinement without pens or paper (and only scant food). Undaunted, he continued to write poems with his own blood in the margins of his cell prayer book and published them on his release. *The New World* is a long utopian narrative that envisions the systemic interdependence of imperialism, capitalism, and war giving way to a just world order founded upon individual liberty and science. Not only does *The New World* mock authorities who imprisoned Jones in a nation ostensibly free – "You have a right to meet petitioning still, – / Just when we choose, – and say – just what we will" – but it also seeks to envision British India through Indian eyes, unmasking official goals to "civilise, reform, redeem!" as "We murdered millions to enrich the few." Moreover, Jones foresees a time when "Sepoy soldiers, waking, band by band, / At last remember they've a fatherland!" and triumph over British oppressors because "God, hope, and history take the Hindhû side!"[2] When Sepoy soldiers indeed rose in 1857, Jones retitled his poem *The Revolt of Hindostan; or, The New World: A Poem*, reprinted it, and supported the rebels' cause.

Jones's refusal to be silenced and his systematic critique of British policy clarify why Karl Marx, exiled in London, should have singled out Jones as "the most talented, consistent and energetic representative of Chartism" he knew.[3] Becoming closely associated with Marx and Friedrich Engels, and contributing poems to the *Red Republican* – the journal in which the first English translation of Marx's *Communist Manifesto* was published in 1850 – Jones exemplifies the shift from Chartism to class consciousness and new radical movements dedicated to overthrowing the capitalist system. Three decades later William Morris, who read Marx's *Das Kapital* in a French translation, likewise coupled political activism with socialist songs and narrative poems. Anarchism, too, found poetic voice at the century's end, in *Liberty Lyrics*, published in 1895 by Louisa Bevington.

More modest reform goals also served as a catalyst for poetry. The Langham Place Circle of the 1850s and 1860s, led by Bessie Parkes, Barbara Bodichon, and Emily Davies, founded the *English Woman's Journal* and later *Victoria Magazine* to provide a voice for women's commitment to educational, economic, and legal reforms. Since the circle included poets Adelaide Procter and Mary Howitt, there was a direct link between poetry and new liberties for women just as poetry was inseparable from Chartism and socialism.

Altogether a strong current of progressive Victorian poetry existed alongside (and challenged) poems that reflected or reinforced the status quo in the state, empire, church, and society. John Stuart Mill's *On Liberty* (1859), *On the Subjection of Women* (1869), and posthumous "Chapters on Socialism" (*Fortnightly Review* [February and April, 1879]) respectively define liberty as the right to do anything that inflicts no active harm on others, advocate full legal and social equality for women, and consider alternatives to capitalism. Such work by a pre-eminent Victorian philosopher had poetic counterparts that likewise sought to envision unencumbered liberty for the society, the individual, and poetry itself. If poets championed liberty in overt political rhetoric or, more subtly, by imagining new social conditions and human development, public debate and political action in turn helped extend the range of the sayable in poetry, an effect already evident when Wordsworth declared, following the French Revolution, that a poet was a man speaking to men and that "humble" life was as profound in its poetic possibilities as heroic or privileged lives. The pressure to admit an ever-greater range of diction and subject matter into poems is another feature of nineteenth-century poetry; from Robert Browning's experiments with language to Swinburne's poems on necrophilia and sado-masochistic pleasure, poets not only supported new freedoms but also took liberties with traditional poetic decorum.

Liberty abroad

To Victorians, Matthew Reynolds observes, Italy could signify a landscape, tourist destination, aesthetic zone, site of Catholic superstition, former empire, or country under the heel of the Austrians.[4] If these multiple associations were useful to poets generally, Italy was an especially productive topic for women, who by moving the scene away from England could exercise their imaginations free of home-bound restrictions. Moreover, since Italy was often personified as an oppressed woman and since all Italians (like British women) were denied the rights of citizenship under Austrian rule, women could obliquely touch on their own dilemmas while exercising the role of sympathy so vital to Victorian poetics and bourgeois femininity.

The most notable response to the Italian Risorgimento ("resurgence"), which eventually led to the expulsion of the Austrians and the unification of Italy in 1861, is *Casa Guidi Windows* (1851) by Barrett Browning. Part I, a prophecy of new liberty and the people's triumph, responds to events of September, 1847, when Grand-Duke Leopold of Tuscany established a national guard as a first step toward a constitution, and a massive procession supporting Italian liberty passed before the Brownings' home at Casa Guidi in Florence. Barrett Browning's attempt to publish this work in *Blackwood's Magazine* in 1848 was rebuffed and later events then overtook her poem. Leopold, who granted a constitution in 1848 and speechified about Italian liberty, fled when the revolution that broke out in Sicily and spread elsewhere faltered; worse, he colluded with Austria and Pope Pius IX (whose brief support of the movement evaporated when a secular Roman republic seemed possible) to re-establish Austrian occupation. Part II was thus written and the whole published in 1851 as a retrospect on revolution and poetic prophecy. A meditation on how to continue seeking liberty in the face of failure, *Casa Guidi Windows* is structured to enact poetically the politics that Barrett Browning advocates.

Her politics are also indebted to her poetics. Like Romantic predecessors, she conceived of poetic imagination or genius as participating in divinity and capable, like God, of creating new outer forms from inward being. Hence innovation, the disruptively new, is a key manifestation of genius and creativity, just as in politics revolutions break with old forms. Yet the organicist conceptual framework she imbibed from Coleridge had also inspired the political theory of Edmund Burke, who in *Reflections on the Revolution in France* (1790) rejected radical revolution because new forms of governance must emerge developmentally from the old. Barrett Browning in both her poetics and politics mediates between revolution and continuity, freedom and law, democracy and inspired leaders, just as a window – her vantage point on the political events unfolding before her – mediates between inside and outside.[5]

Such mediation is evident in her Preface. She terms *Casa Guidi Windows* a "story of personal impressions," implying a developmental plot, yet provides "No continuous narrative"; she expresses "shame" for having "believed, like a woman, some royal oaths," then connects "discrepancies" between belief and actuality to universal human nature and its shared "interval between aspiration and performance, between faith and disillusion, between hope and fact." If she quotes a "broken prophecy" from Ralph Waldo Emerson's elegy for his dead son, "Threnody," thus obliquely introducing the crucial motif of the child, she also ends by reaffirming her original prophecy: "The future of Italy shall not be disinherited."[6]

In the poem itself she immediately fuses poetics and politics by considering the song needed to enunciate a new political vision. A child singing "*O bella libertà, O bella*" sets her song in motion, and rather than recirculating the tired metaphor of Italy as a tragic, suffering woman – a Niobe or Juliet – she follows the example of the child:

> The hopeful child, with leaps to catch his growth,
> Sings open-eyed for liberty's sweet sake!
> And I, a singer also from my youth,
> Prefer to sing with these who are awake.
> ...
> We do not serve the dead – the past is past.
> God lives, and lifts His glorious mornings up
> Before the eyes of men awake at last.   (1.153–6, 217–19)

Just as the biblical music of Jubal gave way to Miriam's and David's songs (1.307–19), just as great Renaissance artists welcomed those who surpassed them (1.362–96), so she now stands "in Italy to-day / Where worthier poets stood and sang before, / I kiss their footsteps yet their words gainsay" (1.49–51). She similarly gainsays the old political order to welcome the new, locating legitimacy not in hereditary rule but in the people's power: "IL POPOLO [the people], – / The word means dukedom, empire, majesty, / And kings in such an hour might read it so" (1.499–501). She also claims that "Better means freer. A land's brotherhood / Is most puissant" (1.658–9) while endorsing both brotherhood and the people's right to rule by figuring the people as a lion: "Roar, therefore! shake your dewlaps dry abroad" (1.670).

These were sentiments and images also circulating in contemporary Chartist verse. Though Part I was ostensibly rejected from *Blackwood's* on the grounds of too much sympathy for Pius IX, its similarity to Chartist sentiments at a time when revolutions were breaking out in Europe and Chartists were marching in England may have made the poem seem dangerous, especially given Barrett Browning's critical prestige after her 1844 *Poems*. Nor was her endorsement of the people's power, rights, and brotherhood the only similarity between *Casa Guidi Windows* and Chartist poems. As in much Chartist verse, Part I asserts the danger of complicity with oppressive rulers ("Austrian Metternich / Can fix no yoke unless the neck agree," 1.662–3), cites papal history to instance the dangers posed by an allied priesthood and king ("priests, trained to rob, / And kings that, like encouraged nightmares, sat / On nations' hearts," 1.907–9), terms "Heroic daring … true success" (1.1215), and above all prophesies the triumph of "this great cause of southern men who strive / In God's name for man's rights, and shall not fail" (1.1201–2).

Very much unlike Chartist poets, however, and like Carlyle in *Heroes and Hero-Worship* (1840), Barrett Browning also contends that success requires a great leader, "God's light organised / In some high soul, crowned capable to lead / The conscious people" (1.761–3), who can inspire

> into all this people round,
> Instead of passion, thought, which pioneers
> All generous passion, purifies from sin,
>   And strikes the hour for. Rise up, teacher! here's
> A crowd to make a nation!   (1.769–73)

Whoever the inspired leader may be, he will require an inspired poet as his compatriot. For the poet's visionary powers can "through all burst and bruits / Of popular passion" continue "Annunciative, reproving, pure, erect," showing the leader "which way your first Ideal bare" (1.1092–3,

1096–7). Alongside her embrace of the people's revolution, rights, and power, then, the poet in Part I also looks for political and poetic geniuses who will effectively hold the people in check. She is even willing momentarily to uphold the authority of Duke and Pope (though highly dubious about both) to achieve a people's freedom.

But of course all comes to naught. As the poet of Part II announces, "I wrote a meditation and a dream, / Hearing a little child sing in the street" (2.1–2). Now she wonders if all Florentines acted the part merely of "little children" who "take up a high strain" only to "sleep upon their mothers' knees again" – though "We thinkers, who have thought for thee, and failed" or "poets, wandered round by dreams" (2.10, 12, 17, 19), did no better. In such admissions the poet risks loss of credibility as poet and as a woman carried away by naïve enthusiasm to support the Grand-Duke: "Absolve me, patriots, of my woman's fault / That ever I believed the man was true!" (2.64–5). But the danger she runs by retaining rather than cutting or revising Part I is her most innovative poetic strategy. Yoking the two parts enables her to forge a "story" from an otherwise discontinuous narrative and to enact her poetics and politics more fully. For the conjoined parts turn the "new" song of Part I into the old out of which a yet newer song must emerge, suggesting ongoing process rather than abortive failure. Moreover, though she excoriates Italians for their "want / Of soul-conviction," their "aims dispersed, / And incoherent means, and valour scant / Because of scanty faith," as well as their "schisms accursed / That wrench these brother-hearts from covenant / With freedom and each other" (2.527–32), Part II newly democratizes poetry and politics by unseating the poet and great leader from their privileged positions above the people in Part I and creating new solidarity with them.

Like the people the poet, too, has failed to be taught, in her case by the past:

> I much repent that, in this time and place
> Where many corpse-lights of experience burn
> From Cæsar's and Lorenzo's festering race,
> To enlighten groping reasoners, I could learn
> No better counsel for a simple case
> Than to put faith in princes ...
> Forgive me, ghosts of patriots, – Brutus, thou,
> Who trailest downhill into life again
> Thy blood-weighted cloak, to indict me with thy slow,
> Reproachful eyes! – for being taught in vain.   (2.70–5, 82–5)

If in Part II she is learning from the mistakes of her first hopes for Italy's freedom, she sees that the people have likewise learned from the immediate past and will no longer invest their hopes for future liberty in the Grand-Duke or, more especially, in the Pope: "Whatsoever deeds they be, / Pope Pius will be glorified in none. / Record that gain, Mazzini!" (2.440–2). But neither does she glorify the republican Mazzini, another potential leader for the future, whose authority she circumscribes by terming him an "extreme theorist" (2.573). Though this characterization might suggest Burkean views (since Burke is hostile to theory in *Reflections on the Revolution*), poetically the epithet enables her to enact newly learned reluctance to trust any leader entirely. As she mediates between failure and gain, old and new truths, so she also mediates – and lessens – the distance between leaders and the people they would inspire.

If succeeding events cast doubt on the revolutionary powers and politics that poetic imagination hailed in Part I, Barrett Browning ultimately reaffirms both through her poem's inward logic. If Part I is a poetic revolution, a new song of Italy that rewrites old tropes, time's passage transforms it into a past from which she learns and out of which she develops a still newer song. Similarly, those who have died fighting in the 1848 revolution, the "patriot Dead" who "only have done well," comprise "seeds of life" that will inspire future fights for liberty (2.657–8, 663), for they will also

> encumber
> The sad heart of the land until it loose
> The clammy clods and let out the Spring-growth
> In beatific green through every bruise.
> The tyrant should take heed to what he doth,
> Since every victim-carrion turns to use,
> And drives a chariot, like a god made wroth,
> Against each piled injustice.   (2.663–70)

The figure of the child, moreover, continues to harbor divine wisdom and anticipate the future. As she gazes upon her English son born in the interval between Parts I and II (a further inscription of ongoing process), she deems him a "blue-eyed prophet" (2.757) and asks him to "Teach me to hope for, what the angels know / When they smile clear as thou dost" (2.750–1), namely, that "New springs of life are gushing everywhere" and bring "Motions" that "signify but growth" (2.762, 766). Italian children, like her own, thus represent "Posterity … smiling on our knees" (2.774). By linking the Italian child singing *"bella libertà"* at the beginning to the English child on which light shines through Casa Guidi windows at the end, Barrett Browning unifies her poetic structure within which the childlike Italians of Part II who failed in their first attempt at revolution but learn from it are aligned with the childlike poet who initially failed to learn from the past and now learns from past and future alike. Insofar as the poet-mother is also linked to past and future through her child and freshly recognizes that posterity emerges from the newly dead past of 1848–9, then poetic prophecy is validated after all:

> I, who first took hope up in this song,
> Because a child was singing one ... behold,
> The hope and omen were not, haply, wrong!
> Poets are soothsayers still.   (2.736–9)

Casa Guidi Windows thus mediates between tradition and revolution, genius and the people, and womanly fallibility and female powers of vision and maternity. Even her poetic medium, the Sicilian sestet (*ababab*), subserves poetic and political mediation. If Barrett Browning adapts the traditional sestet she innovates upon it, rejecting a customary six-stanza poem to unfold long verse paragraphs regulated by inward thought rather than inherited limits. The Sicilian sestet's three alternating rhymes likewise register recurrence and continuity but also enact incremental change with the fresh triple rhymes of each new sestet. The form looks to the past, then, including sonnet tradition, but can also suggest revolution, for it was in Palermo, Sicily, that revolution first broke out in 1848 before spreading northward.

After 1851 three principal leaders of the Risorgimento emerged: Giuseppe Garibaldi, the heroic fighter of 1848–9 who in 1860 liberated Sicily and Naples from Bourbon rule and made Italian unification possible; Camillo Cavour, the Prime Minister of Piedmont who relied on ceaseless negotiation and coalitions to create favorable conditions for a unified free Italy; and Giuseppe Mazzini, the radical republican forced into exile in England from 1837 until the 1848 revolution, and again after it failed, but who led resistance to Austria through his journalism and political organizing.

Even though Swinburne shared the republican principles of Mazzini, his personal hero since Oxford undergraduate days, Swinburne sets aside specific leaders in "A Song in Time of Revolution. 1860." He glances toward Garibaldi's liberation of Naples and Sicily in affixing "1860" to his title, but otherwise generalizes the principle of revolution across national boundaries and subordinates political analysis to lyricism. As he told William Bell Scott in January, 1861, "I think it about my best lyrical piece of work."[7] Devoting scant attention to those waging revolution beyond noting the sounds of their feet, laughter, and shouting, Swinburne instead concentrates on priests and kings.

But this strategy is central to his purpose: the poem is a performative song that defrocks priests, displaces kings, and ritually executes both. Lyricism and revolutionary action thus coalesce. Swinburne establishes this frame of reference in his opening anapestic couplets:

> The heart of the rulers is sick, and the high-priest covers his head:
> For this is the song of the quick that is heard in the ears of the dead.
>
> The poor and the halt and the blind are keen and mighty and fleet:
> Like the noise of the blowing of wind is the sound of the noise of
>   their feet.   (1–4)

His second line fashions song into an instrument bringing death to kings and priests, for only when they are already dead do they hear it. Line 3 stages the reversals and upended order crucial to revolutions, since the formerly weak and excluded now command power. And line 4 establishes the crucial metaphoric and performative framework of the poem. Just as the rhythm of marching feet parallels poetic meter, the "wind" itself has long figured breath and utterance. Both the poet and revolutionaries, then, are conjoined to sound and to each other in the verbal music and cadences of Swinburne's verse; and the recurring wind carrying sound to the frightened priests and kings is at once an invisible, unstoppable force of revolution and, self-referentially, the sounds of the poem itself.

When the wind in which they are joined "is thwart in [the] feet" of kings and priests (33), obstructing and felling them, the song and wind become a smiting sword that kills:

> The sword, the sword is made keen; the iron has opened its mouth;
> The corn is red that was green; it is bound for the sheaves of the south.
>
> The sound of a word was shed, the sound of the wind as a breath
> In the ears of the souls that were dead, in the dust of the deepness of death;
> …
> Where the sword was covered and hidden, and dust had grown in its side,
> A word came forth which was bidden, the crying of one that cried:
>
> The sides of the two-edged sword shall be bare, and its mouth shall be red,
> For the breath of the face of the Lord that is felt in the bones of the
>   dead.   (35–8, 43–6)

The exulting song that unloosens the bones of kings shares the anapests and sadistic pleasures of "Dolores," and it is no surprise that Edmund Gosse later remembered undergraduates shouting out stanzas of "Dolores" and "Song in Time of Revolution" along Cambridge streets.[8] But in "Song in Time of Revolution" sadism and affronts to elders serve a more directly political purpose and imbue lyricism itself with political force.

In both Barrett Browning's and Swinburne's poems devoted to the Risorgimento poetic structure, metaphor, and music are intrinsic to politics, not a decorative flourish added to political declamation. Adopting a range of stances, the poems tacitly challenge each other while engaging events and struggles beyond poetry's bounds. Barrett Browning ends *Casa Guidi Windows* by critiquing Britain's imperialistic displays at the Great Exhibition and domestic obsession with property (which has also thwarted Italians' risking all for freedom). In *Poems and Ballads* Swinburne groups his political poems of 1866 amidst rather than separate from those that inspired most outrage, especially "Anactoria" and "Dolores," calling attention to the politics of domestic decorum and censorship as well as of kings and priests by this juxtaposition.

Liberty at home

After the failure of Chartism in 1848 there were no more mass demonstrations demanding new liberties. But the remaining decades were not politically quiescent – nor free of smaller-scale political action. Eliza Cook's "A Song for the Workers (Written for the Early Closing Movement)," which avers that "Right is up and asking / Loudly for a juster lot" (57–8), was included in her 1853 *Poems*; and Ernest Jones, Ellen Johnston, Janet Hamilton, and Joseph Skipsey continued to keep workers' issues before readers. Henry Mayhew's *London Labour and the London Poor*, initially serialized in the *Morning Chronicle* (October 19, 1849–December 12, 1850), then continued in weekly installments (December 14, 1850–February 21, 1852), extended middle-class interest in workers' lives. Only very gradually did urban workers enter poetry as distinct individuals, however.

Arthur Munby, a graduate of Trinity College, Cambridge and son of a wealthy solicitor, is best known for his photographs of Hannah Cullwick. Aroused by the sight of women performing manual labor, he eventually married Cullwick, a maid-of-all-work, but kept their marriage secret, allowing Hannah to continue servant's duties in their household.[9] Though committed to dubious class politics in his marriage, Munby nonetheless confronted and unsettled readers with his realistic portrayals of what it meant to scrub, wash, and carry away ashes so that middle-class families could enjoy clean homes. As the late-Victorian poet Philip Bourke Marston reports, Munby's "anger has been aroused because writers who treat of persons in humble life have too much idealized them – have not sufficiently insisted on the hard, red, and oftentimes dirty hands which are incident to manual labor."[10] Rather than fetishizing dirt, as some of Munby's photographs and poems do, "'Followers not Allowed'" (*Once a Week* [January 7,

1865], illustrated G. J. Pinwell) exposes middle-class hypocrisy and argues for greater justice for servants.

Munby situates the poem between poetry and the prosaic by yoking an irregular meter that reads like prose with an *abab* rhyme scheme. But his shrewdest strategy is adopting the dramatic monologue and its capacity for irony to expose the class prejudice and exploitive practices of the former mistress of servant Hannah Cullender. At first the employer seems to champion Hannah's dignity, importuning her middle-class friends to listen to Hannah's words even if Hannah is a "coarse and homely ... very drudge," the "lines of grace ... shockingly distorted" in her "clumsy frame."[11] The former mistress is concerned that on holiday Hannah spoke to strange men on the streets, though Hannah ("and mind, / She said it meekly" [30–1]) assures her that she's no younger than her mistress was when she married: "It's the taking wage, / And doing work, and bothering, that tells, / And makes one coarse. But still, it makes us strong" (36–8).

Making use of this assertive strength, Hannah contrasts the mistress's rules for her daughter, who with a brewer "was free to court, like anything: / Why, things was left o' purpose, as I heard, / For them to meet" (43–5), with servants' rules: "My misiss play'd a different game to that: / 'Twas, 'Oh, no! There's no followers allow'd / In *this* house'" (48–50). Fearful of losing her place if she continued to see her lover, Hannah sent him away. But she now asserts that it would be "A rare good job, to let a servant maid / Live honest, then, and have her sweethearts free, / Like ladies have" (61–3), after which the mistress abruptly intervenes:

> I began
> To find this babble tedious. Generally
>   One thinks of servants as a race who live
> By labour and new bonnets; and, indeed,
>   How could our households be at peace and thrive,
> If they had sweethearts too?   (82–7)

Though conceding that if servants' souls contain "Some frozen germ" of the "full-grown love which fashions and controls / The hearts of us fair ladies," then "I think we ought to cherish it, you know" (93–7), the speaker condemns herself and her ilk out of her own mouth, exposing her selfishness and the injustice of forcing servants to surrender basic liberties in order to earn a living.

John Davidson's "Thirty Bob a Week" (*Yellow Book* [July, 1894]), a dramatic monologue spoken by a petty clerk, is much better known, especially after T. S. Eliot's pronouncement that "Davidson had a great theme, and also found an idiom which elicited the greatness of the theme, which endowed this thirty-bob-a-week clerk with a dignity that would not have appeared if a more conventional poetic diction had been employed. The personage that Davidson created in this poem has haunted me all my life, the poem is to me a great poem for ever."[12] Like Kipling's *Barrack-Room Ballads*, "Thirty Bob a Week" absorbs the diction and rhythms of the music hall, but Davidson conjoins them to a clerk's almost existential vision of the meaninglessness and impossibility of his life. Rather than detailing the skimping, fretting, and small humiliations that beset the underpaid clerk, Davidson relies on memorable imagery and the clerk's controlled anguish. Each morning "like a mole" the clerk journeys "in the dark, / A-travelling along the underground" from his ironically named "Pillar'd Halls" in "Suburbean Park" (13–15), the subterranean path standing in for his subhuman conditions and living hell. His inward rage and desire, which, he freely concedes –

> I step into my heart and there I meet
>   A god-almighty devil singing small,
> Who would like to shout and whistle in the street,
>   And squelch the passers flat against the wall;
> If the whole world was a cake he had the power to take,
>   He would take it, ask for more, and eat it all   (43–8) –

illuminate his condition as much as his self-disgust with the "simpleton" who "fell in love and married in his teens" on only thirty bob a week, at which he is "stuck" (49, 52).

Unsparingly, he claims that "No Adam was responsible for me, / Nor society, nor systems, nary one" (69–70). He persists only because he has created an imaginative myth and life philosophy whereby he willed himself into life: "Because I chose to be the thing I was"; "I was the love that chose my mother out; / I joined two lives and from the union burst" (76, 79–80). But the myth of total self-reliance never obscures the impossible terms on which he lives:

> But the difficultest go to understand,
>   And the difficultest job a man can do,
> Is to come it brave and meek with thirty bob a week,
>   And feel that that's the proper thing for you.
> It's a naked child against a hungry wolf;
>   It's playing bowls upon a splitting wreck;
>   …
> And we fall, face forward, fighting, on the deck.   (87–92, 96)

His honesty and will to go on are tantamount to heroism, hence Davidson's deliberate martial metaphor at the close.

The clerk has an auditor to whom he refers more than once: "I ain't blaspheming, Mr. Silver-tongue; / I'm saying things a bit beyond your art"; "With your science and your books and your the'ries about spooks"; "[my] most engrugious notion of the world, / ... leaves your lightning 'rithmetic behind" (31–2, 35, 63–4). Though "art" might refer to the poet and "spooks" to a member of the Society of Psychical Research (founded 1882), the reference to science and arithmetic suggests a statistician. Charles Booth integrated statistics, interviews, and sociological maps to produce *Life and Labour of the People of London* beginning in 1889. Booth's purpose was to show "the numerical relation which poverty, misery and depravity bear to regular earnings and comparative comfort, and to describe the general conditions under which each class lives."[13] Davidson's poem resonates within this textual and social context, adding literary force to the injustice of hard work for wages insufficient to support life so that others can prosper. The clerk's interviewer learns all he needs to know about the clerk's way of life and locale but receives a surplusage in the form of poetic language, rhythm, and psychological suggestion that exceed strict docketing and analysis and expose the limits of measure, whether statistical or monetary.

Efforts to combat social injustices for workers quickened in the final decades of the century: in 1864 Karl Marx founded the International Working Men's Association in London; in 1884 William Morris broke from the Social Democratic Federation, which he had briefly joined, to help found the Socialist League. The League's official publication was *Commonweal*, in which Morris's narrative poem *The Pilgrims of Hope* appeared from March, 1885 to July 3, 1886. It relays a tale of conversion, martyrdom, and prophecy, but redemption comes through socialism rather than Christianity.

Richard, the illegitimate son of a rich man and his mistress, and Richard's unnamed wife, a former agricultural worker, leave the countryside for London. There a greedy lawyer embezzles the legacy Richard has from his father just when Richard is converted to socialism and speaks out at the carpentry shop where he works. Fired for expressing his views, he, his wife, and young son sink ever closer to poverty, especially after Richard is arrested at a political rally, until they are befriended by a wealthy convert to the cause named Arthur. Eventually Arthur and Richard's wife fall in love, to the dismay of all three, and when the Paris Commune forms at the end of the Franco-Prussian War (1870–1), they all leave for Paris and subordinate their personal anguish to a greater cause. Arthur and Richard's wife are killed amidst the Commune's fall, and Richard returns to the countryside not to retreat, but to raise his son and regain his own strength so that "two men there might be hereafter to battle against the wrong" (XIII.87).

In common with much Chartist verse, Morris's poem links revolution to natural cycles to create a sense of inevitability. In Section I, "Message of the March Wind," Richard compares the "hope of the people [that] now buddeth and groweth" to "the seed of midwinter, unheeded, unperished, / Like the autumn-sown wheat 'neath the snow lying green," as well as to his and his wife's love and "the babe 'neath thy girdle that groweth unseen" (I.56–61). When they arrive in Paris and witness the people's joy, Richard thinks back to his own birth and asserts, "For this in our country spring / Did the starlings bechatter the gables, and the thrush in the thorn-bush sing, / ... this was the promise of spring-tide, & the new leaves longing to burst" (XI.59–60, 63). Even though the Commune falls and Richard loses his wife, his narrative ends against the backdrop of the hay's harvesting as he rededicates himself to socialism and prepares for a greater battle ahead. This final section, like the close of *Casa Guidi Windows*, also symbolically links a child to posterity – "my soul is seeing the day / When those who are now but children the new generation shall be" – and prophesies future victory: "I cling to the love of the past and the love of the day to be, / And the present, it is but the building of the man to be strong in me" (XIII.8–9, 88–9).

The psychological portrayal of Richard, his wife, and Arthur is less nuanced than that of the clerk in "Thirty Bob a Week." Rather, the poem's greatest complexity lies in its intertextuality, which embraces not only the *Communist Manifesto* and *Commonweal* but also Morris's earlier poems. *Pilgrims of Hope* features chivalric battle motifs ("the bickering points of steel, and the horses shifting about / 'Neath the flashing swords of the captains," III.73–4) and the vividly colored natural scenes for which Morris was admired as poet and designer: "The forks shine white in the sun round the yellow red-wheeled wain" (VIII.9). The hexameters of Sections III to XIII also look back to those in *The Story of Sigurd the Volsung* (1876).

Above all, however, Morris integrates a love triangle and a character named Arthur into his socialist narrative, thus overtly echoing the love triangles of Arthur, Guenevere, and Launcelot in *Defence of Guenevere and Other Poems* (1858), and Kiartin, Bodli, and Gudrun in "The Lovers of Gudrun" from *The Earthly Paradise* (1868–70), his most popular poetic work. Romance in social problem literature is often considered a sop to the literary marketplace or bourgeois ideology, hence the many critiques of the romance plot in Gaskell's novel *Mary Barton* (1848). Morris, however, did not publish his poem as a commercial venture but as a league publication read principally by those who already supported socialism.

The deliberate echo of his earlier verse enabled Morris to model, and enact, two key themes: conversion and the necessity of speaking out for socialism. Section V is entitled "New Birth" and adopts Christian language to mark Richard's revelation of socialism's promise: "Of peace and good-will he told"; "I was born once long ago: I am born again to-night" (V.99, 126). Section VI then represents the challenge of proselytizing for the new faith and the likely consequences all workers face in pursuing it:

> to others I needs must speak
> (Indeed, they pressed me to that while yet I was weaker than weak).
> So I began the business, and in street-corners I spake
> To knots of men. Indeed, that made my very heart ache,
> So hopeless it seemed ...
>   one of my shopmates heard
> My next night's speech in the street, and passed on some bitter word,
> And that week came a word with my money: "You needn't come
>   again."   (VI.91–5, 125–7)

By so deliberately echoing his earlier poetry yet forcefully advocating for socialism in his first extended poem after becoming a socialist, Morris underscores his own conversion and speaks out from within his aesthetic "workshop" of poetry. The love triangle in *Pilgrims of Hope* and Richard's continuing love for his wife despite knowing that she loves another additionally reinforces socialist repudiation of individual ownership and places the cause above personal need.[14] Creating continuity between this and his earlier poems also enables Morris to reach a literary audience who might be drawn to socialism through his poetry. His success with the former, at least, is evident in the February, 1886 *Athenaeum*; Morris's poem, it asserts, deals "with the Socialist propaganda, in which [he] is taking a share. Politics apart, the poem is full of the old qualities – perfect rapport with nature, admirable sketching of scenery, pathos, and simple diction ... in the large anapæstic measure of '*Sigurd the Volsung*.'"[15] Politics can no more be taken "apart" from *The Pilgrims of Hope*, however, than its poetry can. Those drawn to a fresh narrative by a poet whose work they admired perforce also listened, like the "knots of men" Richard addresses, to a recent convert's political message.

William Morris's name appears in the front matter of Louisa Bevington's *Liberty Lyrics* (1895), which advertises *Liberty: A Journal of Anarchist Communism* (to which Morris and Bevington contributed along with Prince Kropotkin and G. B. Shaw) and a penny *Liberty Pamphlet* that pairs Morris's "Why I am a Communist" with Bevington's "Why I am an Expropriationist" (i.e., opponent to private property). Morris parted from anarchists such as Bevington because he did not accept terrorist violence as a legitimate means of change. Still, Morris and Bevington are usefully linked through their intersections in print culture, their poetic participation in late-century radical politics, and their range of poetic strategies. Like Morris's own, Bevington's politics could take a lyrical turn, as in the first of two quatrains of "The Most Beautiful Thing":

> The most beautiful thing around or above
> Is Love, true Love:
> The beautiful thing can more beautiful be
> If its life be free.

Here the anarchist principle of freedom intensifies beauty and emotion in lines themselves aesthetically heightened by the unfettered enjambment of the first and third lines and strong alliteration.

Like Morris also, Bevington adopts Christian language to articulate her political cause; she goes further, however, in recruiting Christ for anarchism, including its violence, in "Dreamers?":

> "Dreamers?" Ah, no! else he was a dreamer,
> Our crucified brother of long, long ago;
> Arrested, and jeered at; "seditious"; "blasphemer";
> And legally slain, lest the people should *know*
> Offence against privileged, orthodox "order,"
> That stirring of crowds by the straight word and true.   (1–6)

Noting Christ's "agonised cry of desertion" on the cross "Lest haply the whole had been suffered in vain" (9–10), Bevington connects his experience to current political violence: "'Tis suffering violence? Yes, in the taking; / Yet, taken, there shall not be fighting again" (15–16). She ends by urging her "comrades" forward amidst "reproach and derision, / To rid the old world of its thraldom and woe," bidding them take hope from "That lone one, our comrade of long, long ago" (17–20).[16] The anarchist principle of honoring individualism while opposing all institutions enables Bevington to adopt a stance of sympathy, that cornerstone of Victorian poetics, toward Christ's suffering, even though she excoriates the church elsewhere in her volume (for example, "In and Out of Church"). Collectively the poems by Munby, Davidson, Morris, and Bevington indicate that Victorian poetry could passionately insist on greater justice and liberty for workers while maintaining a commitment to poetry as such.

Liberty for women

The most important Victorian poem making the case for women's rights is *Aurora Leigh*, which addresses feminist issues and demonstrates through its verve, ambition, and poetic achievement that women are not a class relative to men but equal in talent. Women poets and suffragists paid tribute to its impact for decades. Louisa Bevington published her first volume of poems under the pseudonym Arbor Leigh, Katherine Bradley (later part of Michael Field) as Arran Leigh. American feminist Susan B. Anthony wrote on the flyleaf of the copy of *Aurora Leigh* she presented to the Library of Congress in 1902, "This book was carried in my satchel for years and read & re-read ... I have always cherished it above all other books."[17] Emily Dickinson in America similarly testified to its power in her letters and the lyric "Her – 'last Poems' – ": "Not on Record – bubbled other, / Flute – or Woman – / So divine."[18]

A special challenge facing women poets who wished to protest injustice or urge greater liberties for women was that doing so could reinforce the very prejudice under which they labored: the assumption that women were excluded from the highest poetic powers and merely expressed spontaneously what they experienced or felt. As George Gilfillan, the champion of working-class poet Alexander Smith, remarked of Felicia Hemans in *Tait's Edinburgh Magazine*, "A *maker* she is not ... Mrs. Hemans' poems are strictly effusions. And not a little of their charm springs from their unstudied and extempore character. This, too, is in fine keeping with the sex of the writer."[19] Such views illuminate the preponderance of dramatic monologues among feminist poems discussed below. By separating the poet from her speaker, a dramatic monologue formally insists on the poet as "*maker*" who crafts a speaker and text rather than presenting feminine "effusions."

Victorian advocacy of women's rights tends to focus on three themes: the double standard applied to women in courtship and sexuality, education, and marriage. If the last two intersected with social and legislative reforms, the first addressed the more nebulous, intractable problem of custom. By inviting readers to imagine alternatives and sympathize with victims of injustice, poetry (like fiction) could help alter traditional gender roles while also consolidating support for specific reforms.

In the paired poems "A Woman's Shortcomings" and "A Man's Requirements" (*Blackwood's Magazine* [October, 1846]), Barrett Browning critiques the double standard and asymmetrical power of men in love relationships. She is careful to do so by also conceding faults in women. Directly rebuking the flirt of "A Woman's Shortcomings" ("Unless you can swear, 'For life, for death!' – / Oh, fear to call it loving!" [31–2]), Barrett Browning adopts a dramatic monologue for "A Man's Requirements" to avoid the "unfeminine" situation of a woman chastising a man in public. The effect of this formal variance is to remind readers that women occupy a range of positions, since the poet and flirt differ. And since the man ostensibly speaking in his own voice is crafted by a woman, masculine authority becomes contingent and susceptible to female appropriation.

Adopting imperative voice, the speaker of "A Man's Requirements" details his expectations of a woman in eleven quatrains and demands nothing less than her whole being:

> Love me, Sweet, with all thou art,
>   Feeling, thinking, seeing;
> Love me in the lightest part,
>   Love me in full being.   (1–4)

Finally, in a sole quatrain, he declares what he will give in exchange:

> Thus, if thou wilt prove me, Dear,
>   Woman's love no fable,
> *I* will love *thee* – half a year –
>   As a man is able.   (41–4)

If it culminates in sarcastic humor (a strategic deflection of "shrill" critique), the poem also structurally mirrors the uneven roles of men and women in courtship in the space it allots to his demands versus what he gives in return.

Suitors were expected to lead active lives apart from courtship; the effects of raising middle-class girls only for courtship and marriage is probed by Augusta Webster in "Faded" (1870), a dramatic monologue uttered by a woman who now knows she will remain unwed. The topic had particular currency after social reformer W. G. Greg pointed out the surplus of women relative to available suitors in "Why are Women Redundant?" (*National Review* [April, 1862]). Florence Nightingale chose not to marry, and Frances Power Cobbe was happy in her domestic housekeeping with another woman. But they were talented intellectuals with adequate financial resources, conditions closed to most middle-class women. By allowing an old maid, long a stock figure in comic literature, to articulate her plight as she addresses a portrait of her younger self, Webster shifts spinsterhood from object to subject, from ridicule to dignity, and from derision to sympathy, even while troubling the realist poetics on which she relies.

For in her poem the two-dimensional portrait of the speaker's younger self, ironically, has more vibrancy and social value than the aging woman dismissed as an unsuccessful copy of the copy:

> Poor imaged mock,
> Thou art more than I to-day; thou hast my right,
> My womanhood's lost right to meet pleased eyes
> And please by being happy …

> Thou hast a being still; but what am I?
> A shadow and an echo – one that was.   (130–3, 137–8)

The old maid frankly envies her young self, but the keynote of her monologue is wonder at the strangeness of such existence, not anger at the cheat
life has practiced on her. If she compares herself to a bankrupt trying to stave
off ruin or a ghost who returns and is unrecognized, she also likens herself
and other old maids to "diswinged flies of the air" (41), a likely allusion to
King Lear: "As flies to wanton boys are we to the gods, / They kill us for their
sport" (IV.i.38–9). "Boys" in a sense also kill women like this speaker, who
become invisible to men once they cease to attract.

One solution to the problem of "redundant" women was to open alternative
careers to them, but careers required adequate education. In contrast to the
broad erudition of Barrett Browning and Webster, who mastered Greek and
Latin, many girls received unsystematic, superficial instruction of the sort
derided in *Aurora Leigh*: "I learnt a little algebra, a little / Of the mathematics, –
brushed with extreme flounce / The circle of the sciences" (1.403–5). In
"The Castaway" Webster represents a similarly inferior education and an
additional injustice that George Eliot portrays in *The Mill on the Floss*
(1860), the sacrifice imposed on sisters so that brothers can flourish:

> I was his sister, prizing him
> As sisters do, content to learn for him
> The lesson girls with brothers all must learn,
> To do without …
> Content with stinted fare and shabby clothes
> And cloistered silent life to save expense,
> Teaching myself out of my borrowed books,
> While he for some one pastime, (needful, true,
> To keep him of his rank; 'twas not his fault)
> Spent in a month what could have given me
> My teachers for a year.   (485–8, 497–503)

That such blatant educational inequities appear in poems written by erudite
women poets underscores that uneducated girls are a social creation, not an
inevitable condition.

Gerald Massey summed up the matter in four lines in "Womankind" (1889),
saying overtly what Barrett Browning and Webster only hint of men:

> Dear things! we would not have you learn too much –
>   Your Ignorance is so charming! We've a notion
> That greater knowledge might not lend you such
>   Sure aid to blind obedience and devotion.

Massey is not the only radical male poet to address women's rights. In Morris's "Defence of Guenevere" the queen scoffs at having been "bought / By Arthur's great name and his little love" (82–3). In *Pilgrims of Hope* Richard's wife glances from her happy marriage to the many thousands for whom "a husband is taken to bed as a hat or a ribbon is worn. / Prudence begets her thousands: 'Good is a housekeeper's life, / So shall I sell my body that I may be matron and wife'" (IV.84–6). If Morris here adopts an economic analysis of marriage consistent with Marxism, he also anticipates Mona Caird's critique of marriage in the August, 1888 *Westminster Review*, in which she asserts that when no alternatives to marriage are available to women, "our common respectable marriage – upon which the safety of all social existence is supposed to rest – will remain, as it is now, the worst, because the most hypocritical, form of woman-purchase."[20]

Caird's essay, along with women's increased entry into universities and professions and social adaptations of Darwinian theory implying that women could evolve into new forms, helped shift the woman question, as earlier debates about women's education and property rights were termed, to the marriage question. Amy Levy's "Xantippe" (1881), Graham R. Tomson's "Ballad of the Bird-Bride" (*Harper's New Monthly Magazine* [January, 1889]), and E. Nesbit's "The Woman's World" (*Shafts* [1892]) all intensify the scrutiny of marriage. Levy opts for the dramatic monologue to reimagine Socrates' shrewish wife as the product of women's exclusion from education and oppression within marriage. Tomson's ballad revises the myth of the swan maiden captured as a bride by the man who steals her feathers to intimate that women are inherently wild and free. When their starving children induce the bird-bride's Eskimo husband to break his promise never to hunt her sister gulls, she reclaims her feathers and flies away with their children, leaving him to grieve his loss. Not coincidentally, the poem also resists contemporary divorce laws by imaging mothers' rather than fathers' rights to their children.

Rather than the distance imparted by dramatic monologue or myth, Nesbit adopts direct lyric expression to claim the liberty without which, J. S. Mill argues in the closing chapter of *On the Subjection of Women* (1869), no human being can assume full dignity. Even abiding love for her husband is inadequate to compensate Nesbit's persona for the diminished subjectivity under which she chafes within marriage:

> I am only you!
> I am yours – part of you – your wife!
> And I have no other life.
>   I cannot think, cannot do,

> I cannot breathe, cannot see;
> There is "us," but there is not "me" –
>   And worst, at your kiss, I grow
>   Contented so.[21]

Here the kiss signifying erotic desire and communion in *Aurora Leigh* or *The Princess* enacts loss of identity. The varying pulse and caesuras of Nesbit's lines formally mirror the woman's restlessness amidst her alienation, while her neurasthenic traits of suffocation and perceptual miasma indicate a disease that is not inherent in her sex but created by marriage itself.

May Kendall's "The Sandblast Girl and the Acid Man" (1894) reverts to the dramatic monologue but uses it to different ends than Webster or Levy. Kendall's monologue, spoken by a sympathetic, love-struck acid man at a stained glass factory, covers a range of feminist and social issues with a light touch, moving readers more through gentle suggestion and sympathy than satire or critique. Yet her very title suggests new terrain for poetry. Besides her unconventional workplace, Kendall reveals the new erotic experiences possible when young men and women began to work alongside each other.

Maggie, the sandblast girl, is serious about work and handles stained glass tracery with finesse. She is also attractive ("Her pretty hair so soft and brown / Is coiled about her shapely head" [37–8]) and has found out the acid man: "And I look up and she looks down, / And both of us go red!" (39–40). For the acid man, however, who is paid only "twenty shillings every week" (49), love and economic analysis are inseparable. Even the socialist newspaper he reads offers no immediate solution to the problem of how to begin saving for marriage when he has a sister to support and Maggie a mother (50–6). The conclusion's uneasy equilibrium between serious social commentary and light romance encapsulates his position and forms a fitting counterpart to his irresolution:

> I'm vastly better off than some!
>   I think of how the many fare
> Who perish slowly, crushed and dumb,
>   For leisure, food and air.
> 'Tis hard, in Freedom's very van,
>   To live and die a luckless churl.
> 'Tis hard to be an acid man,
>   *Without* a sandblast girl!   (65–72)

As the reference to "Freedom's very van" indicates, the social changes that make it possible for Maggie and the acid man to work together are incomplete. Kendall at once gives voice to new subject positions; vividly portrays women pursuing active lives outside marriage (in contrast to "Faded"); represents, as in "Thirty Bob a Week," the struggle to support life on low wages; and, like Morris in *Pilgrims of Hope*, merges elements of socialism and feminism.

Taking liberties

As Kendall's monologue indicates, Victorian reforms, altered living conditions, and increased mobility helped democratize poetic discourse. But the attempt to incorporate sexual detail into poetry met resistance and, at worst, outrage and censorship. As noted in Chapter 3, Thackeray rejected even "Lord Walter's Wife" (1861) on the grounds that Barrett Browning's depiction of "unlawful passion" would offend readers. Barrett Browning retorted that "the corruption of our society requires not shut doors and windows but light and air: and that it is exactly because pure and prosperous women choose to *ignore* vice that miserable women suffer wrong by it everywhere."[22] The intersection of empire and feminism would soon alter this condition. Having recognized the importance of sanitation during the Crimean War, military and political leaders next turned to the problem of venereal disease among soldiers. Reasoning that morale would suffer if soldiers were subjected to genital inspection, legislators instead forced the practice upon the prostitutes whom they deemed already degraded. The Contagious Diseases Acts of 1864, 1866, and 1869 empowered police to arrest suspected prostitutes and force them into inspections and "lock hospitals" if they were contagious. In effect any unaccompanied woman who did not satisfy a policeman's standards of respectability could be arrested and undergo the most intimate of invasive procedures.

The CD acts (as they are often termed) led in a straight line to suffragism; as Josephine Butler, the movement's leader, remarked in the May 9, 1870 *Shield*, the official newspaper of the Anti-Contagious Disease Acts Association, "it was a Parliament of men only who made this law ... Men alone met in committee over it ... it is time that women should arise and demand their most sacred rights in regard to their sisters."[23]

The movement also had literary consequences. As women began to speak about gynecology and prostitution in public meetings attended by men, censorship of illicit sexuality in middle-class fare was increasingly untenable. Not coincidentally, two poems named after prostitutes appeared in 1870, the same year *The Shield* began publication: "Jenny," by D. G. Rossetti, and "The Castaway," by Webster. Numerous poems about prostitutes followed, including A. Mary F. Robinson's "The Scape-Goat" (1884), Oscar Wilde's

"The Harlot's House" (*Dramatic Review* [April 11, 1885]), and Mathilde Blind's "The Russian Student's Tale" (1891) and "Noonday Rest" (1895). If Barrett Browning was temporarily silenced by Thackeray, changing social conditions enabled the "coarse English" names that Eulalie knows all too well in "The Castaway" (62–5) to be named.

Spasmodic poetry, sensation fiction, and newspaper divorce and criminal reports also helped inspire greater latitude in literature from the 1860s onward. But a single work did more in one fell swoop to widen the bounds of poetry than gradual developments. Ironically, as Swinburne remarked, no one objected to "Faustine," which encompasses debauchery, lesbianism, and sadism, when it appeared in the May 31, 1862 *Spectator*: "I have heard that even the little poem of 'Faustine' has been to some readers a thing to make the scalp creep and the blood freeze. It was issued with no such intent. Nor do I remember that any man's voice or heel was lifted against it when it first appeared … in the *Spectator* newspaper for 1862. Virtue, it would seem, has shot up surprisingly in the space of four years or less."[24] But when "Faustine" appeared alongside "Anactoria," "Hermaphroditus," "Fragoletta," and "Dolores" in *Poems and Ballads* (1866), John Morley declared that Swinburne

> is either the vindictive and scornful apostle of a crushing iron-shod despair, or else he is the libidinous laureate of a pack of satyrs. Not all the fervour of his imagination, the beauty of his melody, the splendour of many phrases and pictures, can blind us to the absence of judgment and reason, the reckless contempt for anything like a balance, and the audacious counterfeiting of strong and noble passion by mad intoxicated sensuality.

Despite his lurid description, Morley found "Dolores" "admirable" for its "sustained power and … music, if hateful on other grounds."[25]

"Dolores" pictures no sex acts or erotic zones, though its ample biting and blood evoke sado-masochism and its sheer excess suggests perversity. Swinburne's is a sexuality of epithet and idea rather than graphic physicality: "Thou art noble and nude and antique; / Libitina thy mother, Priapus / Thy father" (50–2). More troubling to contemporaries was the way Swinburne adapted the epithets that structure the Litany of the Blessed Virgin Mary and Feast of the Seven Sorrows (for example, "Mystical rose," "Queen of Martyrs") but inverted them into pagan equivalents. Dolores, like Mary, is "Our Lady of Pain," "mystic and somber," and associated with suffering and death. But Dolores is also a "mystical rose of the mire" (7–8, 21). She is not a specific deity or person but an ageless principle that merges death and sex, pleasure

and pain – a poetic insight decades in advance of Freud's theory of eros and
thanatos, the sex instinct wed to the death instinct:

> [Love and death] laughed, changing hands in the measure,
>> And they mixed and made peace after strife;
> Pain melted in tears, and was pleasure;
>> Death tingled with blood, and was life.
> Like lovers they melted and tingled,
>> In the dusk of thine innermost fane;
> In the darkness they murmured and mingled,
>> Our Lady of Pain.   (177–84)

Three decades later, when Arthur Symons similarly applied an epithet of
the Virgin Mary to a prostitute in "Stella Maris," critics were still outraged.
Swinburne's decision to hurl his poem before the public in 1866 amounts to
interventionist, even revolutionary, rhetoric. "Dolores" exposes another cause
of Swinburne's desire to extend the limits of the sayable, the burden of literary
belatedness: "Old poets outsing and outlove us" (339); "we match not the
dead men that bore us / At a song, at a kiss, at a crime" (387–8). The number
of lines in "Dolores" that open onto an infinite regress of imagination
motivate an intercessory prayer that, if granted, will give poets something
new about which to write:

> There are sins it may be to discover,
>> There are deeds it may be to delight.
> What new work wilt thou find for thy lover,
>> What new passions for daytime or night?
> What spells that they know not a word of
>> Whose lives are as leaves overblown?
> What tortures undreamt of, unheard of,
>> Unwritten, unknown?   (73–80)

In enduring the brunt of critical attacks and becoming a byword for
rebellion and resistance, Swinburne opened new topics, sensations, stances,
and techniques to subsequent Victorian poets. As Kathy Psomiades points
out, for example, "Swinburne creates women who are looked at yet somehow
not seen, are visible yet not visually accessible," an immensely important
technique to women poets, who could infuse sensuality into poetry without
objectifying the female or male figure.[26] By helping to collapse norms of
poetic decorum that had prevailed since the reaction against seventeenth-
century libertine poets like Aphra Behn or John Wilmot, Earl of Rochester,
Swinburne prepared for literary modernism, which would complete
Swinburne's iconoclastic project by radically breaking up old poetic forms

and technique as well as making use of the new discursive freedoms Swinburne pioneered. Swinburne, of course, advocates revolution while maintaining strict regularity of form: each stanza of "Dolores" features seven predominantly anapestic trimeter lines and a concluding dimeter with an *ababcdcd* rhyme scheme. Victorians' incomplete iconoclasm should not veil the degree to which they both imagined and took liberties in their poems, not only at the *fin de siècle*, as the following chapter demonstrates, but throughout Victoria's reign.

Chapter 9

Resisting rhetoric: art for art's sake

Waste not your Hour, nor in the vain pursuit
Of This and That endeavour and dispute;
        Better be jocund with the fruitful Grape
Than sadden after none, or bitter, Fruit.
        Edward FitzGerald, *The Rubáiyát of Omar Khayyám* (1872)

For that dim brow and lingering hand
Come from a more dream-heavy land,
A more dream-heavy hour than this.
        W. B. Yeats, "He Remembers Forgotten Beauty"[1]

If aestheticism mandated poetry's suspension of religious and moral purpose
in favor of form and beauty as ends in themselves, newer attitudes toward
sexual relations, degeneration, and the artistic temperament driven by
Darwinian science and commodity culture intensified this development at
century's end. Evolutionary theory, for example, prompted debate about
which elements in human nature – and British culture – were fittest to survive.
In "The New Hedonism" Grant Allen argued that full "self-development"
meant that the "sex instinct," which drove humans to the highest levels of
intellectual and aesthetic creativity, should be elevated over "self-sacrifice."[2]
Contrary to this optimistic coupling of sexual liberty and artistic excellence,
Max Nordau and others linked contemporary art to "degenerates" characterized by inability to tell right from wrong and male "emotionalism": "a commonplace line of poetry or of prose sends a shudder down his back; he falls
into raptures before indifferent pictures or statues."[3]

Nordau might be describing the poet-aesthete Bunthorne in Gilbert and Sullivan's comic opera *Patience* (1881); it was to promote *Patience* in America that the D'Oyly Carte opera company hired Oscar Wilde (on whom Bunthorne was partly based) to tour America and speechify about aestheticism while sporting velvet knee breeches and holding a lily. Nordau of course missed the obvious point that men like Bunthorne and Wilde were enacting roles not necessarily grounded in biology. Nordau's widely reviewed work nonetheless suggested an intrinsic relation among effeminacy, degeneracy, and poetry that would incite a recoil from all three after 1895.

Aestheticism was situated as an alternative to and critique of Victorian capitalism and commodity culture but could be as easily co-opted by the market as anything else. Readers and gallery visitors who heeded the call of beauty wanted to purchase what they could not create themselves. Their need for discerning guides opened a market niche for poets and painters, so that another feature of aestheticism was its close tie to print commodities: poems, decorated books, and periodical columns. The paradoxical relation of aestheticism to commodity culture is captured in Andrew Lang's "Ballade of Blue China," the title poem of his 1880 volume. D. G. Rossetti had begun collecting blue-and-white ware in the 1860s, prizing its dim luster and blurred outlines; the vogue spread, and as an undergraduate Wilde quipped, "I find it harder and harder every day to live up to my blue china" – a remark reprinted in *Punch* (October 30, 1880) and circulated at large.[4] Lang's poem is a tacit riposte to Wilde. If his second and third stanzas playfully evoke the fantastic figures on porcelain, making art out of art, his first stanza touts a prized purchase that exposes aestheticism's stake in the marketplace:

> There's a joy without canker or cark,
> There's a pleasure eternally new,
> 'Tis to gloat on the glaze and the mark
> Of china that's ancient and blue;
> Unchipp'd all the centuries through
> It has pass'd, since the chime of it rang,
> And they fashion'd it, figure and hue,
> In the reign of the Emperor Hwang.   (1–8)

Lang's light touch informs all twenty-two ballades of his volume, and he added ten more in 1881, mocking the surplus in his title: "XXII and X: XXXII Ballades in Blue China." As noted in Chapter 2, the ease with which Lang and Dobson turned out witty piece after piece itself suggested poetic manufacture, an apt complement to commodities in blue china.

Aestheticism likewise bore a contradictory relationship to rhetoric. Art for art's sake clearly implied a retreat from public debates into self-enclosed aesthetic realms. *The Rubáiyát of Omar Khayyám* rejects "dispute" (214) while Morris avows in the "Apology" of *The Earthly Paradise*, "Of Heaven or Hell I have no power to sing, / I cannot ease the burden of your fears" (1–2). Rather than a prophet who utters eternal truths to guide contemporaries, Morris identifies himself as a "Dreamer of dreams, born out of my due time" and asks, "Why should I strive to set the crooked straight?" (22–3). Though *Pilgrims of Hope* (1885) would ardently distinguish right from wrong, *The Earthly Paradise* aims only "to build a shadowy isle of bliss" (38), an enclosed aesthetic precinct of mimetic "shadows."

Paradoxically, however, Morris also rebuts Carlyle's definition of poets in *Heroes and Hero-Worship* (1840) and Barrett Browning's in *Aurora Leigh* (1856): "the only truth-tellers now left to God, / The only speakers of essential truth" (1.859–60). To assert the claims of aestheticism against prominent mid-Victorian authors was in part to engage in contemporary debates from which aesthetes ostensibly sought escape. As *Patience* and *Punch*'s circulation of Wilde's epigram on blue china indicate, aestheticism was not only a serious literary development but also a vogue and flash point. In Gilbert and Sullivan's operetta Bunthorne's flamboyant effeminacy is contrasted with Heavy Dragoons, hyper-masculine imperial soldiers who troop through the first act aghast that women should flutter about Bunthorne and ignore them. Even the vegetable dyes that gave Pre-Raphaelite costume and paintings a distinctive hue are satirized when Bunthorne terms himself "A greenery-yallery, Grosvenor Gallery, / Foot-in-the-grave young man!"[5] Aestheticism did not stay in a bounded autotelic zone but also entered (and functioned as a) late-century public discourse. To illuminate its discursive function, this chapter examines aestheticism, decadence, and rhetoric in four phases: mid-century aestheticism, the importation of French theories of *l'art pour l'art*, the infusion of same-sex desire into aestheticism and decadence, and the proto-modernist strategies of the Celtic Twilight.

Aestheticism at mid-century: *The Rubáiyát of Omar Khayyám* versus Tractarian poetics

In 1859 few readers noticed when Edward FitzGerald published his translation of Persian quatrains by Omar Khayyám, the twelfth-century poet and astronomer born in what we know as Iran. Refashioning a Persian poet was uniquely suited to enunciate an agnostic life philosophy at mid-century. FitzGerald could claim fidelity to the original as his excuse, and a Muslim poet would hardly endorse Christianity in any case. For Omar, Moses and Jesus are merely historical prophets who conveniently provide metaphors for spring: "the WHITE HAND

OF MOSES on the Bough / Puts out, and Jesus from the Ground suspires" (1859: 15–16). FitzGerald's Omar concedes that he earlier sought, like Tennyson in *In Memoriam*, to pierce the "Veil" shrouding "Human ... Fate" (1859: 124, 126), but he found the task pointless. His faith now centers on the grape:

> How long, how long, in infinite Pursuit
> Of This and That endeavour and dispute?
>   Better be merry with the fruitful Grape
> Than sadden after none, or bitter, Fruit.   (1859: 153–6)

Rejecting the reason and logic on which public debate depends (1859: 159–60), Omar instead underscores the human transience that renders all life goals moot. Those alive in the present "make merry in the Room" vacated by predecessors and must in turn "beneath the Couch of Earth / Descend, ourselves to make a Couch – for whom?" (1859: 85, 87–8). It is a fitting note for a translator, whose secondariness and belatedness are implicit in his task. Omar offers no grand passions, no prophetic insights, merely transient pleasures and loquacity (his own and the pots' regarding their potter) unharnessed to higher purpose.

Even in its first, shorter version, FitzGerald's work flew in the face of middle-class Victorian culture, an effect intensified by quatrains added in the second (1868), third (1872), and fourth (1879) editions. (Because FitzGerald sometimes subtracted quatrains as well, there is no authoritative text, an apt corollary to Omar's universe for which no definitive scriptures suffice.) In contrast to the sanctifying of Victorian commerce in the Great Exhibition, Omar advises, "let the Credit go" since "those who husbanded" their wealth "And those who flung it to the winds" end up alike (1872: 51, 57–8).

Equally indifferent to piety, he rejects the agency of prophets: "Who rose before us, and as Prophets burn'd, / Are all but Stories" (1868: 270–1). Indeed, he anticipates J. S. Mill's contention in "On Nature" (1874) that God cannot be all-loving and omnipotent. Justifying his attachment to drink despite Islamic law, Omar suggests that the grape's "Juice [is] the growth of God" and hence "A Blessing" – or, if not, "why, then, Who set it there?" (1868: 249, 51–2). One of his imagined clay pots adds that its Creator would surely not "Beset the Road I was to wander in, / ... with Predestin'd Evil round / ... and then impute my Fall to Sin" (1868: 346–8). The *Rubáiyát* even echoes Milton's Satan and anticipates Wilde's view of knowledge as a creative construct ("The Critic as Artist") when Omar sends his "Soul through the Invisible" only to conclude, "'Myself am Heav'n and Hell': / Heav'n but the Vision of fulfill'd Desire, / And Hell the Shadow of a Soul on fire" (1868: 281, 284–6). *The Rubáiyát of Omar Khayyám* spurns the sacramental view of nature crucial to Tractarian poetics and heaven itself, which it terms "some After-reckoning ta'en on trust" (1868: 254). The poem elicited no debate or outrage, however, especially when the first edition sold so few copies that FitzGerald's publisher knocked it down to a penny a pamphlet.

After obtaining a remaindered copy of FitzGerald's *Rubáiyát* in 1861, D. G. Rossetti told Swinburne about it, and they soon circulated copies to others, including William Morris.[6] By 1868, when the *Rubáiyát* received a new edition, its world-weariness chimed with that of the highly popular *Earthly Paradise*, which resembled the *Rubáiyát* in making work from the past available in sonorous English. Even Omar's frank agnosticism failed to shock after readers had had nine years to absorb Darwin's *Origin*, published the same year as FitzGerald's first edition. Safely distanced from contemporary debates through its status as translation, and decorously mute on issues of sexuality, the *Rubáiyát* nonetheless acted as a solvent loosening the ties between poetry and moral purpose – especially after the immense popularity it attained by century's end.

Foreign diversions: Swinburne and French decadence

Swinburne played a crucial role not only in opening poetry to new sexual content but also in bringing theorized accounts of *l'art pour l'art* to Britain. Doing so necessarily involved him in persuasive discourse and poetic rhetoric (in Ricoeur's sense of generating new perspectives through imagination) in Victorian periodicals. His review of *Les fleurs du mal* in the September 6, 1862 *Spectator*, never republished during his lifetime, attracted no more animus than "Faustine" in the same paper. Yet Swinburne's articulation of *l'art pour l'art* is unmistakable. Six years before Morris's Apology to *The Earthly Paradise* asked "Why should I strive to set the crooked straight?" (23), Swinburne averred, "a poet's business is presumably to write good verses, and by no means to redeem the age and remould society."[7] Almost thirty years before Wilde contended in "A Preface to *Dorian Gray*" (*Fortnightly Review* [March, 1891]) that "There is no such thing as a moral or an immoral book. Books are well written, or badly written. That is all,"[8] Swinburne asserted of Baudelaire's poems on a decapitated corpse, prayers to Satan, and serpentine female beauty that "The main charm of the book is, upon the whole, that nothing is wrongly given, nothing capable of being re-written or improved on its own ground." More than thirty years before Arthur Symons associated decadence with "moral perversity" in "The Decadent Movement in Literature,"[9] Swinburne remarked that Baudelaire's poetry revealed "the sides on which nature looks unnatural" and focused on "the perverse happiness and wayward sorrows of exceptional people." Baudelaire's excellence, Swinburne concludes, resides in the "supreme excellence of words" – the beauty of his materials irrespective of content, a key premise of *fin-de-siècle* aestheticism and decadence.

Tellingly, Swinburne also anticipates W. B. Yeats in explicitly repudiating rhetoric, which Swinburne connects to mass media and popular taste. "A French poet," he asserts, "is expected to believe in philanthropy, and break off on occasion in the middle of his proper work to lend a shove forward to some theory of progress." But if a reader could "swallow a sonnet like a moral prescription – then clearly the poet supplying these intellectual drugs would be a bad artist; indeed, no real artist, but a huckster and vendor of miscellaneous wares." In contrast to the insistence of E. S. Dallas that "Great poetry" is meant "for the multitude,"[10] Swinburne advocates an elitist, noncommerical art for the few.

Yet Swinburne placed this essay in a periodical known for its moral probity, amid pages devoted to news of the week and theology, which Swinburne's text entered like a flaming brand meant to fix attention and spur reaction. He acknowledged, moreover, that however consummate in aesthetic terms, Baudelaire's poetry had itself become a site of intense rhetoric, since it had "been so violently debated over, so hauled this way and that by contentious critics." Swinburne's review is thus highly rhetorical, shaped to persuade not only by its dispassionate tone and rigorous logic ("Concede the starting point, and you cannot have a better runner") but also by its concession (if not recommendation) that *Les fleurs du mal* could after all be read in moral terms.

By the time "Ave atque vale," the elegy prompted by Baudelaire's death, appeared in the *Fortnightly Review* (January, 1868), Swinburne occupied a far different position in readers' eyes. In 1862 he had produced only two plays and a sprinkling of *Spectator* poems. In 1868 he was the notorious author of *Poems and Ballads*. One reason he could not reprint his 1862 essay on Baudelaire in the wake of his death (August 31, 1867) was that it referred to the "foolish and shameless prosecution" of the first edition of *Les fleurs du mal* that resulted in its being "withdrawn before anything like a fair hearing had been obtained for it." Now that his Moxon edition of *Poems and Ballads* had been suppressed to avoid prosecution, any mention of Baudelaire's experience would signal overt self-reference.

A classical elegy named after a Catullus poem distanced Swinburne from controversy while enabling him to identify with Baudelaire and respond to his own attackers. The full title of the Catullan original is "Frater, ave atque vale," which Tennyson would adopt for the lyric mourning his brother Charles Tennyson Turner. Swinburne's brotherhood lies outside "natural" reproduction and family ties. He claims Baudelaire as a brother in art and persecution, and his allusion to Catullus invokes a Roman poet known equally for supernal lyric beauty and obscenities, precisely the coupling he had praised in *Les fleurs du mal* and been attacked for in *Poems and Ballads*:

> Shall I strew on thee rose or rue or laurel,
>   Brother, on this that was the veil of thee?
>   ...
> Thou sawest, in thine old singing season, brother,
>   Secrets and sorrows unbeheld of us;
>   ...
> For thee, O now a silent soul, my brother,
>   Take at my hands this garland, and farewell.
>
>   (1–2, 23–4, 188–9)

Swinburne further deepens his identification with Baudelaire by referring to the "Lesbian promontories" and "barren kiss of ... wave to wave" above the hidden grave of Sappho, the "supreme head of song," whose kisses were likewise "salt and sterile" (15–16, 18–19). Here he doubly alludes to Baudelaire's "Lesbos" in *Les fleurs du mal* and his own "Anactoria," the dramatic monologue most often singled out for abuse in 1866. His tribute to Baudelaire is itself a form of eulogy or rhetoric of praise, and he imagines not merely the Muses but Apollo himself, god of poetry, "bending us-ward with memorial urns" (130) to pay tribute to Baudelaire and "save thy dust from blame and from forgetting" (147). To the degree that Swinburne identifies himself with Baudelaire, his poem places both poets under the benison of Apollo's protection.

If underwritten by a clear rhetorical purpose, "Ave atque vale" nonetheless enacts the aesthetics of *l'art pour l'art* far more successfully than Swinburne's 1862 review. Weaving together a poetic text in which echoes of *Les fleurs du mal*, Catullus, pastoral elegy, and his own verse intermingle, Swinburne creates a tissue of language that belongs less to a single poet than to the inclusive domain of literariness as such. Swinburne never implies that mourning or reading Baudelaire's verse provides access to the dead poet's self or soul, and he explicitly refuses elegy's conventional consolation of immortality:

> Thou art far too far for wings of words to follow,
>   Far too far off for thought or any prayer.
>   What ails us with thee, who art wind and air?
> What ails us gazing where all seen is hollow?
>   Yet with some fancy, yet with some desire,
>   Dreams pursue death as winds a flying fire,
> Our dreams pursue our dead and do not find.   (89–95)

At the elegy's end, therefore, Swinburne consigns Baudelaire to the silence and nothingness to which all will succumb:

> Content thee, howsoe'er, whose days are done;
>   There lies not any troublous thing before,
>   Nor sight nor sound to war against thee more,
> For whom all winds are quiet as the sun,
>   All waters as the shore.   (194–8)

Only in the material trace of the text itself can something be saved from death, "Not thee, O never thee, in all time's changes, / Not thee, but this the sound of thy sad soul, / The shadow of thy swift spirit, this shut scroll" (100–2). These material remains, ink on paper, alone provide "communion" with "thy song" (104). In so emphasizing the materiality of texts yet their ability to evoke haunting sounds and rhythms not part of the actual page, Swinburne instates an alternative form of mystery and ghostliness intrinsic to poetry itself. Since he and Baudelaire are one as "brothers," Swinburne also denies that his own readers encounter anything more than "shadow" and "sound," visual signs of voicing in print rather than Swinburne's essential self. In this way he also effectively removes poetry and the poet's self from the public realm of controversy despite its environing print context.

By September, 1872, when his essay on *L'année terrible* by Victor Hugo appeared in the *Fortnightly*, Swinburne had backtracked from strict commitment to *l'art pour l'art*. While maintaining that the "rule of art is not the rule of morals" and that "positive excellence" remains the first requirement of any artwork, he contends that "moral or religious passion" and commitment to "the ethics or the politics of a nation or an age" are consistent with art's integrity and that Dante, Milton, and Shelley were "pleased to put their art to such use."[11] In introducing Baudelaire and the key tenet of aestheticism into Britain in the 1860s, however, Swinburne had already diverted energies from Tractarianism and the mid-Victorian poetics of sympathy into the foreign terrain of French decadence and an ideal of art detached from rhetoric. To the degree that he necessarily adopted rhetoric to persuade readers of the new movement's viability he merely confirmed from another standpoint the inherent contradictoriness of aestheticism in an era of print culture.

Platonic and Sapphic strains: same-sex desire in Pater, Symonds, Michael Field, and Wilde

When Swinburne thanked Walter Pater for his earliest essays in *Fortnightly Review*, Pater "replied to the effect that he considered them as owing their inspiration entirely to the example of [Swinburne's] own work in the same line" – further evidence of Swinburne's important role in *fin-de-siècle* aestheticism and decadence.[12] Pater became the movement's key theorist and exponent when his *Fortnightly* essays, along with two from *Westminster Review*, were gathered with unpublished work into *Studies in the History of the Renaissance* (1873). Attuned to the relentless biological, chemical, and psychological processes of life documented by contemporary scientists, Pater made life's transience a central premise:

> What is the whole physical life in [one] moment but a combination of natural elements to which science gives their names? But those elements, phosphorus and lime and delicate fibres, are present not in the human body alone: we detect them in places most remote from it. Our physical life is a perpetual motion of them – the passage of the blood, the waste and repairing of the lenses of the eye, the modification of the tissues of the brain under every ray of light and sound ... Or if we begin with the inward world of thought and feeling, the whirlpool is still more rapid, the flame more eager and devouring.

These conditions permit no direct access to truth but only impressions of constantly changing forms, and within the stream of glancing, ever shifting consciousness these impressions "burn and are extinguished with our consciousness of them" until consciousness itself comprises a "strange, perpetual, weaving and unweaving of ourselves." The scientific empiricism undergirding this model of consciousness also informs Pater's contention that humans are not defined by their common senses or sympathies but by their isolation, "that thick wall of personality through which no real voice has ever pierced on its way to us" until "each mind keep[s] as a solitary prisoner its own dream of a world."[13]

Within such an intellectual framework the poetics of sympathy are rendered moot. In contrast to Arnold, who had urged in "The Function of Criticism" that "to see the object as in itself it really is" forms the basis of criticism, Pater repositions the question within subjectivist psychology, asking, "What is this song or picture, this engaging personality presented in life or in a book, to *me*? What effect does it really produce on me?"[14] Art here ceases to utter universal truths and instead creates an impression on a particular mind through forms crafted by artists who have similarly filtered impressions through their personalities. In a flash Pater also theorizes the grounds on which criticism ceases to provide objective commentary on transcendent art and itself becomes an impressionist artwork, creating via the critic's subjective response to aesthetic experience a new expression of personality.

Within a worldview founded on transience, the aim of life is not to prepare for an afterlife but to intensify experience in the short time available:

> A counted number of pulses only is given to us of a variegated, dramatic life ... To burn always with [a] hard, gem-like flame, to maintain this

ecstasy, is success in life. In a sense it might even be said that our failure is to form habits: for, after all, habit is relative to a stereotyped world … Of such wisdom, the poetic passion, the desire of beauty, the love of art for its own sake, has most. For art comes to you proposing frankly to give nothing but the highest quality to your moments as they pass, and simply for those moments' sake.[15]

L'art pour l'art here becomes a life philosophy as well as a stance on art.

In the course of articulating his aesthetic theory in 1873 Pater also opened a space for same-sex desire. Swinburne's "Dolores" and "Anactoria" had inserted transgressive desires into exquisitely crafted verse, but Pater muted controversy by introducing same-sex desire under the guise of classical studies, an accepted component of elite male education, book reviews, and criticism. His candor was grounded in his philosophy, for he elevated beauty of form and expression over moral purpose and avoided "habits" by looking to less common or naturalized experience. One of Pater's earliest *Fortnightly* essays was "The Poetry of Michelangelo" (November, 1871). Plato's contention that love between men is superior to men's love for women (since the last involves reproduction, which also characterizes animals and can involve self-interest) is central to Michelangelo's sonnets. Their homoeroticism is clear in the conclusion of the sonnet addressed to Tommaso Cavalieri, in which the poet declares himself "An armèd Knight's captive and slave confessed."[16] In choosing to write about Michelangelo's poems rather than his sculpture or frescoes, Pater establishes same-sex desire as a frame of reference, a focus confirmed when he remarks that "it is the Platonic tradition rather than Dante's that has moulded Michelangelo's verse." Pater goes further when he asserts that "Beneath the Platonic calm of the sonnets there is latent a deep delight in carnal form and colour … He who spoke so decisively of the supremacy in the imaginative world of the unveiled human form had not been always, we may think, a mere Platonic lover."[17]

In his earlier essay on Johann Joachim Winckelmann (*Westminster Review* [January, 1867]), the eighteenth-century scholar who turned study of classical art toward Greece rather than Rome, Pater similarly remarks, "That his affinity with Hellenism was not merely intellectual, that the subtler threads of temperament were inwoven in it, is proved by his romantic, fervent friendships with young men." To illustrate the point he quotes this passage from Winckelmann as "characteristic": "those who are observant of beauty only in women, and are moved little or not at all by the beauty of men, seldom have an impartial, vital, inborn instinct for beauty in art."[18]

Pater was attacked for his "Conclusion" to *Studies in the History of the Renaissance* even though the principal cause of offense – the adjuration to "burn always with [a] hard, gemlike flame" and experience as many intense pulsations of life as possible – had appeared without incident in his *Westminster Review* notice of *The Earthly Paradise* (1868). The implicit hedonism of a book by an Oxford don, however, was deemed dangerous to young men, and Pater suppressed the "Conclusion" in the second edition (1877). But at no time was he asked to suppress the essays on Winckelmann and Michelangelo, which focused on art and interpretation. Same-sex desire, then, successfully entered public discourse in the guise of aesthetic criticism, Greek studies, and philosophy, with important consequences for the later development of aestheticism and decadence.

In a note to his essay on Michelangelo Pater comments that "The sonnets have been translated into English, with much skill, and poetic taste, by Mr. J. A. Symonds."[19] Though his complete edition of sonnets did not appear until 1878, those to which Pater alludes appeared in the September, 1872 *Contemporary Review*, the same periodical in which Robert Buchanan attacked "The Fleshly School of Poetry" (October, 1871). That the eminently respectable, theologically inclined *Contemporary Review* should be hospitable both to Buchanan and to translations of homoerotic verse attests yet again to the dialogism of Victorian print culture. Symonds is today best known for his memoirs, which reveal his struggles as a married father of four and self-aware homosexual to live honestly and with dignity in an inhospitable era. Tellingly, his memoirs were not published until 1984, though he and Havelock Ellis coauthored a scientific study entitled *Sexual Inversion* (with Symonds's personal experiences presented as a case study) in 1897. Poetry and commentary on homosexual themes in art offered earlier outlets to Symonds, including the two-volume *Studies of the Greek Poets* (1873) and *New and Old: A Volume of Verse* (1880). "From Friend to Friend" in the latter praises "soul-commingling friendship passion-fraught" that may be inspired by "heaven-born fire that lights / Love in both breasts from boyhood" (8–9, 14), but "Vintage" exemplifies the degree to which impressionist poetry could, like Pater's essays, become suffused with oblique homoeroticism.

The lyric features a sensuous Greek realm in which light plays upon radiant landscapes and nubile bodies. The title literally refers to a grape harvest but also alludes to Keats's "Ode to a Nightingale": "Oh, for a draught of vintage ... / a beaker full of the warm South, / Full of the true, the blushful Hippocrene" (11, 15–16). The poem opens with the speaker's discovery of a faun, half man and half goat, "lying neath the vines" (1). Though Tennyson warns readers to "Arise and fly / The reeling faun, the sensual feast" in *In Memoriam* (118.25–6), Symonds's persona instead pursues the "fair and jocund" faun (3) who "bade me reach / My hand to his, and drew me through the screen / Of clusters intertwined with glistening green" (5–7). Within the enclosed bower to which they retreat, "flickering" light illuminates the faun's beauty: "With purple grapes and white his comely head / Was crowned, and in his hand a bunch he pressed / Against the golden glory of his breast" (12–14).

From their retreat they spy youths and maidens harvesting grapes, but the poem ends with a lovely boy:

> a beardless boy
> Tuning his melancholy lute-strings sung
>   A wild shrill song, that spake of only joy,
>   But was so sad that virgins cold and coy
> Melted, and love mid sorrow-sweetness fell
> On careless hearts that felt the powerful spell.   (23–8)

"[C]areless hearts" is shrewdly vague, allowing for reference both to formerly indifferent maidens but also to the hidden voyeurs now without a care in the presence of rich beauty. "Vintage" offers no inducements to morality, not even a definite theme; self-consciously minor, it pictures in mellifluous verse the fleeting pleasures of language, imagination, and sensuous male beauty. Overt advocacy of homosexual relations, in contrast to poetry that decorously fused aestheticism and same-sex desire, continued to shock, however: Symonds's earlier defense of pederasty in *Studies of the Greek Poets* inspired such outrage that he was forced to withdraw his candidacy for the Oxford Professorship of Poetry in 1876.

Long Ago (1889), by Michael Field, circulates same-sex desire within a very different cultural context. Lesbian sexuality had been omitted from the Labouchere Amendment to the Criminal Law Amendment Act of 1885, which outlawed "acts of gross indecency between men." The same year, as Yopie Prins notes, Dr. Henry Wharton published an edition of Sappho that reconstructed textual fragments and provided a literal translation. Insofar as Michael Field pair a Greek line from Wharton's edition with an accompanying lyric, *Long Ago* is positioned within the ambit of scholarship.[20] Yet their celebration of sensuality and song also registers allegiance to aestheticism, as do the decorative qualities of the book itself. Its elegant white vellum cover is stamped in gold with a roundel of an archaic Greek woman identified as Sappho by Greek letters. Some lyrics, like "Come, Gorgo, put the rug in place" (XXXV), merely gaze with pleasure upon a woman "in [her] grace, / Dark, virulent, divine" (3–4), something of a counterpart to the homoerotic gaze in Symonds's "Vintage." Though the beautiful Gorgo is rebuked for priding herself on a precious ring, pride functions less as moral flaw than an occasion for the Sapphic persona to praise physical charms far exceeding mere ornament.

"Atthis, my darling" (XIV) dares more, suggesting the consummation of same-sex desire. Its first stanza echoes, while revising, the situation of lovers in Wordsworth's "Strange fits of passion have I known" and Tennyson's *Maud* (1.520–6), who pass from contemplating the beloved asleep in her bed to thinking her dead. In Michael Field's lyric Atthis leaves her bed, and the ensuing silence inspires terror in her Sapphic lover: "a great fear and passion shook / My heart lest haply thou wert dead" (3–4). Atthis, active, whereas Lucy and Maud are passive, has gone to gather a love-tribute: "To pluck me iris thou had'st sprung / Through galingale and celandine" (9–10). But the speaker will have no substitute for the woman herself: "Away, away, the flowers I flung / And thee down to my breast I drew" (11–12). The poem ends by insisting on their passionate embrace all night long:

> My darling! Nay, our very breath
> Nor light nor darkness shall divide;
> Queen Dawn shall find us on one bed,
> Nor must thou flutter from my side
> An instant, lest I feel the dread,
> Atthis, the immanence of death.   (13–18)

Death here emphasizes the desolating effects of physical separation from Atthis and a rationale for enjoying sensuous delights while they can; oblique allusion to the "little death" of orgasm also seems likely. In the Wordsworth and Tennyson poems, in contrast, death is the uncanny twin of sexuality and passion, the unwanted end-result of dimly understood psychological process. Forgoing the aggressive violence of Swinburne's Sappho in "Anactoria," Michael Field's Sappho is as candid about lesbian desire for consummation. Lyric XIV thus imparts a specific lesbian inflection to Michael Field's assertion in the Preface to *Long Ago* that Sappho is "the one woman who has dared to speak unfalteringly of the fearful mastery of love."[21] Not until the modernist poems of Amy Lowell would highly crafted poems express lesbian eroticism with such vehemence, candor, and lyric assurance.

Wilde began *The Sphinx* (1894) in the 1870s but did not finalize it for publication until 1892, after *The Picture of Dorian Gray* had appeared in *Lippincott's Magazine* (July, 1890) and been attacked for homoeroticism in a *Scots Observer* review: "it is not made sufficiently clear that the writer does not prefer a course of unnatural iniquity to a life of cleanliness, health, and sanity. The story – which deals with matters only fitted for the Criminal Investigation Department or a hearing *in camerâ* – is discreditable alike to author and editor."[22] Wilde countered such charges with an aesthetic manifesto entitled "A Preface to *Dorian Gray*" in *Fortnightly Review* (March, 1891), then affixed it to his revised novel. Pater's influence is clear in Wilde's declarations that "The critic is he who can translate into another manner or a new material his impression of beautiful things" and that "The highest as the lowest form of criticism is a mode of autobiography." Wilde also turns Pater's subjective model of interpretation against his attackers – "Those who find ugly meanings in beautiful things are corrupt without being charming" – adding, "It is the spectator, and not life, that art really mirrors." Finally, he insists, as had Swinburne before him, on the complete detachment of art from moral purpose: "There is no such thing as a moral or an immoral book … All art is quite useless."[23]

The role of the spectator is also crucial in *The Sphinx*. Wilde's representation of a Greek rather than Egyptian sphinx enables him to incorporate key elements of decadence that Arthur Symons identified in 1893: "an intense self-consciousness, a restless curiosity in research, an over-subtilizing refinement upon refinement, a spiritual and moral perversity."[24] Whereas the Egyptian sphinx is a wingless male, the Greek bears a female head and breasts atop the winged body of a lion. As "half woman and half animal!" (12), the sphinx is a hybrid monstrosity both in body and sexuality, combining erotic, nurturing, naked female breasts with the masculine sinew and ferocity of a lion (see Figure 6).

If the very title denotes monstrosity, Wilde depicts "restless curiosity" when the young student in whose room the sphinx crouches, blinking and silent, poses question after question about her former lovers. The student's scenarios include necrophily –

> Or did you while the earthen skiffs dropped down the grey Nilotic flats
> At twilight and the flickering bats flew round the temple's triple glyphs
>
> Steal to the border of the bar and swim across the silent lake
> And slink into the vault and make the Pyramid your Lúpanar [brothel]
>
> (59–62) –

sadomasochistic bestiality –

> And take a tiger for your mate, whose amber sides are flecked with black,
> And ride upon his gilded back in triumph through the Theban gate,
>
> And toy with him in amorous jests, and when he turns, and snarls, and gnaws,
> O smite him with your jasper claws! and bruise him with your agate breasts!
>
> (145–8) –

and homoeroticism between the Emperor Hadrian and his beloved male slave:

Figure 6   Charles Ricketts, cover design for Oscar Wilde, *The Sphinx*, illustrated by Charles Ricketts (London: Elkin Matthews and John Lane, 1894)

> Sing to me of that odorous green eve when couching by the marge
> You heard from Adrian's gilded barge the laughter of Antinous
>
> And lapped the stream and fed your drouth and watched with hot and
>   hungry stare
> The ivory body of that rare young slave with his pomegranate mouth!
>
> (33–6)

The student also wonders if the sphinx has enjoyed a lesbian bestial relationship with her counterpart, the Chimera, a female monster with the heads of a lion, goat, and serpent: "from the brick-built Lycian tomb what horrible

Chimaera came / With fearful heads and fearful flame to breed new wonders from your womb?" (51–2).

But the sphinx is principally a metaphor of literariness and a character from literature. When Oedipus successfully answers the question posed to him by the Theban sphinx about what creature walks on four legs in infancy, two in maturity, and three in senescence – man – the sphinx dashes herself to death. The student in Wilde's poem resembles Oedipus in his youth but *he* asks the questions and, because this sphinx remains steadfastly inscrutable, he gets no answers: "Get hence! I weary of your sullen ways, / I weary of your steadfast gaze, your somnolent magnificence" (149–50). The sphinx, Nicholas Frankel suggests, comes to represent textual inscrutability itself, the capacity to signify endlessly but to divulge no definite meaning, especially because Wilde's words were given a material setting so dominated by the visual decoration of Charles Ricketts that it impeded the reading process.[25] Here art is truly "useless."

If the verbal–visual text of *The Sphinx* and its irreducible mysteries hark back to the materiality and self-referentiality of text in Swinburne's "Ave atque vale," Wilde's casting the poem as a dramatic monologue and reversing the roles of questioner and sphinx from the Oedipus myth extend Paterian critical premises. In seeking to penetrate the sphinx's riddle as one might read a text, the student reveals his own personality rather than decoding a timeless truth: "Get hence, you loathsome Mystery! Hideous animal, get hence! / You wake in me each bestial sense, you make me what I would not be. / You make my creed a barren sham, you wake foul dreams of sensual life" (167–9). Here, too, "It is the spectator, and not life, that art really mirrors." The poetics of sympathy would force Wilde's readers into the same position as the student, imagining what he imagines and seeking *his* underlying psychological disposition. Not surprisingly, mainstream reviewers operating within this critical paradigm recoiled, and the *Daily News* remarked that "Considerations of space, and, we are reluctantly compelled to admit of decency" precluded a full accounting of the work.[26] Reading protocols advocated by aesthetes and Decadents, in contrast, allowed readers to appreciate the literary possibility of a sphinx's monstrosity and riddling inscrutability fused into a unified but perverse literary text that both invites and resists reading and gazing.

The terms on which Wilde was read changed even more radically after Wilde was arrested on charges of gross indecency with another man in April, 1895, the sequel to Wilde's unsuccessful libel suit against the Marquess of Queensberry, the father of Lord Alfred Douglas, who characterized Wilde as a "Somdomite" (*sic*) on a card left at Wilde's club. When Queensberry located rent boys (prostitutes) and others to testify against him, Wilde was forced to withdraw his suit and was bankrupted by court costs. Then, after a second criminal trial, he was convicted and sentenced to two years' hard labor.

The trials and conviction were a catastrophe not only for Wilde and the liberties of homosexuals but also for aestheticism and decadence. In effect the trial transformed Wilde's and kindred literary texts into "the lowest form of criticism," that is, into a "mode of autobiography," crudely literalizing and fixing as fact what had been presented as fleeting impressions of infinite suggestion. As the first trial transcript indicates, reviews and Wilde's own writing were introduced as evidence – the recoil of rhetoric so to speak after its attempted expulsion from art by Swinburne, Pater, Wilde, Symons, and others. Even the name of Walter Pater was brought into the courtroom when Edward Carson, representing the Marquess of Queensberry, repeatedly pressed Wilde to concede that *Dorian Gray* could be construed to involve sodomy:

WILDE: It had been pointed out to me not by any newspaper criticism
            or anything, but by the only critic of this century I set high,
            Mr. Walter Pater, he had pointed out to me that a certain passage
            was liable to misconstruction.
CARSON: In what respect?
WILDE: In every respect.
CARSON: In what respect?
WILDE: In the respect that it would convey the impression that the sin of
            Dorian Gray was sodomy.[27]

In the wake of such scandal and ruin aestheticism and decadence collapsed as public literary movements. Poetry itself, which had become closely associated with Wilde and aestheticism, came under suspicion and was instantly a less desirable feature in many newspapers and magazines. Under the circumstances *l'art pour l'art* retreated, though by no means disappearing, and the *fin de siècle* was poised to assume the terms assigned by W. B. Yeats in his autobiographical narrative of the 1890s: "The Tragic Generation."

W. B. Yeats and the resources of myth

Despite Wilde's trial *The Savoy* continued to embrace aestheticism and decadence – though this little magazine survived for only eight numbers. It was coedited by Arthur Symons and Aubrey Beardsley, who in 1895 was fired as art editor of *The Yellow Book* because his work too readily evoked decadence. The title and publisher of *The Savoy* were similarly daring. The Savoy Hotel, as readers of newspaper trial reports knew, was frequented by Wilde and Douglas and associated with rent boys. Publisher Leonard Smithers, who became

Wilde's publisher after his release from prison, partly derived his income from selling pornography, so that proprietor and title alike mockingly signaled impropriety. When bookseller W. H. Smith decided to boycott *The Savoy*, its brief life ended.

Symons and Beardsley were quite serious and uncompromising in their aesthetic principles, and their joint venture hosted a poem that outlived the periodical (and its own first title). "O'Sullivan Rua to Mary Lavell," W. B. Yeats's poem in the July, 1896 *Savoy*, became "Michael Robartes Remembers Forgotten Beauty" in *The Wind among the Reeds* (1899) and is today known as "He Remembers Forgotten Beauty." "O'Sullivan Rua" anglicizes Eoghan Rua Ó Súilleabháin, the eighteenth-century Irish Gaelic poet and visionary. Yeats's *Savoy* title thus indicates a poet speaking across time and languages, in many ways the subject of the poem. Only when the poet embraces the woman here designated as Mary Lavell, ceasing to gaze at her, does he discover what she embodies: "When my arms wrap you round, I press / My heart upon the loveliness / That has long faded in the world" (1–3). If he sees former power, beauty, love, and worship that have waned, the poet's vision equally apprehends the inception of passions, producing simultaneous, layered moments and meanings rather than temporal narratives of loss:

> The jeweled crowns that kings have hurled
> In shadowy pools, when armies fled;
> The love-tales wrought with silken thread
> By dreaming ladies upon cloth
> That has made fat the murderous moth;
> The roses that of old time were
> Woven by ladies in their hair,
> Before they drowned their lovers' eyes
> In twilight shaken with low sighs;
> The dew-cold lilies ladies bore
> Through many a sacred corridor
> Where a so sleepy incense rose
> That only God's eyes did not close.   (4–16)[28]

As Yeats says of the Michael Robartes poems in *Wind among the Reeds* (which reprints the *Savoy* text, excepting its references to drowned lovers' eyes and a Christian God), "Michael Robartes is the pride of the imagination brooding upon the greatness of its possessions, or the adoration of the Magi."[29] Yeats's poem telescopes multiple times, sights, and sighs into a woman who is and is not of the present; for her beauty embodies a transhistorical reality that can be accessed only through indirection and imagination: "For that dim brow and lingering hand / Come from a more dream-heavy land, / A more dream-heavy hour than this" (17–19). The woman's beauty is the locus and symbol of mythic time – all time and no time. In the beloved's sighs, accordingly, the poet hears all beauty sighing out its transience, yet he simultaneously recuperates beauty's abiding power in a closing vision of "seraphs, brooding, each alone, / A sword upon his iron knees, / On [Beauty's] most lonely mysteries" (24–6).

The images of defeat and conquest, crowns and moth-eaten cloth, flowers and incense create a symbolist poem that gestures toward the unsayable through a series of discrete, simple images. Their accumulating associations, along with Yeats's distinctive cadences and language, evoke a "dream-heavy," surreal imaginative tableau. Yeats's poetic techniques derive not only from the Continental symbolist movement but also from his commitment to Irish folklore and myth, a commitment inseparable from his support of Irish nationalism and the revival of Irish culture. Nonetheless, his poem adumbrates a larger transition from Victorian to modernist poetics, especially its reliance on myth to suggest permanent forms of mind and imagination removed from didacticism or social debate.

Greek myth was also important to Romantic and Victorian poets, but myth in mid-nineteenth-century poems tends to function differently from Irish myth in Yeats's poem. Barrett Browning's "A Musical Instrument" and Tennyson's "Tithonus," for example, adapt a single myth to depict the suffering inseparable from poetic creativity or the burden of age in the presence of youth. Many Victorians also saw in Tithonus' lament a moral warning against undue ambition or pride: "Why should a man desire in any way / To vary from the kindly race of men[?]" (28–9). The representation of a recurring female principle that transmigrates from body to body, race to race, in Swinburne's "Faustine" and "Dolores" more fully anticipates Yeats's mythic simultaneity, its gesturing through multiple specific references toward a vantage point outside time. Swinburne's frame of reference, however, remains largely classical and less obviously indebted to anthropological concepts of the primitive and the synthetic mythography of James Frazer's *The Golden Bough* (1890).

The obliquity that in Yeats's *Savoy* poem provides access to mythic consciousness hidden in the depths of mind parallels another key force that shaped twentieth-century poetics, Freudian psychoanalysis. Freud himself, of course, found myth indispensable, as the Oedipus complex indicates. Freud's psychodynamic model and the archetypes of Freud's sometime colleague, Carl Jung, assume a layering of mentality, the deepest, most primitive parts of which can never be accessed directly. Hence the unconscious, the driving force of conscious life, can be expressed only in displacements and doublings, often in the form of dreams. Interpreting the drives and appetites of the unconscious demands that the psychoanalyst intuitively discern amidst the fragments, images, and erratic narratives of the patient's self-report a pattern indicating some underlying trauma or disturbance.

Synthetic models of myth and Freudian theory, both so important to poetry in the twentieth century, may also illuminate modernists' energetic hostility to what they decried as "rhetoric" in Victorian poetry. Within a Freudian model any attempt to articulate consciously conceived ideas in poetry or address social debates verges on bad faith because it entails writing poetry from the mind's surface rather than its depths. The sincerity and sympathy lauded by Victorian critics, even if grounded in nuanced language, rhythm, and form, could seem similarly illusory, even self-deceptive, within a Freudian model that posits a mediating ego poised between an unruly, inaccessible unconscious and a superego that passively conforms to – and mandates – cultural inhibitions. In their attempts to represent fundamental desires and drives that surface only as fragmentary images and perceptions, modernists developed new poetic strategies that have often struck readers (then and now) as obscure and difficult, since their work often demands patient attention to starkly juxtaposed images, like the hyacinth girl and professional clairvoyant in Section I of *The Waste Land*, or layered snatches of thought and narrative through which underlying symbolic meaning may gradually be construed. Modernists, however, did not always give due credit to the multiple signifying layers of Victorian poetry – or to their own investments in public debates and contemporary media.

The poems of Robert Browning and Gerard Manley Hopkins also repudiate transparency, and both poets, unsurprisingly, have been championed by modernists. Most Victorian poetry, moreover, can be fruitfully read in psychoanalytic terms. Doing so, however, requires academic training – a far cry from the contention of E. S. Dallas that great poetry is meant for the multitude rather than the few. As this study has suggested throughout, Victorian poetry's integration into mass print culture encouraged and tacitly confirmed Dallas's assertion, and produced by juxtaposition, and often by design, poetry deeply enmeshed with the pressing issues of its time. For this, Victorian poetry was often dismissed by modernists as no more than "rhetoric." Seen within the context of Victorian print culture, however, Victorian poetry emerges as a dynamic body of work notable for multiple perspectives, nuanced forms and language, and persistent orientation toward contingency and questioning. Revisiting poetry in this context helps readers today recuperate the dynamism, vibrancy, and liveliness that defined Victorian poetry in its own day.

Part III

Coda   Close readings

Chapter 10

Elizabeth Barrett Browning, *Aurora Leigh*

It is one of the longest poems in the world, and there is not a dead line in it.   A. C. Swinburne[1]

[*Aurora Leigh* is] the greatest poem which the century has produced in any language.   John Ruskin[2]

Early in 1845 Elizabeth Barrett Browning began to envision "a sort of novel-poem – a poem as completely modern as 'Geraldine's Courtship,' running into the midst of our conventions, & rushing into drawingrooms & the like 'where angels fear to tread'; – & so, meeting face to face & without mask, the Humanity of the age, & speaking the truth as I conceive of it, out plainly."[3] By form alone Barrett Browning announces her allegiance to modernity in the resulting poem. *Aurora Leigh* self-consciously melds poetic and novelistic narrative into an innovative hybrid medium that, like so many Victorian novels, turns on class relations and social reform. Its novel-plot can be readily summarized.

Aurora, born to a well-educated Englishman and blue-eyed Florentine, loses her mother at age four and is raised by her Italian nurse and heartbroken father (who teaches her from his books) until he too dies when she is thirteen. Aurora then travels to England to live with her maiden aunt, who attempts to suppress Aurora's Italian passions and subject her to rigid feminine discipline. Aurora survives thanks to the nurturing presence of nature glimpsed from her window, and above all her discovery of poetry, a scintillation of the universe and revelation of her true vocation. The vocation of her nearby cousin Romney Leigh, the idealistic heir to the Leigh estate, is reform to alleviate poverty. When he proposes to Aurora on her twentieth birthday he dismisses poetry as mere ornament in a world crying for material help, and women's poetry as a more trivial form of ornamentalism. Fiercely asserting the integrity of her vocation and poetry's centrality to life, Aurora rejects him and, when her aunt shortly thereafter dies and leaves her homeless and penniless, spurns the wealth Romney seeks to bestow upon her. Aurora then departs for London to pursue her literary career.

She encounters Romney and his reforming mission again when Lady Waldemar, the passionate, voluptuously beautiful aristocrat who is in love with him, calls on Aurora to express alarm over Romney's impending marriage to Marian Erle, the illegitimate daughter of a hard-drinking itinerant laborer and his long-suffering companion. To Romney this marriage is less about love than a symbolic union of social privilege and the underclass. The intended wedding, however, turns into a riot when Marian Erle, persuaded by the inveiglements of Lady Waldemar to abandon a marriage of which she is unworthy, deserts Romney at the altar.

Eighteen months later Aurora still has not seen her cousin but has developed her craft while supporting herself through journalism and is attaining stature as a poet. When she hears that Romney is soon to marry Lady Waldemar, who parades her close relation to Romney, as well as an expanse of undraped bosom, before Aurora at a soirée, Aurora finds continued residence in England impossible and leaves for Italy just as her most mature work is being published.

First, however, she stops in Paris, and discovers Marian Erle and her infant son in a Parisian market. Marian, it turns out, was betrayed by Lady Waldemar's maid, who arranged for Marian to be raped and sold to a brothel. Marian has escaped the brothel but not pregnancy, and Aurora now adopts Marian and her son as family members, taking them to Florence. Italy under-scores all the intimacies Aurora has lost, and she increasingly regrets her alienation from Romney, whom it is becoming clear she loves, despite her protests to the contrary or her prior inability to reconcile poetic vocation with marriage. Imagining moment by moment that Romney is marrying Lady Waldemar, Aurora becomes depressed, even neurasthenic. This time her poetic vision does not suffice to grasp the realities of the situation: Romney has never ceased loving her and is impervious to the erotic charms of Lady Waldemar. He has been changed, however, by Aurora's newest poem, which convinces him that poetry's cosmic perspective complements material reform. Still programmatically reformist, he turns Leigh Hall into an egalitarian com-mune. The impoverished residents' enculturation cannot accommodate his utopian scheme, however, and they eventually burn Leigh Hall to the ground. Romney is blinded (like Rochester in *Jane Eyre*) when he is struck on the head while escaping.

Romney materializes beside the lonely Aurora in her Florentine tower one evening to recant his early dismissal of her poetry (though not his enduring love), claim Marian as his wife, and adopt Marian's child. He is stymied in this final attempt to impose rational reform on the poor when Marian Erle rejects him because she does not love him and will not allow her beloved son to be superseded by legitimate children. Aurora, disabused of the notion that Romney has married Lady Waldemar and newly aware of his blindness, recants her earlier dismissal of passion and, acting on her new conviction that embodied love must complement inward spiritual vision, declares her love for Romney. The novel-poem closes as the embracing lovers model a partnership, in which poetry and justice, visionary and material realities, man and woman count equally; and the New Jerusalem's glowing walls that Aurora describes symbolize the new poetic, erotic, social, and spiritual order to which she and Romney dedicate their lives.

If the summable plot of *Aurora Leigh* confirms its kinship to the realist novel, the poem is also a blank-verse modern epic nearly 11,000 lines long that begins *in medias res* and ends with a cosmic vision – though the traditional twelve books are reconfigured into nine. *Aurora Leigh* shares with Milton's *Paradise Lost* the aim of articulating the proper relation of humanity to the divine, and with Virgil's *Aeneid* the aim of defining the proper state and family ties on which the state rests. Aurora, however, synthesizes the three roles that Virgil separately allocates to Dido, a ruler as well as desiring woman whose heart breaks amidst loneliness; Lavinia, the destined wife; and Camilla, the woman warrior who goes to battle as an equal alongside men. (In Virgil, of course, only the wife survives.) Rather than consolidating imperial power like the *Aeneid*, *Aurora Leigh* critiques British power relations – though the narrative never quite overcomes horror at the thought of contact with the unwashed and unlovely poor.

Aurora Leigh is also a Spasmodic epic insofar as it elevates poetic imagination to the status of epic action; hence the poetics Aurora announces in Book 5 forms the poem's preliminary climax. As Herbert Tucker and Kirstie Blair observe, *Aurora Leigh* evades the excesses of Spasmodism because Barrett Browning ironizes her speaker when the poem shifts from retrospective narration to confessional diary in Book 5, which tilts the narrative poem toward the dramatic monologue and its limited persona.[4] Even Aurora's repressive aunt and the spiteful Lady Waldemar understand Aurora's feelings for Romney better than she does herself until the very end.

Madame de Staël's *Corinne* (1807), the novel about a romance between a Scottish peer and Italian woman poet, is a source text for the poem's novelistic element, but the story of a poet's origins, development, and resolution of personal crisis looks back to Wordsworth's *The Prelude*, published only six years before *Aurora Leigh*. Barrett Browning's autobiographical epic alludes to Wordsworth's "Ode: Intimations of Immortality" in the first ten lines when Aurora glances toward her childhood. Marian Erle's story repeatedly echoes *The Prelude* itself. When Marian flees from the squire to whom her mother attempts to sell her, nature seems to pursue her as it does the boy Wordsworth in the famous boat-stealing scene:[5] "Trees, fields, turned on her and ran after her; / She heard the quick pants of the hills behind, / Their keen air pricked her neck" (3.1078–80). Aurora compares the shock of encountering Marian's face in Paris to the resurfacing of a drowned face, a parallel to the drowned man shooting to the surface of a lake in *The Prelude* (5.442–59):

> God! what face is that?
>
> ...
>
> It was as if a meditative man
> Were dreaming out a summer afternoon
> And watching gnats a-prick upon a pond,
> When something floats up suddenly, out there,
> Turns over ... a dead face, known once alive ...   (6.226, 235–9)

Barrett Browning's selection of France as the site where Aurora begins to resolve the breakdown of her former ideals and assumptions may itself owe something to *The Prelude* and its narrative of idealism, then destructive disenchantment occasioned by the French Revolution. But it is to Wordsworth's larger project of tracing a poet's development and asserting the transcendent powers of poetic imagination that *Aurora Leigh* is primarily indebted. Customarily, as Linda Peterson points out, Barrett Browning innovates as she appropriates, merging Wordsworth's autobiographical Romantic epic with the materials of the novel, the dramatic monologue, and the poetess narrative of Letitia Landon in *A History of the Lyre*.[6]

To be understood in any depth, *Aurora Leigh* demands to be read in its entirety. It also demands to be read *as* poetry. Keats, by whose soul Aurora swears (1.1003–10), wrote to Shelley in 1820, "'load every rift' of your subject with ore."[7] The "ore" of *Aurora Leigh* dwells in the densely layered echoes embedded in individual passages and the imagery that structures this long work.

Only in retrospect, for example, is it possible to register the degree to which the opening lines forecast the whole:

> Of writing many books there is no end;
> And I who have written much in prose and verse
> For others' uses, will write now for mine, –
> Will write my story for my better self
> As when you paint your portrait for a friend,
> Who keeps it in a drawer and looks at it
> Long after he has ceased to love you, just
> To hold together what he was and is.   (1.1–8)

The first three lines forge a crucial link among writing, identity, and process, and position "writing" (the poem's first substantive word) as a form of infinitude that transcends a given moment or writer. Lines 2 to 3 establish writing as a past and future act for Aurora ("I ... have written," [I] "will write") and so introduce the "double vision" that will define her poetics and the poem while also signaling the poem's hybrid form allied to "prose and verse." An epic simile describing the intended effect of Aurora's poetic autobiography (5–8) additionally announces the poem's ambitions and classical lineage. Yet that epic simile also embodies autobiographical confession with another double frame of reference. Aurora writes when she fears she has lost the love of Romney (whose rescue of an heirloom portrait resembling Aurora the lines may ironically foreshadow) and blends herself with him in language. Her verbal self-portrait may hold together her prior and present identity, but it can also be presented to Romney – the double referent of the "better self" for whom she writes – as a material tie between them. Lines that seem merely introductory thus arc in several directions and introduce the themes of art, erotic relations, and double vision while also prefiguring other portraits that will play a central philosophical and aesthetic role in the poem. The opening lines also forecast the present-tense narration to which Aurora will return in Book 5.

The striking portrait of Aurora's dead mother that soon follows is another key passage. It represents the psychic ground on which Aurora's self, womanhood, and art are formed, since the portrait is at once a primal childhood memory, a bounded image within which multiple femininities resonate, an articulation of the inseparable link between sacred and profane, a commentary on art's transcendence and insufficiency, and a bravura "notional" ekphrasis (that is, verbal recreation of a fictional art work)[8] that has an important afterlife in modernist poetry:

> The painter drew it after she was dead,
> And when the face was finished, throat and hands,
> Her cameriera carried him, in hate
> Of the English-fashioned shroud, the last brocade
> She dressed in at the Pitti ...
>   I, a little child, would crouch
> For hours upon the floor with knees drawn up,
> And gaze across them, half in terror, half
> In adoration, at the picture there, –
> That swan-like supernatural white life
> Just sailing upward from the red stiff silk
> Which seemed to have no part in it nor power
> To keep it from quite breaking out of bounds ...

And as I grew
In years, I mixed, confused, unconsciously,
Whatever I last read or heard or dreamed,
Abhorrent, admirable, beautiful,
Pathetical, or ghastly, or grotesque,
With still that face ... which did not therefore change,
But kept the mystic level of all forms,
Hates, fears, and admirations, was by turns
Ghost, fiend, and angel, fairy, witch, and sprite,
A dauntless Muse who eyes a dreadful Fate,
A loving Psyche who loses sight of Love,
A still Medusa with mild milky brows
All curdled and all clothed upon with snakes
Whose slime falls fast as sweat will; or anon
Our Lady of the Passion, stabbed with swords
Where the Babe sucked; or Lamia in her first
Moonlighted pallor, ere she shrunk and blinked
And shuddering wriggled down to the unclean;
Or my own mother, leaving her last smile
In her last kiss upon the baby-mouth
My father pushed down on the bed for that, –

(1.128–32, 135–42, 146–66)

Rather than an infant sensorium that blends with the audible strains of the River Derwent in Wordsworth's *Prelude* (1.269–81), in *Aurora Leigh* the future poet's girlhood emotions, reading, thoughts, and dreams – in short Aurora's conscious and unconscious self – converge on and with a dead image of the dead maternal body that paradoxically springs into uncanny life-forms ranging from the divine to the abject. The maternal body forever out of reach, which not even art can fully recuperate, haunts, terrifies, yet also empowers the daughter by sparing her nothing. It confronts her with the stark mortality of flesh that rots after death but likewise with flesh that can through similarly unspeakable (publicly at least) sexuality miraculously create and nurture new life. It teaches invention founded on female rather than masculine models and suggests a near-infinitude of possible forms. Allowing for the female as destroyer (fiend, witch, Medusa, Lamia) and preserver (angel, Psyche, Madonna), it opens a wide space of psychic and embodied action for the daughter and confronts her with the mysteries of evil and good, life and death, flesh and eternity. Insofar as the mother is aligned with a supernatural swan and Muse the pictured female body also bespeaks Jovian powers of creation recorded in the tale of Leda and the swan, and epic tradition tied to the resulting birth of Helen.

This astonishing ekphrasis anticipates another ekphrastic passage crucial to modernism, Walter Pater's description of *La Gioconda* in his essay on Leonardo Da Vinci, which W. B. Yeats reprinted as the first poem in *The Oxford Book of Modern Verse*:

> She is older than the rocks among which she sits;
> Like the Vampire,
> She has been dead many times,
> And learned the secrets of the grave;
> And has been a diver in deep seas,
> And keeps their fallen day about her;
> And trafficked for strange webs with Eastern merchants;
> And, as Leda,
> Was the mother of Helen of Troy,
> And, as St. Anne,
> Was the mother of Mary;
> And all this has been to her but as the sound of lyres and flutes,
> And lives
> Only in the delicacy
> With which it has moulded the changing lineaments,
> And tinged the eyelids and the hands.[9]

Pater, too, discerns the blending of sacred and profane, of seductive allure, horror, and shelter in the painted image of a woman. In *Aurora Leigh*, however, the maternal portrait is important for setting up a reservoir of echoes that span the poem and counter its prodigious narrative length with an effect of poetic simultaneity. The baby kisses and nursing breasts imaged in the maternal portrait, for example, resurface in Book 5's opening invocation of the body's dignity and power (5.14–18) and climactic image of the "full-veined, heaving, double-breasted Age" from which all suck (5.213–22).

Psychologically the maternal portrait functions similarly to the "chora" theorized by Julia Kristeva, a pre-verbal, "mobile" phase in which the child experiences no boundaries between self and the mother prior to attaining mature linguistic awareness.[10] Poetically the portrait's reservoir of female images generates Lady Waldemar and Marian, who mirror aspects of Aurora herself. If Lady Waldemar calls Aurora "'the Muse'" (3.363), Aurora identifies her as Lamia, and the thought that Romney "loves / The Lamia-woman" (7.151–2) impels Aurora to her first confession of love:

> Would I show
> The new wife vile, to make the husband mad?
> No, Lamia! shut the shutters, bar the doors
> From every glimmer on thy serpent-skin!

> I will not let thy hideous secret out
> To agonize the man I love – I mean
> The friend I love ... as friends love.   (7.168–74)

Lady Waldemar is also Medusa, whose letter to Aurora in the last book strikes like "twenty stinging snakes" so that "I stood / Dazed" (9.175–7). But then Aurora herself (or is it the gentle Marian?) has the effect of Medusa on Romney when he happens upon both while Marian is pledging to be his "true wife":

> Before I answered he was there himself.
> I think he had been standing in the room
> And listened probably to half her talk,
> Arrested, turned to stone, – white as stone.   (4.269–73)

Marian Erle, who insists that she was "murdered" by rape (6.809–13), is like the maternal portrait a dead-undead corpse:

> To go down with one's soul into the grave,
> To go down half dead, half alive, I say,
> And wake up with corruption, ... cheek to cheek
> With him who stinks since Friday! There it is,
> And that's the horror of't, Miss Leigh.   (6.1199–1203)

Marian is the "Abhorrent" (1.149) defiled woman with an illegitimate child whom Aurora discovers in a marketplace. She is also "Our Lady of the Passion, stabbed with swords / Where the Babe sucked" (1.160–1), and whom Aurora identifies with the Madonna: "I'll find a niche / And set thee there, my saint, the child and thee, / And burn the lights of love before thy face" (7.126–8). If the maternal portrait says so much about the poet and woman Aurora becomes through its psychic, intellectual, and aesthetic effects on her, the portrait is also a poetic site containing, as it were, the entire narrative that follows.

The poem casts up a double set of portraits in Book 3, which telescope Aurora's relation to art, erotic love, and the divine into another set of metaphors. Sent to Aurora by the painter Vincent Carrington, they form a "double vision" of the imprisoned Danaë to whom Jove came as a shower of gold, impregnating her with the hero Perseus:

> A tiptoe Danae, overbold and hot,
> Both arms a-flame to meet her wishing Jove
> Halfway, and burn him faster down; the face
> And breasts upturned and straining, the loose locks
> All glowing with the anticipated gold.
> Or here's another on the self-same theme.
> She lies here – flat upon her prison-floor,

The long hair swathed about her to the heel
Like wet sea-weed. You dimly see her through
The glittering haze of that prodigious rain,
Half-blotted out of nature by a love
As heavy as fate. I'll bring you either sketch.
I think, myself, the second indicates
More passion.   (3.122–35)

Aurora concurs, adding the crucial point that Danaë is both herself and Jove, woman and creator:

Surely. Self is put away,
And calm with abdication. She is Jove,
And no more Danae – greater thus. Perhaps
The painter symbolises unaware
Two states of the recipient artist-soul,
One, forward, personal, wanting reverence,
Because aspiring only.   (3.135–41)

Unready to embrace her own sexuality and desire, Aurora finds the first Danaë "forward," "wanting reverence." Danaean flames nonetheless rekindle in the same book when she opposes Lady Waldemar's assertion that "love's coarse" (3.455) and avers,

I love love: truth's no cleaner thing than love.
I comprehend a love so fiery hot,
It burns its natural veil of August shame,
And stands sublimely in the nude, as chaste
As Medicean Venus.   (3.702–6)

Aurora harbors a Danaë within but as yet a chaste one. The double Danaë portrait metaphorically indicates that to realize herself as poet and woman Aurora will have to own desire and receive love, as in the second Danaë portrait, as well as aspire to divinity through poetry.

By the outset of Book 5 Aurora is acknowledging sexuality's power – "spring's delicious trouble in the ground, / Tormented by the quickened blood of roots, / And softly pricked by golden crocus-sheaves" – which is driven by cosmic force and mirrored in the "human heart's large seasons" and "all that strain / Of sexual passion, which devours the flesh / In a sacrament of souls" (8–10, 13–16). Emotionally desolate in Book 7, she begins to rate love higher than art and now summons Jove and flame yet still conceives love only in passive terms suggested by Io rather than an active–passive Danaë who shares in Jove's creative power:

> Art itself,
> We've called the larger life, must feel the soul
> Live past it. For more's felt than is perceived,
> And more's perceived than can be interpreted,
> And Love strikes higher with his lambent flame
> Than Art can pile the faggots.
>   Is it so?
> When Jove's hand meets us with composing touch,
> And when at last we are hushed and satisfied,
> Then Io does not call it truth, but love?   (7.889–97)

Romney's sudden presence reanimates the Jove–Danaë metaphor but Book 8 radically restages its gender relations. If in the double portraits Danaë becomes Jove, Romney now becomes Danaë to Aurora's Jovian creativity, and his words echo both Book 3 and Aurora's paean to sexuality in Book 5:

> Poet, doubt yourself,
> But never doubt that you're a poet to me
> From henceforth. You have written poems, sweet,
> Which moved me in secret, as the sap is moved
> In still March-branches, signless as a stone:
> But this last book o'ercame me like soft rain
> Which falls at midnight, when the tightened bark
> Breaks out into unhesitating buds
> And sudden protestations of the spring.   (8.590–8)

The chiastic exchange of male and female, creation and receptivity, and fire and life-giving rain in the two Danaë portraits is completed in Book 9, when Aurora at last unites the visionary poet to the woman's body alive with the electric sparks of passion:

> While we two sat together, leaned that night
> So close my very garments crept and thrilled
> With strange electric life, and both my cheeks
> Grew red, then pale, with touches from my hair
> In which his breath was.   (9.820–4)

The Danaë portraits have a minor role in the novelistic plot of *Aurora Leigh*. Romney long suspects that Aurora loves their creator, Vincent Carrington, but in Book 7 Carrington becomes engaged to Kate Ward, a student of Aurora's poetic and personal style, whose eyes are painted into the Danaë portraits (7, 583–7, 603–10). Poetically, however, the portraits infuse female desire into the poem through recurring images and echoes until the poet and desire merge in Book 9.

The Jovian reference in the Danaë portraits and their metaphoric demonstration that a woman can enter into divine creativity ("She is Jove, / And no more Danae," a representation of "the recipient artist-soul") forms part of a cluster of Jovian and related references that assert the woman poet's privileged relation to divinity and society. Barrett Browning thus redefines the woman poet by repudiating chastity or mourning as the grounds enabling her to sing. When Aurora contends in Book 5 that "The artist's part is both to be and do" and to live a "twofold life" of passive suffering and godlike creation (5.367, 81), she echoes the twy-natured Danaë who is both recipient and active. Shortly after the Danaë–Jove portraits are introduced, when desire remains a threat to the developing poet, Aurora affirms that she carries the seeds of Jove within in an artistic rather than embodied sense:

> I felt it in me where it burnt,
> Like those hot fire-seeds of creation held
> In Jove's clenched palm before the worlds were sown, –
> But I – I was not Juno even! my hand
> Was shut in weak convulsion, woman's ill,
> And when I yearned to loose a finger – lo,
> The nerve revolted. 'Tis the same even now:
> This hand may never, haply, open large,
> Before the spark is quenched, or the palm charred,
> To prove the power not else than by the pain.
> It burnt, it burns – my whole life burnt with it,
> And light, not sunlight and not torchlight, flashed
> My steps out through the slow and difficult road.   (3.251–63)

That Barrett Browning resorts to Greek myth to represent the poet's role and worldview indicates her debt to the Romantic legacy of Keats's *The Fall of Hyperion* or Shelley's *Prometheus Unbound*. Throughout, in fact, *Aurora Leigh* is profoundly indebted to Romantic concepts of poetic imagination and the poet; these, too, underscore the poet's links to divinity and society. According to Coleridge the "primary" imagination is "the living Power and prime Agent of all human Perception ... a repetition in the finite mind of the eternal act of creation in the infinite I AM."[11] Coleridge identifies God with infinite, ongoing creation and poetic imagination with limited (because finite) participation in godhead. In a passage that looks back to the Jove–Danaë portraits and Jovian creation (3.251–63), forward to the "lava-lymph" of God ever pouring Himself into new forms (5.3–6), Aurora similarly speculates,

> What, if even God
> Were chiefly God by living out Himself
> To an individualism of the Infinite,
> Eterne, intense, profuse, still throwing up
> The golden spray of multitudinous worlds
> In measure to the proclive weight and rush
> Of His inner nature, – the spontaneous love
> Still proof and outflow of spontaneous life?   (3.750–7)

Aurora Leigh also echoes the Romantic writing of Thomas Carlyle (cited in 5.156), especially *Sartor Resartus*. Carlyle posits a spiritual reality at the center of the universe that can be apprehended only indirectly, through symbol, which he defines as "some embodiment and revelation of the Infinite," since "the Universe" itself "is but one vast Symbol of God." For those able to participate in divinity and create symbols, "Highest of all Symbols are those wherein the Artist or Poet has risen into Prophet, and all men can recognise a present God." Yet even these "Highest" symbols "wax old" and must constantly be formed anew.[12] Aurora echoes this doctrine of symbols and the poet's link to the divine in Book 5:

> There's not a flower of spring
> That dies ere June but vaunts itself allied
> By issue and symbol, by significance
> And correspondence, to that spirit-world
> Outside the limits of our space and time,
> Whereto we are bound. Let poets give it voice
> With human meanings.   (5.120–6)

These Romantic premises clarify why Aurora and the poem so passionately insist that the material reform Romney pursues is hopelessly inadequate. Merely material means omit the spiritual idea that gives form to life (or poems) and links humanity to God and the universe: "Without the spiritual, observe, / The natural's impossible – no form, / No motion" (7.773–5). Romantic premises also underlie the inseparability of erotic relations, reform, and art in *Aurora Leigh*: each involves body and soul, spiritual idea and the idea's expression in embodied form.

Hence Aurora's commitment to double vision –

> To see near things as comprehensively
> As if afar they took their point of sight,
> And distant things as intimately deep
> As if they touched them   (5.185–8) –

brings the cosmic and palpable into relation with each other throughout. If Romney's materialist reform is incomplete, so is ministering to the soul alone. The physical and spiritual union of Aurora and Romney in marriage thus joins female and male, body and soul, vision and work in a new union that makes perceptible the embodied spiritual poetics on which *Aurora Leigh* is premised.

Theirs will be, emphatically, a working marriage. Aurora repudiates passivity on philosophical grounds:

> Be sure no earnest work
> Of any honest creature, howbeit weak,
> Imperfect, ill-adapted, fails so much,
> It is not gathered as a grain of sand
> To enlarge the sum of human action used
> For carrying out God's end. No creature works
> So ill, observe, that therefore he's cashiered.
> The honest, earnest man must stand and work,
> The woman also – otherwise she drops
> At once below the dignity of man,
> Accepting serfdom. Free men freely work.
> Whoever fears God, fears to sit at ease.   (8.705–16)

This passage, too, reflects the influence of Carlyle and their shared belief that transcendent spirit expresses itself through material forms. Like God, Carlyle argues, humanity must express its inward idea and spirit through its outward works: "here, in this poor, miserable, hampered, despicable Actual, wherein thou even now standest, here or nowhere is thy Ideal: work it out therefrom; and working, believe, live, be free." The kind of work matters less than that "the Form thou give it be heroic, be poetic."[13]

Barrett Browning adds an essential element to Carlyle: "The woman also." Tracing Carlylean precepts to their logical conclusion, she arrives at feminism; i.e., excluding women from work condemns them to social and spiritual enslavement and degradation: "she drops / At once below the dignity of man, /Accepting serfdom" (8.713–14). The point applies with added force to Aurora because she is a poet and so participates in divine truth:

> For the truth itself,
> That's neither man's nor woman's, but just God's.
> ...
> Truth, so far, in my book; the truth which draws
> Through all things upwards – that a twofold world
> Must go to a perfect cosmos. Natural things

> And spiritual, – who separates those two
> In art, in morals, or the social drift,
> Tears up the bond of nature and brings death,
> Paints futile pictures, writes unreal verse,
> Leads vulgar days, deals ignorantly with men,
> Is wrong, in short, at all points.   (7.752–3, 761–9)

Aurora moves beyond the traditional association of women with nature and the body by manifesting female vision and agency in a poem that validates her vocation and high purpose. If society benefits from Aurora's utterance of truth and fashioning new forms to help the world forward, double vision necessitates attention to individual as well as social or cosmic benefits. She observes the injunction of "a twofold world" by being both Danaë and Jove, honoring at once her womanhood and divine gift.

Romantic poetics, finally, are crucial to the poem's hybrid form. Its "prose" element – the lengthy narrative and storyline – is the temporal working-out of a synchronous idea behind the whole. It is the body, so to speak, of the poem, while the proliferating symbols and metaphors bespeak its soul. In this sense, too, the poem enacts a double vision. Barrett Browning's formal innovation is likewise underwritten by Romantic poetics. Only by casting off outworn forms and inventing the new can she fulfill the model of creativity and poetic vision her poem articulates. Sustained creativity, however, must be embodied locally as well as in grand designs. On one hand her resonating imagery serves to "load every rift with ore" because it intensifies (by accumulating) associated meanings as the poem develops; on the other hand, as noted earlier, the maternal and Danaë portraits counterpoint temporal narrative with synchronous images. But each new evocation of an underlying image pattern also exemplifies ongoing creation because each successive evocation casts an underlying idea into a new form, as in this example from Book 3:

> I stood up straight and worked
> My veritable work. And as the soul
> Which grows within a child makes the child grow, –
> Or as the fiery sap, the touch from God,
> Careering through a tree, dilates the bark
> And roughs with scale and knob, before it strikes
> The summer foliage out in a green flame –
> So life, in deepening with me, deepened all
> The course I took, the work I did.   (3.327–35)

Crucial themes and ideas in *Aurora Leigh* – the doctrine of work, the poet's imaginative participation in the divine, the soul's spiritual reality expressed outwardly in the body – are all evident here. But the "fiery" divine "touch" flaming out into new life and the intersection of the natural and divine replay key elements of the Danaë–Jove portrait introduced earlier in the same book. In this passage and throughout, Barrett Browning works both as Romantic poet and Victorian storyteller, enunciating a double vision in a novel-poem that embodies and narrates the compelling importance of poetry, social justice, and erotic relations.

Chapter 11

Ernest Dowson, "*Vitae summa brevis spem nos vetat incohare longam*" and Thomas Hardy, "Friends Beyond"

Both "*Vitae summa brevis spem nos vetat incohare longam*" (1896) by Ernest Dowson and "Friends Beyond" (1898) by Thomas Hardy concern the transience of human life and desire. Yet their styles differ markedly, a result of the alternative poetic traditions out of which they worked. Dowson was a member of the Rhymers' Club, along with W. B. Yeats, Lionel Johnson, Arthur Symons, John Davidson, and Richard Le Gallienne. Yeats records the group's aesthetic criterion of "poetry that was, before all else, speech or song," and their attempt "to write like the poets of the Greek Anthology, or like Catullus, or like the Jacobean Lyrists ..."[1] That is, the group aimed for compression, elegance, refinement, and lyricism rather than moral statement or social purpose. Their aesthetic touchstones are clear in "*Vitae summa brevis*," given in its entirety below:

> They are not long, the weeping and the laughter,
>> Love and desire and hate:
> I think they have no portion in us after
>> We pass the gate.
>
> They are not long, the days of wine and roses:
>> Out of a misty dream
> Our path emerges for a while, then closes
>> Within a dream.

Dowson signified the importance of "*Vitae summa brevis*" by placing it prior to the dedication page of his 1896 *Verses*, so that this lyric formed the keynote for his first published collection.

Dowson's two quatrains attain the epigrammatic force of lyrics in the Greek Anthology, but his title comes from line 15 of Horace's Ode I.iv. As Rowena Fowler explains, Horace's "words are addressed to Sestius, a young man of fortune, in the context of a meditation on the interruption of the joys of spring by the inevitable coming of 'pallida Mors,'" or pale death.[2] Jad Adams, who connects Dowson's lyric to "a depth of feeling about death and the brevity of life which it is more than tempting to see as informed by the death of his parents and the insistent intimations of his own mortality brought on by … disease," translates the Horatian line forming his title as "How should hopes be long, when life is short."[3] Though Horace originated the *carpe diem* or seize-the-day theme, "*Vitae summa brevis*" is not a *carpe diem* poem despite its images of wine and flowers. It is a poem uttered from the far side of pleasure, on the cusp of death. The speaker looks back not only on life's pleasures of "Love and desire," metaphorically reiterated as "the days of wine and roses," but also on life's disappointment and sadness, its "hate" and "weeping." "They are not long" twice underscores transience and the emotions' irrelevance after death, while death's finality attains greater emphasis from the poem's image of a gate – which opens only one way, into death, and allows no return.

The second quatrain's reference to dreams on either side of life recalls Prospero's famous lines in *The Tempest*: "We are such stuff / As dreams are made on, and our little life / Is rounded with a sleep."[4] Dowson gives a bleaker, because narrower, account; in his lyric life shrinks to a mere "path" that fleetingly "emerges" from one vague dream until it reaches the gate and passes into another. The vagueness of that dream registers secular skepticism; though Dowson converted to Roman Catholicism in 1891, his lyric suggests no larger meaning in life or compensation for its sorrows. The lyric's very brevity drives home its principal point – as if indeed there were nothing more to say of existence than what can be expressed in eight brief lines.

Yet the harsh message is delivered in lines of extraordinary grace and liquidity. Yeats's reference to "Jacobean lyrists" in describing the goals of the Rhymers' Club is apt, for if Dowson draws upon classical tradition for his title and theme, he also creates a latter-day counterpart to the elegance and con-cinnity of Robert Herrick's famous six-line poem, "Upon Julia's Clothes":

> When as in silks my *Julia* goes,
> Then, then (me thinks) how sweetly flowes
> That liquefaction of her clothes.
> Next, when I cast mine eyes and see
> That brave Vibration each way free;
> O how that glittering taketh me![5]

The lyric effects of Dowson's poem derive in part from its falling rhythm of pentameter–trimeter–pentameter–dimeter quatrains, a metrical mirroring at each quatrain's close of life's brevity. The pentameter lines, moreover, are marked by extremely subtle cadences. The first line, for example, might be read or

> Théy are not lóng, the wéeping ánd the láughter

or

> Théy are nót lóng, the wéeping and the láughter

or even

> Théy áre not lóng, the wéeping ánd the láughter,

this last creating one of Dowson's trademark alexandrines (an extra foot inserted into a pentameter line). These strong yet unfixed cadences confirm Geoffrey Tillotson's contention that in his "loosening of rhythm" Dowson resembles Yeats and T. S. Eliot.[6] The only strictly regular lines, in fact, are the closing iambic dimeters. Thus in "*Vitae summa brevis*" temporary metrical unpredictability succumbs to fixed, inescapable rhythms in the quatrains' final lines, creating a metrical counterpart to life's brief play and death's inevitability within the poem itself.

Equally strategic are the lyric's use of feminine or masculine endings and enjambment. Only its shorter, even-numbered lines end with stressed (masculine) syllables; brevity thus has more force than length, which gives way to falling rhythms and metrical instability. In the first quatrain, lines 1 and 2, which announce life's brief sway, pause or are end-stopped. Only when readers "pass" via the enjambed third line to a point beyond the gate in line 4 is it clear that death slips into the poem during the enjambment. "After" might have been followed by "many years" or "age descends"; instead it rushes without pause into death. In the second quatrain only the first line is end-stopped, so that the passage from one dream into another, final dream is unimpeded and frighteningly fluent. The poem's own musical flow of rhythm and *abab* rhymes are thus complicit in its bleak vision that carries readers easily and all too swiftly along to a dead stop.

In striking contrast to "*Vitae summa brevis*," Hardy's "Friends Beyond" eschews mellifluous elegance and is likely to seem rough and clumsy on a first reading:

> William Dewy, Tranter Reuben, Farmer Ledlow late at plough,
> > Robert's kin, and John's, and Ned's,
> And the Squire, and Lady Susan, lie in Mellstock churchyard now!

Reviewers more accustomed to the urbane poetics of Dowson and other *fin-de-siècle* authors were shocked by Hardy's deliberately rugged work in *Wessex Poems* (1898). The *Saturday Review* complained of "many slovenly, slipshod, uncouth verses"; the *Westminster Gazette* found several poems "clumsy in execution and harsh in sound"; the *Pall Mall Gazette* complained that Hardy's meters were "rough hacking."[7] His rougher music, however, befits a poem set in rural England and drawing upon the novel, dialect poetry, and hymns more than classical tradition.

For late-Victorian readers "Friends Beyond" would have been inseparable from *Under the Greenwood Tree*, Hardy's novel of 1872 republished with a new Preface in 1896 as part of Hardy's *Wessex Novels* – to which *Wessex Poems* two years later formed a poetic counterpart. *Under the Greenwood Tree* depicts William Dewy at a hale seventy years old, playing his bass viol in the Mellstock Quire (or choir) in which his son Reuben, the tranter or carrier, sings tenor, and his grandson Dick plays treble violin. Robert Penny, the shoemaker, is also a member of the choir; and when the musicians set off to sing carols on Christmas Eve, they stop first at Farmer Ledlow's, whose wife is later seen at the Christmas Day church service silently "reckon[ing] her week's marketing expenses during the first lesson."[8]

One focus of the novel is the romance between Dick Dewy and Fancy Day, who has newly returned to Mellstock to serve as schoolmistress. Another is the historical displacement of the rural choir by the innovation of a single organ – a less robust, more sedate musical offering that redirected attention from the traditional musicians' gallery at the back of the church to the pulpit at the front. After the new vicar, Mr. Maybold, announces that the choir will be disbanded, Tranter Reuben exclaims to him, "if you or I, or any man, was to shake your fist in father's face this way, and say, 'William, your life or your music!' he'd say, 'My life!' Now that's father's nater all over; and you see, sir, it must hurt the feelings of a man of that kind for him and his bass-viol to be done away wi' neck and crop."[9]

Here is the unpolished rural dialect that forms part of the lexicon of "Friends Beyond." In the poem, however, William and Reuben Dewy, Farmer and Mrs. Ledlow are dead and buried, everything dearest to them in life now an irrelevance:

W. D.	– "Ye mid burn the wold bass-viol that I set such vallie by."
	...
Far.	– "Ye mid zell my favourite heifer, ye mid let the charlock grow,
	Foul the grinterns, give up thrift."
Wife.	– "If ye break my best blue china, children, I shan't care or ho."

(16, 22–4)

Even when all the dead form a post-mortem choir, they are as indifferent to the music they sang in life as they are to those who survive them:

All.   – "We've no wish to hear the tidings, how the people's fortunes shift;
                What your daily doings are;
     Who are wedded, born, divided; if your lives beat slow or swift.

     "Curious not the least are we if our intents you make or mar,
                If you quire to our old tune,
     If the City stage still passes, if the weirs still roar afar."   (25–30)

Hardy's poem thus invokes his novel's characters and customary pursuits only to drain them of life and passion.

The implications and effect of this strategy are ambiguous, however. Hardy's poem refers readers to his novel yet explodes that work's liveliness. Rather than endorsing his fiction, the poet may be bidding farewell to it. Yet the poem also situates his created characters as a lingering presence in cultural memory. In this respect the poem implicitly considers the past's larger relation to the present, the grounding of memory in external loci, and the chilly fact of human transience.

The poem acquires further ambiguity and dramatic force because the voices of the dead are heard by an unnamed narrator who has survived their deaths and yearns after his "friends" of the title: "'Gone,' I call them, gone for good, that group of local hearts and heads" (4). The narrator is usually assumed to be Hardy, but the role is equally consistent with Dick Dewy, who as a member of the choir has special reason to recall those "gone for good" and to hear suggestions of their voices in the wind or rhythms of dripping water. Whether or not the narrator conforms to the dramatic principle Hardy announced in his Preface to *Wessex Poems* – "The pieces are in a large degree dramatic or personative in conception"[10] – the ironic point of "Friends Beyond" remains that the living are no longer regarded as friends by the dead, who instead maintain death's superiority to life. Death, these ghostly voices suggest, turns the inherent failure of life into triumph by ending all cares and fears:

     "We have triumphed: this achievement turns the bane to antidote,
                Unsuccesses to success,
     Many thought-worn eves and morrows to a morrow free of thought.

     "No more need we corn and clothing, feel of old terrestial stress;
                Chill detraction stirs no sigh;
     Fear of death has even bygone us: death gave all that we possess."
                                                                    (10–15)

Their indifference elevates them to the status of Epicurean gods who (as in the closing stanzas of Tennyson's "The Lotos-Eaters") look upon earthly matters with utter disregard: "with very gods' composure" they "ignor[e] all that haps beneath the moon" (31, 33). In this sense the characters of *Under the Greenwood Tree* offer consolation to the narrator – and to readers – by resituating death as a gift.

But the consolation comes at a high price, setting at naught more conventional scenarios of heaven and the survival instinct itself. Though James Richardson suggests that "the voices of the dead" are "redeemed and brought into focus by the warmth of what is past ('noon-heat breathes it back from walls'), and that the noiseless breathing shades imperceptibly into whispering,"[11] the setting also highlights the uncanny nature of the narrator's colloquy, and potentially positions the dead as revenants who haunt and whisper seductively to the narrator. To adopt the dead's perspective, after all, requires dying away from life. If the dead are luring the narrator to their perspective, the poem sounds a distinctly *fin-de-siècle* note (given other representations of the undead in the 1890s), and the sudden lyricism that enters the poem along with dead voices acquires a less comforting function:

> Yet at mothy curfew-tide,
> And at midnight when the noon-heat breathes it back from walls
>   and leads,
>
> They've a way of whispering to me – fellow-wight who yet abide –
>   In the muted, measured note
> Of a ripple under archways, or a lone cave's stillicide.   (5–9)

Though "stillicide" designates the ceaseless dripping of water within a cave, its eerie resemblance to "suicide" befits the poem's uncanny liminal border between night and morning, winds blowing through cemetery archways, and the presence of moths that suggest both decay and a death's-head. The poem thus hovers unsteadily between a scene of haunting and the recuperation of comforting, if comically ironic, voices. Such ambiguity retroactively rewrites the title as a question of whether those "beyond" the gate of death can be "friends" and familiars.

The interdependence of "Friends Beyond" and *Under the Greenwood Tree* also brings music to the fore as a feature of the novel and the poem itself. In his 1896 preface to the novel Hardy says nothing of the romance between Dick Dewy and Fancy Day; instead he emphasizes the musicians' enactment of a communal aesthetic and their love of art:

> Under the old plan, from half a dozen to ten full-grown players, in addition to the numerous more or less grown-up singers, were officially occupied with the Sunday routine, and concerned in trying their best to make it an artistic outcome of the combined musical taste of the parish ... The zest of these bygone instrumentalists must have been keen and staying, to take them, as it did, on foot every Sunday after a toilsome week

through all weathers to the church, which often lay at a distance from
their homes. They usually received so little in payment for their performances that their efforts were really a labour of love.[12]

This emphasis on communal taste, repudiation of elite cultural authority, and
endorsement of art for its own sake also illuminates the "music," or sonic
features, of "Friends Beyond."

Though the regularly chiming rhymes of "Friends Beyond" enforce Hardy's
theme of rural music, they take the form of *terza rima* (*aba bcb* etc.), the
intricate chain of rhymed tercets used by Dante in *The Divine Comedy* and
Shelley in "Ode to the West Wind." Yoking homely diction and a rhyme
scheme that glances toward supernal achievements in medieval and
Romantic poetry enables Hardy to hint at the artfulness that lurks in his
provincial scene and apparent simplicity. Dante's and Shelley's poems both
represent, like "Friends Beyond," the relation of life to death within the cosmos,
but Hardy's poem lacks Dante's faith in an ordered universe of sin and
salvation. The narrator concedes that "the Trine allow" life's "crosses," only
to add parenthetically, "(Why, none witteth)" (32–3).

Shelley's atheistic universe within which destruction and creation are balanced seems closer to "Friends Beyond," and Shelley also provides a precedent
for integrating Gothic supernaturalism into deeply personal feeling. In Shelley's
ode seeds carried by the wind are buried until spring, "Each like a corpse within
its grave," while dead leaves are driven before the wind's "unseen presence" "like
ghosts from an enchanter fleeing" (2–3, 7–8). Ultimately a prayer for the poet's
regeneration, Shelley's poem ends hopefully: "If winter comes, can spring be far
behind?"(70). Hardy's adoption of *terza rima* may suggest similar hopefulness,
but the regeneration after burial he represents is unconventional comfort at best.

Rather than the iambic pentameter usually accompanying *terza rima*,
Hardy's tercets are formed from two outer trochaic octameter catalectic lines
and a middle line half as long. Trochaic octameter catalectic became familiar
from Tennyson's "Locksley Hall" and Barrett Browning's "Lady Geraldine's
Courtship." Robert Browning combined this meter with tercets in a poem of
particular relevance to "Friends Beyond," "A Toccata of Galuppi's."
Browning's tinkling rhythm represents the sounds emanating from a keyboard
as an unnamed speaker plays the eighteenth-century music composed by
Baldassare Galuppi and considers the Venetians who once listened to his
music only to die with no trace or any self-evident significance in their lives:

> Then they left you for their pleasure: till in due time, one by one,
> Some with lives that came to nothing, some with deeds as well undone,
> Death stepped tacitly and took them where they never see the sun.

But when I sit down to reason, think to take my stand nor swerve,
While I triumph o'er a secret wrung from nature's close reserve,
In you come with your cold music till I creep thro' every nerve.   (28–33)

Galuppi's music, like Hardy's poem, underscores the transience of all existence
and the tragic pointlessness of so much passion in the past, though music, so
closely associated with emotion, remains. If "Friends Beyond" alludes to both
Shelley and Browning through its formal features, the more hopeful glance
toward "Ode to the West Wind" is counterbalanced by darker possibilities.

The trochaic tetrameter middle lines of Hardy's tercets, however, recall the
print versions of some famous English hymns in church hymnals, for example,
Charles Wesley's eighteenth-century "Lo, he comes with clouds descending":

> Lo! he comes with clouds descending,
>   Once for favoured sinners slain;
> Thousand thousand saints attending
>   Swell the triumph of his train:
>   Alleluya!
> God appears, on earth to reign.

Another is the famous Victorian Christmas hymn for children, "Once in royal
David's City," by Cecil Frances Alexander:

> Once in royal David's city
>   Stood a lowly cattle shed,
> Where a Mother laid her Baby
>   In a manger for his bed:
> Mary was that Mother Mild,
> Jesus Christ her little Child.[13]

The meter of Hardy's tercets, then, echoes both high art (the poetry of
Tennyson, Browning, and Barrett Browning) and humble common hymns
performed by choirs and members of congregations across Britain – a ghostly
echo of the sounds once emanating from William Dewy and the Mellstock
Quire. Yet in the poem the dead no longer care for hymns. For that matter, the
trochaic tetrameter rhythm of printed hymns is lost when congregations sing
the words set to music. That only the trochaic tetrameter rhythm of printed
hymns remains in "Friends Beyond" underscores the sundering of text from
living voices yet again. The multivalent associations of Hardy's *terza rima* and
trochaic octameter–tetrameter catalectic meter, like the poem's tone and setting, make grasping the drift of "Friends Beyond" surprisingly difficult. For it
may by turns seem hopeful and acerbic, comic and grim, nostalgic and alien,
familiar and uncanny.

If Dowson and Hardy make subtle use of form to craft unsentimental poems about human transience, they do so within very different aesthetic frameworks. Dowson's phrases ("days of wine and roses," "gone with the wind"[14]) have passed into common currency through their adaptation by popular fiction and films, yet his work is directed more toward the connoisseur than the common reader. His Latin titles presume a highly educated audience and exclude those ignorant of Latin (or lacking anthologies with footnotes). Any reader can access his quatrains, but his subtle cadences and enjambment are likely to be best appreciated by those familiar with poetic tradition. In appealing to the initiated, moreover, Dowson's lyric anticipates modernist verse. Indeed, after Geoffrey Tillotson asserted that T. S. Eliot's "The Hollow Men" echoes Dowson, Eliot wrote a letter to the *Times Literary Supplement* stating, "This derivation had not occurred to my mind, but I believe it to be correct, because the lines he quotes have always run in my head, and because I regard Dowson as a poet whose technical innovations have been underestimated."[15]

Hardy instead crafts a poetry of plain-spokenness and rural scenes, and most obviously draws upon demotic sources including the novel, dialect poetry, and hymnody. A major innovator nonetheless, Hardy follows the precedent of Robert Browning in demonstrating that subtle poetic effects can be achieved through rough music and harsh colloquialisms as well as plangent mellifluousness. His poems are thus important precursor texts for Robert Frost in America and Philip Larkin in England. If Hardy's poetry is at least as complex as Dowson's, Hardy telegraphs a retreat from connoisseurship by explicitly linking poetry to popular print forms.

Yet Hardy and Dowson together more fully suggest the legacy of Victorian poetry than either could do individually. Their differences represent in little the stunning richness of poetic production in Victorian Britain, its many-voicedness, its intersections with mass media (even in Dowson's case in light of Margaret Mitchell's *Gone with the Wind*), and above all the debate it initiates about form, perspective, change, and the possibilities of reading.

Glossary

For definitions of poetic forms, see Chapter 2.

anapest	metrical foot of two unstressed syllables and one stressed syllable (x x /)
anaphora	repeated initial word(s) in successive lines
blank verse	unrhymed iambic pentameter
caesura	internal pause in a poetic line (indicated by a pivot in thought or syntax or by punctuation)
catalectic	omission of final syllable in a poetic line
dactyl	metrical foot of one stressed and two unstressed syllables (/ x x)
dimeter	metrical line of two feet
ekphrasis	verbal description of visual art
end-stopped	line of poetry terminating in punctuation or, more emphatically, one in which meter, syntax, and sense culminate
enjambment	continuation of sense and syntax with no intervening punctuation from one line to the next; run-on lines
feminine rhyme	rhyme in which final syllable is unstressed
half-rhyme	near rhyme (e.g., "fully," "unruly") in which vowel sounds are not identical
heptameter	metrical line of seven feet
hexameter	metrical line of six feet
iamb	metrical foot of one unstressed and one stressed syllable (x /)
masculine rhyme	rhyme in which final syllable is stressed
meter	literally, measure; indicates an underlying pattern of rhythm governing poetic lines (in English verse, line length is dictated by the number of feet, and a foot by a regular pattern of stressed and unstressed syllables)
octameter	metrical line of eight feet
pentameter	metrical line of five feet
rhyme scheme	pattern of recurring terminal sounds in poetic lines (with each new sound assigned a letter in alphabetical order; e.g., the *abba* stanza of *In Memoriam*)
spondee	metrical foot of two accented syllables (/ /)
tetrameter	metrical line of four feet
trimeter	metrical line of three feet
trochee	metrical foot of one stressed and one unstressed syllable (/ x)

Notes

Introducing Victorian poetry

1. Arthur Quiller-Couch, Preface, in *The Oxford Book of Victorian Verse* (Oxford: Clarendon Press, 1912), pp. viii–ix.
2. Richard D. Altick, *The English Common Reader: A Social History of the Mass Reading Public, 1800–1900*, 2nd edn. (Columbus: Ohio State University Press, 1998), pp. 386–7, 392–5, 357.
3. Joseph Bristow, "Whether 'Victorian' Poetry: A Genre and Its Period," *Victorian Poetry*, 42.1 (Spring, 2004), 81–109.
4. James Joyce, *Ulysses* (New York: Modern Library, 1961), p. 50; Ezra Pound, *Literary Essays* (New York: New Directions Books, 1968), p. 11; W. B. Yeats, *Essays and Introductions* (New York: Collier Books Edition, 1968), p. 497.
5. Stuart Curran, "Romantic Poetry: Why and Wherefore?" *The Cambridge Companion to British Romanticism*, ed. Stuart Curran (Cambridge: Cambridge University Press, 1993), p. 226.
6. Martin Hewitt, "Why the Notion of Victorian Britain *Does* Make Sense," *Victorian Studies*, 48.3 (Spring, 2006), 395–438.
7. Virginia Woolf, "Mr. Bennett and Mrs. Brown," in *The Hogarth Essays*, comp. Leonard S. Woolf and Virginia S. Woolf (London: Hogarth Press, 1928), p. 5.
8. Wolfgang Schivelbusch, *The Railway Journey: The Industrialization of Time and Space in the Nineteenth Century*, 2nd English edn. (Berkeley: University of California Press, 1986), p. 9.
9. Ian Carter, *Railways and Culture in Britain: The Epitome of Modernity* (Manchester: Manchester University Press, 2001), pp. 8, 10, 24–5; Schivelbusch, *The Railway Journey*, pp. 65–6; Altick, *The English Common Reader*, pp. 88–9.
10. Hallam Tennyson, *Alfred, Lord Tennyson: A Memoir*, 2 vols. (London: Macmillan, 1897), Vol. I, p. 195.
11. Robin Gilmour, *The Victorian Period: The Intellectual and Cultural Context of English Literature 1830–1890* (Harlow: Longman Group, 1993), pp. 120–1, 126.
12. George Henry Lewes, *Studies in Animal Life*, Cornhill Magazine, 1 (April–June, 1860), 438–47, 598–607, 682–90; *Punch*, November 10, 1860, p. 182.
13. Philip Davis, *The Oxford English Literary History. Volume 8. 1830–1880: The Victorians* (Oxford: Oxford University Press, 2002), p. 5.

14. Altick, *The English Common Reader*, pp. 1, 277; Alan C. Dooley, *Author and Printer in Victorian England* (Charlottesville: University Press of Virginia, 1992), p. 1.

15. Linda K. Hughes and Michael C. Lund, *The Victorian Serial* (Charlottesville: University Press of Virginia, 1991), pp. 1–14 and *passim*.

16. Altick, *The English Common Reader*, p. 296.

17. *Ibid.*, p. 357.

18. *Aurora Leigh*, 3:66–87, 204–46, 299–343; 5:84–155.

19. Isobel Armstrong, *Victorian Poetry: Poetry, Poetics and Politics* (London: Routledge, 1993), pp. 4–7, 12–15.

20. Herbert F. Tucker, "From Monomania to Monologue: 'St. Simeon Stylites' and the Rise of the Victorian Dramatic Monologue," *Victorian Poetry*, 22.2 (Summer, 1984), 121–37; Armstrong, *Victorian Poetry*, pp. 13–15.

21. J. M. Ludlow, "Trade Societies and the Social Science Association"; Christina G. Rossetti, "Up-Hill"; [R. S. C. Chermside], "The Ghost He Didn't See," *Macmillan's Magazine*, 3 (February, 1861), 324–5.

22. *Living Age*, July 26, 1862, p. 148.

23. Quiller-Couch, ed., *Oxford Book of Victorian Verse*, p. 470.

1. Victorian experimentalism

1. Ekbert Faas, *Retreat into the Mind: Victorian Poetry and the Rise of Psychiatry* (Princeton: Princeton University Press, 1988), pp. 12–13, 47, 59.

2. [W. J. Fox], review of Alfred Tennyson, *Poems, Chiefly Lyrical*, *Westminster Review*, 14 (January, 1831), 215–16.

3. *Ibid.*, p. 216.

4. "Z." [Robert Browning], "Johannes Agricola," *Monthly Repository*, n.s., 10 (January, 1836), 45.

5. Isobel Armstrong, *Victorian Poetry: Poetry, Poetics and Politics* (London: Routledge, 1993), pp. 325–6; Susan Brown, "The Victorian Poetess," in *The Cambridge Companion to Victorian Poetry*, ed. Joseph Bristow (Cambridge: Cambridge University Press, 2000), pp. 182–5.

6. Marjorie Stone, "Elizabeth Barrett Browning and the Garrisonians: 'The Runaway Slave at Pilgrim's Point', The Boston Female Anti-Slavery Society, and Abolitionist Discourse in the *Liberty Bell*," in *Victorian Women Poets*, ed. A. Chapman (Cambridge: D. S. Brewer, 2003), pp. 52–3.

7. J. Westland Marston, review of Alfred Tennyson, *The Princess*, *Athenaeum*, January 1, 1848, p. 8.

8. Hallam Tennyson, *Alfred, Lord Tennyson: A Memoir*, 2 vols. (London: Macmillan, 1897), Vol. I, p. 254.

9. "Mr. Browning's Latest Poetry," *North British Review*, 51 (October, 1869), 112; Faas, *Retreat into the Mind*, p. 24.

10. Philip Kelley and Ronald Hudson, eds., *The Brownings' Correspondence* (Winfield, KS: Wedgestone Press, 1984–), 16 vols. to date, Vol. IX, p. 25.

11. H. Tennyson, *Alfred, Lord Tennyson*, Vol. I, pp. 396, 402.

12. R. J. Mann, *Tennyson's "Maud" Vindicated: An Explanatory Essay* (1856), quoted in *Tennyson: The Critical Heritage*, ed. John D. Jump (London: Routledge and Kegan Paul, 1967), p. 199.

13. Tennyson, *Maud, and Other Poems* (London: Edward Moxon, 1855), p. 1.

14. Gerard Manley Hopkins, "The Starlight Night," in *The Oxford Book of Victorian Verse*, ed. Arthur Quiller-Couch (Oxford: Clarendon Press, 1912), p. 691.

15. Gerard Manley Hopkins, "Author's Preface," in *Poems of Gerard Manley Hopkins*, ed. Robert Bridges, 2nd edn. (London: Oxford University Press, 1930), p. 4.

16. Walt Whitman, *Poems by Walt Whitman*, ed. William Michael Rossetti (London: John Camden Hotten, 1868), pp. vii–viii, 1–2; Walt Whitman Archive, "Published Works," www.whitmanarchive.org/works.

17. Reviews of Walt Whitman, *Poems by Walt Whitman*, *Athenaeum*, April 25, 1868, pp. 585–6; and *Chambers's Journal of Popular Literature, Science and Arts*, July 4, 1868, pp. 420–5.

18. William Wordsworth, "Preface to the Second Edition of *Lyrical Ballads*," in *Wordsworth: Poetical Works* (Oxford: Oxford University Press, 1988), p. 734.

19. Ezra Pound, *The Cantos of Ezra Pound* (New York: New Directions, 1979), p. 6; Walt Whitman, *Complete Poetry and Collected Prose* (New York: Viking Press, 1982), pp. 217, 247.

20. S. T. Coleridge, *Biographia Literaria*, ed. James Engell and W. Jackson Bate, 2 vols. (Princeton: Princeton University Press, 1983), Vol. I, p. 156 n. 1.

21. T. and D. C. Sturge Moore, eds., *Works and Days: From the Journal of Michael Field* (London: John Murray, 1933), p. 16.

22. Arthur Symons, "The Decadent Movement in Literature," *Harper's New Monthly Magazine*, 87 (November, 1893), 858–9.

23. Arthur Symons, *The Symbolist Movement in Literature*, rev. edn. (New York: E. P. Dutton, 1919), p. 4.

24. David Goslee, "New(-) Man as Old Man in the *Dream of Gerontius*," *Renascence: Essays on Values in Literature*, 52.4 (Summer, 2000), 275–6.

2. Victorian dialogues with poetic tradition

1. Richard Jenkyns, *The Victorians and Ancient Greece* (Cambridge, MA: Harvard University Press, 1980), p. 194.

2. A. A. Markley, *Stateliest Measures: Tennyson and the Literature of Greece and Rome* (Toronto: University of Toronto Press, 2004), p. 14.

3. George Grote, *A History of Greece*, 4th edn., 12 vols., Vol. I (London: John Murray, 1854), pp. 50–6.

4. Margot K. Louis, "Gods and Mysteries: The Revival of Paganism and the Remaking of Mythography through the Nineteenth Century," *Victorian Studies*, 47 (2005), 345–6.

5. Dora Greenwell, *Camera obscura* (London: Daldy, Isbister and Co., 1876), pp. 9–12.

6. Walter Pater, "The Myth of Demeter and Persephone," *Fortnightly Review*, n.s. 19 (January, 1876), p. 87.

7. William Irvine and Park Honan, *The Book, the Ring, and the Poet* (New York: McGraw-Hill, 1974), p. 119.

8. Markley, *Stateliest Measures*, p. 60.

9. Matthew Arnold, Preface to the First Edition of *Poems* (1853), in *Arnold: The Complete Poems*, 2nd edn., ed. Kenneth Allott and Miriam Allott (London: Longman, 1979), pp. 654–6.

10. Percy Bysshe Shelley, "A Defence of Poetry," in *Essays, Letters from Abroad, Translations and Fragments*, 2 vols., ed. Mrs. [Mary] Shelley (London: Edward Moxon, 1840), Vol. I, p. 57.

11. Dorothy Mermin, *Elizabeth Barrett Browning: The Origins of a New Poetry* (Chicago: University of Chicago Press, 1989), pp. 241–5.

12. *Athenaeum*, September 17, 1870, p. 364.

13. Robert Pattison, *Tennyson and Tradition* (Cambridge, MA: Harvard University Press, 1979).

14. Theocritus, Idyll 7, in *Theocritus*, trans. A. S. F. Gow (Cambridge: Cambridge University Press, 1952), p. 63.

15. Virgil, *The Georgics*, 3.392–5, trans. L. P. Wilkinson (London: Penguin, 1982), p. 112.

16. [Arthur Hugh Clough], "Recent English Poetry," *North American Review*, 77 (July, 1853), 18.

17. Herbert Tucker, "Epic," in *A Companion to Victorian Poetry*, ed. R. Cronin, A. Chapman, and A. Harrison (Oxford: Blackwell, 2002), p. 25.

18. Review of William Morris, *The Life and Death of Jason*, *Athenaeum*, June 15, 1867, p. 780.

19. Simon Dentith, *Epic and Empire in Nineteenth-Century Britain* (Cambridge: Cambridge University Press, 2006), pp. 8–10.

20. [W. E. Gladstone], review of Alfred Tennyson, *Idylls of the King*, *Quarterly Review*, 106 (October, 1859), 468; anon., review of Tennyson, *Idylls of the King*, *Spectator*, December 25, 1869, p. 1531.

21. James T. Knowles, "Tennyson's Arthurian Poem," *Spectator*, January 1, 1870, pp. 15–17; Henry Alford, review of Tennyson, *Idylls of the King*, *Contemporary Review*, 13 (January, 1870), 104–25.

22. Review of Robert Browning, *The Ring and the Book*, Vol. I, *Saturday Review*, December 26, 1868, p. 833; [H. Buxton Forman], "Robert Browning and the Epic of Psychology," *London Quarterly Review*, 32 (July, 1869), 336.

23. [Robert Buchanan], review of Browning, *The Ring and the Book*, *Athenaeum*, March 20, 1869, p. 399.

24. Irvine and Honan, *The Book, the Ring, and the Poet*, pp. 413, 418.
25. Review of Elizabeth Barrett Browning, *Aurora Leigh*, *British Quarterly Review*, 25 (January, 1857), 263.
26. Thomas Percy, Preface to *Reliques of Ancient English Poetry*, 3 vols. (London: J. Dodsley, 1765), Vol. I, p. x.
27. William Wordsworth, "Essay, Supplementary to the Preface (1815)," in *Wordsworth: Poetical Works* (Oxford: Oxford University Press, 1988), p. 749.
28. "Child Waters," in Percy, *Reliques of Ancient English Poetry*, Vol. III, pp. 58–65.
29. Marjorie Stone, *Elizabeth Barrett Browning* (New York: St. Martin's Press, 1995), pp. 125–7.
30. *Ibid.*, pp. 96, 132.
31. Quoted by Christopher Ricks in Alfred Tennyson, *The Poems of Tennyson*, ed. Christopher Ricks, 2nd edn., 3 vols. (Harlow: Longman, 1987), Vol. I, p. 394.
32. Kathy Alexis Psomiades, "'The Lady of Shalott' and the Critical Fortunes of Victorian Poetry," in *The Cambridge Companion to Victorian Poetry*, ed. Joseph Bristow (Cambridge: Cambridge University Press, 2000), pp. 25–45.
33. "Witch of Wokey," in Percy, *Reliques of Ancient English Poetry*, Vol. I, p. 335.
34. Tricia Lootens, "Victorian Poetry and Patriotism," in Bristow, *The Cambridge Companion to Victorian Poetry*, pp. 258–9.
35. Oscar Wilde, *The Complete Letters of Oscar Wilde*, ed. Merlin Holland and Rupert Hart-Davis (London: Fourth Estate, 2000), p. 956.
36. John Stokes, *In the Nineties* (Chicago: University of Chicago Press, 1989), p. 110.
37. Ellen L. O'Brien, *Crime in Verse: The Poetics of Murder in the Victorian Era* (Columbus: Ohio State University Press, 2008), pp. 39, 104–5.
38. Wilde, *Complete Letters*, p. 964.
39. Anne Janowitz, *Lyric and Labour in the Romantic Tradition* (Cambridge: Cambridge University Press, 1998), pp. 134–5, 138, 141.
40. "Songs for the People. / No. XVII. / A Chartist Chorus," *Northern Star*, June 6, 1846, p. 3; available at *Nineteenth Century Serials Edition*, www.ncse.ac.uk/index.html.
41. Brian Maidment, ed., *Poorhouse Fugitives: Self-Taught Poets and Poetry in Victorian Britain* (Manchester: Carcanet, 1987), pp. 67–73.
42. Natalie M. Houston, "Valuable by Design: Material Features and Cultural Value in Nineteenth-Century Sonnet Anthologies," *Victorian Poetry*, 37 (1999), 245.
43. Emily Pfeiffer, "Among the Hebrides," in *Poems* (London: Strahan, 1876), p. 58.
44. [John Dennis], "The English Sonnet," *Cornhill Magazine*, 25 (May, 1872), 595.
45. Alison Chapman, "Sonnet and Sonnet Tradition," in Cronin, Chapman, and Harrison, *A Companion to Victorian Poetry*, p. 106.
46. Jan Marsh, *Christina Rossetti: A Writer's Life* (New York: Viking, 1995), p. 471.
47. Yopie Prins, *Victorian Sappho* (Princeton: Princeton University Press, 1999), p. 179.
48. Dante Alighieri, *The New Life*, trans. D. G. Rossetti, in *Dante Gabriel Rossetti: Collected Poetry and Prose*, ed. Jerome McGann (New Haven: Yale University Press, 2003), p. 292.

49. Jerome McGann, *Dante Gabriel Rossetti and the Game that Must Be Lost* (New Haven: Yale University Press, 2000), pp. xv–xvi, 7.

50. Dante Gabriel Rossetti, *Letters of Dante Gabriel Rossetti*, 5 vols., ed. Oswald Doughty and John Robert Wahl (Oxford: Clarendon Press, 1965–7), Vol. II, p. 850.

51. Matthew Arnold, "The Function of Criticism at the Present Time," in *Lectures and Essays in Criticism*, ed. R. H. Super (Ann Arbor: University of Michigan Press, 1962), pp. 283–4.

52. James K. Robinson, "A Neglected Phase of the Aesthetic Movement: English Parnassianism," *PMLA*, 68 (1953), 739.

53. May Probyn, "Grandmother," in *Ballades and Rondeaus, Chants Royal, Sestinas, Villanelles, &c*, ed. Gleeson White (London: Walter Scott, [1887]), p. 49.

54. May Probyn, "Villanelle"; and Graham R. Tomson, "Villanelle," in White, *Ballades and Rondeaus*, pp. 263, 273.

3. The impress of print: poems, periodicals, novels

1. Arthur Henry Hallam, "On Some of the Characteristics of Modern Poetry, and on the Lyrical Poems of Alfred Tennyson," *Englishman's Magazine*, 1 (August, 1831), 616.

2. Antiquus [J. S. Mill], "What is Poetry?" *Monthly Repository*, n.s., 7 (January, 1833), 61–2, 64.

3. David Masson, "Theories of Poetry," *North British Review*, 19 (1853), 298.

4. *Ibid.*, 310, 315–16, 322–3.

5. E. S. Dallas, *The Gay Science*, 2 vols. (London: Chapman and Hall, 1866), Vol. I, p. 127.

6. "Literature," *Leader*, April 7, 1855, p. 329.

7. Margaret Forster, *Elizabeth Barrett Browning: A Biography* (London: Chatto and Windus, 1988), p. 357.

8. Julia Markus, ed., *Casa Guidi Windows* (New York: Browning Institute, 1977), p. xxxvi.

9. Alice Meynell, "Mr. W. E. Henley's Poems," *Merry England*, 11 (June, 1888), 93; William Fredeman, "Rossetti's 'In Memoriam': An Elegiac Reading of *The House of Life*," *Bulletin of the John Rylands Library*, 47 (1964–5), 298.

10. M. H. Spielmann, *The History of Punch* (New York: Greenwood Press, 1969), pp. 332–3.

11. Christina Rossetti, *The Letters of Christina Rossetti*, ed. Anthony H. Harrison, 4 vols. (Charlottesville: University Press of Virginia, 1997–2004), Vol. I, p. 190.

12. Edgar Finley Shannon, Jr., *Tennyson and the Reviewers: A Study of His Literary Reputation and of the Influence of the Critics upon His Poetry 1827–1851* (Cambridge, MA: Harvard University Press, 1952), pp. 91–2.

13. Herbert F. Tucker, "Glandular Omnism and Beyond: The Victorian Spasmodic Epic," *Victorian Poetry*, 42 (2004), 429–31.

14. Alexander Smith, *A Life Drama*, Scene 4, *Critic*, May 15, 1852, p. 260.

15. [George Henry Lewes], "Literature," *Leader*, September 18, 1852, p. 903.

16. Florence S. Boos, "'Spasm' and Class: W. E. Aytoun, George Gilfillan, Sydney Dobell, and Alexander Smith," *Victorian Poetry*, 42 (2004), 556–8.

17. Richard Cronin, "The Spasmodics," in *A Companion to Victorian Poetry*, ed. R. Cronin, A. Chapman, and A. Harrison (Oxford: Blackwell, 2002), p. 301.

18. "Thomas Maitland" [Robert Buchanan], "The Fleshly School of Poetry: Mr. D. G. Rossetti," *Contemporary Review*, 18 (October, 1871), 335, 338.

19. D. G. Rossetti, "The Stealthy School of Criticism," *Athenaeum*, December 16, 1871, pp. 792–4.

20. Simon Eliot, *Some Patterns and Trends in British Publishing 1800–1919*, Occasional Papers of the Bibliographical Society, 8 (London: The Bibliographical Society, 1994), pp. 44–7, 106.

21. [Arthur Hugh Clough], "Recent English Poetry," *North American Review*, 77 (July, 1853), 2–3.

22. M. M. Bakhtin, "Epic and Novel," in *The Dialogic Imagination*, ed. Michael Holquist, trans. Caryl Emerson and Michael Holquist (Austin: University of Texas Press, 1981), pp. 5–7.

23. Elizabeth Barrett Barrett to Robert Browning, February 27, 1845, in Philip Kelley and Ronald Hudson, eds., *The Brownings' Correspondence* (Winfield, KS: Wedgestone Press, 1984–), 16 vols. to date, Vol. X, pp. 102–3.

24. Geoffrey Tillotson, *Mid-Victorian Studies* (London: Athlone Press, 1965), p. 134; Patrick Scott, ed., *The Bothie: Arthur Hugh Clough, the Text of 1848* (St. Lucia: University of Queensland Press, 1976), pp. 42 n. 141, 43 n. 23.

25. William St. Clair, *The Reading Nation in the Romantic Period* (Cambridge: Cambridge University Press, 2004), pp. 210, 214–15.

26. S. T. Coleridge, *Biographia Literaria*, ed. James Engell and W. Jackson Bate, 2 vols. (Princeton: Princeton University Press, 1983), Vol I, p. 304; Shelley, "A Defence of Poetry," in *Essays, Letters from Abroad, Translations and Fragments*, 2 vols., ed. Mrs. [Mary] Shelley (London: Edward Moxon, 1840), Vol. I, p. 57; Thomas Carlyle, "The Hero as Poet," in *On Heroes, Hero-Worship, and the Heroic in History* (1840), ed. John Chester Adams (Boston: Houghton Mifflin, 1907), pp. 107–8.

27. Matthew Reynolds, *The Realms of Verse 1830–1870: English Poetry in a Time of Nation-Building* (Oxford: Oxford University Press, 2001), pp. 16–18, 47–67.

28. Joanne Shattock, "Reviewing Generations: Professionalism and the Mid-Victorian Reviewer," *Victorian Periodicals Review*, 35 (2002), 397.

29. David Masson, *British Novelists and Their Styles* (Cambridge: Macmillan, 1859), pp. 1–2.

30. [H. L. Mansel], "Sensation Novels," *Quarterly Review*, 113 (1863), 251–3.

31. Jennifer Carnell, *The Literary Lives of Mary Elizabeth Braddon: A Study of Her Life and Work* (Hastings: The Sensation Press, 2000), p. 102.

32. M. E. Braddon, *Garibaldi and Other Poems* (London: Bosworth and Harrison, 1861), pp. 269–71.

33. Clyde Kenneth Hyder, ed., *Swinburne Replies: Notes on Poems and Reviews, Under the Microscope, Dedicatory Epistle* (Syracuse, NY: Syracuse University Press, 1966), pp. 57–8.

34. [Thomas Spencer Baynes], "Swinburne's Poems," *Edinburgh Review*, 134 (July, 1871), 94–5.

35. [Mortimer Collins], *A Letter to the Right Hon. Benjamin Disraeli, M.P.* (London: John Camden Hotten, 1869), p. 18.

36. Review of *The Ring and the Book*, *Month*, 2 (December, 1869), 622; [Mortimer Collins], review of *The Ring and the Book*, *British Quarterly Review*, 49 (April, 1869), 456–7.

37. Henry James, "The Novel in 'The Ring and the Book,'" *Quarterly Review*, 217 (1912), 74–5, 78–80.

38. Linda Peterson, "Domestic and Idyllic," in *A Companion to Victorian Poetry*, ed. Cronin, Chapman, and Harrison, pp. 42–58.

Introduction to Part II

1. W. B. Yeats, "Modern Poetry" (1936), in *Essays and Introductions* (New York: Macmillan, 1961), p. 497.

2. John Henry Raleigh, *Matthew Arnold and American Culture* (Berkeley: University of California Press, 1957), p. 61.

3. Anthony J. Cascardi, "*Judgment*: Arts of Persuasion and Judgment. Rhetoric and Aesthetics," in *A Companion to Rhetoric and Rhetorical Criticism*, ed. Walter Jost and Wendy Olmsted (Oxford: Blackwell, 2004), pp. 294–6.

4. Paul Ricoeur, "Rhetoric – Poetics – Hermeneutics," in *Rhetoric and Hermeneutics in Our Time*, ed. Walter Jost and Michael J. Hyde (New Haven, CT: Yale University Press, 1997), pp. 65–6.

5. Martin F. Tupper, "On Compensation," in *Proverbial Philosophy*, in *Tupper's Complete Poetical Works* (Boston: Crosby, Nichols, Lee, and Co., 1860), p. 20.

4. Poetry, technology, science

1. Edward P. Mead, "The Steam King", *Northern Star*, February 11, 1843, p. 3, lines 25–8.

2. Marshall Berman, *All that Is Solid Melts into Air: The Experience of Modernity* (Harmondsworth: Penguin, 1988), p. 15.

3. William Paley, *Natural Theology; or, Evidences of the Existence and Attributes of the Deity*, 12th edn. (London: J. Faulder, 1809), pp. 1, 3.

4. Francis Darwin, ed., *The Life and Letters of Charles Darwin*, 2 vols. (New York: D. Appleton and Co., 1905), Vol. II, p. 115.

5. Edward P. Mead, "The Steam King," in *Poorhouse Fugitives: Self-Taught Poets and Poetry in Victorian Britain*, ed. Brian Maidment (Manchester: Carcanet, 1987), pp. 41–2.

6. Joseph Skipsey, *Carols, Songs, and Ballads* (London: Walter Scott, 1888), p. 108.

7. Ellen Johnston, *Autobiography, Poems and Songs* (Glasgow: William Love, 1867), pp. 100–1.

8. [Caroline Norton], *A Voice from the Factories* (London: John Murray, 1836), pp. x, vi; reprinted in *Victorian Women Writers Project*, www.indiana.edu/~letrs/vwwp/Norton/voic.html.

9. Ernest Jones, "The Factory Town," *The Labourer*, 1.2 (February, 1847), 49–52.

10. William Allingham, *Life and Phantasy* (London: Reeves and Turner, 1889), pp. 71–2.

11. Ana Parejo Vadillo, *Women Poets and Urban Aestheticism: Passengers of Modernity* (Basingstoke: Palgrave Macmillan, 2005), pp. 2–3, 8–9.

12. Barri J. Gold, "The Consolation of Physics: Tennyson's Thermodynamic Solution," *PMLA*, 117 (2002), 449–64.

13. Hallam Tennyson, *Alfred, Lord Tennyson: A Memoir*, 2 vols. (London: Macmillan, 1897), Vol. II, p. 35.

14. E. Burnet Tylor, "Wild Men and Beast-Children," *Anthropological Review*, 1 (1863), 21, 30.

15. Charles Darwin, *On the Origin of Species by Means of Natural Selection; or, The Preservation of Favoured Races in the Struggle for Life* (New York: New American Library, 1958), p. 166.

16. *Ibid.*, pp. 375–6.

17. S. T. Coleridge, *Biographia Literaria*, ed. James Engell and W. Jackson Bate, 2 vols. (Princeton: Princeton University Press, 1983), Vol. I, p. 285.

18. Mathilde Blind, *The Ascent of Man* (London: Chatto and Windus, 1889), pp. 7–8, 50, 53–8, 106; reprinted in *Victorian Women Writers Project*, www.indiana.edu/~letrs/vwwp/blind/ascent.html.

19. *Ibid.*, pp. 10–11, 28, 46.

20. Blind, *Shelley: A Lecture* (1870), quoted in James Diedrick, "Mathilde Blind," *Dictionary of Literary Biography 199: Victorian Women Poets*, ed. William B. Thesing (Detroit: Gale Group, 1999), p. 33.

21. Blind, *Ascent of Man*, pp. 13, 95–7, 103–4.

22. *Ibid.*, pp. 103–4.

5. Poetry and religion

1. John Henry Newman, review of *The Theatre of the Greeks*, *London Review*, 1.1 (January, 1829), 169.

2. [David Masson], "Theories of Poetry and a New Poet," *North British Review*, 19 (August, 1853), 314.

3. Matthew Arnold, Preface, in *God and the Bible* (London: Smith, Elder, 1884), p. vii.

4. G. B. Tennyson, *Victorian Devotional Poetry: The Tractarian Mode* (Cambridge, MA: Harvard University Press, 1981), pp. 82, 198, 226–9.

5. Simon Eliot, *Some Patterns and Trends in British Publishing 1800–1919*, Occasional Papers of the Bibliographical Society, 8 (London: The Bibliographical Society, 1994), pp. 44–7.

6. Quoted in G. B. Tennyson, *Victorian Devotional Poetry*, p. 116.

7. *Ibid.*, p. 83.

8. Quoted in Owen Chadwick, *The Spirit of the Oxford Movement: Tractarian Essays* (Cambridge: Cambridge University Press, 1990), p. 88.

9. *Ibid.*, pp. 90–5.

10. Sarah Flower Adams, "Nearer, My God, To Thee," in *Hymns and Anthems*, ed. W. J. Fox (London: Charles Fox, 1841), No. LXXXV.

11. Cecil Frances Alexander, *Poems*, ed. William Alexander (London: Macmillan, 1896), pp. 14–15.

12. Quoted in J. R. Watson, *The English Hymn: A Critical and Historical Study* (Oxford: Oxford University Press, 1997), p. 443.

13. Quoted in John Ferns, "Frances Ridley Havergal," in *Dictionary of Literary Biography 199: Victorian Women Poets*, ed. William B. Thesing (Detroit: Gale Group, 1999), p. 162.

14. Frances Ridley Havergal, *Loyal Responses; or, Daily Melodies for the King's Minstrels* (London: James Nisbet and Co., 1878), pp. 9–10.

15. Hallam Tennyson, *Alfred, Lord Tennyson: A Memoir*, 2 vols. (London: Macmillan, 1897), Vol. II, p. 170.

16. Emily Brontë, *The Poems of Emily Brontë*, ed. Derek Roper with Edward Chitham (Oxford: Oxford University Press, 1995), p. 270.

17. G. B. Tennyson, *Victorian Devotional Poetry*, pp. 108–9.

18. *Ibid.*, p. 80.

19. Alfred H. Miles, ed., *The Poets and the Poetry of the Century: Robert Bridges and Contemporary Poets* (London: Hutchinson and Co., 1893), pp. 165–70.

20. Julia Saville, *A Queer Chivalry: The Homoerotic Asceticism of Gerard Manley Hopkins* (Charlottesville: University Press of Virginia, 2000), p. 5.

21. Elizabeth Barrett Browning, Preface, in *The Seraphim and Other Poems: The Complete Works of Mrs. E. B. Browning*, ed. Charlotte Porter and Helen A. Clarke, 6 vols. (New York: G. D. Sproul, 1901), Vol. I, p. 164.

22. Barrett Browning, Preface, in *Poems* (1844), in *ibid.*, Vol. II, pp. 143–4.

23. Cynthia Scheinberg, *Women's Poetry and Religion in Victorian England: Jewish Identity and Christian Culture* (Cambridge: Cambridge University Press, 2002), pp. 4, 22, 28, 33–4, 44–8, 65–6.

24. Linda Hunt Beckman, *Amy Levy: Her Life and Letters* (Athens: Ohio University Press, 2000), p. 315 n. 39.

25. Scheinberg, *Women's Poetry and Religion in Victorian England*, pp. 230–2.

26. Daniel A. Harris, "Hagar in Christian Britain: Grace Aguilar's 'The Wanderers,'" *Victorian Literature and Culture*, 27.1 (1999), 143–69.

27. *Ibid.*, 144–5.

6. Poetry and the heart's affections

1. Isobel Armstrong, *Victorian Scrutinies: Reviews of Poetry, 1830–1870* (London: Athlone Press, 1972), pp. 9–14.
2. Adam Smith, *An Inquiry into the Nature and Causes of the Wealth of Nations*, 3rd edn., 3 vols. (Edinburgh: A. Constable and Co., 1806), Vol. II, p. 242.
3. Louis Althusser, "Ideology and Ideological State Apparatuses" (1970), in *A Critical and Cultural Theory Reader*, ed. Antony Easthope and Kate McGowan (Toronto: University of Toronto Press, 1992), p. 52.
4. James Eli Adams, "Victorian Sexualities," in *A Companion to Victorian Literature and Culture*, ed. Herbert F. Tucker (Oxford: Blackwell, 1999), pp. 127–8.
5. Isobel Armstrong, "Msrepresentation: Codes of Affect and Politics in Nineteenth-Century Women's Poetry," in *Women's Poetry, Late Romantic to Late Victorian: Gender and Genre, 1830–1900*, ed. Isobel Armstrong and Virginia Blain (Basingstoke: Macmillan, 1999), pp. 20–1.
6. Jerome McGann, *The Poetics of Sensibility: A Revolution in Literary Style* (Oxford: Clarendon Press, 1996), pp. 7, 109, 136–8, 146–7, 169.
7. Paula Feldman, "The Poet and the Profits: Felicia Hemans," in Armstrong and Blain, *Women's Poetry, Late Romantic to Late Victorian*, pp. 87–9.
8. Richard Cronin, *Romantic Victorians: English Literature, 1824–1840* (Basingstoke: Palgrave, 2002), p. 107; Herbert F. Tucker, "House Arrest: The Domestication of English Poetry in the 1820s," *New Literary History*, 25.3 (Summer, 1994), 541–5.
9. Glennis Stephenson, *Letitia Landon: The Woman behind L. E. L.* (Manchester: Manchester University Press, 1995), pp. 47–8; Cynthia Lawford, "Diary," *London Review of Books*, September 21, 2000, pp. 36–7.
10. Linda H. Peterson, "Rewriting *A History of the Lyre*: Letitia Landon, Elizabeth Barrett Browning and the (Re)Construction of the Nineteenth-Century Woman Poet," in Armstrong and Blain, *Women's Poetry, Late Romantic to Late Victorian*, pp. 115–29.
11. Coventry Patmore, *The Angel in the House: The Betrothal* (London: J. W. Parker and Son, 1854), pp. 72–3.
12. Richard Holt Hutton, review of Coventry Patmore, *The Angel in the House*, *North British Review*, 28 (May, 1858), 538, 543.
13. E. Nesbit, *Lays and Legends* (London: Longmans, Green, and Co., 1887), p. 38.
14. Ellen Johnston, *Autobiography, Poems, and Songs* (Glasgow: William Love, 1867), pp. 44–5.
15. Eliza Ogilvy, "A Natal Address to My Child, March 19th 1844," in *Victorian Women Poets: An Anthology*, ed. Angela Leighton and Margaret Reynolds (Oxford: Blackwell, 1995), pp. 300–1.
16. Samantha Matthews, *Poetical Remains: Poets' Graves, Bodies, and Books in the Nineteenth Century* (Oxford: Oxford University Press, 2004), pp. 257, 261.
17. Caroline Norton, *The Dream, and Other Poems*, 2nd edn. (London: Henry Colburn, 1841), pp. 77–95.

18. Philip Kelley and Ronald Hudson, eds., *The Brownings' Correspondence* (Winfield, KS: Wedgestone Press, 1984–), 16 vols. to date, Vol. IX, pp. 349, 380.

19. Charles Dickens, *David Copperfield* (1849–50), Chapters 45, 48.

20. Linda H. Peterson, "Alice Meynell's *Preludes*, or Preludes to What Future Poetry?" *Victorian Literature and Culture*, 34 (2006), 410.

21. Alfred Tennyson, *The Princess* (London: Edward Moxon, 1847), p. 158.

22. Meg Tasker, "*Aurora Leigh*: Elizabeth Barrett Browning's Novel Approach to the Woman Poet," in *Tradition and the Poetics of Self in Nineteenth-Century Women's Poetry*, ed. Barbara Garlick (Amsterdam: Rodopi, 2002), p. 36.

23. Anthony Hecht, *The Hard Hours: Poems* (New York: Athenaeum, 1967), p. 17.

7. Poetry and empire

1. Arthur Conan Doyle, *Songs of Action* (New York: Doubleday and McClure, 1898), p. 3.

2. Frances Browne, *The Star of Attéghéi, The Vision of Schwartz, and Other Poems* (London: Edward Moxon, 1844), p. 69.

3. Speranza (Lady Wilde), "A Lament for the Potato," *Poems of Speranza*, 2nd edn. (Glasgow: Cameron and Ferguson, n.d. [1871?]), p. 63; reprinted in *Victorian Women Writers Project*, www.indiana.edu/~letrs/vwwp/wilde/speranza.html#p63.

4. Review of William Burge, *Observations on the Supreme Appellate Jurisdiction of Great Britain*, British and Foreign Review, 11 (May, 1841), 288.

5. Michael Leapman, *The World for a Shilling: How the Great Exhibition of 1851 Shaped a Nation* (London: Headline Book Publishing, 2001), p. 106.

6. *Ibid.*, pp. 23, 82, 134–7, 142.

7. Gerald Massey, "Kings Are but Giants because We Kneel," *The Friend of the People*, March 8, 1851, reprinted in *Voices of Freedom and Lyrics of Love* (London: J. Watson, 1851), pp. 70–1; "They Are but Giants while We Kneel," in *The Ballad of Babe Christabel with Other Lyrical Poems*, 4th edn. (London: David Bogue, 1854), pp. 170–3.

8. Martin Tupper, "The Indian Martyrs," *London Journal*, October 10, 1857, p. 95.

9. Quoted in Jennifer Carnell, *The Literary Lives of Mary Elizabeth Braddon: A Study of Her Life and Work* (Hastings: The Sensation Press, 2000), p. 97.

10. Jan Marsh, *Christina Rossetti: A Writer's Life* (New York: Viking, 1995), pp. 194–6.

11. [Christina] Rossetti, "The Round Tower at Jhansi. – June 8, 1857," *Once a Week*, 1 (August 13, 1859), 140.

12. Virginia Blain, ed., *Victorian Women Poets: A New Annotated Anthology* (Harlow: Pearson Education, 2001), p. 87.

13. Emily Pfeiffer, *Under the Aspens* (London: Kegan Paul, Trench, and Co., 1882), pp. 98–104.

14. Robert Buchanan, "The Voice of the Hooligan," *Contemporary Review*, 76 (December, 1899), quoted in Steve Attridge, *Nationalism, Imperialism, and*

Identity in Late Victorian Culture: Civil and Military Worlds (New York: Macmillan, 2003), p. 70.

15. Henry Newbolt, *Clifton Chapel and Other School Poems* (London: John Murray, 1908), pp. 8–9.

16. D. G. Rossetti, "The Burden of Nineveh," *Oxford and Cambridge Magazine*, 1 (August, 1856), 512–16.

17. James T. Knowles, Letter to the Editor, *Spectator*, January 1, 1870, pp. 15–17.

18. Review of *Idylls of the King*, *Victoria Magazine*, 14 (February, 1870), 381.

19. Review of *Idylls of the King*, *Dublin University Magazine*, 54 (April, 1860), 498–9; "King Arthur and His Round Table," *Blackwood's Edinburgh Magazine*, 88 (September, 1860), 337.

20. Herbert F. Tucker, "The Epic Plight of Troth in *Idylls of the King*," *ELH*, 58 (1991), 701–20.

21. [William Gladstone], review of *Idylls of the King*, *Quarterly Review*, 106 (October, 1859), 468.

8. Poetic liberties

1. Ernest Jones, "The March of Freedom," *The Labourer*, 3 (March, 1848), 101–8, lines 1–3.

2. Ernest Jones, *The New World: A Democratic Poem*, *Notes to the People*, 1 (March, 1851), 5–6, 11.

3. Karl Marx, "The Chartists," *New York Daily Tribune*, August 25, 1852, p. 6.

4. Matthew Reynolds, *The Realms of Verse 1830–1870: English Poetry in a Time of Nation-Building* (Oxford: Oxford University Press, 2001), pp. 75–85.

5. Isobel Armstrong, "*Casa Guidi Windows*: Spectacle and Politics in 1851," in *Unfolding the South: Nineteenth-Century British Women Writers and Artists in Italy*, ed. Alison Chapman and Jane Stabler (Manchester: Manchester University Press, 2003), pp. 51–3.

6. Elizabeth Barrett Browning, Preface to *Casa Guidi Windows*, in *The Complete Works of Mrs. E. B. Browning*, ed. Charlotte Porter and Helen A. Clarke, 6 vols. (New York: G. G. Sproul, 1901), Vol. III, pp. 249–50.

7. A. C. Swinburne, *The Swinburne Letters*, ed. Cecil Y. Lang, 6 vols. (New Haven: Yale University Press, 1959–62), Vol. I, p. 43.

8. Edmund Gosse, *The Life of Algernon Charles Swinburne* (New York: Macmillan, 1917), pp. 160–1.

9. Anne McClintock, *Imperial Leather: Race, Gender and Sexuality in the Colonial Contest* (New York: Routledge, 1995), pp. 132–7.

10. Philip Bourke Marston, "A Realistic Poet," *Atlantic Monthly*, 49 (April, 1882), 515.

11. Arthur Munby, *Verses New and Old* (London: Bell and Daldy, 1865), pp. 72–6, lines 8–9, 12).

12. T. S. Eliot, Preface, in *John Davidson: A Selection of His Poems*, ed. Maurice Lindsay (London: Hutchinson, 1961), p. vii.

13. Charles Booth, *Labour and Life of the People*, 2 vols., 3rd edn. (London: Williams and Norgate, 1891), Vol. I, p. 6.
14. Florence S. Boos, "Narrative Design in *The Pilgrims of Hope*," in *Socialism and the Literary Artistry of William Morris*, ed. Florence S. Boos and Carole G. Silver (Columbia: University of Missouri Press, 1990), p. 162.
15. "Literary Gossip," *Athenaeum*, February 20, 1886, p. 264.
16. L. S. Bevington, *Liberty Lyrics* (London: James Tochatti "Liberty" Press, 1895), pp. 7–8, reprinted in *Victorian Women Writers Project*, www.indiana.edu/~letrs/ vwwp/bevington/liberty.html.
17. Quoted in Elizabeth Barrett Browning, *Aurora Leigh*, ed. Margaret Reynolds (New York: W. W. Norton, 1996), p. viii.
18. Ellen Moers, *Literary Women: The Great Writers* (Garden City, NY: Anchor Books, 1977), pp. 84–9.
19. [George Gilfillan], "Female Authors, No. 1 – Mrs. Hemans," *Tait's Edinburgh Magazine*, n.s., 14 (1847), quoted in *The Woman Question: Society and Literature in Britain and America 1837–1883*, ed. Elizabeth K. Helsinger, Robin Lauterbach Sheets, and William Veeder, 3 vols. (Chicago: University of Chicago Press, 1983), Vol. III, p. 29.
20. Mona Caird, "Marriage," *Westminster Review*, 130 (August, 1888), 195.
21. E. Nesbit, *Lays and Legends*, Second Series (London: Longmans, Green, and Co., 1892), p. 109.
22. Margaret Forster, *Elizabeth Barrett Browning: A Biography* (London: Chatto and Windus, 1988), p. 357.
23. Josephine Butler, Letter to the Editor, *The Shield*, May 9, 1870, p. 80.
24. A. C. Swinburne, *Notes on Poems and Reviews* (London: John Camden Hotten, 1866), p. 14.
25. [John Morley], review of A. C. Swinburne, *Poems and Ballads*, *Saturday Review*, August 4, 1866, pp. 145–7, reprinted in *Swinburne: The Critical Heritage*, ed. Clyde K. Hyder (New York: Barnes and Noble, 1970), pp. 29, 26.
26. Kathy Alexis Psomiades, *Beauty's Body: Femininity and Representation in British Aestheticism* (Stanford: Stanford University Press, 1997), p. 70.

9. Resisting rhetoric: art for art's sake

1. W. B. Yeats, "He Remembers Forgotten Beauty", *The Savoy*, 3 (July, 1896), 67.
2. Grant Allen, "The New Hedonism," *Fortnightly Review*, n.s., 55 (March, 1894), 377–92.
3. Max Nordau, *Degeneration* (New York: D. Appleton and Co., 1895), p. 19.
4. Richard Ellmann, *Oscar Wilde* (New York, Alfred A. Knopf, 1988), pp. 45, 135.
5. W. S. Gilbert, *Patience*, Act 2, in *The Savoy Operas* (London: Macmillan, 1952), p. 196.
6. Christopher Decker, Introduction, in Edward Fitzgerald, *The Rubáiyát of Omar Khayyám: A Critical Edition*, ed. Christopher Decker (Charlottesville: University Press of Virginia, 1997), p. xxxiv.

7. A. C. Swinburne, review of Charles Baudelaire, *Les fleurs du mal*, *Spectator*, September 6, 1862, pp. 998–1000.

8. Oscar Wilde, "A Preface to *Dorian Gray*," *Fortnightly Review*, n.s. 49 (March, 1891), 480.

9. Arthur Symons, "The Decadent Movement in Literature," *Harper's New Monthly Magazine*, 87 (November, 1893), 859.

10. E. S. Dallas, *The Gay Science*, 2 vols. (London: Chapman and Hall, 1866), Vol. I, p. 127.

11. A. C. Swinburne, review of Victor Hugo, *L'année terrible*, *Fortnightly Review*, n.s. 12 (September, 1872), 257–8.

12. A. C. Swinburne to John Morley, April 11, 1873, in *The Swinburne Letters*, ed. Cecil Y. Lang, 6 vols. (New Haven: Yale University Press, 1959–62), Vol. II, p. 241.

13. Walter Pater, "Conclusion," in *Studies in the History of the Renaissance*, reprinted in *The Renaissance*, ed. Adam Phillips (Oxford: Oxford University Press, 1986), pp. 150–2.

14. "Preface," in *ibid.*, p. xxix.

15. "Conclusion," in *ibid.*, pp. 152–3.

16. Michelangelo di Lodovico Buonarroti Simoni, *The Sonnets of Michael Angelo Buonarroti*, trans. John Addington Symonds, 2nd edn. (London: Smith, Elder, 1904), p. 33.

17. Walter Pater, "The Poetry of Michelangelo," *Studies in the History of the Renaissance*, pp. 52, 55.

18. Pater, "Winckelmann," in *Studies in the History of the Renaissance*, pp. 122–3.

19. Pater, "The Poetry of Michelangelo," in *ibid.*, p. 53.

20. Yopie Prins, *Victorian Sappho* (Princeton: Princeton University Press, 1999), pp. 52–3, 74, 80–1.

21. Michael Field, Preface, in *Long Ago* (Portland, ME: Thomas B. Mosher, 1897), p. vi.

22. Review of Oscar Wilde, *The Picture of Dorian Gray*, *Scots Observer*, July 5, 1890, p. 181.

23. Wilde, "A Preface to *Dorian Gray*," 480–1.

24. Symons, "The Decadent Movement in Literature," 858–9.

25. Nicholas Frankel, *Oscar Wilde's Decorated Books* (Ann Arbor: University of Michigan Press, 2000), pp. 158–70.

26. Quoted in Merlin Holland, ed., *The Real Trial of Oscar Wilde: The First Uncensored Transcript of The Trial of Oscar Wilde vs. John Douglas (Marquess of Queensberry), 1895* (New York: Fourth Estate, 2003), p. 323 n. 230.

27. *Ibid.*, pp. 78–9.

28. W. B. Yeats, "O'Sullivan Rua to Mary Lavell," *The Savoy* (July, 1896), 67.

29. Quoted in R. F. Foster, *W. B. Yeats: A Life*, 2 vols., Vol. I: *The Apprentice Mage* (Oxford: Oxford University Press, 1997), pp. 214–15.

10. Elizabeth Barrett Browning, *Aurora Leigh*

Additional close readings are available at the online "Supplement to *The Cambridge Introduction to Victorian Poetry*," http://lib.tcu.edu/urn/:ths2009061801.

1. A. C. Swinburne, *The Complete Works of Algernon Charles Swinburne*, ed. Edmund Gosse and Thomas J. Wise, 20 vols. (London: W. Heinemann Ltd., 1925–7), Vol. XVI, p. 4.
2. John Ruskin, *The Works of John Ruskin*, ed. E. T. Cook and Alexander Wedderburn, 39 vols. (New York: Longmans Green, 1903–12), Vol. XV, p. 227.
3. Philip Kelley and Ronald Hudson, eds., *The Brownings' Correspondence* (Winfield, KS: Wedgestone Press, 1984–), 16 vols. to date, Vol. X, pp. 102–3.
4. Herbert F. Tucker, "Glandular Omnism and Beyond: The Victorian Spasmodic Epic," *Victorian Poetry*, 42 (2004), 443–6; Kirstie Blair, "Spasmodic Affections: Poetry, Pathology, and the Spasmodic Hero," *Victorian Poetry*, 42 (2004), 486–8.
5. William Wordsworth, *The Prelude*, 1.372–88.
6. Linda Peterson, "Rewriting *A History of the Lyre*: Letitia Landon, Elizabeth Barrett Browning and the (Re)Construction of the Nineteenth-Century Woman Poet," in Isobel Armstrong and Virginia Blain (Basingstoke: Macmillan, 1999), pp. 115–32.
7. John Keats, *Selected Poems and Letters*, ed. Douglas Bush (Cambridge, MA: Houghton Mifflin, 1959), p. 298.
8. John Hollander, *The Gazer's Spirit: Poems Speaking to Silent Works of Art* (Chicago: University of Chicago Press, 1995), pp. 4, 7–10, 30.
9. Walter Pater, "Mona Lisa," in *The Oxford Book of Modern Verse, 1892–1935*, ed. W. B. Yeats (New York: Oxford University Press, 1937), p. 1.
10. Julia Kristeva, *The Kristeva Reader*, ed. Toril Moi (New York: Columbia University Press, 1986), pp. 93–4.
11. S. T. Coleridge, *Biographia Literaria*, ed. James Engell and W. Jackson Bate, 2 vols. (Princeton: Princeton University Press, 1983), Vol. I, p. 304.
12. Thomas Carlyle, *Sartor Resartus* (London: Grant Richards, 1902), pp. 189, 192–3.
13. *Ibid.*, p. 167.

11. Ernest Dowson, *"Vitae summa brevis spem nos vetat incohare longam"* and Thomas Hardy, "Friends Beyond"

1. W. B. Yeats, *The Autobiography of William Butler Yeats* (New York: Macmillan, 1978), p. 200; W. B. Yeats, BBC broadcast, October 11, 1936, quoted in Norman Alford, *The Rhymers' Club: Poets of the Tragic Generation* (Basingstoke: Macmillan, 1994), p. 51.
2. Rowena Fowler, "Ernest Dowson and the Classics," *Yearbook of English Studies*, 3 (1973), 249.
3. Jad Adams, *Madder Music, Stronger Wine: The Life of Ernest Dowson, Poet and Decadent* (London: I. B. Tauris, 2000), p. 120.
4. William Shakespeare, *The Tempest*, IV.i.156–8.
5. Robert Herrick, *Hesperides* (1648), in *Seventeenth-Century Verse and Prose, Volume One: 1600–1660*, ed. Helen C. White, Ruth C. Wallerstein, and Ricardo Quintana (Toronto: Macmillan, 1970), p. 256.

6. [Geoffrey Tillotson], "Ernest Dowson," *Times Literary Supplement* (January 3, 1935), 6.

7. Quoted in James Gibson, "*Wessex Poems*, 1898," in *The Achievement of Thomas Hardy*, ed. Phillip Mallett (Basingstoke: Macmillan, 2000), p. 112.

8. Thomas Hardy, *Under the Greenwood Tree*, ed. Tim Dolin (London: Penguin, 1998), p. 32.

9. *Ibid.*, p. 67.

10. Thomas Hardy, Preface, in *Wessex Poems and Other Verses* (London: Harper, 1898), p. vi.

11. James Richardson, *Thomas Hardy: The Poetry of Necessity* (Chicago: University of Chicago Press, 1977), p. 122.

12. Hardy, *Under the Greenwood Tree*, p. 161.

13. *The English Hymnal Service Book* (London: Oxford University Press, 1962), pp. 180, 254.

14. Ernest Dowson, "*Non sum qualis eram bonae sub regno Cynarae*," line 13.

15. T. S. Eliot, Letter to the Editor, *Times Literary Supplement*, January 10, 1935, p. 21.

Further reading

Anthologies

Armstrong, I. and Bristow, J. *Nineteenth-Century Women Poets*, Oxford: Clarendon Press, 1996

Boos, F. *Working-Class Women Poets in Victorian Britain*, Peterborough, ON: Broadview Press, 2008

Collins, T. and Rundle, V. *The Broadview Anthology of Victorian Poetry and Poetic Theory*, Peterborough, ON: Broadview Press, 1999

Cunningham, V. *The Victorians: An Anthology of Poetry and Poetics*, Oxford: Blackwell Publishers, 2000

Karlin, D. *The Penguin Book of Victorian Verse*, Harmondsworth: Penguin Books, 1997

Leighton, A. and Reynolds, M. *Victorian Women Poets*, Oxford: Blackwell Publishers, 1995

Maidment, B. *The Poorhouse Fugitives: Self-Taught Poets and Poetry in Victorian Britain*, Manchester: Carcanet, 1987

O'Gorman, F. *Victorian Poetry: An Annotated Anthology*, Oxford: Blackwell Publishers, 2004

Ricks, C. *The New Oxford Book of Victorian Verse*, Oxford: Oxford University Press, 1987

General studies and surveys

Armstrong, I. *Victorian Poetry: Poetry, Poetics and Politics*, London: Routledge, 1993

Armstrong, I. and Blain, V., eds. *Women's Poetry, Late Romantic to Late Victorian: Gender and Genre, 1830–1900*, New York: St. Martin's Press, 1999

Bevis, M. *The Art of Eloquence*, Oxford: Oxford University Press, 2007

Bristow, J., ed. *The Cambridge Companion to Victorian Poetry*, Cambridge: Cambridge University Press, 2000

Chapman, A., ed. *Victorian Women Poets*, Cambridge: D. S. Brewer, 2003

Christ, C. *Victorian and Modernist Poetics*, Chicago: University of Chicago Press, 1984

Cronin, R., Chapman, A., and Harrison, A., eds. *A Companion to Victorian Poetry*, Oxford: Blackwell, 2002

Douglas-Fairhurst, R. *Victorian Afterlives: The Shaping of Influence in Nineteenth-Century Literature*, Oxford: Oxford University Press, 2002

Griffiths, E. *The Printed Voice of Victorian Poetry*, Oxford: Clarendon Press, 1989

Harrison, A. *Victorian Poets and Romantic Poems: Intertextuality and Ideology*, Charlottesville: University Press of Virginia, 1990

Hughes, L. K., ed. "Whither Victorian Poetry?" *Victorian Poetry*, special issues, 41 (2003), 459–645; 42 (2004), 1–109

Leighton, A. *Victorian Women Poets: Writing against the Heart*, Charlottesville: University Press of Virginia, 1992

Reynolds, M. *The Realms of Verse 1830–1870: English Poetry in a Time of Nation-Building*, Oxford: Oxford University Press, 2001

Shaw, W. D. *The Lucid Veil: Poetic Truth in the Victorian Age*, London: Athlone Press, 1987

Slinn, E. W. *Victorian Poetry as Cultural Critique*, Charlottesville: University of Virginia Press, 2003

Poetic form

General

Campbell, M. *Rhythm and Will in Victorian Poetry*, Cambridge: Cambridge University Press, 1999

Tucker, H. "The Fix of Form: An Open Letter," *Victorian Literature and Culture*, 27 (1999), 531–5

"Of Monuments and Moments: Spacetime in Nineteenth-Century Poetry," *Modern Language Quarterly*, 58 (1997), 269–97

Dramatic monologue

Faas, E. *Retreat into the Mind: Victorian Poetry and the Rise of Psychiatry*, Princeton: Princeton University Press, 1988

Langbaum, R. *The Poetry of Experience: The Dramatic Monologue in Modern Literary Tradition*, New York: Random House, 1957

Mermin, D. *The Audience in the Poem: Five Victorian Poets*, New Brunswick, NJ: Rutgers University Press, 1983

Shires, L., ed. "The Dramatic 'I' Poem," *Victorian Poetry*, special issue, 22 (1984), 97–226

Sinfield, A. *Dramatic Monologue*, London: Methuen, 1977

Victorian poetry and classical tradition

Bush, D. *Mythology and the Romantic Tradition in English Poetry*, New York: Pageant Book Company, 1957

Dentith, S. *Epic and Empire in Nineteenth-Century Britain*, Cambridge: Cambridge University Press, 2006

Hurst, I. *Victorian Women Writers and the Classics: The Feminine of Homer*, Oxford: Oxford University Press, 2006

Jenkyns, R. *The Victorians and Ancient Greece*, Cambridge, MA: Harvard University Press, 1980

Markley, A. *Stateliest Measures: Tennyson and the Literature of Greece and Rome*, Toronto: University of Toronto Press, 2004

Maxwell, C. *The Female Sublime from Milton to Swinburne*, Manchester: Manchester University Press, 2001

Prins, Y. *Victorian Sappho*, Princeton: Princeton University Press, 1999

Tucker, H. *Epic: Britain's Heroic Muse 1790–1910*, Oxford: Oxford University Press, 2008

Turner, F. *The Greek Heritage in Victorian Britain*, New Haven: Yale University Press, 1981

Modern forms and tradition

Bold, A. *The Ballad*, London: Methuen, 1979

Friedman, A. *The Ballad Revival: Studies in the Influence of Popular on Sophisticated Poetry*, Chicago: University of Chicago Press, 1961

Janowitz, A. *Lyric and Labour in the Romantic Tradition*, Cambridge: Cambridge University Press, 1998

Holmes, J. *Dante Gabriel Rossetti and the Late Victorian Sonnet Sequence: Sexuality, Belief and the Self*, Aldershot: Ashgate, 2005

Lootens, T. *Lost Saints: Silence, Gender, and Victorian Literary Canonization*, Charlottesville: University Press of Virginia, 1996

Mermin, D. "The Damsel, the Knight, and the Victorian Woman Poet (1986)," in *Victorian Women Poets: A Critical Reader*, ed. Angela Leighton, Oxford: Blackwell, 1996, 198–214

Phelan, J. *The Nineteenth-Century Sonnet*, Basingstoke: Palgrave Macmillan, 2005

Print culture

Altick, R. *The English Common Reader: A Social History of the Mass Reading Public, 1800–1900*, 2nd edn., Columbus: Ohio State University Press, 1998

Armstrong, I. *Victorian Scrutinies: Reviews of Poetry, 1830–1870*, London: Athlone Press, 1972

Brake, L. *Print in Transition, 1850–1910: Studies in Media and Book History*, Basingstoke: Palgrave, 2001
   Subjugated Knowledges: Journalism, Gender and Literature in the Nineteenth Century, New York: New York University Press, 1994
Demoor, M. *Their Fair Share: Women, Power, and Criticism in the Athenaeum, from Millicent Garrett Fawcett to Katherine Mansfield, 1870–1920*, Aldershot: Ashgate, 2000
Easley, A. "Tait's Edinburgh Magazine in the 1830s: Dialogues on Gender, Class, and Reform," *Victorian Periodicals Review*, 38 (2005), 263–79
Erickson, L. *The Economy of Literary Form: English Literature and the Industrialization of Publishing, 1800–1850*, Baltimore: Johns Hopkins University Press, 1996
Fraser, H., Green, S., and Johnston, J., *Gender and the Victorian Periodical*, Cambridge: Cambridge University Press, 2003
Hughes, L. K. "What the *Wellesley Index* Left Out: Why Poetry Matters to Periodicals," *Victorian Periodicals Review*, 40.2 (Summer, 2007), 91–125
LaPorte, C. and J. R. Rudy, eds. "Spasmodic Poetry and Poetics," *Victorian Poetry*, special issue, 42.4 (Winter, 2004), 421–583
Ledbetter, K. *Tennyson and Victorian Periodicals: Commodities in Context*, Aldershot: Ashgate, 2007
Roberts, A. *Romantic and Victorian Long Poems: A Guide*, Aldershot: Ashgate, 1999
Robson, C. "Standing on the Burning Deck: Poetry, Performance, History," *PMLA*, 120 (2005), 148–62
St. Clair, W. *The Reading Nation in the Romantic Period*, Cambridge: Cambridge University Press, 2004

Poetry, science, technology

Dawson, G., ed. "Science and Poetry," *Victorian Poetry*, special issue, 41.1 (Spring, 2003), 1–172
Peterfreund, S. "Robert Browning's Decoding of Natural Theology in 'Caliban upon Setebos,'" *Victorian Poetry*, 43 (2005), 317–31
Rudy, J. *Electric Meters: Victorian Physiological Poetics*, Athens: Ohio University Press, 2009

Poetry and religion

Blair, K., ed. *John Keble in Context*, London: Anthem, 2004
Blair, K. and Mason, E., eds. "Tractarian Poets," *Victorian Poetry*, special issue, 44.1 (Spring, 2006), 1–116
Knight, M., and Mason, E. *Nineteenth-Century Religion and Literature: An Introduction*, Oxford: Oxford University Press, 2006

Melnyk, J. *Victorian Religion: Faith and Life in Britain*, Westport, CT: Praeger, 2008

Melnyk, J., ed. *Women's Theology in Nineteenth-Century Britain: Transfiguring the Faith of Their Fathers*, New York: Garland, 1998

Nixon, J., ed. *Victorian Religious Discourse: New Directions in Criticism*, Basingstoke: Palgrave Macmillan, 2004

Tamke, S. *Make a Joyful Noise unto the Lord: Hymns as a Reflection of Victorian Social Attitudes*, Athens: Ohio University Press, 1978

Tennyson, G. B. *Victorian Devotional Poetry: The Tractarian Mode*, Cambridge, MA: Harvard University Press, 1981

Wheeler, M. *Death and the Future Life in Victorian Literature and Theology*, Cambridge: Cambridge University Press, 1990

Poetry and the heart's affections

Ball, P. *The Heart's Events: The Victorian Poetry of Relationships*, London: Athlone Press, 1976

Blair, K. *Victorian Poetry and the Culture of the Heart*, Oxford: Clarendon Press, 2006

Cronin, R. *Romantic Victorians: English Literature, 1824–1840*, Basingstoke: Palgrave, 2002

Edmond, R. *Affairs of the Hearth: Victorian Poetry and Domestic Narrative*, London: Routledge, 1988

McSweeney, K. *Supreme Attachments: Studies in Victorian Love Poetry*, Aldershot: Ashgate, 1998

Poetry and empire

Bevis, M. "Fighting Talk: Victorian War Poetry," in *The Oxford Handbook of British and Irish War Poetry*, ed. Tim Kendall, Oxford: Oxford University Press, 2007, 7–33

Brantlinger, P. *Rule of Darkness: British Literature and Imperialism, 1830–1914*, Ithaca, NY: Cornell University Press, 1988

Graham, C. *Ideologies of Epic: Nation, Empire, and Victorian Epic Poetry*, Manchester: Manchester University Press, 1998

Kiernan, V. "Tennyson, King Arthur, and Imperialism," in *Culture, Ideology, and Politics: Essays for Eric Hobsbawm*, ed. Raphael Samuel and Gareth Stedman Jones, London: Routledge, 1982, 126–48

King, K. R. and W. Morgan. "Hardy and the Boer War: The Public Poet in Spite of Himself," *Victorian Poetry*, 17 (1979), 66–83

Parry, A. *The Poetry of Rudyard Kipling: Rousing the Nation*, Buckingham: Open University Press, 1992

Smith, M. Van Wyck. *Drummer Hodge: The Poetry of the Anglo-Boer War (1899–1902)*, Oxford: Oxford University Press, 1978

Poetic liberties

Boos, F. "'Nurs'd Up amongst the Scenes I have Describ'd': Political Resonances in the Poetry of Working-Class Women," in *Functions of Victorian Culture at the Present Time*, ed. C. L. Krueger, Athens: Ohio University Press, 2002, 137–56

Boos, F., ed. "The Poetics of the Working Classes," *Victorian Poetry*, special issue, 39.2 (Summer, 2001), 103–389

Brown, S. "Economical Representations: Dante Gabriel Rossetti's 'Jenny,' Augusta Webster's 'A Castaway,' and the Campaign against the Contagious Diseases Acts," *Victorian Review*, 17 (1991), 78–95

Finn, M. C. *After Chartism: Class and Nation in English Radical Politics 1848–1874*, Cambridge: Cambridge University Press, 1993

Joyce, P. *Visions of the People: Industrial England and the Question of Class 1848–1914*, Cambridge: Cambridge University Press, 1991

Thain, M. and A. I. P. Vadillo, eds. "Fin de Siècle Literary Culture and Women Poets," *Victorian Literature and Culture*, special issue, 34.2 (September, 2006), 389–684

Weiner, S. K. *Republican Politics and English Poetry, 1789–1874*, Basingstoke: Palgrave Macmillan, 2005

Art for art's sake

Bristow, J., ed. *The Fin-de-siècle Poem: English Literary Culture and the 1890s*, Athens: Ohio University Press, 2005

Denisoff, D. *Aestheticism and Sexual Parody, 1840–1940*, Cambridge: Cambridge University Press, 2001

Freedman, J. *Professions of Taste: Henry James, British Aestheticism, and Commodity Culture*, Palo Alto, CA: Stanford University Press, 1990

Gray, E. *The Poetry of Indifference: From the Romantics to the Rubáiyát*, Amherst: University of Massachusetts Press, 2005

Leighton, A. *On Form: Poetry, Aestheticism, and the Legacy of a Word*, Oxford: Oxford University Press, 2007

Marshall, G., ed. *The Cambridge Companion to the Fin-de-siècle*, Cambridge University Press, 2007

Nelson, J. G. *The Early Nineties: A View from the Bodley Head*, Cambridge, MA: Harvard University Press, 1971

   Publisher to the Decadents: Leonard Smithers in the Careers of Beardsley, Wilde, Dowson, University Park: Pennsylvania University Press, 2000

Stetz, M., and Lasner, M. S. *England in the 1890s: Literary Publishing at the Bodley Head*, Washington, D.C., Georgetown University Press, 1990

Thain, M. "Modernist *Homage* to the *Fin de siècle*," *Yearbook of English Studies*, 37.1 (January, 2007), 22–40

Aurora Leigh

Brown, S. "*Paradise Lost and Aurora Leigh*," *SEL: Studies in English Literature*, 37 (1997), 723–40

Laird, H. "*Aurora Leigh*: An Epical Ars poetica," in *Critical Essays on Elizabeth Barrett Browning*, ed. S. Donaldson, New York: G. K. Hall, 1999, 275–90

Mermin, D. *Elizabeth Barrett Browning: The Origins of a New Poetry*, Chicago: University of Chicago Press, 1989

Reynolds, M., Introduction, in *Aurora Leigh*, ed. M. Reynolds, Athens: Ohio University Press, 1992, 1–77

Thomas Hardy

Langbaum, R. "Browning and Hardy," *Studies in Browning and His Circle*, 17 (1989), 15–22

Mallett, P., ed. *Palgrave Advances in Thomas Hardy Studies*, Basingstoke: Palgrave Macmillan, 2004

Taylor, D. *Hardy's Metres and Victorian Prosody*, Oxford: Clarendon Press, 1988
  Hardy's Poetry, 1860–1928, New York: Columbia University Press, 1981
  "Thomas Hardy and Thomas Gray: The Poet's Currency," *ELH: English Literary History*, 65.2 (1998), 451–77

Ernest Dowson

Snodgrass, C. "Aesthetic Memory's Cul-de-Sac: The Art of Ernest Dowson," *English Literature in Transition, 1880–1920*, 35.1 (1992), 26–53

Weiner, S. K. "Sight and Sound in the Poetic World of Ernest Dowson," *Nineteenth-Century Literature*, 60.4 (March, 2006), 481–509

Cambridge Introductions to Literature

This series is designed to introduce students to key topics and authors.
Accessible and lively, these introductions will also appeal to readers who want
to broaden their understanding of the books and authors they enjoy.

Ideal for students, teachers, and lecturers
Concise, yet packed with essential information
Key suggestions for further reading

Authors

Jane Austen *Janet Todd*

Samuel Beckett *Ronan McDonald*

Walter Benjamin *David Ferris*

J. M. Coetzee *Dominic Head*

Joseph Conrad *John Peters*

Jacques Derrida *Leslie Hill*

Emily Dickinson *Wendy Martin*

George Eliot *Nancy Henry*

T. S. Eliot *John Xiros Cooper*

William Faulkner *Theresa M. Towner*

F. Scott Fitzgerald *Kirk Curnutt*

Michel Foucault *Lisa Downing*

Robert Frost *Robert Faggen*

Nathaniel Hawthorne *Leland S. Person*

Zora Neale Hurston *Lovalerie King*

James Joyce *Eric Bulson*

Herman Melville *Kevin J. Hayes*

Sylvia Plath *Jo Gill*

Edgar Allan Poe *Benjamin F. Fisher*

Ezra Pound *Ira Nadel*

Jean Rhys *Elaine Savory*

Edward Said *Conor McCarthy*

William Shakespeare *Emma Smith*

Shakespeare's Comedies *Penny Gay*

Shakespeare's History Plays *Warren Chernaik*

Shakespeare's Tragedies *Janette Dillon*

Harriet Beecher Stowe   *Sarah Robbins*
Mark Twain   *Peter Messent*
Edith Wharton   *Pamela Knights*
Walt Whitman   *M. Jimmie Killingsworth*
Virginia Woolf   *Jane Goldman*
W. B. Yeats   *David Holdeman*

Topics

The American Short Story   *Martin Scofield*
Comedy   *Eric Weitz*
Creative Writing   *David Morley*
Early English Theatre   *Janette Dillon*
English Theatre, 1660–1900   *Peter Thomson*
Francophone Literature   *Patrick Corcoran*
Modern British Theatre   *Simon Shepherd*
Modern Irish Poetry   *Justin Quinn*
Modernism   *Pericles Lewis*
Narrative (second edition)   *H. Porter Abbott*
The Nineteenth-Century American Novel   *Gregg Crane*
Postcolonial Literatures   *C. L. Innes*
Postmodern Fiction   *Bran Nicol*
Russian Literature   *Caryl Emerson*
Scenography   *Joslin McKinney and Philip Butterworth*
The Short Story in English   *Adrian Hunter*
Theatre Historiography   *Thomas Postlewait*
Theatre Studies   *Christopher Balme*
Tragedy   *Jennifer Wallace*
Victorian Poetry   *Linda K. Hughes*

Lightning Source UK Ltd.
Milton Keynes UK
UKHW020955130422
401491UK00017B/620